Fodor's New SECOND EDITION

Colorado

Jordan Simon

"When it comes to information on regional history, what to see and do, and shopping, these guides are exhaustive."

—*USAir Magazine*

"Usable, sophisticated restaurant coverage, with an emphasis on good value."
—Andy Birsh, *Gourmet Magazine* columnist

"Valuable because of their comprehensiveness."
—*Minneapolis Star-Tribune*

"Fodor's always delivers high quality...thoughtfully presented...thorough."
—*Houston Post*

"An excellent choice for those who want everything under one cover."
—*Washington Post*

D0869033

Portions of this book appear in *Fodor's The Rockies*.

Fodor's Travel Publications, Inc.
New York • Toronto • London • Sydney • Auckland

ON THE ROAD WITH FODOR'S

A GOOD TRAVEL GUIDE is like a wonderful traveling companion. It's charming, it's brimming with sound recommendations and solid ideas, it pulls no punches in describing lodging and dining establishments, and it's consistently full of fascinating facts that make you view what you've traveled to see in a rich new light. In the creation of *Fodor's Colorado*, we at Fodor's have gone to great lengths to provide you with the very best of all possible traveling companions—and to make your trip the best of all possible vacations.

About Our Writers

The information in these pages is the product of exhaustive research by our extraordinary writers.

Jordan Simon defected to the world of journalism in 1987. A former contributing editor of *TAXI* magazine, he has written for *Fodor's Caribbean and Virgin Islands, Elle, Travel and Leisure, Snow Country, Food Arts, Caribbean Travel & Life, Los Angeles, USAir, Town & Country, Physicians Travel & Meeting Guide, Ski, Modern Bride, International Entertaining, Wine Country International, California,* and other publications. He is food and wine editor of *Ski Impact,* author of *Fodor's Branson* and the *Gousha/USA Today Ski Atlas,* co-author of the upcoming *Celestial Seasonings* cookbook (Random House Value Publishing), and director of the International Ski Film & Video Festival, held annually in Colorado.

The following people and organizations provided invaluable assistance and resources—not to mention wonderful company—along the way: Peggy Mahoney (Continental Airlines); Gina Kroft (Crested Butte); Mike Smedley (Purgatory/Durango); Barb Jennings and Stacey Kramer (Steamboat); Barb Loken, Andrea Box, and Mike Shim-Konis (Telluride); Pat Peeples, Jim Feldhaus, Carol Frangos Johnson, Paul Witt, Rob Perlman, and Joel Heath (Vail/Beaver Creek); Paula Sheridan, Joan Christensen, and Julie Klein (Winter Park); Jim Felton (Keystone/A-Basin); Kristen Kopplin (Copper Mountain); Rachel Flood and Carol Cannon (Breckenridge); Killeen Russell, Jennifer Gardner, and Bobbie Jacobs (Aspen/Snowmass); Kent Zimmerman and Laura Myers (Boulder); Karin Gamba (Glenwood Springs); Kathleen Donnelley (Trinidad); Dean Dennis (Pueblo); Kristin Bricker (Colorado Springs); Jodi Miller (Alamosa); George Turner (Cañon City); Susie Blackhurst and Sally Anderson (Estes Park); Debbie Kovalik and Barb Bowman (Grand Junction); Rod Zang (Rifle); Rick Hamman (for introducing me to Colorado wines); Ron and Patti Rudolph (for their company); Jerry and Barbara Alley Simon (for the obvious—and for getting me on skis); Holly Rouillard Johnson and Kathleen Brown (for their expertise); and Claire Walter and Lois Friedman (for their encouragement).

What's New

A New Design

If this is not the first Fodor's guide you've purchased, you'll immediately notice our new look. More readable and easier to use than ever? We think so—and we hope you do, too.

New Takes on Colorado

Controversy has plagued the opening of the new Denver International Airport. Originally scheduled to open in December 1993, but plagued by delays (most stemming from a faulty state-of-the-art baggage-handling system), the $4+ billion facility finally opened its gates February 28, 1995. Denverites were furious about cost overruns, placing the blame squarely on Mayor Wellington Webb and his predecessor, the current Secretary of Transportation Federico Peña, who approved the project. Allegations of greed and graft ran rampant, as did the jokes. (A few samples: "DIA is D.O.A."; "Oh what a tangled Webb we weave..."; and "Denver's Invisible Airport.") While some still grumble about the distance from town (twice that of Stapleton) and fare increases (airport fees to carriers are significantly higher—a cost transferred to passengers), early reports are favorable. Aesthetically, the airport, which boasts a $7 million art collection in its halls and an unusual tent-like roof, is stunning; technologically (despite the initial baggage woes), it is the most advanced facility in America thanks to increased runway capacity and other efficiencies. These should eliminate many of the delays and cancellations that made Stapleton itself the butt of several jokes.

Let Us Do Your Booking

Our writers have scoured Colorado to come up with an extensive and well-balanced list of the best B&Bs, inns, resorts, and hotels, both small and large, new and old. But you don't have to beat the bushes to come up with a reservation. Now we've teamed up with an established hotel-booking service to make it easy for you to secure a room at the property of your choice. It's fast, it's free, and confirmation is guaranteed. If your first choice is booked, the operators can line up your second right away. Just call 1–800/FODORS–1 or 1–800/363–6771 (0800–89–1030 in Great Britain; 0014–800–12–8271 in Australia; 1–800/55–9101 in Ireland).

Travel Updates

In addition, just before your trip, you may want to order a Fodor's Worldview Travel Update. From local publications all over Colorado, the lively, cosmopolitan editors at Worldview gather information on concerts, plays, opera, dance performances, gallery and museum shows, sports competitions, and other special events that coincide with your visit. See the order blank at the back of this book, call 800/799–9609, or fax 800/799–9619.

And in Colorado

The last few years have been tumultuous for Colorado, which is still suffering repercussions from the late-1992 passage of Amendment 2, which outlawed civil rights legislation for special-interest groups. It was specifically targeted at gays and in turn angered liberal groups who called for a boycott of the state. The move was moderately successful: Colorado lost over $100 million of convention business through 1998. However, its effects were ameliorated somewhat by an influx of right-wing convention business and by a fine 1992-93 ski season. Although Amendment 2 was de-

clared unconstitutional in 1993 by the state Supreme Court, Colorado appealed. In February 1995, the U.S. Supreme Court agreed to hear arguments the following fall, with its decision expected in early 1996. Activists have threatened another state boycott should the nation's highest court rule in favor of Amendment 2.

So far there are no new developments for 1996: no major building, no imminent closures, no controversial amendments. But after the roller-coaster ride Coloradans have taken the past few years, they're staying tuned.

How to Use This Guide

Organization

Up front is the **Gold Guide,** comprising two sections on gold paper that are chock-full of information about traveling within your destination and traveling in general. Both are in alphabetical order by topic. **Important Contacts A to Z** gives addresses and telephone numbers of organizations and companies that offer destination-related services and detailed information or publications. Here's where you'll find information about how to get to Colorado from wherever you are. **Smart Travel Tips A to Z,** the Gold Guide's second section, gives specific tips on how to get the most out of your travels, as well as information on how to accomplish what you need to in Colorado.

Chapters in *Fodor's Colorado* are arranged by region. Each chapter covers exploring, shopping, sports, dining, lodging, and arts and nightlife and ends with a section called Essentials, which tells you how to get there and get around and gives you important local addresses and telephone numbers.

Stars

Stars in the margin are used to denote highly recommended sights, attractions, hotels, and restaurants.

Restaurant and Hotel Criteria and Price Categories

Restaurants and lodging places are chosen with a view to giving you the cream of the crop in each location and in each price range.

For restaurants:

CATEGORY	RESORTS AND CITIES	TOWNS AND COUNTRY
$$$$	over $40	over $35
$$$	$30–$40	$25–$35
$$	$20–$30	$15–$25
$	under $20	under $15

All prices are for a three-course meal, excluding drinks, service, and tip.

For hotels:

CATEGORY	RESORTS AND CITIES	TOWNS AND COUNTRY
$$$$	over $350	over $225
$$$	$250–$350	$150–$225
$$	$125–$250	$90–$150
$	under $125	under $90

All prices are for a standard double room in high season, excluding tax and service.

Hotel Facilities

Note that in general you incur charges when you use many hotel facilities. We wanted to let you know what facilities a hotel has to offer, but we don't always specify whether or not there's a charge, so when planning a vacation that entails a stay of several days, it's wise to ask what's included in the rate.

Hotel Meal Plans

Assume that hotels operate on the European Plan (EP, with no meals) unless we note that they use the American Plan (AP, with all meals), the Modified American Plan (MAP, with breakfast and dinner daily), or the Continental Plan (CP, with a Continental breakfast daily).

Dress Code in Restaurants

In general, we note a dress code only when men are required to wear a jacket or a jacket and tie.

Credit Cards

The following abbreviations are used: **AE,** American Express; **D,** Discover; **DC,** Diners Club; **MC,** MasterCard; and **V,** Visa.

Please Write to Us

Everyone who contributed to *Fodor's Colorado* has worked hard to make the text accurate. All prices and opening times are based on information supplied to us at press time, and Fodor's cannot accept responsibility for any errors that may have occurred. The passage of time will bring changes, so it's always a good idea to call ahead and confirm information when it matters—particularly if you're making a detour to visit specific sights or attractions. When making reservations at a hotel or inn, be sure to mention if you have a disability or are traveling with children, if you prefer a private bath or a certain type of bed, or if you have specific dietary needs or any other concerns.

Were the restaurants we recommended as described? Did our hotel picks exceed your expectations? Did you find a museum we recommended a waste of time? We would love your feedback, positive and negative. If you have complaints, we'll look into them and revise our entries when the facts warrant it. If you've happened upon a special place that we haven't included, we'll pass the information along to the writers so they can check it out. So please send us a letter or postcard (we're at 201 East 50th Street, New York, New York 10022). We'll look forward to hearing from you. And in the meantime, have a wonderful trip!

Karen Cure
Editorial Director

Colorado

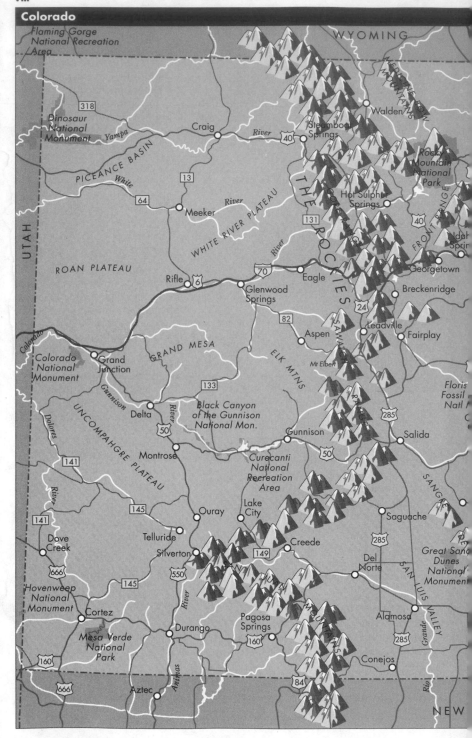

WYOMING

Flaming Gorge
National Recreation
Area

Dinosaur
National
Monument

318

Craig

Yampa River

40

Steamboat
Springs

Walden

MEDICINE BOW MOUNTAINS

PICEANCE BASIN

White

13

64

Meeker

River

WHITE RIVER PLATEAU

Rocky
Mountain
National
Park

Hot Sulphur
Springs

131

FRONT RANGE

40

Idah
Spri

ROAN PLATEAU

Rifle

6

Glenwood
Springs

70

Eagle

River

THE ROCKIES

Georgetown

Breckenridge

24

82

Aspen

ELK MTNS

SAWATCH

Leadville

Fairplay

Colorado

Colorado
National
Monument

Grand
Junction

GRAND MESA

Gunnison

133

Mt Elbert

285

RANGE

Floris
Fossil
Natl I

Dolores

UNCOMPAHGRE PLATEAU

Delta

River

50

Black Canyon
of the Gunnison
National Mon.

Gunnison

50

Salida

SANGRE

141

Montrose

Curecanti
National
Recreation
Area

Saguache

River

141

145

Ouray

Lake
City

285

Del
Norte

Great Sand
Dunes
National
Monument

Dove
Creek

666

Telluride

Silverton

550

Creede

149

285

SAN LUIS VALLEY

Hovenweep
National
Monument

Cortez

145

River

SAN JUAN

Pagosa
Springs

Alamosa

Grande

285

Mesa Verde
National
Park

160

Durango

MOUNTAINS

160

Conejos

666

Animas

Aztec

84

Rio

NEW

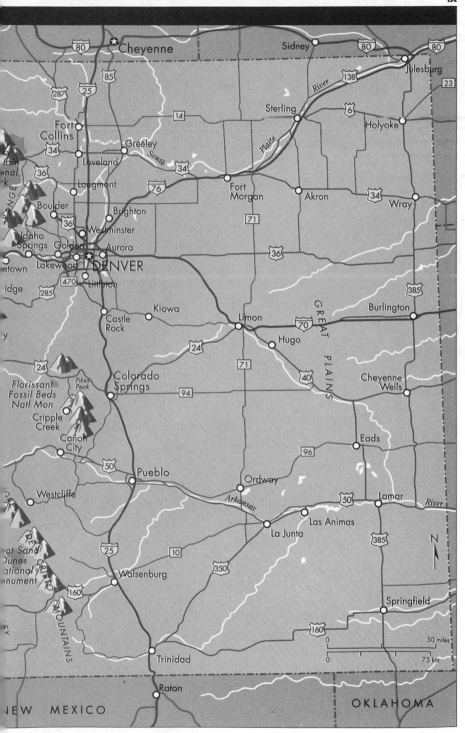

The United States

CANADA

BRITISH COLUMBIA
ALBERTA
SASKATCHEWAN
MANITOBA

Vancouver
Victoria
Seattle
Olympia
WASHINGTON
Portland
Salem
OREGON
Spokane
Columbia R.
Calgary
Regina
Winnipeg

Trans-Canada Hwy.

Great Falls
Missouri R.
MONTANA
Helena
Billings
NORTH DAKOTA
Fargo
Bismarck

IDAHO
Boise
Snake R.
WYOMING
SOUTH DAKOTA
Pierre
Missouri R.

Carson City
Sacramento
San Francisco
NEVADA
Salt Lake City
UTAH
Cheyenne
Denver
NEBRASKA
Lincoln

Fresno
Colorado R.
Colorado Springs
COLORADO
KANSAS

CALIFORNIA
Santa Barbara
Los Angeles
Las Vegas
Flagstaff
Santa Fe
OKLAHOMA
Oklahoma City

San Diego
ARIZONA
Phoenix
Albuquerque
NEW MEXICO
Amarillo

PACIFIC OCEAN
BAJA CALIFORNIA
SONORA
Tucson
El Paso
CHIHUAHUA
Rio Grande
Dallas
TEXAS
Austin
San Antonio

RUSSIA
ARCTIC OCEAN

Bering Strait
Bering Sea
Nome
ALASKA
Fairbanks
CANADA
MEXICO
COAHUILA

ALEUTIAN ISLANDS
Anchorage
Juneau
NUEVO LEON
TAM-AULIPAS

PACIFIC OCEAN

0   400 miles
0   400 km
N

Honolulu
Oahu
Maui
HAWAII
Hawaii
PACIFIC OCEAN

IMPORTANT CONTACTS A TO Z

An Alphabetical Listing of Publications, Organizations, and Companies That Will Help You Before, During, and After Your Trip

No single travel resource can give you every detail about every topic that might interest or concern you at the various stages of your journey—when you're planning your trip, while you're on the road, and after you get back home. The following organizations, books, and brochures will supplement the information in *Fodor's Colorado.* For related information, including both basic tips on visiting Colorado and background information on many of the topics below, study Smart Travel Tips A to Z, the section that follows Important Contacts A to Z.

A

AIR TRAVEL

The major gateway to Colorado is the new **Denver International Airport** (☎ 303/342–2000 or 800/247–2336, TTY 800/688–1333), replacing Stapleton; it possesses the best facilities for predicting and handling weather of any airport in the world. Flying time is 4 hours from New York, 2½ hours from Chicago, and 2 hours from Los Angeles.

CARRIERS

Carriers serving Denver International Airport include **American Air-**lines (☎ 800/433–7300), **Continental** (☎ 800/525–0280), **TWA** (☎ 800/221–2000), **United** (☎ 800/221–1212), and **USAir** (☎ 800/428–4322), with commuter airline links to smaller airports in the region.

For inexpensive, no-frills flights, contact **MarkAir** (☎ 800/627–5247) or **Midwest Express** (☎ 800/452–2022).

From the United Kingdom, airlines serving Colorado include **American Airlines** (☎ 0345/789–789), **British Airways** (☎ 0181/897–4000 or 0345/222–111), **Continental** (☎ 0800/776–464), **Delta Airlines** (☎ 0800/414–767), **Northwest** (☎ 01293/561–000), **TWA** (☎ 0800/222–222), **United Airlines** (☎ 0181/990–9900), and **Virgin Atlantic** (☎ 01293/747–747).

COMPLAINTS

To register complaints about charter and scheduled airlines, contact the U.S. Department of Transportation's **Office of Consumer Affairs** (400 7th St. NW, Washington, DC 20590, ☎ 202/366–2220 or 800/322–7873).

PUBLICATIONS

For general information about charter carriers, ask for the Office of Consumer Affairs' brochure **"Plane Talk:**

Public Charter Flights." The Department of Transportation also publishes a 58-page booklet, **"Fly Rights"** (Consumer Information Center, Dept. 133-B, Pueblo, CO 81009; $1.75).

For other tips and hints, consult the Consumers Union's monthly **"Consumer Reports Travel Letter"** (Box 53629, Boulder CO 80322, ☎ 800/234–1970; $39 a year) and the newsletter **"Travel Smart"** (40 Beechdale Rd., Dobbs Ferry, NY 10522, ☎ 800/327–3633; $37 a year); *The Official Frequent Flyer Guidebook,* by Randy Petersen (4715-C Town Center Dr., Colorado Springs, CO 80916, ☎ 719/597–8899 or 800/487–8893; $14.99 plus $3 shipping); *Airfare Secrets Exposed,* by Sharon Tyler and Matthew Wonder (Universal Information Publishing; $16.95 plus $3.75 shipping from Sandcastle Publishing, Box 3070-A, South Pasadena, CA 91031, ☎ 213/255–3616 or 800/655–0053); and *202 Tips Even the Best Business Travelers May Not Know,* by Christopher McGinnis (Irwin Professional Publishing, 1333 Burr Ridge Parkway, Burr Ridge, IL 60521, ☎ 800/634–3966; $10 plus $3 shipping).

World Time Zones

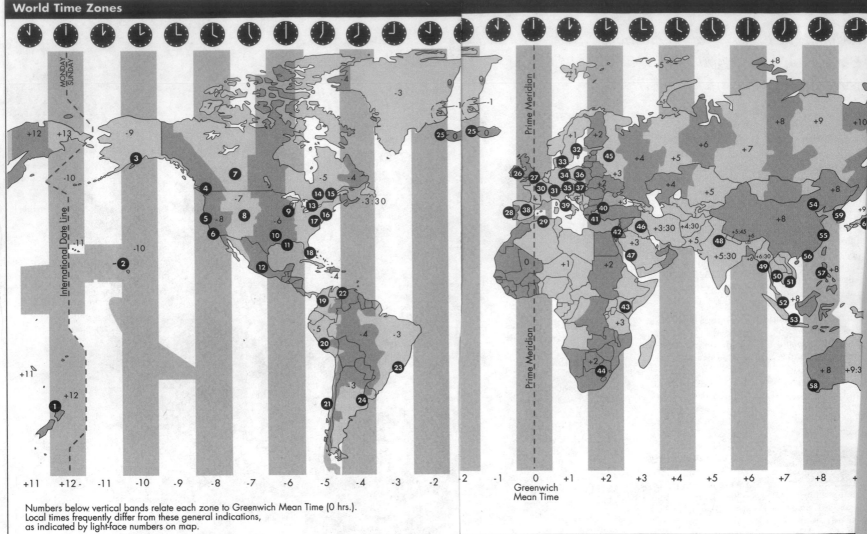

Numbers below vertical bands relate each zone to Greenwich Mean Time (0 hrs.).
Local times frequently differ from these general indications,
as indicated by light-face numbers on map.

Algiers, **29**
Anchorage, **3**
Athens, **41**
Auckland, **1**
Baghdad, **46**
Bangkok, **50**
Beijing, **54**

Berlin, **34**
Bogotá, **19**
Budapest, **37**
Buenos Aires, **24**
Caracas, **22**
Chicago, **9**
Copenhagen, **33**
Dallas, **10**

Delhi, **48**
Denver, **8**
Djakarta, **53**
Dublin, **26**
Edmonton, **7**
Hong Kong, **56**
Honolulu, **2**

Istanbul, **40**
Jerusalem, **42**
Johannesburg, **44**
Lima, **20**
Lisbon, **28**
London
(Greenwich), **27**
Los Angeles, **6**
Madrid, **38**
Manila, **57**

Mecca, **47**
Mexico City, **12**
Miami, **18**
Montréal, **15**
Moscow, **45**
Nairobi, **43**
New Orleans, **11**
New York City, **16**

Ottawa, **14**
Paris, **30**
Perth, **58**
Reykjavík, **25**
Rio de Janeiro, **23**
Rome, **39**
Saigon (Ho Chi Minh
City), **51**

San Francisco, **5**
Santiago, **21**
Seoul, **59**
Shanghai, **55**
Singapore, **52**
Stockholm, **32**
Sydney, **61**
Tokyo, **60**

Toron
Vanco
Vienn
Warsa
Wash
Yange
Züric

WITHIN COLORADO

Regional carriers include **Mesa** (☎ 800/637–2247), **Midwest Express** (☎ 800/452–2022), **Delta/SkyWest** (☎ 800/221–1212), which flies out of Salt Lake City, and **United Express** (☎ 800/241–6522 or 800/662–3736).

B

BETTER BUSINESS BUREAU

For local contacts, consult the **Council of Better Business Bureaus** (4200 Wilson Blvd., Arlington, VA 22203, ☎ 703/276–0100).

BUS TRAVEL

Greyhound Lines (☎ 800/231–2222) operates bus service to Colorado from many points in the United States.

WITHIN COLORADO

Greyhound Lines operates regular intercity routes with connections from Denver. Smaller bus companies provide service within local areas. One such line is **Springs Transit Management** in Colorado Springs (☎ 719/475–9733).

C

CAR RENTAL

Major car-rental companies represented in Colorado include **Alamo** (☎ 800/327–9633, 0800/272–2000 in the United Kingdom); **Avis** (☎ 800/331–1212, 800/879–2847 in Canada); **Budget** (☎ 800/527–0700, 0800/181–181 in the United Kingdom); **Dollar**

(known as Eurodollar outside North America, ☎ 800/800–4000, 0181/952–6565 in the United Kingdom); **Hertz** (☎ 800/654–3131, 800/263–0600 in Canada, 0181/679–1799 in the United Kingdom); and **National** (☎ 800/227–7368, 0181/950–5050 in the United Kingdom, where it is known as Europcar). Rates in Denver begin at $32.00 a day and $148.00 a week for an economy car with unlimited mileage.

CHILDREN AND TRAVEL

FLYING

Look into **"Flying with Baby"** (Third Street Press, Box 261250, Littleton, CO 80126, ☎ 303/595–5959; $5.95 plus $1 shipping), cowritten by a flight attendant. **"Kids and Teens in Flight,"** free from the U.S. Department of Transportation's Office of Consumer Affairs, offers tips for children flying alone. Every two years the February issue of **Family Travel Times** (see Know-How, below) details children's services on three dozen airlines.

GAMES

The gamemeister, Milton Bradley, has games to help keep little (and not so little) children from fidgeting while riding in planes, trains, and automobiles. Try packing the Travel Battleship sea battle game ($7), the vertical strategy game Travel Connect Four ($8), the Travel Yahtzee dice game ($6), the Travel

Trouble dice and board game ($7), or the Travel Guess Who mystery game ($8).

KNOW-HOW

Family Travel Times, published four times a year by Travel with Your Children (TWYCH, 45 W. 18th St., New York, NY 10011, ☎ 212/206–0688; annual subscription $40), covers destinations, types of vacations, and modes of travel.

The **Family Travel Guides** catalogue (PO Box 6061, Albany, CA 94706, ☎ 510/527–5849; $1 postage) lists about 200 books and articles on family travel. **Great Vacations with Your Kids,** by Dorothy Jordon and Marjorie Cohen (Penguin USA, 120 Woodbine St., Bergenfield, NJ 07621, ☎ 201/387–0600 or 800/253–6476; $13), and **Traveling with Children—And Enjoying It,** by Arlene K. Butler (Globe Pequot Press, Box 833, 6 Business Park Rd., Old Saybrook, CT 06475, ☎ 203/395–0440, 800/243–0495, or 800/962–0973 in CT; $11.95 plus $3 shipping) help plan your trip with children, from toddlers to teens. Also check **Take Your Baby and Go! A Guide for Traveling with Babies, Toddlers and Young Children,** by Sheri Andrews, Judy Bordeaux, and Vivian Vasquez (Bear Creek Publications, 2507 Minor Ave., Seattle, WA 98102, ☎ 206/322–7604 or 800/326–6566; $5.95 plus $1.50 shipping). TWYCH (see above) also publishes *Skiing with Children* ($29).

TOUR OPERATORS

Contact **Rascals in Paradise** (650 5th St., Suite 505, San Francisco, CA 94107, ☎ 415/978–9800 or 800/872–7225).

If you're outdoorsy, look into **Ecology Tours** (c/o the Audubon Center of the North Woods, Box 530, Sandstone, MN 55072, ☎ 612/245–2648), which mix travel and nature study; Audubon Society family summer camps and **Ecology Workshops** (613 Riversville Rd., Greenwich, CT 06831, ☎ 203/869–2017), as well as programs from **American Wilderness Experience** (Box 1486, Boulder, CO 80306, ☎ 303/444–2622 or 800/444–0099) and **Wildland Adventures** (3516 N.E 155th St., Seattle, WA 98155, ☎ 206/365–0686 or 800/345–4453).

CUSTOMS

CANADIANS

Contact **Revenue Canada** (2265 St. Laurent Blvd. S, Ottawa, Ontario, K1G 4K3, ☎ 613/993–0534) for a copy of the free brochure *"I Declare/Je Déclare"* and for details on duties that exceed the standard duty-free limit.

U.K. CITIZENS

HM Customs and Excise (Dorset House, Stamford St., London SE1 9NG, ☎ 0171/202–4227) can answer questions about U.K. customs regulations and publishes *"A Guide for Travellers,"* detailing standard procedures and import rules.

D
FOR TRAVELERS
WITH DISABILITIES

COMPLAINTS

To register complaints under the provisions of the Americans with Disabilities Act, contact the U.S. Department of Justice's **Public Access Section** (Box 66738, Washington, DC 20035, ☎ 202/514–0301, FAX 202/307–1198, TTY 202/514–0383).

IN THE U.K.

Contact the **Royal Association for Disability and Rehabilitation** (RADAR, 12 City Forum, 250 City Rd., London EC1V 8AF, ☎ 0171/250–3222) or **Mobility International** (Rue de Manchester 25, B–1070 Brussels, Belgium, ☎ 32/02/410–6297), an international clearinghouse of travel information for people with disabilities.

LOCAL INFO

Colorado's **Wilderness on Wheels** (7125 W. Jefferson Ave., Lakewood, CO 80235, ☎ 303/988–2212) can help answer accessibility questions and plan outings.

ORGANIZATIONS

FOR TRAVELERS WITH HEARING IMPAIRMENTS➤ Contact the **American Academy of Otolaryngology** (1 Prince St., Alexandria, VA 22314, ☎ 703/836–4444, FAX 703/683–5100, TTY 703/519–1585).

FOR TRAVELERS WITH MOBILITY PROBLEMS➤

Contact the **Information Center for Individuals with Disabilities** (Fort Point Pl., 27–43 Wormwood St., Boston, MA 02210, ☎ 617/727–5540, 800/462–5015 in MA, TTY 617/345–9743); **Mobility International USA** (Box 10767, Eugene, OR 97440, ☎ and TTY 503/343–1284; FAX 503/343–6812), the U.S. branch of an international organization based in Belgium (*see below*) that has affiliates in 30 countries; **MossRehab Hospital Travel Information Service** (1200 W. Tabor Rd., Philadelphia, PA 19141, ☎ 215/456–9603, TTY 215/456–9602); the **Society for the Advancement of Travel for the Handicapped** (347 5th Ave., Suite 610, New York, NY 10016, ☎ 212/447–7284, FAX 212/725–8253); the **Travel Industry and Disabled Exchange** (TIDE, 5435 Donna Ave., Tarzana, CA 91356, ☎ 818/344–3640, FAX 818/344–0078); and **Travelin' Talk** (Box 3534, Clarksville, TN 37043, ☎ 615/552–6670, FAX 615/552–1182).

FOR TRAVELERS WITH VISION IMPAIRMENTS➤ Contact the **American Council of the Blind** (1155 15th St. NW, Suite 720, Washington, DC 20005, ☎ 202/467–5081, FAX 202/467–5085) or the **American Foundation for the Blind** (15 W. 16th St., New York, NY 10011, ☎ 212/620–2000, TTY 212/620–2158).

PUBLICATIONS

Several free publications are available from the

U.S. Information Center (Box 100, Pueblo, CO 81009, ☎ 719/948–3334): **"New Horizons for the Air Traveler with a Disability"** (address to Dept. 355A), describing legally mandated changes; the pocket-size **"Fly Smart"** (Dept. 575B), good on flight safety; and the Airport Operators Council's worldwide **"Access Travel: Airports"** (Dept. 575A).

Fodor's **Great American Vacations for Travelers with Disabilities** (available in bookstores, or call 800/533–6478; $18) details accessible attractions, restaurants, and hotels in U.S. destinations. The 500-page **Travelin' Talk Directory** (Box 3534, Clarksville, TN 37043, ☎ 615/552–6670; $35) lists people and organizations who help travelers with disabilities. For specialist travel agents worldwide, consult the **Directory of Travel Agencies for the Disabled** by Helen Hecker (Twin Peaks Press; Disability Bookshop, Box 129, Vancouver, WA 98666, ☎ 206/694–2462 or 800/637–2256; $19.95 plus $3.50 shipping and handling). The Sierra Club publishes **Easy Access to National Parks** (730 Polk St., San Francisco, CA 94109, ☎ 415/776–2211 or 800/935–1056; $16 plus $3 shipping).

TRAVEL AGENCIES AND TOUR OPERATORS

The Americans with Disabilities Act requires that travel firms serve the needs of all travelers. However, some agencies and operators specialize in making group and individual arrangements for travelers with disabilities, among them **Access Adventures** (206 Chestnut Ridge Rd., Rochester, NY 14624, ☎ 716/889–9096), run by a former physical-rehab counselor. In addition, many general-interest operators and agencies (*see* Tour Operators, *below*) can arrange vacations for travelers with disabilities.

FOR TRAVELERS WITH HEARING IMPAIRMENTS➤ One agency is **International Express** (7319-B Baltimore Ave., College Park, MD 20740, ☎ and TTY 301/699–8836, FAX 301/699–8836), which arranges group and independent trips.

FOR TRAVELERS WITH MOBILITY PROBLEMS➤ A number of operators specialize in working with travelers with mobility problems: **Access Tours** (Box 2985, Jackson, WY 83001, ☎ 307/733–6664 in summer; 2440 S. Forest, Tucson, AZ 85713, ☎ 602/791–7977 winter–mid-May), which organizes national park tours; **Hinsdale Travel Service** (201 E. Ogden Ave., Suite 100, Hinsdale, IL 60521, ☎ 708/325–1335 or 800/303–5521), a travel agency that will give you access to the services of wheelchair-user and traveler Janice Perkins; and **Wheelchair Journeys** (16979 Redmond Way, Redmond, WA 98052, ☎ 206/885–2210), which can handle arrangements worldwide.

FOR TRAVELERS WITH DEVELOPMENTAL DISABILITIES➤ Contact the nonprofit **New Directions** (5276 Hollister Ave., Suite 207, Santa Barbara, CA 93111, ☎ 805/967–2841).

DISCOUNT CLUBS

Options include **Entertainment Travel Editions** (Box 1068, Trumbull, CT 06611, ☎ 800/445–4137; fee $28–$53, depending on destination); **Great American Traveler** (Box 27965, Salt Lake City, UT 84127, ☎ 800/548–2812; $49.95 annually); **Moment's Notice Discount Travel Club** (163 Amsterdam Ave., Suite 137, New York, NY 10023, ☎ 212/486–0500; $25 annually, single or family); **Privilege Card** (3391 Peachtree Rd. NE, Suite 110, Atlanta, GA 30326, ☎ 404/262–0222 or 800/236-9732; $74.95 annually); **Travelers Advantage** (CUC Travel Service, 49 Music Sq. W, Nashville, TN 37203, ☎ 800/548–1116 or 800/648–4037; $49 annually, single or family); and **Worldwide Discount Travel Club** (1674 Meridian Ave., Miami Beach, FL 33139, ☎ 305/534–2082; $50 annually for family, $40 single).

DRIVING

AUTO CLUBS

The **American Automobile Association (AAA)** offers maps, route planning, and emergency road service to its members; members of Britain's Automobile Association (BAA) are granted reciprocal privileges. To join AAA, look in local phone directories under AAA for the nearest club, or contact the national organization (1000 AAA Dr., Heathrow, FL 32746-5063, ☎ 407/444-7000 or 800/222-4357 in the United States; 800/336-4357 in Canada).

ROAD CONDITIONS

For current road conditions, call the **Colorado State Highway Department** (☎ 303/639-1111 within a two-hour drive of Denver; 303/639-1234 statewide).

E

EMERGENCIES

Dialing 911 will summon police, fire, and ambulance services throughout the state of Colorado.

G

GAY AND
LESBIAN TRAVEL

ORGANIZATIONS

The **International Gay Travel Association** (Box 4974, Key West, FL 33041, ☎ 800/448-8550), a consortium of 800 businesses, can supply names of travel agents and tour operators.

PUBLICATIONS

The premier international travel magazine for gays and lesbians is *Our World* (1104 N. Nova Rd., Suite 251, Daytona Beach, FL 32117, ☎ 904/441-5367; $35 for 10 issues). The 16-page monthly *"Out & About"* (☎ 212/645-6922 or 800/929-2268; $49 for

10 issues) covers gay-friendly resorts, hotels, cruise lines, and airlines.

TOUR OPERATORS

Cruises and resort vacations are handled by **Toto Tours** (1326 W. Albion, Suite 3W, Chicago, IL 60626, ☎ 312/274-8686 or 800/565-1241), which has group tours worldwide.

TRAVEL AGENCIES

The largest agencies serving gay travelers are **Advance Travel** (10700 Northwest Freeway, Suite 160, Houston, TX 77092, ☎ 713/682-2002 or 800/695-0880);**Islanders/Kennedy Travel** (183 W. 10th St., New York, NY 10014, ☎ 212/242-3222 or 800/988-1181); **Now Voyager** (4406 18th St., San Francisco, CA 94114, ☎ 415/626-1169 or 800/255-6951); and **Yellowbrick Road** (1500 W. Balmoral Ave., Chicago, IL 60640, ☎ 312/561-1800 or 800/642-2488). **Skylink Women's Travel** (746 Ashland Ave., Santa Monica, CA 90405, ☎ 310/452-0506 or 800/225-5759) works with lesbians.

I

INSURANCE

Travel insurance covering baggage, health, and trip cancellation or interruptions is available from **Access America** (Box 90315, Richmond, VA 23286, ☎ 804/285-3300 or 800/284-8300); **Carefree Travel Insurance** (Box 9366, 100 Garden City Plaza, Garden City, NY 11530, ☎ 516/294-0220 or 800/323-

3149); **Near Services** (Box 1339, Calumet City, IL 60409, ☎ 708/868-6700 or 800/654-6700); **Tele-Trip** (Mutual of Omaha Plaza, Box 31716, Omaha, NE 68131, ☎ 800/228-9792); **Travel Insured International** (Box 280568, East Hartford, CT 06128-0568, ☎ 203/528-7663 or 800/243-3174); **Travel Guard International** (1145 Clark St., Stevens Point, WI 54481, ☎ 715/345-0505 or 800/826-1300); and **Wallach & Company** (107 W. Federal St., Box 480, Middleburg, VA 22117, ☎ 703/687-3166 or 800/237-6615).

IN THE U.K.

The **Association of British Insurers** (51 Gresham St., London EC2V 7HQ, ☎ 0171/600-3333; 30 Gordon St., Glasgow G1 3PU, ☎ 0141/226-3905; Scottish Provident Bldg., Donegall Sq. W, Belfast BT1 6JE, ☎ 01232/249176; and other locations) gives advice by phone and publishes the free *"Holiday Insurance,"* which sets out typical policy provisions and costs.

L

LODGING

For comprehensive statewide accommodation information, contact the **Colorado Hotel and Lodging Association** (999 18th St., Suite 10472, Denver, CO 80202, ☎ 303/297-8335). For information about hotels near national parks, contact state tourism offices or the **National Park Service** national headquarters (Office of Public Inquiries, Box 37127, Washington, DC 20013, ☎ 202/208–4747) or its Rocky Mountain regional office (12795 W. Alameda Pkwy., Lakewood, CO 80225, ☎ 303/969–2000).

APARTMENT AND VILLA RENTAL

Among the companies to contact are **At Home Abroad** (405 E. 56th St., Suite 6H, New York, NY 10022, ☎ 212/421–9165); **Rent-a-Home International** (7200 34th Ave. NW, Seattle, WA 98117, ☎ 206/789–9377 or 800/488–7368); and **Vacation Home Rentals Worldwide** (235 Kensington Ave., Norwood, NJ 07648, ☎ 201/767–9393 or 800/633–3284). Members of the travel club **Hideaways International** (767 Islington St., Portsmouth, NH 03801, ☎ 603/430–4433 or 800/843–4433; $99 annually) receive two annual guides plus quarterly newsletters, and arrange rentals among themselves.

GUEST RANCHES

For lists of ranches, contact the **Colorado Dude/Guest Ranch Association** (Box 300, Tabernash, CO 80478, ☎ 970/724–3653).

HOME EXCHANGE

Principal clearinghouses include **HomeLink International/Vacation Exchange Club** (Box 650, Key West, FL 33041, ☎ 305/294–1448 or 800/638–3841; $60 annually), which gives members four annual directories,

with a listing in one, plus updates; **Intervac International** (Box 590504, San Francisco, CA 94159, ☎ 415/435–3497; $65 annually), which has three annual directories; and **Loan-a-Home** (2 Park La., Apt. 6E, Mount Vernon, NY 10552, ☎ 914/664–7640; $35–$45 annually), which specializes in long-term exchanges.

HOTELS

Colorado has experienced a hotel building boom during the past 12 years. **Doubletree** (☎ 800/222–8733), **Holiday Inn** (☎ 800/465–4329), **Marriott** (☎ 800/228–9290), **Ramada** (☎ 800/228–2828), **Red Lion Hotels and Inns** (☎ 800/547–8010), **Sheraton** (☎ 800/325–3535), **Stouffer** (☎ 800/468–3751), and **Westin** (☎ 800/228–3000) all have relatively new properties in major Colorado cities. **Courtyard by Marriott** (☎ 800/321–2211) and **Embassy Suites** (☎ 800/362–2779) offer suite accommodations in Denver.

INNS AND BED-AND-BREAKFASTS

For complete lists and booking information, contact the professional association **Distinctive Inns of Colorado/Bed and Breakfast Colorado** (Box 10472, Colorado Springs, CO 80932, ☎ 800/866–0621).

MOTELS

Nationally recognized chains include **Best Western** (☎ 800/528–1234), **Days Inn** (☎ 800/325–2525), **La Quinta Inns** (☎ 800/531–

5900), **Motel 6** (☎ 505/891–6161), **Quality Inn** (☎ 800/228–5151), **Rodeway Inn** (☎ 800/221–2222), **Super 8 Motel** (☎ 800/848–8888), and **Travelodge** (☎ 800/255–3050).

M
MONEY MATTERS

ATMS

For specific **Cirrus** locations in the United States and Canada, call 800/424–7787. For U.S. **Plus** locations, call 800/843–7587 and enter the area code and first three digits of the number you're calling from (or of the calling area where you want an ATM).

WIRING FUNDS

Funds can be wired via **American Express MoneyGram**SM (☎ 800/926–9400 from the United States and Canada for locations and information) or **Western Union** (☎ 800/325–6000 for agent locations or to send using MasterCard or Visa, 800/321–2923 in Canada).

P
PASSPORTS
AND VISAS

U.K. CITIZENS

For fees, documentation requirements, and to get an emergency passport, call the **London Passport Office** (☎ 0171/271–3000). For visa information, call the **U.S. Embassy Visa Information Line** (☎ 0891/200–290; calls cost 49p per minute or 39p per minute cheap rate) or write the **U.S. Embassy Visa Branch** (5 Upper

Grosvenor St., London W1A 2JB). If you live in Northern Ireland, write the **U.S. Consulate General** (Queen's House, Queen St., Belfast BTI 6EQ).

PHOTO HELP

The **Kodak Information Center** (☎ 800/242–2424) answers consumer questions about film and photography. Pick up the *Kodak Guide to Shooting Great Travel Pictures* (Random House, ☎ 800/733–3000; $16.50), which gives you tips on how to take travel pictures like a pro.

R

RAIL TRAVEL

Amtrak (☎ 800/872–7245) connects Colorado to both coasts and all major American cities, with trains that run through Denver.

S

SENIOR CITIZENS

EDUCATIONAL TRAVEL

The nonprofit **Elderhostel** (75 Federal St., 3rd Floor, Boston, MA 02110, ☎ 617/426–7788), for people 60 and older, has offered inexpensive study programs since 1975. The nearly 2,000 courses cover everything from marine science to Greek myths and cowboy poetry. Fees for programs in the United States and Canada, which usually last one week, run about $300, not including transportation.

ORGANIZATIONS

Contact the **American Association of Retired**

Persons (AARP, 601 E St. NW, Washington, DC 20049, ☎ 202/434–2277; $8 per person or couple annually). Its Purchase Privilege Program gets members discounts on lodging, car rentals, and sightseeing, and the AARP Motoring Plan furnishes domestic trip-routing information and emergency road-service aid for an annual fee of $39.95 per person or couple ($59.95 for a premium version).

For other discounts on lodgings, car rentals, and other travel products, along with magazines and newsletters, contact the **National Council of Senior Citizens** (1331 F St. NW, Washington, DC 20004, ☎ 202/347–8800; membership $12 annually) and *Mature Outlook* (6001 N. Clark St., Chicago, IL 60660, ☎ 312/465–6466 or 800/336–6330; subscription $9.95 annually).

PUBLICATIONS

The 50+ Traveler's Guidebook: Where to Go, Where to Stay, What to Do, by Anita Williams and Merrimac Dillon (St. Martin's Press, 175 5th Ave., New York, NY 10010, ☎ 212/674–5151 or 800/288–2131; $12.95), offers many useful tips. **"The Mature Traveler"** (Box 50400, Reno, NV 89513, ☎ 702/786–7419; $29.95), a monthly newsletter, covers travel deals.

STUDENTS

GROUPS

Major tour operators include **Contiki Holidays**

(300 Plaza Alicante, Suite 900, Garden Grove, CA 92640, ☎ 714/740–0808 or 800/466–0610).

HOSTELING

Contact **Hostelling International–American Youth Hostels** (733 15th St. NW, Suite 840, Washington, DC 20005, ☎ 202/783–6161) in the United States; **Hostelling International–Canada** (205 Catherine St., Suite 400, Ottawa, Ontario K2P 1C3, ☎ 613/237–7884) in Canada; and the **Youth Hostel Association of England and Wales** (Trevelyan House, 8 St. Stephen's Hill, St. Albans, Hertfordshire AL1 2DY, ☎ 01727/855215 and 01727/845047) in the United Kingdom. Membership ($25 in the United States, C$26.75 in Canada, and £9 in the United Kingdom) gets you access to 5,000 hostels worldwide that charge $7–$20 nightly per person.

ID CARDS

To be eligible for discounts on transportation and admissions, get the **International Student Identity Card** (ISIC) if you're a bona fide student or the **International Youth Card** (IYC) if you're under 26. In the United States, the ISIC and IYC cards cost $16 each and include basic travel accident and illness coverage, plus a toll-free travel hot line. Apply through the Council on International Educational Exchange (*see* Organizations, *below*). Cards are available for $15 each in Canada from **Travel Cuts**

(187 College St., Toronto, Ontario M5T 1P7, ☎ 416/979–2406 or 800/667–2887) and in the United Kingdom for £5 each at student unions and student travel companies.

ORGANIZATIONS

A major contact is the **Council on International Educational Exchange** (CIEE, 205 E. 42nd St., 16th Floor, New York, NY 10017, ☎ 212/661–1450) with locations in Boston (729 Boylston St., 02116, ☎ 617/266–1926); Miami (9100 S. Dadeland Blvd., 33156, ☎ 305/670–9261); Los Angeles (1093 Broxton Ave., 90024, ☎ 310/208–3551); 43 other college towns nationwide; and the United Kingdom (28A Poland St., London W1V 3DB, ☎ 0171/437–7767). Twice a year, it publishes *Student Travels* magazine. The CIEE's Council Travel Service offers domestic air passes for bargain travel within the United States and is the exclusive U.S. agent for several student-discount cards.

Campus Connections (325 Chestnut St., Suite 1101, Philadelphia, PA 19106, ☎ 215/625–8585 or 800/428–3235) specializes in discounted accommodations and airfares for students. The **Educational Travel Centre** (438 N. Frances St., Madison, WI 53703, ☎ 608/256–5551) offers rail passes and low-cost airline tickets, mostly for flights departing from Chicago.

In Canada, also contact **Travel Cuts** (*see above*).

T
TOUR OPERATORS

Among the companies selling tours and packages to Colorado, the following have a proven reputation, are nationally known, and offer plenty of options.

FROM THE U.K.

Among those companies you might consider as you plan your trip to Colorado are **Cosmosair** (Ground Floor, Dale House, Tiviot Dale, Stockport, Cheshire SK1 1TB, ☎ 0161/480–5799); **Kuoni Travel** (Kuoni House, Dorking, Surrey RH5 4AZ, ☎ 01306/742–222, FAX 01306/744–222); **Premier Holidays** (Premier Travel Center, Westbrook, Milton Rd., Cambridge CB4 1YQ, ☎ 01223/516–688, FAX 01223/516 615); **Ramblers Holidays, Ltd.** (Box 43, Welwyn Garden City, Hertfordshire AL8 6PQ, ☎ 01707/331–133, FAX 01707/333–276); **Travelpack** (Clarendon House, Clarendon Rd., Eccles, Manchester M30 9AL, ☎ 0161/707–4404, FAX 0161/707–4403); and **Trek America, Ltd.** (Trek House, The Bullring, Deddington, Banbury, Oxon OX15 OTT, ☎ 01869/338–777, FAX 01869/338–846).

GROUP TOURS

For deluxe escorted tours of Colorado, contact **Maupintour** (Box 807, Lawrence KS 66044, ☎ 800/255–4266 or 913/843–1211) and **Tauck Tours**

(11 Wilton Rd., Westport, CT 06880, ☎ 800/468–2825 or 203/226–6911). Another operator falling between deluxe and first-class is **Globus** (5301 S. Federal Circle, Littleton, CO 80123, ☎ 800/221–0090 or 303/797–2800). In the first-class and tourist range, contact **Collette Tours** (162 Middle St., Pawtucket, RI 02860, ☎ 800/832–4656 or 401/728–3805); and **Mayflower Tours** (1225 Warren Ave., Downers Grove, IL 60515, ☎ 708/960–3430 or 800/323–7604). For budget and tourist class programs, try **Cosmos** (*see* Globus, *above*).

ORGANIZATIONS

The **National Tour Association** (546 E. Main St., Lexington, KY 40508, ☎ 606/226–4444 or 800/755–8687) and **United States Tour Operators Association** (USTOA, 211 E. 51st St., Suite 12B, New York, NY 10022, ☎ 212/750–7371) can provide lists of member operators and information on booking tours.

PACKAGES

Independent vacation packages are available from major airlines and tour operators. Contact **American Airlines Fly AAway Vacations** (☎ 800/321–2121); **Certified Vacations** (Box 1525, Fort Lauderdale, FL 33302, ☎ 305/522–1414 or 800/233–7260); **Continental Airlines Grand Destinations** (☎ 800/634–5555); **Delta Dream Vacations** (☎ 800/872–7786); **Globetrotters**

THE GOLD GUIDE / IMPORTANT CONTACTS

(139 Main St., Cambridge, MA 02142, ☎ 617/621–9911 or 800/999–9696); **Kingdom Tours** (300 Market St., Kingston, PA 18704, ☎ 717/283–4241 or 800/872–8857); **United Vacations** (☎ 800/328–6877); and **USAir Vacations** (☎ 800/455–0123). **Funjet Vacations** based in Milwaukee, Wisconsin, and **Gogo Tours** in Ramsey, New Jersey, sell packages to Colorado available through travel agents only.

PUBLICATIONS

Consult the brochure **"On Tour"** and ask for a current list of member operators from the National Tour Association (*see* Organizations, *above*). Also get a copy of the **"Worldwide Tour & Vacation Package Finder"** from the National Tour Association (*see* Organizations, *above*) and the Better Business Bureau's **"Tips on Travel Packages"** (Publication No. 24-195; 4200 Wilson Blvd., Arlington, VA 22203; $2).

For one-of-a-kind Western itineraries with stays at unique inns and ranches, contact **Off the Beaten Path** (109 E. Main St., Bozeman, MT 59715, ☎ 406/586–1311, ☎ 406/587–4147). The company customizes trips for individual travelers that include little-known attractions and restaurants.

THEME TRIPS

ADVENTURE➤ **All Adventure Travel** (5589 Arapahoe, No. 208, Boulder, CO 80303,

☎ 800/537–4025), with more than 80 tour operator members, can satisfy virtually any special interest in Colorado.

BICYCLING➤ Bike tours of Colorado are available from **Backroads** (1516 5th St., Suite A550, Berkeley, CA 94710, ☎ 510/527–1555 or 800/462–2848) and **Cycle America** (Box 485, Cannon Falls, MN 55009, ☎ 800/245–3263).

CAMPING➤ For Western U.S. camping trips in the company of travelers from all over the globe, check out the programs of **Trek America** (Box 470, Blairstown, NJ 07825, ☎ 908/362–9198 or 800/221–0596).

NATURE➤ For learning vacations in one of Colorado's national parks, contact the **National Audubon Society** (National Environmental Education Center, 613 Riversville Rd., Greenwich, CT 06831, ☎ 203/869–2017) and the **National Wildlife Federation** (1400 16th St. NW, Washington, DC 20036, ☎ 703/790–4363 or 800/432–6564). **Questers Worldwide Nature Tours** (275 Park Ave. S, New York, NY 10010, ☎ 212/673–3120 or 800/468–8668) has nature tours with all the comforts of home.

RIVER RAFTING➤ Contact **OARS** (Box 67, Angels Camp, CA 95222, ☎ 209/736–4677) for a complete selection of Colorado trips.

TRAVEL AGENCIES

For names of reputable agencies in your area, contact the **American Society of Travel Agents** (1101 King St., Suite 200, Alexandria, VA 22314, ☎ 703/739–2782).

IN THE U.K.

Travel agencies that offer cheap fares to Colorado include **Trailfinders** (42–50 Earl's Court Rd., London W8 6FT, ☎ 0171/937–5400), **Travel Cuts** (295a Regent St., London W1R 7YA, ☎ 0171/637–3161), and **Flightfile** (49 Tottenham Court Rd., London W1P 9RE, ☎ 0171/700–2722).

V

VISITOR
INFORMATION

Contact the **Colorado State Tourist Office** (☎ 800/433–2656) to receive a vacation planner and **TravelBank Colorado** (Box 200594, Denver, CO 80220, ☎ and fax 303/320–8550) for information via modem. In Canada, call the **U.S. Travel and Tourism Office** (480 University Ave., Suite 602, Toronto, Ontario M5G IV2, ☎ 416/595–0335, FAX 416/595–5211).

In the U.K., also contact the **United States Travel and Tourism Administration** (Box 1EN, London W1A 1EN, ☎ 0171/495–4466). For a free USA pack, write the USTTA at Box 170, Ashford, Kent TN24 0ZX). Enclose stamps worth £1.50.

W

WEATHER

For current conditions and forecasts, plus the local time and helpful travel tips, call the **Weather Channel Connection** (☎ 900/932–8437; 95¢ per minute) from a Touch-Tone phone.

SMART TRAVEL TIPS A TO Z

Basic Information on Traveling in Colorado and Savvy Tips to Make Your Trip a Breeze

The more you travel, the more you know about how to make trips run like clockwork. To help make your travels hassle-free, Fodor's editors have rounded up dozens of tips from our contributors and travel experts all over the world, as well as basic information on visiting Colorado. For names of organizations to contact and publications that can give you more information, *see* Important Contacts A to Z, *above*.

A
AIR TRAVEL

If time is an issue, **always look for nonstop flights,** which require no change of plane. If possible, **avoid connecting flights,** which stop at least once and can involve a change of plane, although the flight number remains the same; if the first leg is late, the second waits.

ALOFT

AIRLINE FOOD➤ If you hate airline food, **ask for special meals when booking.** These can be vegetarian, low-cholesterol, or kosher, for example; commonly prepared to order in smaller quantities than standard catered fare, they can be tastier.

SMOKING➤ Smoking is banned on all flights within the United States of less than six hours' duration and on all Canadian flights; the ban also applies to domestic segments of international flights aboard U.S. and foreign carriers.

CUTTING COSTS

The Sunday travel section of most newspapers is a good source of deals.

CONSOLIDATORS➤ Consolidators, who buy tickets at reduced rates from scheduled airlines, sell them at prices below the lowest available from the airlines directly—usually without advance restrictions. Sometimes you can even get your money back if you need to return the ticket. Carefully read the fine print detailing penalties for changes and cancellations. If you doubt the reliability of a consolidator, **confirm your reservation with the airline.**

MAJOR AIRLINES➤ The least-expensive airfares from the major airlines are priced for round-trip travel and are subject to restrictions. You must usually **book in advance and buy the ticket within 24 hours** to get cheaper fares, and you may have to **stay over a Saturday night.** The lowest fare is subject to availability, and only a small percentage of the plane's total seats are sold at that price. It's good to **call a number of airlines,** and **when you are quoted a good price,** **book it on the spot**—the same fare on the same flight may not be available the next day. Airlines generally allow you to change your return date for a $25 to $50 fee, but most low-fare tickets are nonrefundable. However, if you don't use it, you can apply the cost toward the purchase price of a new ticket, again for a small charge.

B
BUSINESS HOURS

Throughout Colorado, most retail stores are open from 9 or 9:30 until 6 or 7 daily in downtown locations and until 9 or 10 in suburban shopping malls. Downtown stores sometimes stay open later on Thursday night. Normal banking hours are weekdays 9–5; some branches are also open on Saturday morning.

C
CAMERAS, CAMCORDERS, AND COMPUTERS

LAPTOPS

Before you depart, **check your portable computer's battery,** because you may be asked at security to turn on the computer to prove that it is what it appears to be. At the airport, you may prefer to **request a manual inspection,** although security X-rays do not harm hard-disk or floppy-disk storage.

PHOTOGRAPHY

If your camera is new or if you haven't used it for a while, **shoot and develop a few rolls of film** before you leave. Always **store film in a cool, dry place**—never in the car's glove compartment or on the shelf under the rear window.

Every pass of film through an X-ray machine increases the chance of clouding. To protect it, carry it in a clear plastic bag and **ask for hand inspection at security.** Such requests are virtually always honored at U.S. airports. Don't depend on a lead-lined bag to protect film in checked luggage—the airline may increase the radiation to see what's inside.

VIDEO

Before your trip, **test your camcorder, invest in a skylight filter to protect the lens, and charge the batteries.** (Airport security personnel may ask you to turn on the camcorder to prove that it's what it appears to be.)

Videotape is not damaged by X-rays, but it may be harmed by the magnetic field of a walk-through metal detector, so **ask that videotapes be hand-checked.**

CHILDREN AND TRAVEL

With dude ranches and many outdoor activities, Colorado is tailor-made for family vacations. But plan ahead, and

involve your youngsters as you outline your trip. When packing, **bring a supply of things to keep them busy** in the car, on the airplane, on the train, or however you are traveling (*see* Children and Travel *in* Important Contacts A to Z, *above*). Driving gives you the option of stopping frequently to let them get out and burn off energy.

Many Colorado resorts have innovative children's programs. Day-care centers and children's ski schools are de rigueur throughout the state. In summer, the Telluride Kids' Academy introduces children to the Old West, with gold panning, rock climbing, and camping in an authentic tepee. Children adore Colorado's special events, from winter carnivals and county fairs to kid-oriented rodeos. If you **plan your itinerary around seasonal festivals,** you'll never lack things to do. In addition, **check local newspapers for special events** mounted by public libraries, museums, parks, and YMCA/YWCAs.

BABY-SITTING

For recommended local sitters, **check with your hotel desk.**

DRIVING

If you are renting a car, **arrange for a car seat when you reserve.** Sometimes they're free.

FLYING

On domestic flights, children under 2 not occupying a seat travel free, and older children

currently travel on the lowest applicable adult fare.

BAGGAGE➢ In general, the adult baggage allowance applies for children paying half or more of the adult fare.

FACILITIES➢ When making your reservation, **ask for children's meals or freestanding bassinets** if you need them; the latter are available only to those with seats at the bulkhead, where there's enough legroom. If you don't need a bassinet, **think twice before requesting bulkhead seats**—the only storage for in-flight necessities is in the inconveniently distant overhead bins.

SAFETY SEATS➢ According to the Federal Aviation Administrations (FAA), it's good to **use safety seats aloft.** Airline policy varies. U.S. carriers allow FAA-approved models, but airlines usually require that you buy a ticket, even if your child would otherwise ride free, because the seats must be strapped into regular passenger seats.

LODGING

Most hotels allow children under a certain age to stay in their parents' room at no extra charge, while others charge them as extra adults; be sure to **ask about the cutoff age.**

CUSTOMS AND DUTIES

IN COLORADO

Foreign visitors age 21 or over may import the following into the

United States: 200 cigarettes or 50 cigars or 2 kilograms of tobacco; 1 U.S. liter of alcohol; gifts valued at $100. Restricted items include meat products, seeds, plants, and fruits. Never carry illegal drugs.

BACK HOME

IN CANADA➤ Once per calendar year, when you've been out of Canada for at least seven days, you may bring in C$300 worth of goods duty-free. If you've been away less than seven days but more than 48 hours, the duty-free exemption drops to C$100 but can be claimed any number of times (as can a C$20 duty-free exemption for absences of 24 hours or more). You cannot combine the yearly and 48-hour exemptions, use the C$300 exemption only partially (to save the balance for a later trip), or pool exemptions with family members. Goods claimed under the C$300 exemption may follow you by mail; those claimed under the lesser exemptions must accompany you.

Alcohol and tobacco products may be included in the yearly and 48-hour exemptions but not in the 24-hour exemption. If you meet the age requirements of the province through which you reenter Canada, you may bring in, duty-free, 1.14 liters (40 imperial ounces) of wine or liquor *or* 24 12-ounce cans or bottles of beer or ale. If you are 16 or older, you may bring in, duty-free,

200 cigarettes, 50 cigars or cigarillos, and 400 tobacco sticks or 400 grams of manufactured tobacco. Alcohol and tobacco must accompany you on your return.

An unlimited number of gifts valued up to C$60 each may be mailed to Canada duty-free. These do not count as part of your exemption. Label the package "Unsolicited Gift—Value Under $60." Alcohol and tobacco are excluded.

IN THE U.K.➤ From countries outside the European Union, including the United States, you may import duty-free 200 cigarettes, 100 cigarillos, 50 cigars or 250 grams of tobacco; 1 liter of spirits or 2 liters of fortified or sparkling wine; 2 liters of still table wine; 60 milliliters of perfume; 250 milliliters of toilet water; plus £136 worth of other goods, including gifts and souvenirs.

D

FOR TRAVELERS
WITH DISABILITIES

When discussing accessibility with an operator or reservationist, **ask hard questions.** Are there any stairs, inside *or* out? Are there grab bars next to the toilet *and* in the shower/tub? How wide is the doorway to the room? To the bathroom? For the most extensive facilities, meeting the latest legal specifications, **opt for newer accommodations,** which more often have been designed with access in mind. Older

properties must usually be retrofitted and may offer more limited facilities as a result. Be sure to **discuss your needs before booking.**

DISCOUNT CLUBS

Travel clubs offer members unsold space on airplanes, cruise ships, and package tours at as much as 50% below regular prices. Membership may include a regular bulletin or access to a toll-free hot line giving details of available trips departing from three or four days to several months in the future. Most also offer 50% discounts off hotel rack rates. Before booking with a club, **make sure the hotel or other supplier isn't offering a better deal.**

DRIVING

The Rockies offer some of the most spectacular vistas and challenging drives in the world. Roads range from multilane blacktop to barely graveled backroad trails; from twisting switchbacks with well-placed guardrails to primitive campgrounds with lanes so narrow that the driver has to back up to the edge of a steep cliff to make a turn. Scenic routes and lookout points are clearly marked, enabling visitors to slow down and pull over to enjoy the views. One can seldom be bored driving through Colorado, since the terrain is so rugged and mountainous.

Highways and the national parks are

crowded during the summer months (June, July, and August), and almost deserted (and occasionally impassable) in winter. Follow the speed limit, drive defensively, and **make sure your gas tank is full,** since distances between gas stations could make running on empty (or in the reserve zone) a not-so-pleasant memory of your trip.

A word to drivers: Roadkills—animals struck by vehicles—are among the more unpleasant sights along the highway. Be aware that deer, elk, and even bears might cross the road just as you're driving by. Exercise caution, not only to save a life, but also to avoid possible extensive damage to your car.

The speed limit is 65 miles per hour on U.S. interstate highways in rural areas and 55 miles per hour in urban zones and on secondary highways. Throughout this book, "CO" refers to state roads, while "CR" is used for county routes.

WINTER DRIVING

Modern highways make mountain driving safe and generally trouble-free even in cold weather. Although winter driving can occasionally present some real challenges, road maintenance is good and plowing is prompt. However, in mountain areas, tire chains, studs, or snow tires are essential. If you're planning to drive into high elevations, be sure to **check the weather forecast** be-

forehand. Even the mountain passes on main highways may be forced to close because of snow. The Colorado State Highway Department has a number to call for road conditions (*see* Driving *in* Important Contacts A to Z, *above*). Be prepared for stormy weather: **carry an emergency kit** containing warm clothes, a flashlight, some food, and perhaps a sleeping bag. If you do get stalled by deep snow, do not leave your car. Wait for help, running the engine only if needed.

H
HEALTH ISSUES

ALTITUDE

You may feel dizzy and weak and find yourself breathing heavily— signs that the thin mountain air isn't giving you your accustomed dose of oxygen. It's good to **drink plenty of water, avoid heavy intake of alcohol and caffeine, and rest often** until you're acclimatized. If you experience severe headaches and nausea, see a doctor. Other altitude-related problems include dehydration and overexposure to the sun due to the thin air.

I
INSURANCE

BAGGAGE

Airline liability for your baggage is limited to $1,250 per person on domestic flights. On international flights, the airlines' liability is $9.07 per pound or $20 per kilogram for

checked baggage (roughly $640 per 70-pound bag) and $400 per passenger for unchecked baggage. Insurance for losses exceeding the terms of your airline ticket can be bought directly from the airline at check-in for about $10 per $1,000 of coverage; note that it excludes a rather extensive list of items, shown on your airline ticket.

FLIGHT

You should **think twice before buying flight insurance.** Often purchased as a last-minute impulse at the airport, it pays a lump sum when a plane crashes, either to a beneficiary if the insured dies or sometimes to a surviving passenger who loses eyesight or a limb. Supplementing the airlines' coverage described in the limits-of-liability paragraphs on your ticket, it's expensive and basically unnecessary. Charging an airline ticket to a major credit card often automatically entitles you to coverage and may also embrace travel by bus, train, and ship.

FOR U.K. TRAVELERS

According to the Association of British Insurers, a trade association representing 450 insurance companies, it's wise to **buy extra medical coverage when you visit the United States.** You can buy an annual travel-insurance policy valid for most vacations during the year in which it's purchased. If you go this route, make sure it covers you if you have a preexisting medical condition or are pregnant.

TRIP

Without insurance, you will lose all or most of your money if you must cancel your trip due to illness or any other reason. Especially if your airline ticket or package tour is nonrefundable and cannot be changed, it's essential that you **buy trip-cancellation-and-interruption insurance.** When considering how much coverage you need, look for a policy that will cover the cost of your trip plus the nondiscounted price of a one-way airline ticket should you need to return home early. Read the fine print carefully, especially sections defining "family member" and "preexisting medical conditions." Also **consider default or bankruptcy insurance,** which protects you against a supplier's failure to deliver. However, such policies often do not cover default by a travel agency, tour operator, or airline if you bought your tour and the coverage directly from the firm in question.

L
LODGING

APARTMENT AND VILLA RENTALS

If you want a home base that's roomy enough for a family and comes with cooking facilities, **consider a furnished rental.** It's generally cost-wise, too, although not always— some rentals are luxury properties (economical

only when your party is large). Home-exchange directories do list rentals—often second homes owned by prospective house swappers—and some services search for a house or apartment for you (even a castle if that's your fancy) and handle the paperwork. Some send an illustrated catalogue and others send photographs of specific properties, sometimes at a charge; up-front registration fees may apply (*see* Lodging *in* Important Contacts A to Z, *above*).

CAMPING

Camping is an invigorating and inexpensive way to tour Colorado. The state is full of state and national parks and forests with sites that range from rustic, with pit toilets and cold running water, to campgrounds with full hookups, bathhouses with hot showers, and paved trailer pads that can accommodate even jumbo RVs. Fees vary, from $6 to $10 a night for tents, up to $21 for RVs, but are usually waived once the water is turned off for the winter. Sometimes site reservations are accepted, and then only for up to seven days (early birds reserve up to a year in advance); more often, they're not. Campers who prefer a more remote setting may camp in the backcountry; it's free but you'll need a permit, available from park visitor centers and ranger stations. If you're visiting in summer, plan well ahead.

The National Parks: Camping Guide ($3.50; Superintendent of Documents, U.S. Government Printing Office, Washington, DC 20402) may be helpful.

In addition, you'll find privately operated campgrounds; their facilities and amenities are usually more extensive (swimming pools are common), reservations are more widely accepted, and nightly fees are higher: $7 and up for tents, $23 for RVs.

GUEST RANCHES

If the thought of sitting around a campfire after a hard day on the range makes your heart beat faster, **consider playing dude** on a guest ranch. These range from wilderness-rimmed working ranches that accept guests and encourage them to pitch in with chores and other ranch activities to luxurious resorts, on the fringes of a small city, with an upscale clientele, swimming pools, tennis courts, and a lively roster of horse-related activities such as breakfast rides, moonlight rides, all-day trail rides, and the like. Rafting, fishing, tubing, and other activities in the surrounding wilderness are usually available, and at working ranches, guests may be able to participate in a cattle roundup. In winter, cross-country skiing and snowshoeing keep guests busy. Lodging can run the gamut from charmingly rustic cabins to the kind of deluxe quarters you expect at a first-class hotel. Meals may be gourmet or plain but hearty. Many ranches offer packages and children's and off-season rates.

HOME EXCHANGE

If you would like to find a house, an apartment, or other vacation property to exchange for your own while on vacation, **become a member of a home-exchange organization,** which will send you its annual directories listing available exchanges and will include your own listing in at least one of them. Arrangements for the actual exchange are made by the two parties to it, not by the organization.

INNS AND BED-AND-BREAKFASTS

Charm is the long suit of inns, which generally occupy a restored older building with some historical or architectural significance. They're usually small, with under 20 rooms, and outside cities. Breakfast may be included in the rates.

B&Bs are private homes whose owners welcome paying guests. They usually have anywhere from two to ten rooms, some with private baths and some with shared facilities, and always serve breakfast at no extra charge. The decor and the hospitality reflect the personalities and tastes of the B&B's owners to an even greater degree than at inns.

RESORTS

Colorado resorts range from fishing lodges to luxury turn-of-the-century showplaces such as the Broadmoor in Colorado Springs. Ski-resort towns throughout the state are home to dozens of facilities in all price ranges; the activities lacking in any individual property can usually be found in the town itself, in summer as well as winter.

M MONEY AND EXPENSES

ATMS

Chances are that you can **use your bank card at ATMs** to withdraw money from an account and get cash advances on a credit-card account if your card has been programmed with a personal identification number, or PIN. Before leaving home, **check in on frequency limits** for withdrawals and cash advances.

On cash advances you are charged interest from the day you receive the money, whether from a teller or an ATM. Transaction fees for ATM withdrawals outside your home turf may be higher than for withdrawals at home.

COSTS

First-class hotel rooms in Denver cost from $75 to $175 a night, although some "value" hotel rooms go for $40 to $60, and, as elsewhere in the United States, rooms in national budget chain motels go for about $40 nightly. Weekend packages, offered by most city hotels, cut prices up to 50% (but may not be available in peak winter or summer seasons). As a rule, costs outside the major cities are lower, except in some of the deluxe resorts. A cup of coffee costs about 75¢, the price for a hamburger runs between $4 and $5, and a beer at a bar generally costs from $2 to $3.

TAX

Sales tax is 3% in Colorado. City and state taxes may also apply to services and purchases; tax varies depending on city and county.

TRAVELER'S CHECKS

Whether or not to buy traveler's checks depends on where you are headed; **take cash to rural areas and small towns, traveler's checks to cities.** The most widely recognized are American Express, Citicorp, Thomas Cook, and Visa, which are sold by major commercial banks for 1% to 3% of the checks' face value—it pays to **shop around.** Both American Express and Thomas Cook issue checks that can be counter-signed and used by you or your traveling companion. Record the numbers of the checks, cross them off as you spend them, and keep this information separate from your checks.

WIRING MONEY

You don't have to be a cardholder to send or receive funds through MoneyGram[SM] from American Express. Just go to a MoneyGram agent, in retail and convenience stores and in American Express Travel Offices. Pay up to $1,000 with cash or a credit card, anything over that in cash. The money can be picked up within 10 minutes in cash or check at the nearest MoneyGram agent. There's no limit, and the recipient need only present photo identification. The cost, which includes a free long-distance phone call, runs from 3% to 10%, depending on the amount sent, the destination, and how you pay.

You can also send money using Western Union. Money sent from the United States or Canada will be available for pickup at agent locations in 100 countries within 15 minutes. Once the money is in the system, it can be picked up at any one of 25,000 locations. Fees range from 4% to 10%, depending on the amount you send.

P
PACKAGES
AND TOURS

A package or tour to Colorado can make your vacation less expensive and more convenient. Firms that sell tours and packages purchase airline seats, hotel rooms, and rental cars in bulk and pass some of the savings on to you. In addition, the best operators have local representatives to help you out at your destination.

A GOOD DEAL?

The more your package or tour includes, the better you can predict the ultimate cost of your vacation. Make sure you know exactly what is included, and **beware of hidden costs.** Are taxes, tips, and service charges included? Transfers and baggage handling? Entertainment and excursions? These can add up.

Most packages and tours are rated deluxe, first-class superior, first class, tourist, or budget. The key difference is usually accommodations. If the package or tour you are considering is priced lower than in your wildest dreams, **be skeptical.** Also, **make sure your travel agent knows the hotels** and other services. Ask about location, room size, beds, and whether the facility has a pool, room service, or programs for children, if you care about these. Has your agent been there or sent others you can contact?

BUYER BEWARE

Each year consumers are stranded or lose their money when operators go out of business—even very large ones with excellent reputations. If you can't afford a loss, take the time to **check out the operator**—find out how long the company has been in business, and ask several agents about its reputation. Next, **don't book unless the firm has a consumer-protection program.** Members of the United States Tour

Operators Association and the National Tour Association are required to set aside funds exclusively to cover your payments and travel arrangements in case of default. Nonmember operators may instead carry insurance; look for the details in the operator's brochure— and the name of an underwriter with a solid reputation. Note: When it comes to tour operators, **don't trust escrow accounts.** Although there are laws governing those of charter-flight operators, no governmental body prevents tour operators from raiding the till.

Next, **contact your local Better Business Bureau and the attorney general's office** in both your own state and the operator's; have any complaints been filed? Last, **pay with a major credit card.** Then you can cancel payment, provided that you can document your complaint. Always **consider trip-cancellation insurance** (*see* Insurance, *above*).

BIG vs. SMALL➤ An operator that handles several hundred thousand travelers annually can use its purchasing power to give you a good price. Its high volume may also indicate financial stability. But some small companies provide more personalized service; because they tend to specialize, they may also be experts on an area.

SINGLE TRAVELERS

Prices are usually quoted per person, based on two sharing a room. If traveling solo, you may be required to pay the full double occupancy rate. Some operators eliminate this surcharge if you agree to be matched up with a roommate of the same sex, even if one is not found by departure time.

USING AN AGENT

Travel agents are an excellent resource. In fact, large operators accept bookings only through travel agents. But it's good to **collect brochures from several agencies,** because some agents' suggestions may be skewed by promotional relationships with tour and package firms that reward them for volume sales. If you have a special interest, **find an agent with expertise in that area;** the American Society of Travel Agents can give you leads in the United States. (Don't rely solely on your agent, though; agents may be unaware of small-niche operators, and some special-interest travel companies only sell direct).

PACKING FOR COLORADO

Informality reigns in Colorado, and casual clothing is acceptable—even expected—in most places. Jeans, sport shirts, and T-shirts fit in almost everywhere, for both men and women. The few restaurants and performing arts events where dressier outfits are required, largely in resorts and larger cities, are the exception.

If you plan to spend much time outdoors, and certainly if you go in winter, choose clothing appropriate for cold and wet weather. Cotton clothing, including denim—although fine on warm, dry days—can be uncomfortable when it gets wet and when the weather's cold. A better choice is clothing made of wool or any of a number of new synthetics that provide warmth without bulk and maintain their insulating properties even when wet. Prepare for winter's below-zero temperatures and pack good boots, warm socks and liners, long johns, a well-insulated jacket, and a warm hat and mittens.

In summer, you'll want shorts during the day. But because early morning and night can be cold, and high passes windy, pack a sweater and a light jacket, and perhaps also a wool cap and gloves. Try layering—a T-shirt under another shirt under a jacket—and peel off layers as you go. For walks and hikes, you'll need sturdy footwear. To take you into the wilds they should have thick soles and plenty of ankle support; if your shoes are new and you plan to spend much time on the trail, break them in at home. Bring a light backpack for day hikes, along with a canteen or water bottle, and don't forget rain gear.

If you attend dances and other events at Native American reservations, dress conservatively—skirts or long pants for women, long pants for men—or you may be asked to leave.

When traveling to mountain areas, **remember that sunglasses and a sun hat are essential at high altitudes;** the thinner atmosphere requires sunscreen with a greater SPF than you might need at lower elevations. Bring an extra pair of eyeglasses or contact lenses in your carry-on luggage, and if you have a health problem, **pack enough medication** to last the trip. **Don't put prescription drugs or valuables in luggage to be checked,** for it could go astray.

LUGGAGE

Free airline baggage allowances depend on the airline, the route, and the class of your ticket; ask in advance. In general, on domestic flights you are entitled to check two bags—neither exceeding 62 inches, or 158 centimeters (length + width + height), or weighing more than 70 pounds (32 kilograms). A third piece may be brought aboard; its total dimensions are generally limited to less than 45 inches (114 centimeters), so it will fit easily under the seat in front of you or in the overhead compartment. In the United States, the FAA gives airlines broad latitude to limit carry-on allowances and tailor them to different aircraft and operational conditions. Charges for excess, oversize, or overweight pieces vary.

SAFEGUARDING YOUR LUGGAGE> Before leaving home, **itemize**

your bags' contents and their worth, and label them with your name, address, and phone number. (If you use your home address, cover it so that potential thieves can't see it.) Inside your bag, **pack a copy of your itinerary.** At check-in, **make sure that your bag is correctly tagged** with the airport's three-letter destination code. If your bags arrive damaged or not at all, file a written report with the airline before leaving the airport.

PASSPORTS AND VISAS

CANADIANS

No passport is necessary to enter the United States.

U.K. CITIZENS

British citizens need a valid passport. If you are staying fewer than 90 days and traveling on a vacation, with a return or onward ticket, you will probably not need a visa. However, you will need to fill out the Visa Waiver Form, 1-94W, supplied by the airline. While traveling, **keep one photocopy of the data page** separate from your wallet and leave another copy with someone at home. If you lose your passport, promptly call the nearest embassy or consulate, and the local police; having the data page can speed replacement.

R RENTING A CAR

CUTTING COSTS

To get the best deal, **book through a travel agent and shop around.**

When pricing cars, **ask where the rental lot is located.** Some off-airport locations offer lower rates—even though their lots are only minutes away from the terminal via complimentary shuttle. You may also want to **price local car-rental companies,** whose rates may be lower still, although service and maintenance standards may not be up to those of a national firm. Also **ask your travel agent about a company's customer-service record.** How has it responded to late plane arrivals and vehicle mishaps? Are there often lines at the rental counter, and, if you're traveling during a holiday period, does a confirmed reservation guarantee you a car?

INSURANCE

When you drive a rented car, you are generally responsible for any damage or personal injury that you cause as well as damage to the vehicle. Before you rent, **see what coverage you already have** under the terms of your personal auto-insurance policy and credit cards. For about $14 a day, rental companies sell insurance, known as a collision damage waiver (CDW), that eliminates your liability for damage to the car; it's always optional and should never be automatically added to your bill.

SURCHARGES

Before picking up the car in one city and leaving it in another, **ask about drop-off charges or one-way**

service fees, which can be substantial. Note, too, that some rental agencies charge extra if you return the car before the time specified on your contract. To avoid a hefty refueling fee, **fill the tank just before you turn in the car.**

FOR U.K. CITIZENS

In the United States you must be 21 to rent a car; rates may be higher for those under 25. Extra costs cover child seats, compulsory for children under 5 (about $3 per day), and additional drivers (about $1.50 per day). To pick up your reserved car you will need the reservation voucher, a passport, a U.K. driver's license, and a travel policy covering each driver.

S SENIOR-CITIZEN DISCOUNTS

To qualify for age-related discounts, **mention your senior-citizen status up front** when booking hotel reservations, not when checking out, and before you're seated in restaurants, not when paying your bill. Note that discounts may be limited to certain menus, days, or hours. When renting a car, **ask about promotional car-rental discounts**—they can net lower costs than your senior-citizen discount.

STUDENTS ON THE ROAD

To save money, **look into deals available through student-ori-**

ented travel agencies. To qualify, you'll need to have a bona fide student ID card. Members of international student groups also are eligible. *See* Students *in* Important Contacts A to Z, *above.*

T
TELEPHONES

The telephone area codes for Colorado are 303, 970, and 719.

Pay telephones cost 25¢ for local calls. Charge phones are also found in many locations. These phones can be used to charge a call to a telephone-company calling card, a credit card, or your home phone, or for collect calls.

LONG DISTANCE

The long-distance services of AT&T, MCI, and Sprint make calling home relatively convenient and let you avoid hotel surcharges; typically, you dial an 800 number in the United States.

W
WHEN TO GO

Summer is one of Colorado's two big seasons. In fact,

transplanted locals have a saying, "We came for the winters, but we stayed for the summers." In many major tourist destinations, hotels fill up, especially in July and August (book well ahead to avoid disappointment). Backcountry campsites fill up, too, from June through Labor Day. Many ski resort towns offer significantly lower rates in summer. Note that many national parks and monuments are either partially or entirely closed October through May.

Winter is also prime time. Ski resorts buzz from December to early April; Christmas week attracts the largest crowds. Driving is chancy, and, although the interstates are kept open, mountain passes are usually closed.

If you don't mind sometimes-capricious weather, spring and fall are terrific; rates drop and crowds are nonexistent. Spring's pleasures are somewhat limited, since snow usually blocks the high country well into June. But spring is a good time for fishing, rafting

on rivers swollen with snowmelt, birding, and wildlife-viewing. In fall, aspen splash the mountainsides with gold, and wildlife come down to lower elevations. The fish are spawning, and the angling is excellent.

CLIMATE

Despite its well-deserved reputation for erratic weather conditions, Colorado averages about 300 days of sunshine each year, making it one of America's sunniest states. While sometimes brutally hot on the plains, summer days are milder in the mountains, where the mercury rarely reaches 90 degrees (remember, though, that the high altitude makes the sun's rays stronger). Evening temperatures drop into the 40s and 50s. Thunderstorms are common over the higher peaks. Spring and fall are usually quite pleasant, with temperatures in the 70s. Winter can be devastatingly cold, often with subzero temperatures on the western slope of the Rockies. What follows are the average daily maximum and minimum temperatures for Aspen.

Climate in Aspen

Jan.	33F	1C	May	64F	18C	Sept.	71F	22C
	6	−14		32	0		35	2
Feb.	37F	3C	June	73F	23C	Oct.	60F	16C
	8	−13		37	3		28	−2
Mar.	42F	6C	July	80F	27C	Nov.	44F	7C
	15	−9		44	7		15	−9
Apr.	53F	12C	Aug.	78F	26C	Dec.	37F	3C
	24	−4		42	6		8	−13

1 Destination: Colorado

INTRODUCTION

TEDDY ROOSEVELT SPOKE OF COLORADO as "scenery to bankrupt the English language." Walt Whitman wrote that its beauty "awakens those grandest and subtlest elements in the human soul." For more than 200 years pioneers, poets and presidents alike have rhapsodized over what an increasing number of "out-of-towners" are learning: that Colorado is one of America's prime chunks of real estate.

Colorado is a state of sharp, stunning contrasts. The Rockies create a mountainous spine that's larger than Switzerland, with 52 eternally snowcapped summits towering higher than 14,000 feet. Yet its eastern third is a sea of hypnotically waving grasslands; its southwest, a vibrant multihued desert, carved with pink and mauve canyons, vaulting cinnamon spires, and gnarled red rock monoliths. Its mighty rivers, the Colorado, Arkansas, and Gunnison, etch deep, yawning chasms every bit as impressive as the shimmering blue-tinged glaciers and jagged peaks of the San Juan, Sangre de Cristo, and Front ranges. Add to this glittering sapphire lakes and jade forests, and you have an outdoor paradise second to none.

Much of the state's visual appeal can also be attributed to the legacy of the frontier and mining days, when gold, silver, and railroad barons left an equally rich treasure trove of Victorian architecture in the lavish monuments they built to themselves. The Old West comes alive in Colorado, where you're practically driving through the pages of a history book. The first Europeans to explore were the Spanish, who left their imprint in the lyrical names and distinctive architecture of the southern part of the state. They were followed by trappers, scouts, and explorers, including some of the legendary names in American history—Zebulon Pike, Kit Carson, Stephen Long, and William Bent—intent on exploiting some of the area's rich natural resources, including vast lodes of gold and silver. In so doing they displaced—and often massacred—the original settlers, Pawnee, Comanche, Ute, and Pueblo, whose ancestors, the Anasazi, fashioned the spectacular, haunting cliff dwellings of Mesa Verde National Park.

The controversy and contentiousness live on. In 1992 Colorado made national headlines when it passed Amendment 2, carefully worded (some say deliberately vague) legislation designed to outlaw antidiscrimination bills. In reality, the amendment was aimed directly at homosexuals, and sought to reverse existing local gay-rights ordinances. (Aspen, Boulder, and Denver were among the first communities in the nation to pass such ordinances.)

In response to the legislation, a boycott was called (and has since been canceled) by liberal and gay/lesbian groups nationwide, with mixed results. The state picked up almost as much convention business from conservative organizations as it lost, and a superb 1992-93 snow season brought skiers in droves. Amendment 2 was declared unconstitutional by the state Supreme Court in 1993. Colorado appealed, and the U.S. Supreme Court agreed to hear arguments in the fall of 1995, with a decision to follow in early 1996.

Indeed, despite the Amendment 2 controversy, Colorado has its progressive side: It was the first state to send a Native American to the Senate in 1992: Ben "Nighthorse" Campbell, himself a figure of controversy for his flamboyant style and mannerisms. Senator Campbell proved to be a maverick in true Colorado tradition when he switched parties from Democratic to Republican upon reaching Congress.

Along with feisty independence, be it right- or left-wing, Coloradans have always displayed an eccentric, even ostentatious streak. State history is animated by stories of fabulous wealth and equally spectacular ruin in the bountiful precious-metal mines. Discovery of gold in 1859 spurred the first major settlement of Colorado, followed by the inevitable railroad lines for transport. When the lodes petered out, many of the thriving communities became virtual ghost towns, until the discovery of black gold in the oil-shale reserves of northwest Colorado and, especially, white gold on the ski slopes.

Today Colorado is a state of unabashed nature lovers and outdoors enthusiasts. Though most people associate the state with skiing, residents have a saying, "We came for the winters, but we stayed for the summers." In addition to skiing and snowmobiling in winter, they climb, hike, bike, fish, and camp in the summer, making Colorado one of America's premier four-seasons destinations.

WHAT'S WHERE

Denver
One of the fastest-growing cities in America, Denver is an appealing blend of high-tech glitz and down-home warmth. It offers some splendid museums; historic homes; the vibrant lower downtown (or LoDo) scene, with galleries, boutiques, brew pubs, and restaurants galore; and miles of greenbelt where all Denver bikes, jogs, and hangs out. It's also conveniently located for day trips to Golden (home of the Coors Brewery and Buffalo Bill's grave) and the Victorian mining towns, Central City and Blackhawk, which allow limited stakes gambling.

I–70 and the High Rockies
Like Denver, the High Rockies region is an invigorating blend of old and new, from evocative Victorian mining towns like Georgetown, Idaho Springs, and Leadville to prefab ski area developments like Copper Mountain, Keystone, and Vail. These and other leading resort towns, like Aspen, Breckenridge, and Steamboat (all of which have lovingly preserved their Victorian past), make the High Rockies one of America's premier sports destinations.

Southwest Colorado
Southwestern Colorado may be the most hauntingly beautiful part of the state, encompassing a range of ecosystems from high alpine to semi-arid desert, with 14,000-foot peaks plummeting to 2,000-foot deep canyons. The area is equally rich architecturally, from the exquisite Victorian gingerbreads of Ouray, Crested Butte, and Telluride (all outdoors meccas, attracting skiers, mountain bikers, and climbers) to the ornate mansions of railroad town Durango to the eerie Anasazi cliff dwellings of Mesa Verde National Park.

South Central Colorado
The attractions in the Colorado Springs area alone draw millions of people to Colorado: Pikes Peak, the U.S. Air Force Academy, the gaudy mullioned houses of turn-of-the-century spa Manitou Springs, the sensuously abstract red rock formations of Garden of the Gods. Within an hour's drive are the fascinating Florissant Fossil Beds, the limited stakes gambling in the old mining town of Cripple Creek, and the astonishing Royal Gorge and its Suspension Bridge.

North Central Colorado
Anchored by the progressive, arty college town of Boulder, the north central part of Colorado sees more than 2 million visitors annually, most of them hiking, climbing, biking, horseback riding, snowmobiling, and cross-country skiing through the spectacular Rocky Mountain National Park.

Northwest Colorado
Probably the least well known section of the state, the Northwest offers both tremendous value and diversity to vacationers. They can explore the dinosaur remains at Dinosaur National Monument; learn more about those giants at Devil's Canyon; white-water raft on the Colorado, Green, and Yampa rivers; enjoy wine tastings at several top-notch vineyards; view Native American petroglyphs at Canyon Pintado; hike and camp amid the gnarled knobby monoliths of Colorado National Monument.

PLEASURES & PASTIMES

You'll probably want to spend your Colorado vacation enjoying the Great Outdoors, or you may want to plan sightseeing activities. Below are some favorite pleasures and pastimes in Colorado. Refer to the appropriate chapters for more detailed descriptions of these and other things to do.

Biking and Four-Wheel Driving

Mountain biking is zooming in popularity, and thousands of people challenge the same Colorado slopes in summer that skiers do in winter. More and more ski areas are opening their chairlifts to bikers and hikers, and actively promoting themselves as summer destination resorts. There are numerous trails winding through the mountain passes, with arduous ascents and exhilarating descents.

Remember: know your limits! Many trails are between 7,500 and 11,000 feet, where oxygen is scarce. They're also frequently desolate; always bring along some food and a canteen of water, as dehydration is a common occurrence at high altitudes. Weather can have a tremendous impact on outdoor activities. Always check the condition of roads and trails, and get the latest weather reports before setting out. Take precautions against heat stroke or exhaustion by resting frequently in shaded areas, and against hypothermia by layering clothing in winter. Ultimately, good physical conditioning is the strongest guard against the elements. Four-wheeling is another great way to explore the unspoiled areas. Jeeping is especially big in the rugged San Juan Mountains in the southwestern part of the state.

Dining

In 1944, a Denver drive-in owner named Louis Ballast grilled a slice of cheese on top of a hamburger and became famous for patenting his invention, the cheeseburger. But the dining scene in Colorado is far more than the "three Bs;" beef, buffalo and burritos. Denver, as befits a vibrantly multi-ethnic city, boasts a dazzling range of cuisines from southwestern to classic French, Italian to Thai. The resort restaurants, even in such isolated towns as Crested Butte, rank among the country's most sophisticated. Whatever you're hankering after, from nova to nouvelle, down home to upscale, you're sure to find it in Colorado. Many restaurateurs emphasize the region's unique assets, imaginatively incorporating indigenous ingredients in their menus and highlighting its frontier heritage by occupying silver barons' mansions or restored bordellos. "Colorado Cuisine" is gaining popularity, with its emphasis on fresh local fish (like rainbow trout and salmon), game (elk, venison, rattlesnake), and produce, combined with sauces and garnishes that create an unlikely yet savory counterpoint to the main ingredients. Depending on the season, it can be hearty and robust, or wonderfully light and perfumed. Much of the local cooking is delicately influenced by Colorado's neighbor to the south, New Mexico, sharing its flavorful blend of Native American, Spanish Colonial, and Anglo traditions, as well as a palpable respect for the land. Be sure to try Colorado's Rocky Mountain oysters (the polite term for what separates a bull from a steer), which are famous (some would say infamous) for their size and taste. Colorado's sugar-sweet Rocky Ford cantaloupes have passionate admirers. Apples, peaches, and pears grown in the Grand, Delta, and San Luis valleys are delicious. Colorado's Western slope also possesses excellent vineyards, and local wines are often featured in the best restaurants. The industry is one of the fastest growing in Colorado. Beer is also popular, and microbreweries are enjoying increasing recognition throughout the Rockies. Often located in or connected with a local pub, some of these breweries produce only enough specialty beers (called microbrews) for their own establishments. Colorado has more microbreweries than any other state, and some of their brews, such as Elk, Venison, and Trout, are available from regular beer outlets. The brew pubs are a great place to hang out and sample savory ales and stouts that have Coors beat by a country mile.

Fishing

Fishing in Colorado's numerous rivers, lakes, and streams is an equally popular activity. Among the abundant cold-water sport fish are several species of trout, including cutthroat, rainbow, lake and brook; kokanee salmon; and mountain whitefish.

Cool-water varieties are walleye, yellow perch, and northern pike. Warm-water sport fish include channel catfish, white crappie and white, largemouth and smallmouth bass. Fishing is legal year-round (though several restrictions apply in Rocky Mountain National Park), but you must obtain a license.

Golfing

Golf is another major warm-weather activity. Duffers usually adore Colorado's superlative championship courses, for the combination of stunning mountain scenery and the additional loft on their drives (which has been known, paradoxically, to drive tennis players crazy). Among the many classic courses are the Broadmoor, Tamarron, Breckenridge Golf Club, Golf Course at Cordillera, Keystone Ranch Golf Club, and Tiara Rado Golf Club.

Hiking

Colorado's 11 national forests, comprising over two thirds of the state–Arapaho, Roosevelt, Grand Mesa, Gunnison, Pike, Rio Grande, Routt, San Isabel, San Juan, Uncompahgre, and White River–abound in recreational and sightseeing activities for tourists, including many sterling trekking opportunities. The Colorado Trail is an incredibly scenic 465-mile route that winds its way from Durango to Denver, popular with both bikers and hikers. Always carry emergency supplies in your backpack: proper equipment includes a flashlight, compass, waterproof matches, first-aid kit, water, extra food, knife, and a light plastic tarp for shelter. Never drink from streams or lakes, unless you boil the water first, or purify it with tablets. Giardia, an intestinal parasite, may be present.

National Parks and Monuments

Colorado boasts two glorious national parks, Rocky Mountain (north of Denver) and Mesa Verde (in the southwest corner). The former celebrates Colorado's sublime wilderness scenery, full of glowering glaciers, glittering alpine lakes, meadows woven with wildflowers, and majestic stands of aspen and evergreens. The latter contains an awe-inspiring collection of hauntingly beautiful ancient cliff dwellings, abandoned by the Anasazi centuries ago, set amid exquisite sandstone and red rock formations. Nothing conveys the ex-traordinary diversity of Colorado's sights and attractions better than its seven national monuments. The range of the state's natural wonders can be seen in the gnarled spires and tortured landscape of the Colorado National Monument, outside Grand Junction; the vast anomalous sweep of the Great Sand Dunes National Monument near Alamosa in the south-central part of the state, over a thousand miles from the Pacific or Gulf of Mexico; the deep gash of the Black Canyon of the Gunnison National Monument; and the eerie remains of prehistoric behemoths at the Dinosaur and Florissant Fossil Beds National Monuments. Colorado's rich history is on display in Bent's Old Fort National Historic Site in La Junta, once the major trading post in the Southwest, and the deserted Anasazi ruins of Hovenweep National Monument, straddling the Colorado–Utah border.

Shopping

The Rocky Mountain region combines a frontier reverence for nature and the country's past with a fascination for ski-resort glitz and a modern love for megamalls and discount outlet shopping centers. Boutiques, galleries, and malls are either right in or nearby the many resort towns and cities covered in this book.

You'll find outlets of many top designers in Denver's malls and department stores, as well as in chic resorts like Aspen and Vail. But the real buys in Colorado, of course, are indigenous artifacts, crafts, and specialties. Western and Native American art galleries (showcasing everything from Navajo weaving to Zuni jewelry, Pueblo pottery to sandpainting) and stores specializing in Western memorabilia and cowboy clothing dot the landscape, especially in the southwest. Beware the numerous "authentic trading posts" lining the roads: While fun and kitschy, they're usually tourist traps with second-rate merchandise.

Skiing and Snowmobiling

Colorado is virtually synonymous with skiing. In fact, 20% of all skier visits throughout the United States in 1991 were recorded in Colorado. Residents and travelers alike claim that the snow—"champagne powder"—is the lightest and fluffiest anywhere. World-famous resorts like Aspen/Snowmass, Vail/Beaver

Creek, Crested Butte, Telluride, Steamboat Springs, Purgatory, Winter Park, Breckenridge, Keystone/Arapahoe Basin, and Copper Mountain are legendary for their variety of terrain and consistently superb conditions. But don't overlook the so-called "Gems of Colorado," smaller resorts (that would be considered quite sizable almost anywhere else) like Wolf Creek, Monarch, Loveland, Ski Sunlight, and Eldora that offer the same pristine snow and far smaller crowds. Most of the areas also include or access cross-country trail networks, as do several of Colorado's numerous dude ranches. If you head out on your own for some backcountry skiing, take the proper gear (repair and first-aid kits, blankets, an avalanche beacon, and lightweight shovel). Always check for the latest snowpack and weather conditions. Snowmobiling is another superb way to explore virgin terrain, especially in Grand County.

White-Water Rafting

The other classic Colorado water sport is white-water rafting. Rivers like the Colorado, Arkansas, and Animas abound in Level IV and V rapids, as well as a gentler stretches for beginners.

FODOR'S CHOICE

No two people will agree on what makes a perfect vacation, but it's fun and helpful to know what others think. We hope you'll have a chance to experience some of Fodor's Choices yourself while visiting Colorado. For detailed information about each entry, refer to the appropriate chapters in this guidebook.

Hotels

★ **The Broadmoor Hotel, Colorado Springs.** This is one America's leading resorts, offering everything from a pampering spa to three punishing golf courses. $$$$

★ **The Ritz-Carlton, Aspen.** It sets the standard for luxury and sophistication in the ultimate glitzy resort town. $$$$

★ **Hotel Jerome, Aspen.** This historic hotel offers plush accommodations with tasteful period decor. $$$$

★ **Hyatt Regency Beaver Creek.** This model ski in/ski out chain property is renowned for its service and its excellent family programs. $$$$

★ **Sonnenalp, Vail.** The owning family, the Fasslers, make the Sonnenalp a true piece of Bavaria in faux-Alpine Vail. $$$

★ **Brown Palace, Denver.** This is the doyenne of historic hotels in Colorado, and it rigorously maintains its standards. $$–$$$

★ **Hotel Boulderado, Boulder.** By far the coziest, most distinctive hotel in Boulder. $$–$$$

★ **Strater Hotel, Durango.** The Strater is a Victoriana dream, with exquisite wainscoting and furnishings throughout. $–$$

Guest Ranches and Retreats

★ **C Lazy U Ranch, Granby.** More a resort than a ranch, the deluxe C Lazy U may well be the best place to learn horseback riding and equestrian events in the United States. $$$$

★ **Home Ranch, Clark.** This refined retreat is a member of Relais et Chateaux, and lives up to that chain's exacting standards for luxury. $$$$

★ **Vista Verde Ranch, Steamboat Springs.** Vista Verde offers a more rustic, down-home ambience in contrast to its upscale neighbor, Home Ranch. $$$$

★ **Irwin Lodge, Crested Butte.** This homey hunting-style lodge offers the ultimate in seclusion and the best powder ski instructors in America. $$–$$$

Inns and B&Bs

★ **The Lodge at Cordillera, Edwards (Vail Valley).** This small, stylish retreat with a European feel offers quiet pampering and luxury, in addition to a superb spa, golf course, cross-country/hiking trail network, and restaurant. $$$–$$$$

★ **Hotel Lenado, Aspen.** This airy, classy B&B is one of Aspen's finest accommodations. $$$

★ **New Hotel Rochester, Durango.** If you like Western memorabilia, you'll love this paean to the Wild West, whose rooms are even named for shoot-em-ups filmed in the area. $$–$$$

★ **Crested Butte Club, Crested Butte.** This delightful hostelry combines an ultra-modern health club with turn-of-the-century splendor. *$$*

★ **Queen Anne Inn, Denver.** This is a wonderfully civilized retreat just a few blocks from the excitement of Denver's downtown. *$–$$*

★ **Eagle River Inn, Minturn.** This charming inn with exquisite Southwestern decor is one of the Vail Valley's best bargains to (cowboy) boot. *$*

★ **St. Elmo Inn, Ouray.** This old miner's hangout in one of Colorado's most ravishing towns gleams with Victorian furnishings. *$*

★ **Williams House, Breckenridge.** Not only is this an adorable dollhouse B&B, but the owners define hospitable. *$*

Restaurants

★ **Alpenglow Stube, Keystone.** This is the finest on-mountain restaurant in the state; it even provides slippers for skiers at lunch. *$$$$*

★ **The Flagstaff House, Boulder.** This is that rare restaurant whose food matches its vaunted views (of downtown Boulder). *$$$$*

★ **Splendido, Beaver Creek.** Very posh, very pricey, and very much worth it for David Wlaford's memorable cuisine, which merrily synthesizes Pacific Rim, Mediterranean, and southwestern influences with aplomb. *$$$$*

★ **Syzygy, Aspen.** Smart but not smart-ass in black and white accents, this is the spot for sensuous jazz and sensuously textured new American food. *$$$$*

★ **Campagna, Telluride.** This intimate trattoria prepares delectable, perfectly grilled Tuscan specialties. *$$$–$$$$*

★ **Soupçon, Crested Butte.** This marvelous bistro is a welcome surprise in Crested Butte, which the *Denver Post* claims has more fine restaurants per capita than anywhere in America. *$$$–$$$$*

★ **Briarhurst Manor, Manitou Springs.** Perhaps the most swooningly romantic restaurant in Colorado: the perfect place to pop the question, or let someone down easily. *$$$*

★ **Antares, Steamboat Springs.** A vibrant addition to Steamboat's dining scene, Antares offers a phenomenal selection of wines by the glass to go with its inventive American regional fare. *$$–$$$*

★ **Terra Bistro, Vail.** Cindy Walt seduces with regional, organic ingredients at this sleek, soaring space in the Vail Athletic Club. *$$–$$$*

★ **Rattlesnake Grill, Denver.** Acclaimed chef-restaurateur Jimmy Schmidt makes a triumphant return to Denver, with the hip, hopping, happening spot with innovative, reasonably priced new American cuisine. *$$*

★ **Ski Tip Lodge, Keystone.** This homey, dollhouse cottage serves memorable five-course meals. *$$*

★ **Lola's Place, Durango.** This intimate cottage is splashed in bold colors; the creative Southwestern food is just as boldly flavored. *$–$$*

★ **El Tesoro, Colorado Springs.** This lovely converted artists' atelier is renowned for its light, flavorful "nouvelle" new Mexican food. *$*

★ **Janey's Chile Wagon, Cañon City.** A paean to kitsch (velvet Elvis paintings, neon parrots), Janey's also cooks up a mean green chile. *$*

★ **Slogar, Crested Butte.** Set in a restored Victorian bordello, awash in lace and plush velour, Slogar serves heaping helpings of some the best fried chicken anywhere. *$*

Nightlife and Après Ski

★ **El Chapultepec, Denver.** Forget the dreary setting; this is the coolest hottest hangout for top jazz artists in town.

★ **Diamond Belle Saloon, Durango.** From player piano to waitresses in period garb to the ornate gilt trim, this is like (high-) stepping out in the 19th century.

★ **One World Café, Telluride.** A joyous celebration of multiculturalism, this joint serves up Thai food and live bands from ska to funk.

★ **Palmo's, Vail.** A great spot for single malt scotches and designer lattes, Palmo's is particularly notable for its exquisite, baroque Menzel woodcarvings.

★ **Phantom Canyon Brew Pub, Colorado Springs.** Set in a fabulous turn-of-the-century warehouse space with cathedral ceilings, this is the new hot spot for everyone from yuppies to retired military in the Springs.

★ **The Station, Grand Junction.** Up-and-coming regional bands, mostly of the very alternative variety, steam into the Station.

★ **Sundance Saloon, Durango.** This is an authentic "scoot your boot" palace, replete with cowpokes in ten-gallon hats and sawdust on the floor.

★ **The Tippler, Aspen.** An old standby, beloved for its theme nights, like Disco Diva.

★ **The Wynkoop Brewery, Denver.** The "Koop" is the quintessential brew-pub experience, from its excellent ales, porters, and stouts to the live cabaret and lively scene.

Views

★ First glimpse of Vail's (I–70 and the High Rockies) famous **Back Bowls** as you come off the lift.

★ **Pikes Peak** (South Central) as seen through the gnarled spires of Garden of the Gods.

★ Gazing down on the cliff dwellings at **Mesa Verde** (Southwest).

FESTIVALS AND SEASONAL EVENTS

Contact state tourism offices (*see* Visitor Information *in* the Gold Guide) for more on these events.

WINTER

DEC.➤ Christmas is the focus. Denver hosts the **World's Largest Christmas Lighting Display,** with 20,000 floodlights washing civic buildings in reds, greens, blues, and yellows (☎ 303/892–1112), while Silverton searches for a yule log at its **Yule Log Celebration** (☎ 303/387–5654 or 800/752–4494). The **Vail Festival of Lights** promotes a whole range of attractions including World Cup ski races, Dickensian carolers, brilliant lighting displays, and Christmas ice-skating spectaculars.

JAN.➤ The big events of the month are Denver's two-week **National Western Stock Show and Rodeo,** the world's largest livestock show, and ski competitions such as the **Steamboat Springs Annual Northwest Bank Cowboy Downhill, the Aspen/ Snowmass Winterskol, and Breckenridge's Ullr Fest and World Cup Freestyle.**

FEB.➤ Steamboat Springs hosts the oldest continuous **Winter Carnival** west of the Mississippi.

SPRING

MAR.➤ Springfield holds one of its two annual **Equinox Festivals** as the sun turns nearby Crack Cave into a sort of Stonehenge, highlighting the ancient Ogam calendar and writings of possible Celtic origin, around AD 471. Over 70 tribes convene for the Denver Pow Wow, with Native American dancers, artisans, and musicians. Charity and celebrity events rope them in at many ski areas, including the **Crested Butte American Airlines Celebrity Ski to Benefit the Cystic Fibrosis Foundation, the Colorado Special Olympics** (at Copper Mountain), **Jimmy Heuga's Mazda Ski Express** (raising money to fight MS) at various areas, and the **Beaver Creek American Ski Classic** (hosted by former president Gerald Ford).

APR.➤ **Kit Carson's Annual Mountain Man Rendezvous** relives the time of the mountain men in a colorful festival in Kit Carson. **A Taste of Vail** showcases that area's superlative restaurants.

MAY➤ Look into the **Fort Vasquez Fur Trappers Rendezvous,** in Platteville, where fur-trading days return with demonstrations, contests, costumes, games, and Native American crafts and dances.

SUMMER

JUNE➤ The **Silly Homebuilt River Raft Race,** held in Las Animas, keeps spectators guessing which improbable floating contraptions will reach the finish line and which will explore the bottom of the Arkansas River, where the event is held. Meanwhile, the season of music festivals and cultural events gets into swing with Telluride's weekend-long **Bluegrass Festival** (☎ 303/728–3041), the **Aspen Music Festival, Steamboat's Western Weekend** (with rodeo events, a country-music festival, chili cook-off, Cowboy Poetry gathering, and more), and **Springs in the Mountains Chamber Music Festival,** Vail's **Bravo! Colorado Music Festival,** Glenwood Springs' **Strawberry Days,** and Grand Junction's **Country Jam.** Also popular in summer is Boulder's **Colorado Shakespeare Festival** (☎ 303/492– 1527), one of the top three in the country.

JULY➤ Colorado celebrates an all-American Fourth of July. Among the largest celebrations is the **Fantastic Fourth in Frisco** (☎ 303/668–5800). Arts events galore continue, including **Dance Aspen, Aspen International Design Conference,** Denver's **Black Arts and Asian Arts Festivals,** Winter Park's **Jazz and American Music Festivals,** and the **Brecken-**

ridge Music Institute Concert Series.

Aug.➤ Rodeos are typical late-summer fare; witness the **Pikes Peak or Bust Rodeo** in Colorado Springs (☎ 719/635–7506, 800/368–4748 outside the state), the state's largest. Country fairs are also big business, especially Pueblo's star-studded state fair. Other top events include the **Estes Park Folk Festival, Music in Ouray Chamber Concert Series,** Telluride's **Jazz Celebration** and **Wild Mushroom Festival,** and the **Bolshoi Academy**'s annual residency in Vail.

AUTUMN

Sept.➤ Cripple Creek's **Aspen Leaf Tours,** free trail tours by Jeep through ghost towns and old gold mines, show off the brilliant mountain aspens (Cripple Creek Chamber of Commerce, ☎ 719/689–2169). The **Denver International Air Show** (☎ 303/892–1112), the country's largest such event, draws jet teams from around the world, antique aircraft, parachutists, high-tech military planes, and aerial acrobats. Other daredevils take to the skies in Colorado Springs' **Hot Air Balloon Classic** and the **Telluride Hang Gliding Festival.** Major **film festivals** take place in Aspen, Breckenridge, and Telluride (one of the world's leading showcases for foreign and independent cinema).

Oct.➤ Oktoberfests and Harvest Celebrations dominate the calendar, most notably Carbondale's **Potato Days,** Haxtun's **Corn Festival,** and the Cedaredge and Penrose **Applefests.**

Nov.➤ Creede's **Chocolate Festival** puts chocolates of every size, shape, and description in every corner of town (☎ 719/658–2374 or 800/327–2102). The Yuletide season is rung in with spectacular **Christmas tree lightings** and parades in Denver, Cañon City, Estes Park, and other locales.

2 Denver

DENVER'S BUILDINGS JUT JAGGEDLY INTO THE SKY-LINE, creating an incongruous setting in a state that prides itself on its pristine wilderness. But for all the high-power, high-rise grandeur displayed downtown, Denver is really a cow town at heart. Throughout the 1960s and '70s, when the city mushroomed on a huge surge of oil and energy revenues, Denverites hustled to discard evidence of their Western past to prove their modernity. The last decade, however, has brought an influx of young, well-educated professionals—Denver has the second-largest number of college graduates per capita in the country—lured by Colorado's outdoor mystique and encouraged by the megalopolis's business prospects.

Most Denverites are unabashed nature lovers whose weekends are often spent skiing, camping, hiking, biking, or fishing. For them, preserving the environment and the city's rich mining and ranching heritage are of equally vital importance to the quality of life. Areas like LoDo—the historic lower downtown—now buzz with jazz clubs, restaurants, and art galleries housed in carefully restored century-old buildings. The culturally diverse populace avidly supports the Denver Art Museum, the Museum of Natural History, and the new Museo de las Americas. The expert acting troupe of the Denver Center Theater Company is at home in both traditional mountings of classics and more provocative contemporary works.

Those who don't know Denver may be in for a few big surprises. Although one of its monikers is the "Mile High City," another is "Queen City of the Plains." Denver is flat, with the Rocky Mountains creating a spectacular backdrop; this combination keeps the climate delightfully mild. Denverites do not spend their winters digging out of fierce snowstorms and skiing out their front doors. They take advantage of a comfortable climate, historic city blocks, a cultural center, and sky's-the-limit outdoor adventures just minutes from downtown. All of these factors make this appealing city more than just a layover between home and the Rockies.

EXPLORING DENVER

Orientation

Most of Denver's top attractions are concentrated downtown, a remarkably compact area that can be toured on foot. However, a car is recommended for exploring outside of downtown proper.

Tour 1: Downtown

Numbers in the margin correspond to points of interest on the Denver map.

★ **Denver** presents its official face to the world at the **Civic Center,** a three-block-long park with lawns, gardens, and a Greek amphitheater
❶ that together form a serene backdrop for the **State Capitol,** which was built in 1894. It was constructed mostly of materials indigenous to Colorado, including marble, granite, and rose onyx. Especially inspiring is the gold-leaf dome, a reminder of the state's mining heritage. Visitors can climb to the balcony for a panoramic view of the Rockies, or merely to the 13th step, which is exactly 1-mile high (above sea level). *1475 Sherman St.,* ☎ *303/866–2604.* ☛ *Free.* ⊙ *Mon.–Sat. 9–4; tours available on the half-hour.*

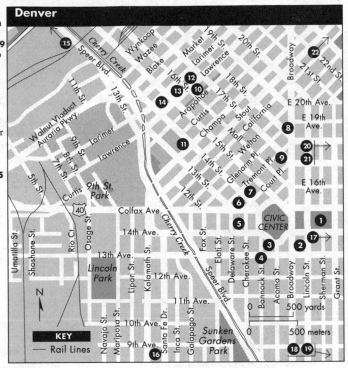

❷ Just off the Civic Center is the **Colorado History Museum,** which contains vibrant depictions of the state's frontier past and how the cultures have collided here. Changing exhibits highlight eras such as the Jazz Age and the Gay '90s; permanent displays include Conestoga wagons, great old touring cars, and an extraordinary time line called "The Colorado Chronicle 1800–1950," which depicts the state's history in amazing detail. The display stretches 112 feet, 6 inches, and dedicates 9 inches to each year. It's crammed with artifacts from rifles to land-grant surveys and old daguerreotypes. *1300 Broadway,* ☎ *303/866–3682.* ☛ *$3 adults, $1.50 children and senior citizens.* ☉ *Mon.–Sat. 10–4:30, Sun. noon–4:30.*

★ ❸ The **Denver Art Museum,** also off the Civic Center park, was remodeled for its 1993 centennial and has superlative, uniquely displayed holdings in Asian, pre-Columbian, Spanish-Colonial, and contemporary Southwestern art. A model of museum design, with dazzling mountain views as a bonus, the museum is intelligently laid out, highly accessible (providing just enough information while emphasizing the aesthetics), and thoughtfully lit. Children will love the imaginative hands-on exhibits and video corners. If there's a flaw here, it's that space for the fine European collection is limited until renovations are completed in 1997. *100 W. 14th Avenue Pkwy.,* ☎ *303/640–2793.* ☛ *$3 adults, $1.50 students and senior citizens, children under 6 and Sat. free.* ☉ *Tues.–Sat. 10–5, Sun. noon–5.*

❹ Close by is the **Byers-Evans House,** an elaborate redbrick Victorian built in 1883 and restored to its pre–World War I condition. It serves as the **Denver History Museum,** offering exciting interactive video exhibits and history programs about the city. *1310 Bannock St.,* ☎ *303/620–4933.* ☛ *$2.50 adults, $1.25 children and senior citizens.* ☉ *Tues.–Sun. 11–3.*

⑤ A few blocks away is Denver's **U.S. Mint,** the source of all those coins stamped with a *D.* Free tours take guests around the facility, where more than 5 billion coins are minted yearly, and where the nation's second-largest hoard of gold is displayed. *W. Colfax Ave. and Chero-kee St., ☎ 303/844–3582. ☛ Free. Tours weekdays 8–3 every 20 min, except during inventory (usually last 2 wks in June).*

⑥ A fascinating detour is to the **Denver Firefighters Museum,** which oc-cupies the space of Denver's first firehouse. All the original items of the trade are displayed here, including uniforms, nets, fire carts and trucks, bells, and switchboards. *1326 Tremont Pl., ☎ 303/892–1100. ☛ $2. ☉ Weekdays 10–2.*

⑦ From here, it's one block up to the tranquil **Trianon Museum and Art Gallery,** and its marvelous collection of 18th- and 19th-century Euro-pean furnishings and objets d'art. The museum also houses a rare gun collection, with pieces dating from the 16th century onward. Guided tours are offered. *335 14th St., ☎ 303/623–0739. ☛ $1. ☉ Mon.–Sat. 10–4.*

★ Walk up to the **6th Street Mall** to pick up one of the free shuttle buses that run the length of downtown, providing a good, quick tour. These buses are the only vehicles allowed on the otherwise pedestrian-only street, which is lined with shady trees, outdoor cafés, historic build-ings, and tempting shops.

★ ⑧ Hop off at Tremont Place and walk a block to the **Museum of West-ern Art,** in a converted frontier-era bordello (on the National Register of Historic Places). It now houses works by those artistic heroes of the Western mythos: Remington, Bierstadt, and Russell, and latter-day mas-ters such as O'Keeffe. The collection is highly distilled; all the vividly composed works are considered by experts to be among the artists' finest and most representative pieces. *1727 Tremont Ave., ☎ 303/296–1880. ☛ $3 adults, $2 students and senior citizens, children under 7 free. ☉ Tues.–Sat. 10–4:30.*

⑨ Catercorner from the museum is the majestic **Brown Palace Hotel** (321 17th St.), Denver's hotel empress, built in 1892 and still considered the city's most prestigious address. Reputedly this was the first atrium hotel in the United States: Its ornate lobby and nine stories are crowned by a stunning Tiffany stained-glass window. (*See* Lodging, *below.*)

As you head back down the mall toward lower downtown, you'll see ⑩ the 330-foot-high **Daniels and Fisher Tower** (16th and Arapahoe Sts.), built to emulate the campanile of St. Mark's Cathedral in Venice. ⑪ Head a block east to Curtis, then south about two blocks to the **Den-ver Performing Arts Complex** (14th and Curtis Sts., ☎ 303/893–4000), a huge, impressively high-tech group of theaters connected by a soaring, glass archway to a futuristic symphony hall. Guided tours are available, but times vary so you must call ahead.

⑫ Return to Arapahoe and go one block to the **Tabor Center,** a festive shopping mall with more than 60 stores and attractions, including fast-food eateries, strolling troubadours, jugglers and fire-eaters, and splash-⑬ ing fountains. Across from Tabor Center is **Writer Square,** whose shops line the entrance to the arched redbrick courtyards of historic ⑭ **Larimer Square** (Larimer and 15th Sts.), Denver's most charming shop-ping district, where some of the city's oldest retail buildings and classi-est specialty shops do business. Larimer Square—actually a street—was saved from the wrecker's ball by a determined preservationist in the

1960s, when the city went demolition-crazy in its eagerness to present a more youthful image.

Larimer runs roughly along a boundary of **LoDo,** an historic lower downtown area now home to art galleries, nightclubs, and restaurants ranging from Denver's most upscale to its most down-home. This part of town was once the city's thriving retail center, then it fell into disuse and slid into slums; in the past few years it has been undergoing a vigorous revival spearheaded not just by avant-garde artists and retailers, but by loft dwellers who have taken over old warehouses here. The handsome new Coors Stadium, home of baseball's Colorado Rockies, has further galvanized the area. Its old-fashioned brick and grillwork facade, ornamented with 41 blue, green, and white terra-cotta columbines (the state flower), was designed to blend in with the surrounding Victorian warehouses.

A little outside the downtown loop (west on 15th St., just past the confluence of the South Platte River and Cherry Creek) is the wonderfully odd **Forney Transportation Museum.** Resembling an abandoned auto yard, the property outside is littered with peeling carriages, corroding cabooses, and classic cycles; inside, in the not-quite-thought-out exhibit rooms, are an 1898 Renault coupe, Teddy Roosevelt's tour car, Aly Khan's Rolls, and a Big Boy steam locomotive, among other collectibles. Strangely enough, there's also a room dedicated to 18th-century military uniforms. Anyone who grew up on model cars or Lionel trains will wander this eccentric museum in a happy daze. *1416 Platte St.,* ☎ *303/433–3643.* ☛ *$4 adults, $3.50 senior citizens, $2 children 12–16, $1 children 5–11.* ⊙ *Mon.–Sat. 10–5, Sun. 11–5.*

From the Forney, take I–25 south, exit east on Sixth Avenue, and head north on Santa Fe Drive. The **Museo de las Americas,** the region's first museum dedicated to the achievements of Latinos in the Americas, has a permanent collection as well as rotating exhibits that cover everything from Hispanics in the state legislature to Latin American women artists in the 20th century. *861 Santa Fe Dr.,* ☎ *303/571–4401.* ☛ *$2 adults, $1 students and senior citizens, children under 13 free.* ⊙ *Tues.–Sat. 10–5.*

Tour 2: East of Downtown

A car is recommended on this tour, as it covers an area more spread out than downtown.

The **Molly Brown House,** on Pennsylvania Street between East 12th and 13th avenues, not far from the capitol, is a Victorian confection that celebrates the life and times of the scandalous, "unsinkable" Molly Brown, heroine of the *Titanic* who courageously saved several lives and continued to provide assistance to survivors back on terra firma. Costumed guides and original furnishings in the museum including flamboyant gilt-edge wallpaper, lace curtains, tile fireplaces, and tapestries) evoke bygone days. A bit of trivia: Margaret Tobin Brown was known as Maggie, not Molly, during her lifetime. Meredith Willson, the composer-lyricist of the musical, *The Unsinkable Molly Brown,* based on Brown's life, thought Molly was easier to sing. *1340 Pennsylvania St.,* ☎ *303/832–4092.* ☛ *$3.* ⊙ *Mon.–Sat. 10–4, Sun. noon–4.*

A few blocks down the street, the Beaux Arts–style **Grant-Humphreys Mansion** is a grandiose, 42-room testament to the proper Denver society that looked down on Molly at the turn of the century. *770 Pennsylvania St.,* ☎ *303/894–2506.* ☛ *$3 adults, $1.50 children 6–17.* ⊙ *Tues.–Fri. 10–2.*

⑲ Head east on Eighth Avenue to the **Denver Botanic Gardens,** a flowering respite from the urban hustle and bustle. A conservatory looms above; among its displays is a re-creation of a tropical rain forest; outside are a Japanese garden, a rock garden, gazebos and arboretums, and gorgeous horticultural displays (at their peak during summer). *1005 York St.,* ☎ *303/331–4010.* ☛ *$3 adults, $1.50 senior citizens, $1 children.* ⊙ *Daily 9–4:45.*

★ Northeast of downtown, between Colorado Boulevard and York Street, along 17th Avenue, is **City Park,** Denver's largest public space of its kind, with rose gardens, lakes, a golf course, tennis courts, and two of the city's most popular attractions: the Denver Zoo and the Denver Museum of Natural History. A shuttle runs between the two.

⑳ The engaging **Denver Zoo** features a nursery for baby animals; a polar bear exhibit, where visitors can watch the animals swim underwater; seal shows; educational programs on endangered species; and the *Zooliner* train, which snakes through the property as guests are given a safari lecture. The 5-acre, $10 million "Primate Panorama" will open in August 1996 for the zoo's centennial and will house more than 25 species of primates in state-of-the-art environments that simulate the animals' natural habitats. *E. 23rd St., between York St. and Colorado Blvd.,* ☎ *303/331–4110.* ☛ *$4 adults, $2 senior citizens and children.* ⊙ *Daily 10–6.*

★ ㉑ The seventh-largest museum in the United States, the **Denver Museum of Natural History,** offers a rich combination of traditional collections—dinosaur remains, a mineralogy display, an Egyptology wing—and intriguing hands-on exhibits such as the "Hall of Life," where you can test your health and fitness on various contraptions. The massive complex includes an IMAX movie theater and the Gates Planetarium. A new permanent exhibit, "Prehistoric Journey," opens in October 1995. Plans call for a walk-through exhibit covering seven stages of the earth's development, with each "envirorama" representing a specific area of North America or Australia at a particular time. *2001 Colorado Blvd.,* ☎ *303/322–7009.* ☛ *To museum: $4 adults, $2 senior citizens and children.* ☛ *To IMAX: $5 adults, $4 senior citizens and children.* ☛ *To planetarium: $3.50 adults, $2.50 senior citizens and children.* ⊙ *Daily 9–5.*

㉒ Return to City Park, and exit north along York Street, then turn west on 30th Avenue to the **Black American West Museum and Heritage Center,** with its revealing collection of documents that depict the vast contributions African Americans made to opening up the West. Nearly a third of the cowboys and many pioneer teachers and doctors were African Americans. *3091 California St.,* ☎ *303/292–2566.* ☛ *$2 adults, $1.50 senior citizens, 75¢ children 12–17, 50¢ children under 12.* ⊙ *Wed.–Fri. 10–2, Sat. noon–5, Sun. 2–5.*

Tour 3: Short Excursion from Denver

Getting There
Central City, as well as Black Hawk, are easily reached by taking I–70 or Highway 6 west from Denver and turning north on CO 119. Both towns can be explored on foot.

Exploring Central City/Black Hawk
★ When limited-stakes gambling was introduced in 1991 to the beautifully preserved old mining towns of **Central City/Black Hawk,** howls of protest were drowned out by cheers from struggling townspeople. Fortunately, strict zoning laws were legislated to protect the towns' ar-

chitectural integrity, and by and large the laws have been successful. However, the general atmosphere may be more raucous today than it was in its heyday in the 1860s, thanks to the steady stream of tour buses and loudly jingling coffers. Gaming here is restricted to blackjack, poker, and slots, and the maximum bet is $5.

There are nearly 40 casinos in Black Hawk and Central City. All are in historic buildings—from jails to mansions—and their plush interiors have been lavishly decorated to re-create the Old West era—a period when this town was known as the "Richest Square Mile on Earth."

The most notable attraction in Black Hawk is the **Lace House,** a superb example of Carpenter Gothic architecture, with signature lacy gingerbread trim. *161 Main St.,* ☎ *303/582–5382.* ☛ *$1.* ✆ *Daily 11–6.*

In Central City, make your first stop the intriguing **Gilpin County Historical Society Museum** (228 E. High St., ☎ 303/582–5283; ☛ $3; open daily 9–5), where photos and reproductions, as well as vintage pieces from different periods of Gilpin County history, paint a richly detailed portrait of life in a typical rowdy mining community.

Around the corner, several attractions line Eureka Street. The **Teller House Casino, Restaurant, and Museum** (120 Eureka St., ☎ 303/582–3800) was once one of the West's ritziest hotels. Upstairs is the opulent room that was occupied by President Grant and, later, by Mae West. Downstairs, the floor of the famous Face Bar is adorned with the portrait of a mystery woman named Madeline, painted in 1936 by Herndon Davis. Some say it was created as a lark, others bet it was done for the price of a drink. Down the block is the glorious **Central City Opera House** (621 17th St., ☎ 303/292–6700), which still hosts performances in the summer.

This area is honeycombed with mines, some of which purportedly still contain rich veins of gold. **The Lost Gold Mine** offers tours of two connected shafts filled with original tools and specimens. The requisite souvenir shop outside sells gold-nugget jewelry. *231 Eureka St.,* ☎ *303/642–7533.* ☛ *$3.50 adults, $1.75 children 5–11.* ✆ *Summer daily 8–8; winter daily 10–6.*

What to See and Do With Children

The Denver Children's Museum is one of the finest of its kind in North America, offering constantly changing hands-on exhibits that lure children into discovery. The biggest attraction is a working television studio, replete with a weather station, a news desk, and a viewing booth where kids can videotape each other and watch the results on "byte"-size monitors. Other interesting aspects of the museum include the "Indians of the Northwest" display, where children can build their own totem poles and the outdoor park with climbing equipment, a year-round ski instruction hill, and a trolley ($2 for adults, $1 for children) that clatters and clangs the 2 miles down the South Platte River to the Forney Transportation Museum. *2121 Crescent Dr.,* ☎ *303/433–7444.* ☛ *$4 children, $3 adults, $1.50 senior citizens over 60.* ✆ *June–Aug., daily 10–5. Sept.–May, Tues.–Sun. 10–5.*

The Denver Zoo (*see* Exploring, *above*).

Elitch Gardens Amusement Park is a Denver family tradition, with three hair-raising roller coasters (one ranked in the nation's top 10); a hand-carved, antique carousel; a 100-foot-high Ferris wheel that provides sensational views of downtown; a high-dive show; summer stock theater; and botanical gardens. Its new downtown location is twice as big as its former site. *I–25 and Speer Blvd.*, ☎ *303/455–4771.* ☛ *$14.95 unlimited ride pass weekdays, $15.95 weekends; chaperon pass (no rides) $8 weekdays, $9 weekends.* ☉ *Weekends mid-Apr.–May; daily June–Labor Day. Hours vary so call ahead.*

Other Points of Interest

★ **Golden,** just 20 minutes west of Denver on I–70 or Highway 6 (W. 6th Ave.), is the destination of thousands of beer lovers who make the pilgrimage to the **Coors Brewery.** One of the world's largest, it was founded in 1873 by Adolph Coors, a 21-year-old German stowaway. The free tour lasts a half hour and explains not only the brewing process, but also how "Rocky Mountain mineral water" (or "Colorado Kool-Aid") is packaged and distributed locally. Informal tastings are held at the end of the tour for those 21 and over; souvenirs are available at the gift shop. *13th and Ford Sts.*, ☎ *303/277–2337.* ☛ *Free.* ☉ *Mon.–Sat. 10–4 (children under 18 must be accompanied by an adult).*

The other favorite Golden attraction is the **Buffalo Bill Grave and Museum.** Contrary to popular belief, Bill Cody never expressed a burning desire to be buried here: The *Denver Post* bought the corpse from Bill's sister, and bribed her to concoct a teary story about his dying wish. Apparently, rival towns were so outraged that the National Guard had to be called in to protect the grave from robbers. The drive up Lookout Mountain to the burial site offers a sensational panoramic view of Denver that alone is worth the price of admission. Adjacent to the grave is a small museum with the usual art and artifacts as well as a run-of-the-mill souvenir shop. *Rte. 5 off I–70 exit 256, or 19th Ave. out of Golden,* ☎ *303/526–0747.* ☛ *$2 adults, $1 children 6–15.* ☉ *May–Oct., daily 9–5; Nov.–Apr., Tues.–Sun., 9–4.*

Just outside of Golden is the **Colorado Railroad Museum,** a must-visit for any choo-choo junkie. More than 50 vintage locomotives and cars are displayed outside. Inside the replica-1880 masonry depot are historical photos and puffing Billy (nickname for steam trains) memorabilia, along with an astounding model train set that steams through a miniature, scaled version of Golden. *17155 W. 44th Ave.*, ☎ *303/279– 4591.* ☛ *$3 adults, $1.50 children under 16.* ☉ *Daily 9–5.*

If you have some extra time while in Golden consider walking down 12th Street, a National Historic District with handsome 1860s brick buildings. Among the monuments is the **Astor House** (corner of 12th and Arapahoe Sts.), a museum with period furnishings, and Colorado's first **National Guard Armory,** which was built in 1913 and is the largest cobblestone building in America.

Other attractions in town include the **Colorado School of Mines** (16th and Maple Sts., ☎ 303/273–3823; open daily 9–4:30), the nation's largest and foremost school of mineral engineering. The lovely campus contains an outstanding geology museum displaying minerals, ore, and gemstones from around the world. Also on campus is the prominent **National Earthquake Center** (1711 Illinois St., ☎ 303/236–1500; tours by appointment weekdays 9–11 and 1–3), which is responsible for recording continental drift and seismic activity. Free tours are available weekdays by appointment.

Wrap up your full day with a stop at **Heritage Square** (Hwy. 40 and 6th Ave., ☎ 303/279–2789), a re-creation of an 1880s frontier town, with an opera house, a narrow-gauge railway train ride, a Ferris wheel, a water slide, specialty shops, and a music hall that stages original comedies and musicals as well as traditional melodramas. A vaudeville-style review ends each evening's entertainment.

SHOPPING

Denver may be the best place in the country for recreational gear and fashions of all stripes. Sporting goods stores hold legendary ski sales around Labor Day.

Shopping Districts and Malls

The posh **Cherry Creek** shopping district is 2 miles from downtown in a pleasant, predominantly residential neighborhood. On one side of First Avenue at Milwaukee Street is the Cherry Creek Shopping Mall, a classy granite-and-glass behemoth that houses some of the nation's top retailers, among them: Abercrombie & Fitch, Bally, Banana Republic, Burberry's, Laura Ashley, Lord & Taylor, Louis Vuitton, Neiman Marcus, Polo/Ralph Lauren, and Saks Fifth Avenue. Across from the Cherry Creek Shopping Mall lies Cherry Creek North, an open-air development of tree-lined streets and shady plazas, with art galleries, specialty shops, and fashionable restaurants.

Historic **Larimer Square** (14th and Larimer Sts.), houses distinctive shops and restaurants. **Writer Square** (1512 Larimer St.) has Tiny Town—a doll-size village inhabited by Michael Garman's inimitable figurines—as well as shops and restaurants. **Tabor Center** (16th St. Mall) is a light-filled atrium whose 60 specialty shops include upscale retailers such as Brooks Brothers and Crabtree & Evelyn, and others that showcase uniquely Coloradan merchandise. It also contains the Bridge Market, which is filled with pushcarts selling everything from Ecuadorian sweaters to endearingly tacky souvenirs. The **Tivoli** (900 Auraria Pkwy., corner of 9th Ave. and Larimer) is a restored historic brewery, with its original pipes and bricks exposed, that houses several moderately priced specialty stores and restaurants.

South of Denver, **Castle Rock Factory Shops** (exit 184 off I–25) offers 25%–75% savings on everything from appliances to apparel at its more than 50 outlets.

Department Stores

Joslins (16th and Curtis Sts., ☎ 303/534–0441) is Denver's oldest department store. The nine **Foley's** department stores throughout metropolitan Denver offer good values; Cherry Creek is their main store in downtown Denver (15 S. Steele St., ☎ 303/333–8555)

Specialty Stores

Antiques

South Broadway between First Avenue and Evans Street, as well as the side streets off this main drag, is chockablock with dusty antiques stores, where patient browsing could net some amazing bargains.

The **Antique Mall of Lakewood** (9635 W. Colfax Ave.) features more than 200 dealer showrooms.

Art and Crafts

LoDo has the trendiest galleries, many in restored Victorian warehouses.

Baobab Tree (1518 Wazee St., ☎ 303/595–0965) sells South African imports, including astonishing masks. **The Art of Craft** (1736 Wazee

St., ☎ 303/292–5564) specializes in such wearable art as hand-painted ties and kimonos. **Made in Colorado** (1060 14th St., ☎ 303/298–7812) offers the state's most intriguing products, from Colorado wines to Native American pottery.

Cherry Creek has its share of chic galleries, including **Pismo** (2727 E. 3rd Ave., ☎ 303/333–7724), which showcases exquisite handblown-glass art.

For Native American arts and crafts, head for **Native American Trading Company** (1301 Bannock St., ☎ 303/534–0771), which has an outstanding collection of weavings, pottery, jewelry, and regional painting. The **Mudhead Gallery** (555 17th St., in the Hyatt, ☎ 303/293–0007; and 321 17th St., in the Brown Palace, ☎ 303/293–3377) sells museum-quality Southwestern art, with an especially fine selection of Santa Clara and San Ildefonso pottery, and Hopi kachinas. Old Santa Fe Pottery's (2485 S. Santa Fe Dr., ☎ 303/871–9434) 20 rooms are crammed with Southwestern art, Mexican masks, and hand-painted ceramic tiles.

Beer
Colorado is considered the center of home brewing, and Denver has five brew pubs, each with its own ambience. If you're feeling heady, stop by the **Wine and Hop Shop** (705 E. 6th Ave., ☎ 303/831–7229) for beginner beer- and wine-making kits and a virtual field of fresh hops and grains, or to goggle at the "wall of malt."

Books
The Tattered Cover (1st Ave. at Milwaukee St., ☎ 303/322–7727) is a must for all bibliophiles. It may be the best bookstore in the United States, not only for the near-endless selection of volumes (more than 400,000 on four stories) and helpful, knowledgeable staff, but for the incomparably refined atmosphere: overstuffed armchairs; reading nooks; and afternoon readings, lectures, and musicales.

Sporting Goods
Gart Brothers Sports Castle (1000 Broadway, ☎ 303/861–1122) is a huge, multistory shrine to Colorado's love of the outdoors. Entire floors are given over to a single sport at this and the many other branches throughout Denver.

Western Wear and Collectibles
Cry Baby Ranch (1428 Larimer, ☎ 303/623–3979) has a rambunctious assortment of '40s and '50s cowboy kitsch. **Denver Buffalo Company** (1109 Lincoln St., ☎ 303/882–0884) has wonderful Western duds and high-quality souvenirs, not to mention a restaurant that specializes in buffalo—low in fat and cholesterol. There's also a gourmet deli serving BuffDogs (hot dogs made with buffalo meat), corned buffalo, and other such specialties. **Miller Stockman** (16th Ave. and California, ☎ 303/825–5339) is an old-line Denver retailer selling the real McCoy.

SPORTS AND THE OUTDOORS

Participant Sports

Cycling and Jogging
Platte River Greenway is a 20-mile-long path for rollerblading, bicycling, and jogging which runs alongside Cherry Creek and the Platte River; much of it runs through downtown Denver. Paved paths wind through lovely **Matthews-Winters Park,** dotted with plaintive pioneer

graves amid the sun-bleached grasses, thistle, and columbine. The **Denver Parks Department** (☎ 303/698–4900) has more suggestions for biking and jogging paths throughout the metropolitan area's 205 parks, including the popular Cherry Creek and Chatfield Lake State Recreation areas.

Golf

Six courses are operated by the City of Denver and are open to the public: **City Park** (E. 25th Ave. and York St., ☎ 303/295–4420), **Evergreen** (29614 Upper Bear Creek, Evergreen, ☎ 303/674–4128); **Kennedy** (10500 E. Hampden Ave., ☎ 303/751–0311); **Overland Park** (S. Santa Fe Dr. and Jewell Ave., ☎ 303/698–4975); **Wellshire** (3333 S. Colorado Blvd., ☎ 303/692–5636); and **Willis Case** (W. 50th Ave. and Vrain St., ☎ 303/458–4877).

Arrowhead Golf Club (10850 W. Sundown Trail, Littleton, ☎ 303/973–9614), 45 minutes from downtown in Roxborough State Park, was designed by Robert Trent Jones and is set impressively among red sandstone spires. **Plum Creek Golf and Country Club** (331 Players Club, Castle Rock, ☎ 303/688–2611) is an 18-hole Pete Dye–designed championship course.

Health Clubs

Denver has more fitness clubs per capita than any other American city. The state-of-the-art **International Athletic Club** (1630 Welton St., ☎ 303/623–2100) is a 65,000-square-foot, full-service facility featuring more than 65 aerobics classes weekly. The club has cardiovascular and fitness equipment; weight training; racquetball, squash, and basketball courts; and a running track, among other features. Guest passes are available at many major hotels.

Hiking

Just 15 miles west of Denver, **Red Rocks Park and Amphitheater** (off U.S. 285 or I–70) is a breathtaking, 70-million-year-old wonderland of vaulting oxblood- and cinnamon-color sandstone spires; the outdoor music stage is set in a natural 8,000-seat amphitheater (with perfect acoustics, as only nature could have designed) that has awed even the likes of Leopold Stokowski and the Beatles. Tickets to concerts are stratospheric, but hiking in this metro Denver park is free.

Mt. Falcon Park (off Hwy. 8, Morrison exit, or U.S. 285, Parmalee exit) looks down on Denver and across at Red Rocks. It's amazingly tranquil, laced with meadows and streams and shaded by conifers. The trails are very well marked.

Tennis

The city has 28 parks with tennis courts. For information call the **Denver Parks Department** (☎ 303/331–4047).

Water Sports

Both **Cherry Creek Marina** (Cherry Creek State Park, Aurora, ☎ 303/779–6144) and **Chatfield Marina** (Chatfield State Park, Littleton, ☎ 303/791–7547) rent sailboats, powerboats, and Windsurfers April–October.

Spectator Sports

Auto Racing

Bandimere Speedway (3501 S. Rooney Rd., Morrison, ☎ 303/697–6001) features NHRA Championship Drag Racing April–September.

Baseball

The **Colorado Rockies,** Denver's National League team, plays April–October in Coors Stadium (off Arapahoe and 21st Sts., ☏ 303/762–543.

Basketball

Denver's NBA franchise team, the **Denver Nuggets,** plays October–April in the McNichols Arena (just west of downtown across I–25, ☏ 303/893–3865).

Football

Denver Broncos, the city's NFL team, plays September–December at Mile High Stadium (just west of downtown across I–25, ☏ 303/433–7466).

Horse Racing

Arapahoe Park (26000 E. Quincy Ave., ☏ 303/690–2400) is the venue for pari-mutuel racing May–September.

DINING

As befits a multiethnic crossroads, Denver offers a dizzying range of eateries: Head for LoDo, 32nd Avenue in the Highland District, or 17th Street for the more inventive kitchens; try Federal Street for cheap ethnic eats—especially Thai and Vietnamese. Throughout Denver, however, you'll find many trendy restaurants offering new American cuisines with an emphasis on indigenous regional ingredients and light, healthful preparations. Denver's hotels also offer some fine restaurants (*see* Lodging, *below*).

Outside Denver, in Central City/Black Hawk, you'll see that virtually every casino has a restaurant with the usual $2.99 daily specials and all-you-can-eat buffets. Nonetheless, there are a few good places to dine.

For price ranges, *see* the Dining price chart *in* On the Road with Fodor's at the front of this guide.

Downtown and Environs

American

$$$ **Strings.** This light, airy restaurant with its wide-open kitchen resembles a SoHo loft. It's a preferred hangout for Denver's movers and shakers as well as visiting celebs, whose autographs hang on the walls. The food is billed as casual contemporary; specialties include spaghetti with caviar, asparagus, and champagne cream sauce or monkfish braised in fennel. ✕ *1700 Humboldt St.,* ☏ *303/831–7310. Reservations required. AE, D, DC, MC, V. Closed Sun. lunch.*

$$$ **Zenith American Grill.** This attractive space has a cool high-tech look—
★ track lighting, striking artwork, black-and-white tables—that contrasts with the conservative design of most Denver establishments. Chef Kevin Taylor produces creative variations on the Southwestern theme, and cleverly lightens the traditional meat-and-potatoes bent of Colorado cuisine. Standouts include a velvety yet fiery smoked corn soup with avocado salsa; Texas venison with caramelized apples; sweet potato custard and spicy sun-dried cherries; and "kick ass" swordfish with Texas BBQ, chili stir fry, and cilantro lime butter. ✕ *1750 Lawrence St.,* ☏ *303/820–2800. Reservations required. AE, MC, V. No lunch weekends.*

$$–$$$ **Rattlesnake Grill.** Renowned restaurateur Jimmy Schmidt has returned
★ to Denver, where his Rattlesnake Club was bitten by the late '80s recession. His new space is impressive: soft track lighting, picture windows overlooking the action on Cherry Creek Mall, and witty color

photos of food as well as black-and-white landscapes. Keith Josefiak's food is a sensational fusion of various American regional cuisines with a soupçon of Provençal flair. You might start with roast garlic and celeriac soup or pheasant quesadillas layered with smoked gouda, scallions, and chili peppers. Among the rotating specials are grilled salmon with chanterelles, and pork loin chop with dried Michigan cherries, roasted shallots, and crispy sage. Tempt your sweet tooth with the white chocolate ravioli served with a hazelnut crème anglaise. ✗ *3000 1st Ave., ☎ 303/377–8000. Reservations advised. AE, MC, V.*

$ **Wazee Supper Club.** Denverites flock to this hip hole for hot jazz and the best pizza in town—crisp yet gooey and bursting with flavor. Some grouse the Wazee has less ambience since it moved down the street, but the exposed brick walls, jet-black tables, and maroon Naugahyde chairs still convey its ultracool tone. ✗ *1600 15th St., ☎ 303/623–9518. No reservations. AE, MC, V.*

$ **The Wynkoop.** This trendy yet unpretentious local institution was
★ Denver's first brew pub, and it's still the best. Try the terrific shepherd's pie or grilled marlin sandwich; wash it down with wilderness wheat ale or sagebrush stout; then repair to the gallery, pool hall, and cabaret for a full night of entertainment. ✗ *1634 18th St., ☎ 303/297–2700. Reservations for 6 or more weekdays; no reservations on weekends. AE, DC, MC, V.*

Asian

$$ **Imperial Chinese.** Papier-mâché lions greet you at the entrance of this sleek Szechuan stunner, probably the best Chinese restaurant in a 500-mile radius. Seafood is the specialty; try the steamed sea bass in ginger or the spicy, fried Dungeness crab. ✗ *1 Broadway, ☎ 303/698–2800. Reservations advised. AE, DC, MC, V. Closed Sun. lunch.*

$ **Chez Thuy Hoa.** The original chef of T-Wa Inn, Hoa "Wa," left to open this simple downtown eatery. The decor isn't much to speak of—a few plants, old-fashioned ceiling fans, and pink napery—but the savory food keeps it packed during lunchtime (you can usually walk right in at dinner). Try the squid in lemongrass; Dungeness crab salad; or egg rolls bursting with ground pork or shrimp, mint, sprouts, and cucumber. ✗ *1500 California St., ☎ 303/623–4809. AE, MC, V. Closed Sun. lunch.*

Continental

$$$ **Augusta.** With sweeping views of downtown and gleaming brass, glass, and marble enhanced by pin spotlights showcasing the striking art, this handsome restaurant is one of the best in the city. Chef Roland Ulber holds sway in the kitchen, reinvigorating classic Continental fare with such imaginative preparations as milk-fed veal medallions topped with foie gras and beautifully set off by a tart lingonberry sauce. At $35, the five-course tasting menu is one of Denver's greatest bargains ($15 more buys a glass of wine to complement each dish). ✗ *1672 Lawrence St., ☎ 303/572–9100. Reservations advised. AE, D, DC, MC, V. Closed lunch.*

$$$ **Cliff Young's.** Although Young no longer oversees operations here,
★ this refined Art Deco restaurant with maroon chairs, dark banquettes, and crisp white napery is still run with meticulous care. Head chef Sean Brasel has introduced Asian and Southwestern touches to the menu, with such specialties as pinwheels of salmon with tangerine ginger compote and wasabi mashed potatoes or seared venison tenderloin with poblano and pumpkin. The new American standbys are still available for devoted regulars, including Colorado rack of lamb and buffalo carpaccio. The dancing to piano and violin music at dinner and the old-school obsequiousness of the wait staff can make the restaurant seem frozen in the 1950s. The ambience is considerably less stuffy (and

the prices far lower) at lunch, when the restaurant becomes a haven for harried executives. ✕ *700 E. 17th Ave.,* ☎ *303/831–8900. Reservations advised. AE, D, DC, MC, V. No lunch weekends.*

$$–$$$ **European Café.** Housed with panache in a converted loft that now gleams with polished brass and crystal, the European Café is a favorite for those attending downtown events. Many of chef Radek Cerny's dishes pay homage to such French master chefs as Georges Blanc and Paul Bocuse, and all are beautifully presented. Try the lamb chops with shiitake mushrooms in Madeira glaze. ✕ *1515 Market,* ☎ *303/825–6555. Reservations advised. AE, D, DC, MC, V. No lunch weekends.*

French

$$$ **Cache Cache.** Chef Jack Goldsmith is a practitioner of *cuisine minceur*— no butter or cream is used in his preparations. But the sunny flavors of Provence explode on the palate thanks to the master's savvy use of garlic, tomato, eggplant, fennel, and rosemary. The lamb loin sandwiched between crisp, potato *galettes* (pancakes) on a bed of spinach and ratatouille is sublime; salads are sensational. ✕ *265 Detroit St.,* ☎ *303/394– 0044. Reservations advised. AE, MC, V. Closed Sun.*

$$$ **Tante Louise.** This longtime Denver favorite, just 15 minutes from downtown by car, resembles an intimate French country home. Fireplaces, candlelight, and classical music attract a mostly over-fifty crowd. One-third of chef Michael Degenhart's menu is French, one-third is new American, and one-third features low-fat dishes. Try the delicate angel-hair pasta and grilled salmon in beurre blanc, or any of the superlative lamb specials. ✕ *4900 E. Colfax Ave.,* ☎ *303/355– 4488. Reservations advised. AE, D, DC, MC, V. Closed Sun.; no lunch except Fri.*

$$ **La Coupole.** This expert French bistro is an oasis in this seedier part of LoDo, where taco joints, abandoned warehouses, and neighborhood bars are the norm. Gleaming brass, black leather banquettes, exposed brick walls, potted plants, lace curtains, and crisp white napery transport happy diners to the Left Bank. Everything is solidly prepared, from monkfish with lobster mayonnaise to chicken breast in morel cream sauce, not to mention a perfect tarte tatin. ✕ *2191 Arapahoe St.,* ☎ *303/297–2288. Reservations advised. AE, D, DC, MC, V. Closed Sun. lunch.*

$$ **Le Central.** This homey bistro calls itself "Denver's affordable French restaurant." The cozy dining rooms are enlivened by brick walls and colorful artwork courtesy of local schoolchildren. While the preparation can be inconsistent, old standbys such as boeuf bourguignon, salmon en croûte, and steak au poivre are dependable. ✕ *112 E. 8th Ave.,* ☎ *303/863–8094. Reservations for 5 or more at dinner. D, MC, V. Closed Mon. lunch.*

Italian

$$ **Barolo Grill.** This restaurant looks like a chichi farmhouse, as if Martha
★ Stewart went gaga over an Italian count: There are dried flowers in brass urns, hand-painted porcelain, and straw baskets everywhere. The food isn't precious in the least, however; it's more like Santa Monica meets San Stefano—bold yet classic, healthful yet flavorful. Choose from wild boar stewed with apricots, risotto croquettes flavored with minced shrimp, or smoked-salmon pizza. The wine list is well-considered and fairly priced. ✕ *3030 E. 6th Ave.,* ☎ *303/393–1040. Reservations advised. AE, MC, V. Closed lunch and Sun. and Mon.*

Mexican

$ **Bluebonnet Café and Lounge.** Its location out of the tourist loop, in a fairly seedy neighborhood southeast of downtown, doesn't stop the crowds (mostly tourists) from lining up early for this restaurant. The early Western, Naugahyde decor and fantastic jukebox set an upbeat mood for killer margaritas and some of the best burritos and green chili in town. ✗ *457 S. Broadway,* ☎ *303/778–0147. No reservations. MC, V.*

Steaks/Western

$$$ **Buckhorn Exchange.** If hunting makes you queasy, don't enter this Den-
★ ver landmark, a shrine to taxidermy where 500 Bambis stare down at you from the walls. The handsome men's-club decor—with pressed tin ceilings, burgundy walls, red-checker tablecloths, rodeo photos, shotguns, and those trophies—probably looks the same as it did when the Buckhorn first opened in 1893. Rumor has it Buffalo Bill was to the Buckhorn what Norm Peterson was to *Cheers.* The dry-aged, prime-grade Colorado steaks are huge, juicy, and magnificent, as is the game. For an appetizer, try the smoked buffalo sausage or black bean soup. ✗ *1000 Osage St.,* ☎ *303/534–9505. Reservations advised. AE, D, DC, MC, V. Closed weekend lunch.*

Outside Denver

Central City/Black Hawk

$$ **Black Forest Inn.** This is an affectionate re-creation of a Bavarian hunting lodge, replete with antlers, tapestries, and cuckoo clocks. Hearty specialties range from fine schnitzel to succulent wild game. Afterward, you can repair to Otto's casino. ✗ *260 Gregory St., Black Hawk,* ☎ *303/279–2333. Reservations advised. MC, V.*

Golden

$ **The Observatory.** This inimitable upstairs café features a retractable roof and 8-inch reflecting telescope for stargazing on warm nights. The menu is simple, with such items as Observa Burgers, Moon Dogs, and UFOs (unusual food orders), and libations such as Black Holes, Milky Ways, and Bailey's Comets. ✗ *29259 Hwy. 40, El Rancho, Golden,* ☎ *303/526–1988. No reservations. AE, MC, V.*

LODGING

Denver has lodging choices from the stately Brown Palace to the commonplace YMCA, with options such as bed-and-breakfasts and business hotels in between. Stapleton properties may very well languish once hotels open near the new Denver International Airport (DIA) in 1997. In addition, Adams Mark Hotels purchased the downtown I. M. Pei–designed Radisson and the old May D&F Department Store across the street in 1994, with plans to convert them into Denver's largest property (more than 1,000 rooms and a state-of-the-art convention center). Unless you're planning a quick escape to the mountains, consider staying in or around downtown, where most of the city's attractions are within walking distance. For price ranges *see* the Lodging chart *in* On the Road with Fodor's at the front of this guide.

$$–$$$ **Brown Palace.** This grande dame of Colorado lodging has housed nu-
★ merous public figures from President Eisenhower to the Beatles. The details are exquisite: A dramatic nine-story lobby is topped with a glorious stained-glass ceiling, and rooms are decorated with Victorian flair, using sophisticated wainscoting and art-deco fixtures. A much needed refurbishment in 1995 replaced faded carpets, linens, and upholstery. The Palace Arms, its formal restaurant, has won numerous awards, including one from *Wine Spectator* magazine. Guests have access to a local health club. 🏨 *321 17th St.,* ☎ *303/297–3111 or 800/321–2599;*

FAX 303/293–9204. 205 rooms, 25 suites. 4 restaurants, 2 bars, concierge. AE, D, DC, MC, V.

$$ Burnsley. Since its face-lift in the 1980s, this 16-story, Bauhaus-style tower has been a haven for executives seeking peace and quiet close to downtown. The tastefully appointed accommodations are all suites and feature balconies and full kitchens. A refurbishment in 1993 brightened up the place, adding floral linens; dusky rose, salmon, and burgundy carpets or upholstery; and old-fashioned riding prints. Many suites have a sofa bed, making this a good bet for families. The swooningly romantic restaurant is a perfect place to pop the question. ☎ *1000 Grant St.,* ☏ *303/830–1000 or 800/231–3915; FAX 303/830–7676. 82 suites. Restaurant, bar, pool. AE, DC, MC, V.*

$$ Cambridge Club Hotel. This 1960s-era luxury suites hotel is on a tree-lined street convenient to downtown, one block from the state capitol building. Each suite is individually decorated with a smart mix of contemporary and traditional furnishings, from Asian to French provincial; all have kitchenettes. Local lobbyists, politicos, and CEOs favor the bar. ☎ *1560 Sherman St.,* ☏ *303/831–1252 or 800/877–1252; FAX 303/831–4724. 28 suites. Restaurant, bar, kitchenettes. AE, D, DC, MC, V.*

$$ Loews Giorgio. The 12-story steel-and-black glass facade conceals the
★ unexpected and delightful Italian Baroque motif within. Rooms are spacious and elegant, with teal colors and blond wood predominating, and such Continental touches as fresh flowers, fruit baskets, and Renaissance-style portraits. The formal Tuscany restaurant serves sumptuous Italian cuisine. Guests may use a nearby health club, and a Continental breakfast is included in the room rate. The only drawback of this property is its location: halfway between downtown and the Denver Tech Center, with little in the immediate vicinity. ☎ *4150 E. Mississippi Ave.,* ☏ *303/782–9300 or 800/345–9172; FAX 303/758–6542. 200 rooms, 19 suites. Restaurant, bar. AE, D, DC, MC, V.*

$$ Warwick Hotel. This stylish business hotel, ideally located on the edge of downtown, offers oversize rooms and suites and features brass and mahogany Thomasville antique reproductions. Most rooms contain wet bars, full refrigerators, and private balconies. A breakfast buffet and access to the health club next door are included in the room rate. ☎ *1776 Grant St.,* ☏ *303/861–2000 or 800/525–2888; FAX 303/832–0320. 145 rooms, 49 suites. Restaurant, bar, pool, concierge. AE, DC, MC, V.*

$$ Westin Hotel Tabor Center. This sleek, luxurious high-rise opens right
★ onto the 16th Street Mall and all the downtown action. Rooms, renovated in 1995, are oversize and done in grays and taupes, with paisley duvets and prints of the Rockies and the Denver skyline on the walls. Each room also has such amenities as an iron and ironing board, a desk pull-out tray for laptop computers, and cable TV and in-room movies. The hotel even buys blocks of tickets for weekend shows at the Denver Performing Arts Complex for guests' exclusive use. ☎ *1672 Lawrence St., 80202,* ☏ *303/572–9100, FAX 303/572–7288. 420 rooms. 2 restaurants, bar, pool, health club, racquetball. AE, D, DC, MC, V.*

$–$$ Castle Marne. This historic B&B, just east of downtown, sits in a shabbily genteel area. Its balconies, four-story turret, and intricate stone and woodwork present a dramatic facade. On the inside, rooms are richly decorated with antiques and artwork. Birdcages, butterfly cases, and old photos of the house are displayed throughout. Most rooms have brass or mahogany beds, throw rugs, tile fireplaces (nonworking), a profusion of dried and fresh flowers, and clawfoot tubs; a few have hot tubs or whirlpool baths. Rooms don't have TVs, but there's one in the common room. A full gourmet breakfast—served in the dining room—is included in the room rate, as is afternoon tea. ☎ *1572 Race St., ☎ 303/331–0621 or 800/926–2763; FAX 303/331–0623. 9 rooms. Business services. AE, D, DC, MC, V.*

$–$$ Oxford Hotel. During the Victorian era this hotel was an elegant fix-
★ ture on the Denver landscape. It has been restored to its former turn-
of-the-century glory: Rooms are uniquely furnished with French and
English period antiques, while the bar re-creates an art-deco ocean liner.
Its location is perfect for those seeking a different, artsy environment.
Complimentary shoe shines, afternoon sherry, and morning coffee and
fruit are among the civilized touches offered here. Although the Oxford is a notch down from the Brown Palace in most respects, it's also
less expensive and is home to McCormick's Fish and Oyster House,
Denver's premier seafood restaurant. ☎ *1600 17th St., ☎ 303/628–
5400 or 800/228–5838; FAX 303/628–5413. 81 rooms. Restaurant, 2
bars, beauty salon. AE, DC, MC, V.*

$–$$ Queen Anne Inn. The Queen Anne occupies two adjacent Victorians
★ north of downtown in the regentrified Clements historic district (some
of the neighboring blocks have yet to be reclaimed). This handsome
property is a delightful, romantic getaway for B&B mavens. Both
houses have handsome oak wainscoting and balustrades, 10-foot
vaulted ceilings, numerous bay or stained-glass windows, and such period furnishings as brass and canopy beds, cherry and pine armoires,
and oak rocking chairs. The best accommodations are the four gallery
suites dedicated to Audubon, Rockwell, Calder, and Remington; each
displays reproductions representative of that artist's work. All rooms
have phones and private baths. A full breakfast and afternoon wine
tastings are offered daily. ☎ *2147 Tremont Pl., ☎ 303/296–6666; FAX
303/296–2151. 10 rooms, 4 suites. AE, D, MC, V.*

$ Comfort Inn/Downtown. The advantages of this well-used hotel are its
reasonable rates and its location in the heart of downtown. Rooms are
somewhat cramped, but renovations completed in 1995 added new car-
peting and draperies throughout. The corner rooms on the upper floors
feature wraparound floor-to-ceiling windows with stunning panoramic
views. A complimentary Continental breakfast is offered. ☎ *401 17th
St., ☎ 303/296–0400 or 800/221–2222; FAX 303/297–0774. 229
rooms. Laundry service. AE, D, DC, MC, V.*

$ Holiday Chalet. Stained-glass windows and homey touches through-
out make this Victorian brownstone exceptionally charming. It's also
conveniently situated in Capitol Hill, the neighborhood immediately
east of downtown. Many of the rooms are furnished with overstuffed
Victorian armchairs in light floral fabrics and such cute touches as straw
hats; some units have tile fireplaces, others have small sitting rooms.
Each room has a kitchenette, which is stocked with breakfast foods.
☎ *1820 E. Colfax Ave., ☎ 303/321–9975 or 800/626–4497. 10
rooms. Kitchenettes. AE, D, DC, MC, V.*

THE ARTS AND NIGHTLIFE

The Arts

Friday's *Denver Post* and *Rocky Mountain News* publish calendars of
the week's events, as does the slightly alternative *Westword,* which is
free and published on Tuesday. **TicketMaster** (☎ 303/830–8497) and
TicketMan (☎ 303/430–1111 or 800/200–8497) sell tickets by phone
to major events, tacking on a slight service charge; the **Ticket Bus** (no
☎), on the 16th Street Mall at Curtis Street, sells tickets from 10 until
6 weekdays, and half-price tickets on the day of the performance.

Dance

The **Colorado Ballet** (☎ 303/237–8888) specializes in the classics; performances are staged at the Denver Performing Arts Complex (14th and Curtis Sts.).

Music

The **Colorado Symphony Orchestra** performs at Boettcher Concert Hall (13th and Curtis Sts., ☎ 303/986–8742); the **Denver Chamber Orchestra** (18th Ave. and Broadway, ☎ 303/825–4911) usually plays at historic Trinity Methodist Church downtown. The **Paramount Theater** (1621 Glenarm Pl., ☎ 303/623–0106) is the site for many large-scale rock concerts. The exquisite **Red Rocks Amphitheater** (☎ 303/572–4704) and **Fiddler's Green** (☎ 303/741–5000) are the primary outdoor concert venues.

Opera

Opera Colorado (☎ 303/778–6464) offers spring and fall seasons, often with internationally renowned artists, at the Denver Performing Arts Complex. **Central City Opera** (621 17th St., Central City, ☎ 303/292–6700), housed in an exquisite Victorian opera house, has the finest of settings.

Theater

The **Denver Performing Arts Complex** (14th and Curtis Sts., ☎ 303/893–3272) houses most of the city's large concert and theater venues. The **Denver Center Theater Company** (14th. and Curtis Sts., ☎ 303/893–4100) offers high-caliber repertory theater, including new works by promising playwrights, at the Bonfils Theatre Complex. **Robert Garner Attractions** (☎ 303/893–4100) brings Broadway road companies to Denver. Among the provocative fringe theaters are **Spark Artists Co-operative** (1535 Platte St., ☎ 303/744–3275), which also has a gallery space; **Eulipions, Inc. Cultural Center** (2425 Welton St., ☎ 303/295–6814), which presents plays by and with African Americans; **Changing Scene Theater** (1527½ Champa St., ☎ 303/893–5775); **Industrial Arts Theatre** (120 W. 1st Ave., ☎ 303/744–3245); **Hunger Artists Ensemble Theater** (Margery Reed Hall, Univ. of Denver, S. University Blvd. and Evans Ave., ☎ 303/893–5438); and **El Centro Su Teatro** (4925 High St., ☎ 303/296–0219).

Nightlife

Downtown and **LoDo** are where most Denverites make the scene. Downtown features more mainstream entertainment, whereas LoDo is home to fun, funky rock clubs and small theaters. Remember that Denver's altitude can intensify your reaction to alcohol.

Cabaret

The **Wynkoop Cabaret** (1634 18th St., downstairs in The Wynkoop Brewpub, ☎ 303/297–2700) offers everything from top-name jazz acts to up-and-coming stand-up comedians, including cabaret numbers.

Comedy Clubs

Comedy Works (1226 15th St., ☎ 303/595–3637) is where Denver comics hone their skills. Well-known performers often drop by. **Chicken Lips Comedy Theater** (1300 17th St., ☎ 303/534–4440) is an improv troupe specializing in topical satire.

Country and Western

The **Grizzly Rose** (I–25 at Exit 215, ☎ 303/295–1330) has miles of dance floor, national bands, and offers two-step dancing lessons. **Cactus Moon** (10001 Grant St., ☎ 303/451–5200) is larger than most venues and offers "Food, Firewater, and Dancin'." **Stampede Mesquite Grill & Dance Emporium** (2430 S. Havana St., ☎ 303/337–6904) is the latest boot-scooting spot.

Dinner Theater

The **Country Dinner Playhouse** (6875 S. Clinton St., ☎ 303/799–1410) serves a meal before the performance, which is usually a Broadway-style show. In Golden, the **Heritage Square Music Hall** (☎ 303/279–7800) has a buffet to go along with an evening of old-fashioned melodrama.

Bars and Clubs

DISCOS

Club Infinity (900 Auraria Pkwy., in the Tivoli Mall, ☎ 303/534–7206) nearly lives up to its name, with five bars and an enormous dance floor swept by laser beams. **Industry** (1222 Glenarm Pl., ☎ 303/620–9554) is the latest hip, happening hip-hop spot, with live techno-rave and house music, packing in Denver's youngest and trendiest. **Deadbeat** (404 E. Evans Ave., ☎ 303/758–6853) is where the cool college crowd goes to get carded.

GAY BARS

Charlie's (900 E. Colfax Ave., ☎ 303/839–8890) offers country-western atmosphere and music at the hottest gay bar in town.

JAZZ

El Chapultepec (20th and Market Sts., ☎ 303/295–9126) is a depressing, fluorescent-lit, bargain-basement Mexican dive. Still, the limos parked outside hint at its enduring popularity: This is where visiting musicians, from Ol' Blue Eyes to the Marsalis brothers, jam after hours. **Brendan's Pub** (1624 Market St., ☎ 303/595–0609) attracts local jazz and blues talents. The **Burnsley Hotel** (1000 Grant St., ☎ 303/830–1000) hops with live jazz several nights a week.

ROCK AND ROLL

There are a number of smoky hangouts in this city, the most popular being the down-home **Herman's Hideaway** (1578 S. Broadway, ☎ 303/777–5840), which showcases local and national acts, with a smattering of reggae, blues, and alternative music thrown in to keep things lively. Also popular are the **Bluebird Theater** (3317 E. Colfax Ave., ☎ 303/322–2308); **Cricket on the Hill** (1209 E. 13th Ave., ☎ 303/830–9020); and the **Mercury Café** (2199 California St., ☎ 303/294–9281), which triples as a marvelous health-food restaurant (sublime tofu fettuccine), fringe theater, and rock club specializing in acoustic sets, progressive, and newer wave music.

SINGLES

Rock Island (Wazee and 15th Sts., ☎ 303/572–7625) caters to the young, hip, and restless. Denver's five brew pubs are always hopping: **Rock Bottom Brewery** (1001 16th St., ☎ 303/534–7616) is the flavor-of-the-month, thanks to its rotating special brews and reasonably priced pub grub.

EXCURSION TO THE EASTERN PLAINS

One-third of Colorado is prairie land—vast stretches of hypnotically rolling corn and wheat fields, Russian thistle, and tall grasses coppered by the sun. This is middle America, where families have been ranching and farming the same plot of land for generations; where county fairs, livestock shows, and high-school football games are the main forms of entertainment; where the Corn and Bible belts stoically tighten a notch in times of adversity.

If you want to get in touch with America's roots, here is a good place to begin. The small one-horse towns such as Heartstrong and Last Chance—names redolent of the heartland—tell an old story, that of the first pioneers who struggled across the continent in search of a better life. The Pony Express and Overland trails cut right through northeast Colorado (James Michener set his epic historical novel *Centennial* in this territory), where even today you'll find weathered trading posts, lone buttes that guided the weary homesteaders westward, and downhome friendly people who take enormous pride in their land and their heritage.

Tour 1: I–76 and Environs

The first major stop on I–76 is **Fort Morgan,** the seat of Morgan County and a major agricultural center for corn, wheat, and sugar beets, the big cash crops in these parts. But its true claim to fame is as band leader Glenn Miller's birthplace. The **Fort Morgan Museum,** on Main Street, is a repository of local history that describes the town's origins in 1864 as a military fort constructed to protect gold miners and displays Miller memorabilia. Items exhibited include artifacts from the Koehler Site, an excavated landfill nearby that revealed a prehistoric campsite, and classic Americana such as a replica of the soda fountain from an old drugstore. On your way out, pick up a historical downtown walking-tour brochure to tell you about some of the handsome homes lining Main Street. *400 Main St.,* ☎ *970/867–6331.* ☛ *$2 adults, $1 children under 13.* ☉ *Weekdays 10–5, Sat. 11–5; in summer also open Sun. 1–4:30.*

Farther along the interstate is **Sterling,** a peaceful, prosperous town of graceful whitewashed houses with porch swings and shady trees that fringe neighborhood streets. Sterling bills itself as "the City of Living Trees," a tribute to local artist Brad Rhea who has chiseled living trees into fanciful works of art: towering giraffes, festive clowns, golfers (at the country club), and minutemen (at the National Armory). Several downtown buildings, listed on the National Register of Historic Places, are supreme examples of turn-of-the-century pioneer architecture; among them is Logan County Courthouse.

The **Overland Trail Museum,** a replica of a classic old fort carved out of rock, offers displays of homesteading life, with painstaking re-creations of a typical blacksmith shop and schoolhouse, as well as exhibits of Plains Natives and pioneer clothing and utensils. *Jct. of Hwy. 6 and I–76,* ☎ *970/522–3895.* ☛ *Free.* ☉ *Mon.–Sat. 9–5, Sun. 10–5.*

The last stop in Colorado is **Julesburg,** called by Mark Twain "the wickedest city in the west," though today it's hard to picture the sleepy town as Sodom and Gomorrah rolled into one. Julesburg is the proud site of the only Pony Express Station in Colorado, duly celebrated at **Fort Sedgwick Depot Museum,** with assorted paraphernalia from mail patches to saddles. *202 W. 1st St.,* ☎ *970/474–2264.* ☛ *Free.* ☉ *Mon.–Sat. and holidays 9–5, Sun. 11–5.*

Tour 2: I–70

An option to the I–76 tour is to travel on I–70, which cuts a swath through the heart of Colorado and traverses much of the same terrain and small-town life as Tour 1. Since both routes are equally enjoyable, consider which attractions interest you to help you choose. The first major community on this route is **Limon,** which is sadly best known as the locale of a ferocious twister that leveled the town in 1990. Admirably, residents banded together and today there are few apparent signs of the devastation.

Limon's rich past is displayed at the **Limon Heritage Museum,** offering collections of saddles, arrowheads, a restored 1924 Puffing Billy coach, and changing photo and graphics exhibits. *E. Ave. and 1st St.,* ☎ *719/775–2373.* ☛ *Free; donations accepted. Hours vary so call ahead.*

Ten miles east of Limon, along I–70, is the **Genoa Tower Museum,** an intriguing oddity that bills itself as the "highest point between the Rockies and the Mississippi." Aside from providing splendid vistas of the plains, the tower houses an eclectic collection of Native American artifacts, fossils, and Elvis Presley memorabilia. Owner Jerry Chubbock says, "If it ain't here, it don't exist." The Ripleyesque display of animal monstrosities seems to support his boast. *Exit 371, off I–70 (follow signs to museum),* ☎ *719/763–2309.* ☛ *$1 adults, 50¢ children under 13.* ⊙ *Daily 8–8.*

The easternmost sizable town along I–70 is **Burlington,** 12 miles from the Kansas border. They take their history seriously here, as evidenced by **Old Town,** a lovingly authentic re-creation of a 1900s Old West village, with more than 20 restored turn-of-the-century buildings complete with antique frontier memorabilia. Daily cancans and weekend gunfights take place in the Longhorn Saloon throughout the summer, as well as rip-roaring melodramas and madam shows (with the occasional cat fight). It's a hoot and a half. *I–70 exit 437,* ☎ *719/346–7382.* ☛ *Free.* ⊙ *Memorial Day–Labor Day, daily 8 AM–9 PM; Labor Day–Memorial Day, daily 9–6.*

Burlington's other main attraction was designated one of Colorado's 13 National Historic Landmarks. The **Kit Carson County Carousel,** in the Burlington Fairgrounds, Memorial Day–Labor Day, is a fully restored and operational carousel hand-carved by the Philadelphia Toboggan Company in 1905. It's one of fewer than 170 carousels to retain its original paint. Forty-six exquisitely detailed creatures bob and weave to the jaunty accompaniment of a 1909 Wurlitzer Monster Military Band Organ. Among the residents here are richly caparisoned camels, fiercely toothsome tigers, and gamboling goats.

Shopping

Most of the towns have at least one artisan whose work is proudly displayed in general stores, specialty shops, and craft fairs—be it a bronze-cast cowboy sculpture or a quilt. (Poking around the local emporia may net you some interesting finds.) **Lourine's** (101 E. 1st St., Otis, ☎ 970/246–3221) is noted for its hand-painted china. **Nelda's Antiques and Treasure Trove** (215/221 N. Interocean Ave., Holyoke, ☎ 970/854–3153) advertises "Scale House Antiques and Oddities, from Rags to Riches." For the best (if hokiest) selection of souvenirs, head for the **Old Town Emporium** (I–70 exit 437, ☎ 719/346–7382), in Burlington.

Sports and the Outdoors.

The northeast offers prime camping, hiking, fishing, and golf opportunities. The many lakes and reservoirs are havens for water-sports enthusiasts interested in everything from waterskiing to windsurfing. Wildlife- and bird-watchers will enjoy the Pawnee National Grasslands and the Cottonwood, Elliott, and Sandstage state wildlife areas, among others. For more information on the areas recommended below, call the chamber of commerce in each community.

Fishing

For exceptional fishing, try any of the following: Bonny Reservoir, Idalia; Jumbo Reservoir, Sedgwick; Kinney Lake, Hugo; North Sterling Reservoir, Sterling; Prewitt Reservoir, Merino; Stalker Lake and State Fish Hatchery, Wray. Trout and bass are plentiful at all locations.

Golf

Fort Morgan Municipal Golf Course (Riverside Park, Fort Morgan, ☎ 970/867–5990), **Riverview Golf Course** (Riverview Rd., Sterling, ☎ 970/522–3035), and **Sterling Country Club** (CO 14, Sterling, ☎ 970/522– 5523) are all 18-hole championship courses with challenging terrain.

Hiking

Most of the land in the region is so flat that the area is nicknamed "the Great American Desert" and "the Outback." However, the monotonous, dreary stretch of CO 71, just north of Fort Morgan, is improbably broken by the Pawnee Buttes that loom on the horizon. The Plains Natives used these twin, sedimentary upthrusts as lookout posts and today they are prime hiking terrain.

Dining

Livestock are a main source of livelihood on the eastern Plains, where billboards proclaim "Nothing satisfies like beef." However, the calorie- and cholesterol-conscious will appreciate the fresh fish that sometimes appears on menus. If all else fails, there's usually a choice between an Arby's and a Dairy Queen. Reservations are not necessary.

For price ranges *see* the Dining price chart *in* On the Road with Fodor's at the front of this guide.

$–$$ **Country Steak-Out.** Fort Morgan's first steak house—a combination between a diner and a barn—looks as if it hasn't changed since the Dust Bowl era. After a long day of following behind pickup trucks with bumper stickers that admonish you to "Eat beef," you might as well succumb to the succulent steaks served here. ✕ *19592 E. 8th Ave., Fort Morgan,* ☎ *970/867–7887. AE, MC, V. Closed Sun. dinner and Mon.*

$ **Fergie's West Inn Pub.** This small, simple restaurant-bar serves up sensational soups and sandwiches, including predictably mouthwatering barbecued beef. ✕ *324 W. Main St., Sterling,* ☎ *970/522–4220. No credit cards. Closed weekends.*

$ **Mr. A's Interstate House.** Locals swear by this glorified truck stop, off I-70. The humongous portions and daily specials define economical. Try the chicken fried steak, biscuits and gravy, or green chili. ✕ *415 S. Lincoln St., Burlington,* ☎ *719/346–8010. AE, MC, V.*

Lodging

In this part of the state you'll find the usual assortment of chain motor lodges, with a few historic B&Bs in the larger towns. For price ranges *see* the Lodging chart *in* On the Road with Fodor's at the beginning of this guide.

$$ **Best Western Sundowner.** This property is a notch above the usual motel, with spacious, tasteful rooms, and several amenities. Continental breakfast is included in the room rate. ▥ *Overland Trail St., Sterling,* ☎ *970/522–6265. 29 rooms. Restaurant, pool, hot tub, exercise room, coin laundry. AE, MC, V.*

$ Best Western Park Terrace. Clean, pleasant rooms with cable TV are what you'll find in this perfectly comfortable, typical motel. ☎ *725 Main St., Fort Morgan,* ☎ *970/867–8256. 24 rooms. Restaurant, pool. AE, MC, V.*

$ Chaparral Budget Host. This serviceable motor lodge is perfectly located right near Old Town, and offers the usual amenities such as cable TV. ☎ *I–70 exit 437, Burlington,* ☎ *719/346–5361. 39 rooms. Pool, hot tub. AE, MC, V.*

$ Crest House. This property has two sections: a small, decently outfitted motel and an exquisite B&B in a lovely old Victorian home, with beveled-glass windows and four-poster beds. Opt for the B&B, though you'll receive the same friendly, thoughtful treatment from the owners wherever you stay. ☎ *516 Division Ave., Sterling,* ☎ *970/522–3753. 5 rooms in house, 9 in motel. AE, MC, V.*

Getting There

The nearest international airports are in Denver (*see* Arriving and Departing by Plane, *below*) and Cheyenne, Wyoming.

By Car
I–70 cuts through the center of Colorado into Kansas, and I–76 angles northeast into Nebraska. If you're driving to Denver from the north or east, follow the itinerary in reverse. If time allows, occasionally get off the main highway and drive the two-lane byways to get a real sense of this region's communities and slower pace of life.

By Bus
Greyhound Lines (☎ 800/231–2222) offers service to several towns throughout the region, including Fort Morgan, Sterling, Limon, and Burlington.

Important Addresses and Numbers
Hospitals
There are medical facilities in Fort Morgan (Colorado Plains Medical Center, 1000 Lincoln St., ☎ 303/867–3391); Sterling (Sterling Regional Medical Center, 615 Fairhurst St., ☎ 970/522–0122); and Burlington (Kit Carson County Memorial Hospital,286 16th St., ☎ 719/346–5311).

Visitor Information
Burlington Chamber of Commerce (480 15th St., Burlington 80807, ☎ 719/346–8070); **Colorado Welcome Center** (48265 I–70, Burlington 80807, ☎ 719/346–5554); **Fort Morgan Area Chamber of Commerce** (300 Main St., Fort Morgan 80701, ☎ 970/867–6702 or 800/354–8660); **Logan County Chamber of Commerce** (Box 1683, Main and Front Sts., Sterling 80751, ☎ 970/522–5070); **Northeast Colorado Travel Region** (420 S. 14th St., Burlington 80807, ☎ 800/777–9075).

DENVER ESSENTIALS

Arriving and Departing by Plane
Airports and Airlines
Denver International Airport (☎ 303/270–1900 or 800/247–2336), or DIA, opened its gates in early 1995, replacing Stapleton. It is served by most major domestic carriers and many international ones, including **Alaska Airlines** (☎ 800/426–0333), **American** (☎ 800/433–7300), **America West** (☎ 800/247–5692), **Continental** (☎ 800/525–0280), **Delta** (☎ 800/221–1212), **Frontier** (☎ 800/432–1359), **Midway** (☎

800/446–4392), **SkyWest** (☎ 800/453–9417), **Mesa** (☎ 800/637–2247), **Northwest** (☎ 800/225–2525), **TWA** (☎ 800/221–2000), **United** (☎ 800/241–6522), and **USAir** (☎ 800/425–4322).

Between the Airport and Downtown

BY BUS

The **Airporter** (☎ 303/333–5833) serves downtown and southeast Denver Tech Center hotels, with 15-minute scheduled departures daily between 6 AM and 10:15 PM to downtown, and 30-minute departures to southeast Denver. **Denver Airport Shuttle** (☎ 303/342–5450), or DASH, serves downtown and several nearby ski areas. The region's public bus service, **Regional Transportation District** (RTD, ☎ 303/299–6000 for route and schedule information; 303/299–6700 for other inquiries) runs **SkyRide** to and from DIA; the trip takes 55 minutes, and the fare is $6. There is a transportation center in the airport just outside baggage claim.

BY TAXI

Taxis to downtown cost $25–$30 from DIA. Call **Metro Taxi** (☎ 303/333–3333), **Yellow Cab** (☎ 303/777–7777), or **Zone Cab** (☎ 303/444–8888).

BY LIMOUSINE

Options include **Admiral Limousines** (☎ 303/296–2003 or 800/828–8680), **Celebrity Limousine** (☎ 303/252–1760 or 800/778–1211), **Denver Limousine Services** (☎ 303/766–0400 or 800/766–2090), **Executive Touring Car** (☎ 303/743–8522 or 800/743–8622). Rates average $25 and up, depending on the type of car.

RENTAL CAR

Alamo (☎ 303/321–1176 or 800/327–9633), **Avis** (☎ 303/839–1280 or 800/331–1212), **Budget** (☎ 303/341-2277 or 800/222–6772), **Dollar** (☎ 303/398–2323 or 800/756–3701), **Hertz** (☎ 303/355–2244 or 800/654–3131), and **National** (☎ 303/342–0717) all have airport and downtown representatives.

Arriving and Departing by Car, Train, and Bus

By Car

Reaching Denver by car is fairly easy, except during rush hour when the interstates (and downtown) get congested. Interstate highways I–70 and I–25 intersect near downtown; an entrance to I–70 is just outside the airport.

By Train

Union Station (17th Ave. at Wynkoop, downtown, ☎ 303/524–2812) has Amtrak service.

By Bus

The **Greyhound Lines** depot is at 1055 19th Street (☎ 303/293–6541 or 800/231–2222).

Getting Around

In downtown Denver, free shuttle-bus service operates about every 10 minutes until 11 PM, running the length of the 16th Street Mall (which bisects downtown) and stopping at two-block intervals. If you plan to spend much time outside downtown, a car is advised, although buses and taxis are available. Even downtown, parking spots are usually easy to find; try to avoid driving in the area during rush hour, when traffic gets heavy.

By Bus or Train

The region's public bus service, **RTD** (*see* Between the Airport and Downtown, *above*) is comprehensive, with routes throughout the metropolitan area. The service also links Denver to outlying towns such as Boulder, Longmont, and Nederland. You can buy bus tokens at grocery stores or pay with exact change on the bus. Fares vary according to time and zone. Within the city limits, buses cost $1 during peak hours (6–9 AM, 4–6 PM), 50¢ at other times. You can also buy a **Cultural Connection Trolley** (☎ 303/299–6000) ticket for $1 at several convenient outlets throughout downtown, from the trolley driver, or from most hotel concierges. The trolley operates daily, every half hour 9–6, linking 18 prime attractions from the Denver Performing Arts Complex downtown to the Denver Natural History Museum in City Park. Tickets are good for one stop. RTD's **Light Rail** service (☎ 303/299–6000) began in October 1994. The original 5.3-mile track links southwest and northeast Denver to downtown; routes are continually expanding; the fare is $1.

By Taxi

Cabs are available by phone and at the airport and can generally be hailed outside major hotels. Companies offering 24-hour service include: **Metro Taxi** (☎ 303/333–3333), $1.40 minimum, $1.40 per mile; and **Yellow Cab** (☎ 303/777–7777), $1.40 minimum, $1.20 per mile.

Guided Tours

Orientation

Gray Line Tour of Denver (☎ 303/289–2841) offers a three-hour city tour, a Denver mountain parks tour, and a mountain casino tour. Tours range from $15 to $40 per person.

Walking Tours

The preservation group **Historic Denver** (1330 17th St., ☎ 303/534–1858) offers tours of old Denver for a $5 fee. Self-guided walking-tour brochures are available from the Denver Metro Convention and Visitors Bureau (*see* Visitor Information *below*).

Important Addresses and Numbers

Police

For nonemergency police assistance, call 303/575–3127.

Emergency Rooms

Rose Medical Center (4567 E. 9th Ave., ☎ 303/320–2121) and **St. Joseph Hospital** (1835 Franklin St., ☎ 303/837–7240) are both open 24 hours.

Doctors

Downtown Health Care (1860 Larimer St., No. 100, ☎ 303/296–2273) is a full medical clinic. **Rose Medical Center** (*see above*) refers patients to doctors, 8–5:30. **Med Search St. Joseph's Hospital** (1835 Franklin St., ☎ 303/866–8000) is a free referral service.

Dentists

Metropolitan Denver Dental Society (3690 S. Yosemite St., ☎ 303/488–0243) offers referrals to dentists; **Centre Dental Associates** (1600 Stout St., No. 1370, ☎ 303/592–1133) is open 8–6, with emergency after-hours care available.

Late-Night Pharmacies

Walgreens (2000 E. Colfax Ave., ☎ 303/331–0917) is open daily, 24 hours.

Visitor Information

The **Denver Metro Convention and Visitors Bureau** (225 W. Colfax Ave., Denver, CO 80202, ☎ 303/892–1112 or 800/888–1990), open weekdays 8–5 and Saturday 9–1, is across from the City and County Building, and provides information and free maps, magazines, and brochures. **Travelers Aid Society** (1245 E. Colfax Ave., ☎ 303/832–8194) offers the same assistance.

3 I-70 and the High Rockies

I-70 IS THE MAJOR ARTERY that fearlessly slices the Continental Divide, passing through or near many of Colorado's most fabled resorts and towns: Aspen, Vail, Breckenridge, Steamboat, Keystone, Snowmass, Copper Mountain, Beaver Creek, Winter Park. True powder hounds intone those names like a mantra to appease the snow gods, speaking in hushed tones of the gnarly mogul runs, the wide-open bowls on top of the world. Here is the image that lingers when most people think of Colorado: a Christmas paperweight come to life, with picture-postcard mining towns and quasi-Tyrolean villages framed by cobalt skies and snowcapped peaks. To those in the know, Colorado is as breathtaking the rest of the year, when meadows are woven with larkspur and columbine, the maroon mountains flecked with the jade of juniper and the ghostly white of aspen.

Like most of Colorado, the High Rockies region is a blend of old and new, of tradition and progress. It is historic towns such as Leadville, whose muddy streets still ring with the lusty laughter from saloons, of flamboyant millionaires who built grandiose monuments to themselves before dying penniless. It's also modern resorts such as Vail, whose history began a mere 30 years ago, yet whose founding and expansion involved risk-taking and egos on as monumental a scale. The High Rockies is fur trappers and fur-clad models, rustlers and Rastafarians, heads of cattle and heads of state. One thing links all the players together: a love of the wide-open spaces, and here, those spaces are as vast as the sky.

EXPLORING I–70 AND THE HIGH ROCKIES

Most visitors on their way to the magnificent ski resorts accessed by I–70 whiz through the Eisenhower Tunnel and cross the Continental Divide without paying much attention to the extraordinary engineering achievements that facilitate their journey. Interstate 70 and the tunnel are tributes to human ingenuity and endurance: Before their completion in the 1970s, crossing the High Rockies evoked the long, arduous treks of the pioneers.

Numbers in the margin correspond to points of interest on the I–70 and the High Rockies map.

❶ **Idaho Springs,** just outside of Denver, is your first stop on I–70, although a more spectacular drive is along U.S. 6, which parallels the interstate and winds through Clear Creek Canyon. In autumn, the quaking aspens ignite the roadside, making this an especially scenic route.

Idaho Springs was the site of Colorado's first major gold strike, which occurred on January 7, 1859. Today, the quaint old town recalls its mining days, especially along downtown's National Historic Landmark District **Miner Street,** the main drag whose pastel Victorians will transport you back a century without too much imagination.

During the Gold Rush days, ore was ferried from Central City via a 22,000-foot tunnel to Idaho Springs. The **Argo Gold Mill** explains the milling process and runs public tours. *2350 Riverside Dr.,* ☎ *970/567–2421.* ✆ *$3.* ☉ *Mid-May–mid-Oct., daily 9–5.*

Just outside town is the **Phoenix Gold Mine,** still a working site. A seasoned miner leads visitors underground, where they can wield 19th-century excavating tools, and dig or pan for gold. Whatever riches guests find are theirs to keep. *Off Trail Creek Rd.,* ☎ *970/567–0422.* ✒ *$5 adults, $3 children under 12.* ☉ *Daily 10–6.*

Idaho Springs presently prospers from its **Hot Springs,** at Indian Springs Resort (302 Soda Creek Rd., ☎ 970/567–2191). Around the springs, known to the Ute natives as the "healing waters of the Great Spirit," are geothermal caves that were used by several tribes as a neutral meeting site. Hot baths and a mineral-water swimming pool are the primary draws for the resort, but the scenery from here is equally fantastic. **Bridal Veil Falls,** within sight of the resort, are spun out as delicately as lace on the rocks. Also close by is the imposing **Charlie Tayler Water Wheel**—the largest in the state—constructed by a miner in the 1890s who attributed his strong constitution to that fact that he never shaved, took baths, or kissed women.

Drive 2 miles west up Fall River Road to **St. Mary's Glacier,** a vision of alpine splendor. In summer the sparkling sapphire lake makes a pleasant picnic spot; in winter, intrepid extreme skiers and snowboarders hike up the glacier and bomb down.

For even more glorious surroundings, take the Mt. Evans Scenic and Historic Byway—the highest paved auto road in America—to the summit of the 14,264-foot-high **Mt. Evans.** The pass winds through scenery of incomparable grandeur: past several placid lakes, one after another every few hundred feet; and vegetation galore, from towering Douglas firs to stunted dwarf bristlecone pines.

❷ West on I–70, then north on U.S. 40 (along the glorious Berthoud Pass) is **Winter Park,** a place that Denverites have come to think of as their own personal ski area. Although it's owned by the City of Denver and makes a favorite day trip—only 67 miles away—it deserves consideration as a destination resort on its own. Winter Park is easily accessible, the skiing and setting are superb, and it offers the best value of any major ski area in the state. It's also equally popular in summer for hiking and biking. Since the glory of the area is its natural setting, and most people come here specifically to enjoy the resources, Winter Park otherwise has few tourist attractions.

The three interconnected mountains—Winter Park, Mary Jane, and Vasquez Ridge—offer a phenomenal variety of terrain. Head to Vasquez Ridge for splendid intermediate cruising; Mary Jane for some of the steepest, most thrilling bumps in Colorado; and Winter Park for a pleasing blend of both. The ski area has worked hard to upgrade its facilities: The elegant **Lodge at Sunspot,** opened in 1993, is one of Colorado's finest on-mountain restaurants.

❸ Just east of the Continental Divide, and just west of the I–70/U.S. 40 junction, is **Georgetown,** also close enough to be a day trip from Denver, but its quiet charms warrant more than a hurried visit. Georgetown rode the crest of the silver boom during the second half of the 19th century. Most of its elegant, impeccably maintained brick buildings, which comprise a National Historic District, date from that period. Fortunately, Georgetown hasn't been tarted up at all, so it provides a true sense of what gracious living meant in those rough-and-tumble times. You can wander the five-square-block downtown on your own, or explore it on horse-drawn trolley, courtesy of the **Rutherford Carriage Service** (☎ 303/569–2675), which runs half-hour tours in the summer, daily between 11 and 4.

The **Hamill House,** home of the silver magnate William Arthur Hamill, is a Gothic Revival beauty that displays most of the original wall cov-

I-70 and the High Rockies

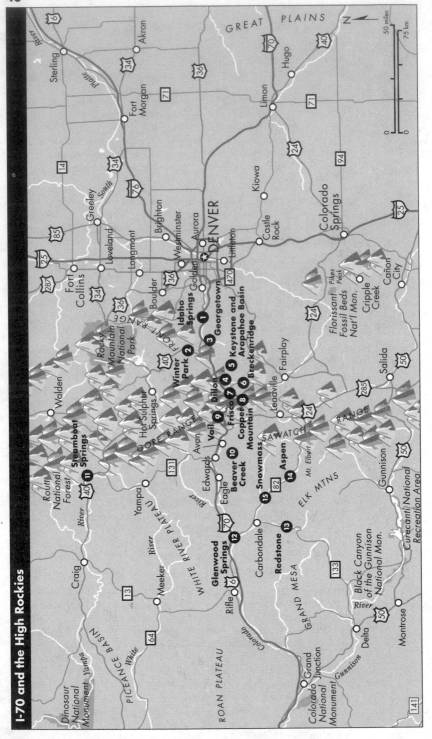

GREAT PLAINS

N

50 miles

75 km

Sterling

Akron

Fort Morgan

Limon

Hugo

Kiowa

Colorado Springs

Greeley

Brighton

Westminster

Aurora

DENVER

Littleton

Castle Rock

Pikes Peak

Cañon City

Cripple Creek

Florissant Fossil Beds Nat'l Mon.

Fort Collins

Boulder

Longmont

Loveland

Golden

Georgetown

Idaho Springs **1**

3

Keystone and Arapahoe Basin **5**

Breckenridge **6**

Fairplay

Salida

Winter Park **2**

4

Dillon **7**

Copper Mountain **8**

Vail **9**

Frisco

Leadville

Mt. Elbert

Avon

Beaver Creek **10**

Snowmass

Aspen **14**

82

SAWATCH RANGE

ELK MTNS

Gunnison

Curecanti National Recreation Area

Rocky Mountain National Park

FRONT RANGE

GORE RANGE

Hot Sulphur Springs

Walden

Steamboat Springs **11**

Routt National Forest

Yampa

Edwards

Eagle

15

Glenwood Springs **12**

Carbondale

Redstone **13**

Black Canyon of the Gunnison National Mon.

Montrose

Delta

Craig

Meeker

WHITE RIVER PLATEAU

Rifle

GRAND MESA

Colorado National Monument

Grand Junction

Gunnison River

PICEANCE BASIN

ROAN PLATEAU

Dinosaur National Monument

Yampa

White River

Colorado River

erings and furnishings; there's also a unique curved glass conservatory. *3rd and Argentine Sts., ☎ 303/569–2840. ☛ $2.50 adults, $1.50 senior citizens, 50¢ children 12–16. ⊙ May–Sept., daily 10–4; Oct.–Apr., weekends noon–4.*

The elaborate **Hotel de Paris,** built almost single-handedly by Frenchman Louis Dupuy in 1875, was one of the Old West's preeminent hostelries. Now a museum, the hotel depicts how luxuriously the rich were accommodated: Tiffany fixtures, lace curtains, and hand-carved furniture re-create an era of opulence. *6th and Griffith Sts., ☎ 303/569–2311. ☛ $2. ⊙ Memorial Day–Oct. 1, daily 9–5; Oct. 2–Memorial Day, weekends noon–4.*

Hop on the **Georgetown Loop Railroad,** a 1920s narrow-gauge steam locomotive that connects the town with the equally historic community of **Silver Plume.** The 6-mile round-trip excursion takes about 70 minutes and winds through vast stands of pine and fir before crossing the 95-foot-high Devil's Gate Bridge, where the track actually loops back over itself as it gains elevation. In Silver Plume, you can tour the **Lebanon Silver Mill and Mine.** *100 Loop Dr., ☎ 303/569–2403. Train operates Memorial Day–Labor Day, daily 10–4; Labor Day–early Oct., weekends 10–4.*

Now get in the car and drive the 20-mile loop of the Guanella Pass Scenic Byway (C.R. 381 and 62) for stunning vistas of the **Mt. Evans Wilderness Area.** Then park yourself at the **Wildlife Viewing Station** by Georgetown Lake, from where you can catch a glimpse of the state's largest herd of rare bighorn sheep.

The western slope of the Rockies (past the Continental Divide) is where the most—and fluffiest—snow falls. As you travel west along I–70, you'll reach one of world's engineering marvels, the 8,941-foot-long **Eisenhower Memorial Tunnel.** Most people who drive through take its presence for granted, but until the first lanes were opened in 1973, the only access route west was the perilous **Loveland Pass,** a twisting, turning roller coaster of a ride. Snow, mud, and a steep grade proved the downfall of many an intrepid motorist. In truly inclement weather, it was impassable, and the east and west slopes were completely cut off from each other.

Authorities first proposed the Eisenhower in 1937 (under a different name, of course). At that time, most geologists warned about unstable rock; for more than three decades their direst predictions came true as rock walls crumbled, steel girders buckled, and gas pockets caused mysterious explosions. When the project was finally completed, more than 500,000 cubic yards of solid granite had been removed from Mt. Trelease. The original cost-estimate in 1937 was $1 million. By the time the second bore was completed in 1979, the tunnel's cost had skyrocketed to $340 million.

A string of superb ski areas now greets you. First is unassuming **Loveland** (*see* Sports and the Outdoors, *below*), a favorite of locals who appreciate the inexpensive lift tickets and short lines. More popular, however, is **Summit County,** a few miles farther on I–70, where four mega-areas—Keystone/Araphoe Basin (A-Basin), Breckenridge, and Copper Mountain—attract skiers from all over the world. There's a saying among Summit County residents: Copper for skiing, Breck for lodging, and Keystone for food. The adage is accurate.

Though the resorts were once marketed together, they are not all owned by the same company. Ralston Purina owns Keystone/A-Basin and purchased Breckenridge in 1993. They plan to link these three areas even more closely. So popular is Summit County, thanks to its incomparable setting, incredible variety of ski terrain, multitude of summer activities, and easy accessibility from Denver, that it welcomes more visitors annually than Aspen and Vail combined. Unfortunately, this creates terrible snarls along I–70, especially on weekends and holidays.

In many respects, Summit County serves as a microcosm of Colorado. It's a combination of grand old mining towns and ultramodern developments, of salty old-timers and yuppies. (Indeed, the county attracts so many young technocrats and professionals it's being touted as the new Silicon Valley.)

4 **Dillon,** just off I–70 on U.S. 6 East, was founded in the 1870s as a stage-coach stop and trading post for miners, but its location has changed twice since the town's conception. Only a decade after it was founded, Dillon was moved closer to the railroad line. Then, in 1955, plans were drawn up to dam the Blue River, hence forming a reservoir to quench Denver's growing thirst. Dillon would end up submerged under 150 feet of water. Once again the town was moved. Foresighted residents decreed that no building in the new location would be higher than 30 feet, so as not to obstruct the view of the reservoir—now gratefully called Dillon Reservoir, or Lake Dillon. The potential tragedy turned into a boon and a boom for the reborn town, stunningly set on pine-blanketed hills mirrored in the sapphire water. There's no pretension to Dillon, just nature lovers and sports enthusiasts who take advantage of all the recreational opportunities their idyllic home affords.

Continue along U.S. 6 to the first two great ski areas of Summit **5** County, **Keystone** and **Arapahoe Basin.** Arapahoe, the farther of the two areas, was the first to be built in Summit County, in the late '40s. Some say it hasn't changed since; the dig refers, in part, to some of Colorado's notoriously slowest lifts. Still, most of A-Basin's dedicated skiers wouldn't have it any other way. It's also America's highest ski area, with a *base* elevation of 10,780 feet. Most of the runs are above timberline, giving it an almost otherworldly feel. Aficionados love the short lift lines, the literally breathtaking views (and altitudes), the whopping 90% intermediate and expert terrain, and the wide-open bowls that stay open into June. A-Basin came under new management in the late '70s, but, aside from some upgrading of facilities, it has remained true to its resolutely un-chic, gnarly self.

Keystone is another matter. Designed to be cruisers' nirvana, with just enough flash to compete with the glamorous resorts, it compares favorably with the stylish if sterile megadevelopments of the Alps—such as France's Les Arcs. For the most part, its planners were sensitive to the environment, favoring mountain colors and materials that blend inconspicuously with the natural surroundings. Keystone has pursued an aggressive policy of expansion, opening the tougher terrain on North Peak (mogul heaven) and The Outback (glade skiing) in an attempt to change its "easy" reputation and provide a balanced ski experience. Keystone has one drawback: Its sprawling base area. To improve this situation, an ambitious $400 million redevelopment plan will, among other things, overhaul the base lodge and create more accommodations at the mountain itself. Keystone is becoming a magnet in summer, too, with a small lake for water sports, a top-ranked golf course, and the same premium service visitors can expect in winter.

Double back on U.S. 6 West until it merges with CO 9 South. In a few **6** miles you'll reach **Breckenridge,** a town that many consider the state's prettiest. In 1859 gold was discovered here, and the town sprang to life. For the next several decades Breckenridge's fortunes rose and fell as its lodes of gold and then silver were mined and exhausted. Still, it's the oldest continuously occupied town on the western slope, and fortunately, its architectural legacy from the mining era remains.

The downtown comprises one of Colorado's largest National Historic Districts, with 254 buildings in the National Register of Historic Places. The district is roughly a compact 12 square blocks, bounded by Main and High streets, Washington Avenue, and Wellington Road. The **Breckenridge Activity Center** (201 S. Main St., ☎ 970/453–5579) and **Summit Historical Society** (309 N. Main St., ☎ 970/453–9022) publish guided tours of more than 40 prominent structures, which range from simple log cabins to false-fronts to Victorians with lacy gingerbread trim, all lovingly restored and painted.

TIME OUT Step back to the '50s, and stop by **Glory Days Café** (311 S. Main St., ☎ 970/453–9495), a tribute to all that is deliriously retro hip from the Eisenhower years, with an authentic 1952 jukebox (and 45s), and cholesterol-laden '50s favorites.

The skiing at Breckenridge, which opened as a resort in 1961, is wonderfully varied over Peaks 7, 8, 9, and 10 of the Tenmile Range. The only downside is the strenuous poling required between Breck's four mountains. There are marvelous bowls and chutes on Peak 8, which is above timberline; gentle sweeping runs on Peak 9; and roller-coaster steeps on Peak 10. Consistent with the town's proud heritage, many runs are named for the old mines, including Bonanza, Cashier, Gold King, and Wellington. Nonetheless, Breck has developed a reputation for embracing the new: One of the first areas to permit snowboarding, it now holds the annual World Snowboarding Championships. Also, for one week each January the town declares itself an independent kingdom during the wild revel called Ullr Fest, which honors the Norse God of snow.

❼ Back on I–70, just past Route 9, lies the funky, low-key town of **Frisco,** an odd hodgepodge of strip malls near the interstate, with a charming downtown district trimmed with restored bed-and-breakfasts and hell-raising bars. Frisco is a good, moderate (and sane) alternative to the glitzier, pricier resorts in the county, and it's worth exploring even if you're staying elsewhere. The **Frisco Historic Park** (Main and 2nd Sts., ☎ 970/668–3428; ☞ Free; open Tues.–Sat. 11–4) re-creates the boom days with a fully outfitted one-room schoolhouse, jail, and log chapel among the seven authentic 19th-century buildings.

❽ A few miles further, off I–70, is **Copper Mountain,** another major ski area. Copper is even more self-contained than Keystone, and is dedicated to skiing, although it's picking up as a summer resort. Many skiers think the award-winning design, perfectly contoured to the natural terrain, is one of the world's best. The layout is ideal: Beginner runs are concentrated on the right side (facing the mountain) of the area, intermediate runs in the center, and expert terrain to the left. Weaker skiers can't get into trouble unless they look for it. Accommodations here are uniformly excellent, the nightlife lively for singles and younger couples, and the variety of activities and programs perfect for families.

Just a hop, skip, and a jump west of Summit County on I–70 is one of America's leading destinations, a playground of former presidents (and vice presidents), consistently ranked the finest ski resort in America, if not the world: **Vail.** The four-letter word means Valhalla for skiers
❾

and conjures up images of the rich and famous enjoying their privileges. Actually, Vail is one of the least likely success stories in skiing. Seen from the village, the mountain doesn't look all that imposing. There are no glowering glaciers, no couloirs and chutes slashed from the rock, not even an Olympian summit shrouded in clouds. Even local historians admit that the Gore Creek Valley in which Vail regally sits was an impoverished backwater, too isolated to play a prominent or colorful role in Colorado history, until the resort's opening in 1962.

In truth, the men who lent their names to the valley and resort deserved more notoriety than notice. Sir St. George Gore (a regrettably appropriate name) was a swaggering, filthy rich, drunken lout of a baronet who went on a three-year bacchanal in the 1850s and butchered every herd of elk and buffalo in sight. Charles Vail, the otherwise obscure chief engineer of the Colorado Highway Department from 1930 to 1945 was—according to townspeople who dealt with him—an ornery cuss who was rumored to accept kickbacks from contractors.

Then, two visionaries appeared on the scene: Pete Seibert, a veteran of the 10th Mountain Division that prepared for alpine warfare in the surrounding Gore and Sawatch ranges during World War II, and Earl Eaton, a uranium prospector who had grown up in and surveyed these very ranges. In 1957 they ascended the mountain now known as Vail, and upon attaining the summit discovered what skiers now salivate over: the Back Bowls, 4,000 acres of open glades formed when the Ute Indians set "spite fires" to the timberland in retaliation for being driven out by ranchers and miners. After five years of bureaucratic red tape and near-financial suicide, Seibert's dream became reality, and Vail resort was created.

Former owner George Gillett calls Vail "one of God's special works," and in reality it is an almost perfect example of mountain-and-village design. The development is remarkably compact, divided into the residential East Vail, the upscale Vail Village, and the more modest utilitarian Lionshead. Vail resembles a quaint Bavarian hamlet, with homey inns and lodges nestled against cozy A-frame chalets and clock towers. This, along with a heavy European bias among both the population and clientele, gives Vail perhaps the most international flavor and flair of any Colorado resort. It's crafted to anticipate a guest's every need, so you'll find a wealth of dining, shopping, and entertainment options at your fingertips. Everyone here is thoroughly professional: friendly without being familiar, knowing their business but not yours. Despite its tony reputation, the resort has actively courted the family trade in recent years. Children love the kids-only amusement parks at the ski area, with 15 acres of ski-through tepee villages, gold mines, and other rides attractions.

Although the mountain has the sheer exhilarating edge in size over nearly every other North American ski area, it's brilliantly and clearly linked by a well-placed network of lifts and trails. There are 1,220 acres of immensely varied runs on the front side alone, but the Back Bowls are truly skiers' heaven: More than twice the skiable terrain accessed from the front, the back side has eye-popping expanses of fluffy white snow that make both intermediates and experts feel they can ski for days and not run into a single soul. Those same slopes have become a mecca for mountain bike fanatics in summer, and the village now hosts a wide variety of festivals year-round.

TIME OUT The **Hubcap Brewery and Kitchen** (Crossroads Shopping Ctr., ☎ 970/476-5757) is Vail's only microbrewery, offering five regular beers (Vail

Pale Ale and Beaver Tail Brown Ale are standouts) and rotating specials. Decor is upscale-diner, with gleaming chrome hubcaps (owner Dean Liotta welcomes additions) adorning the walls. The food is mostly superior pub grub such as calamari, chicken wings, and quesadillas.

At cosmopolitan Vail the emphasis is on luxury, although the pre-fab buildings are beginning to show their age. The best sightseeing is window-shopping, ogling the deluxe merchandise and the consumers—a delightful rather than daunting experience. While you're here, there are two tourist attractions worth visiting. The **Betty Ford Alpine Gardens** (183 Gore Creek Dr., ☎ 970/476–0103; donations accepted; open Memorial Day–Labor Day, daily 9–7) are an oasis of forsythia, heather, wild roses, and shrubs, and have the distinction of being the highest public alpine gardens in the world. The **Colorado Ski Museum/Ski Hall of Fame** (15 Vail Rd., ☎ 970/476–1876; donations accepted; open Tues.–Sat. 9–5) traces the development of the sport throughout the world, with an emphasis on Colorado's contributions. Fascinating displays include century-old skis and tows, early ski fashions, and an entire room devoted to the 10th Mountain Division.

The rest of Vail Valley is composed of solid working-class towns such as **Avon, Eagle, Edwards,** and **Minturn,** which is enjoying a renaissance thanks to the influx of savvy artists and entrepreneurs who have opened several superb galleries and the **Minturn Cellars** winery. There is, however, one exception—**Beaver Creek,** an exclusive four-season development that gives even Utah's ultra-posh Deer Valley a run for its cash flow. It's been open since 1980, and is finally emerging from big sister Vail's shadow. The rap used to be that Beaver Creek was even more immaculately groomed than its soigné clientele. However, when Beaver Creek developed the 110-acre Grouse Mountain in 1991, the resort's reputation changed. With more than 40% of its terrain now rated advanced, skiers flock here on powder days to seek out Grouse and famed runs such as Birds of Prey. Beginners and intermediates can still find the same pampering on the slopes they receive elsewhere in the resort, which is often blissfully uncrowded even on Vail's most congested days. Plans to link Beaver Creek's trail system with that of nearby Arrowhead (*see* Skiing *in* Sports and the Outdoors, *below*) by the 1996–97 season will create one of the state's finest family areas.

Beaver Creek's sublime setting, luxurious accommodations, gourmet restaurants, and world-class golf course designed by Robert Trent Jones make the resort equally popular in summer, especially with families and couples. Elegant without being ostentatious, Vail's quietly glamorous little sister appeals to a select settled crowd, and everything at Beaver Creek lives up to its billing, from the billeting to the bill of fare.

A few miles west, past the town of Edwards, the narrow, winding Route 131 squirrels north from I–70 through the **Yampa Valley.** The lush, wide-open spaces and vistas are both gorgeous and lonely, relieved only by the occasional odd rock formation thrusting up from the ground. This is cattle country, a land of jade forests, jagged outcroppings, and streams silvered by the sun and skirting the **Flat Tops Wilderness Area,** a high, flat mountaintop crowned with a lava dome that glaciers have sculpted into a stunning series of steep cliffs and deep gashes.

TIME OUT   **Antlers Café** (Main St., Yampa, no ☎) is owned by Mike Benedict who is, by his own admission, a crusty old codger. Women couldn't sit at the handsome old bar until 1970 ("This ain't no brothel," Mike growled, "and I ain't got no cabaret license."). There's no question where some of his sympathies lie: Amidst the trophies, potbellied stove, antique jukebox, and cash register are such signs as "If you're hungry and out of work, eat an environmentalist." Mike's an equal-opportunity insulter, though, with a delightfully sly grin ("Never mind the dog," reads another sign, "beware of owner."). He'll say you owe him 25 bucks for a photo: He means it!

⓫ After driving another 30–40 minutes north on Route 131, you'll arrive at **Steamboat Springs,** followed closely by **Steamboat Mountain Village.** Steamboat is aptly nicknamed Ski Town, U.S.A., since the town has "sent" more athletes to the Winter Olympics than any other ski resort in America. Presently, the tally is more than 30, the most famous probably being silver medalist (in the 1972 slalom) Billy Kidd, whose irrepressible grin and 10-gallon hat are instantly recognizable. When he's around, Kidd conducts daily tours of the mountain.

Speaking of the mountain, keep in mind that the part that's visible from the base area is only the tip of the iceberg, and much more terrain lies concealed in back. Steamboat is famed for its eiderdown-soft snow; in fact, the term "champagne powder" was coined here to describe the area's unique feathery dumps, the result of Steamboat's fortuitous position between the arid desert to the west and the moisture-magnet of the Continental Divide to the east, where storm fronts duke it out.

If you're looking for hellacious steeps and menacing couloirs, you won't find them in Steamboat, but you will find perhaps the finest tree skiing in America. Beginners and intermediates rave about the wide-open spaces of Sunshine Bowl and Storm Peak. Steamboat also earns high marks for its comprehensive children's programs, the Kidd Center for Performance Skiing (where you can learn demanding disciplines like powder, mogul, and tree skiing), and two of Colorado's best on-mountain restaurants, Hazie's and Ragnar's.

The modern Steamboat Mountain Village is attractive enough, if lacking in personality: a maze of upscale condos, boutiques, and bars. To its credit, though, this increasingly "hot" destination has retained its down-home, Western friendliness, providing the trappings while avoiding the trap of a premium resort. That may have to do with Steamboat Springs itself, a mere 10-minute drive away, where Stetson hats are sold for use and not for souvenirs. Steamboat's origins are not as a mining town but as a ranching and farming community, setting it apart from a Breckenridge or an Aspen. It has its share of Victorian buildings, most of them fronting Lincoln Avenue, the main drag, but they were built to be functional rather than ornamental.

The **Tread of Pioneers Museum,** in a beautifully restored federal building, is an excellent spot to bone up on local history, and includes ski memorabilia dating back to the turn of the century, when Carl Howelsen opened Howelsen Hill, still the country's preeminent ski-jumping facility. *8th and Oak Sts.,* ☎ *970/879–2214.* ☛ *$2.50 adults, $1 children 6–12.* ☉ *Daily 11–5.*

The entrance to Steamboat from the mountain is roughly marked by the amusingly garish '50s neon sign from the Rabbit Ears Motel, and the unmistakable stench of sulphur. The town got its name from French trappers who, after hearing the bubbling and churning hot springs, mistakenly thought a steamboat was chugging up the Yampa River.

There are more than 100 hot springs in the immediate vicinity; the **Steamboat Visitor Center** (12th St. and Lincoln Ave., ☎ 970/879–4301) publishes a fun and informative walking tour guide that describes many of the spots. The two most famous are the **Steamboat Springs**

Health and Recreation Hot Springs (Lincoln Ave., ☎ 970/879–1828; ☛ $5; open daily 7 AM 8 PM) in town; and the **Strawberry Park Natural Hot Springs** (Strawberry Park Rd., ☎ 970/879–0342; ☛ $5; open daily 8 AM–midnight), 7 miles out of town. The springs may not be as restorative as legend claims, but the inspiring views of the surrounding pristine forest certainly are.

In summer, Steamboat serves as the gateway to magnificent **Routt National Forest,** which offers a wealth of activities from hiking to mountain biking to fishing. Among the nearby attractions are the 283-foot **Fish Creek Falls** and the splendidly rugged **Mt. Zirkel Wilderness Area.** To the north, two sparkling man-made lakes, **Steamboat** and **Pearl,** offer a variety of water sports, including fishing and sailing.

Return the way you came and head west on I–70 to reach the natural and man-made 15-mile-long **Glenwood Canyon.** Nature began the work as the Colorado River carved deep buff-tinted granite, limestone, and quartzite gullies—brilliantly streaked with lavender, rose, and ivory. This process took a half-billion years. Then man stepped in, seeking a more direct route west. In 1992, the work on I–70 through the canyon was completed at a cost of almost $500 million. Much of the expense was attributable to the effort to preserve the natural landscape as much as possible. When contractors blasted cliff faces, for example, they stained the exposed rock to simulate nature's weathering. Biking trails were also created, providing easy access to the hauntingly beautiful **Hanging Lake Recreation Area.** Here Dead Horse Creek sprays ethereal flumes from curling limestone tendrils into a startlingly turquoise pool, as jet-black swifts dart to and fro. It's perhaps the most transcendent of several idyllic spots now reachable on bike or foot. The intrepid can scale the delicate limestone cliffs, pocked with numerous caverns and embroidered with pastel-hued gardens.

I–70 snakes through the canyon on its way to a famed spa that forms the western apex of a triangle with Vail and Aspen. Once upon a time, **⑫** **Glenwood Springs** was every bit as tony as those chic resorts are today, attracting a faithful legion of the pampered and privileged who came to enjoy the waters (the world's largest natural hot springs), said to cure everything from acne to rheumatism.

Today the entrance to town and its once-splendid prospects of a fertile valley fringed by massive peaks is marred by the proliferation of malls, motels, and fast-food outlets. Remnants of her glory days can still be seen in the grand old **Hotel Colorado** (526 Pine St., ☎ 970/945–6511), regally commanding the vaporous pools from a patrician distance. Modeled after the Villa de Medici in Italy, the property opened its doors in 1893 to become the fashionable retreat of its day. Teddy Roosevelt even made it his unofficial "Little White House" in 1905, and so began the Teddy Bear craze, when a chambermaid stitched together tatters for the President after he returned empty-handed from an exhausting hunt.

The **Yampah Hot Springs,** near the hotel, were discovered by the Ute Indians (Yampah is Ute for "Big Medicine"), and are still popular today. Even before the heyday of the Hotel Colorado, western notables from Annie Oakley to Doc Holliday came to take the curative waters. In Doc's case, however, the cure didn't work, and six months after his arrival in 1887 he died broke, broken-down, and tubercular. (He lies in Linwood Cemetery, a half-mile east of town.) The smaller pool is 100 feet long and maintained at 104 degrees; the larger is more than two city blocks long (405 feet), and contains in excess of a million gallons of constantly filtered water that is completely refilled every six hours, and maintained at a soothing 90 degrees. *Pine St.,* ☎ *970/945–7131.* ☞ *$6.25 adults, $4 children 3–12.* ☉ *Memorial Day–Labor Day, daily 7:30 AM–10 PM; Labor Day–Memorial Day, 9 AM–10 PM.*

Two blocks down the street, the **Yampah Spa and Vapor Caves** is a series of three natural underground steam baths. The same 124-degree springs that supply the pool flow under the cave floors. Each chamber is successively hotter than the last; you can scoop mud from the walls for a cleansing facial, as you purify your body (and soul, according to Ute legend). A variety of spa treatments from massages to body wraps is also available. *709 E. 6th St.,* ☎ *970/945–0667.* ☞ *$7.75 for caves alone, more for various treatments.* ☉ *Daily 9–9.*

Twenty minutes south of Glenwood Springs, off Route 82 along Route 117, is another Colorado gem, the small but satisfying **Ski Sunlight,** a favorite of locals who enjoy the varied terrain, sensational views, and lack of pretension. The ratio of shredders (snowboarders) to downhillers here is quite high, as Sunlight has a reputation for "radical air."

At **Carbondale,** Route 82 splits, and Route 133 veers south on its way to **Redstone,** a charming artists' colony whose streets are lined with pretty galleries and boutiques, and whose boundaries are ringed by impressive sandstone cliffs from which the town draws its name. Its history dates back to the late 19th century when J. C. Osgood, director of the Colorado Fuel and Iron Company, built **Cleveholm Manor** (now known as **Redstone Castle**) to entertain the other titans of his day, such as John D. Rockefeller, J. P. Morgan, and Teddy Roosevelt. Among the home's embellishments are gold-leaf ceilings, maroon velvet walls, silk brocade upholstery, marble and mahogany fireplaces, Persian rugs, and Tiffany chandeliers. Today, the hotel is in the National Register of Historic Places, and is open to the public. Stay a night amid baronial splendor in one of the rooms favored by a Roosevelt or a Rockefeller. *58 Redstone Blvd.,* ☎ *970/963–3408.*

Osgood's largesse extended to his employees, for whom he constructed one of the first planned communities, a utopian model in its day. The **Redstone Inn** (82 Redstone Blvd., ☎ 970/963–2526), designated a National Historic Place, is a fine example of the magnate's generosity. Though this structure pales in comparison to the castle, its flourishes include a Tudor bell tower and sumptuous Victorian furnishings. You can also stay overnight at the cozy, relaxing inn.

Meanwhile, Route 82 continues southeast and skirts the Roaring Fork River on its way to **Aspen,** one of the world's fabled resorts and practically a byword for glitz, glamour, and glorious skiing. To the uninitiated, Aspen and Vail are virtually synonymous. To residents, a rivalry exists, despite the current détente that led to the formation of the Aspen/Vail Premier Passport (an interchangeable ski pass that includes a one-way transfer). Comparisons are admittedly odious and at best superficial, though a few instructive generalizations can be made.

The most obvious distinction is the look: Vail is a faux-Bavarian development, Aspen an authentic Victorian mining town. Vail is a lower-key, discreet, relaxed, and relaxing retreat. In see-and-be-seen Aspen, the only bad press is no press (the season doesn't seem to begin without some tabloid scandal). Vail is politicians—where Gerald Ford, Dan Quayle, and John Sununu fled to escape the cares of state. Aspen is recording stars and Hollywood—where Don Johnson and Melanie Griffith remarried (and divorced) and Barbra Streisand took a stand against controversial Amendment 2.

Aspen is a slave to fashion, so much so that the term "Aspen formal" was coined to describe the combination of dressing for the elements (ski hat, wool mittens) and for success (dinner jacket, evening gown). Locals tend to be either violently beautiful or merely wealthy, but fashionable takes on many meanings in Aspen. It's always been a magnet for cultural and countercultural types. After all, bad-boy gonzo journalist Hunter S. Thompson is one of the more visible citizens; and one of Aspen's most beloved figures is unrepentant hippie John Bennett, who tools around in his "Ultimate Taxi" (it's plastered with 3-D glasses, crystal disco balls, and neon necklaces and redolent of dry ice and incense). You'll find everyone from "social x-rays" with Vogue exteriors and vague interiors to long-haired musicians in combat boots and fatigues. To be fair, most Aspenites couldn't care less: Theirs is a freewheeling, tolerant town that welcomes diversity of personal expression. It's all part of the Aspen mystique. Ultimately, it doesn't matter what you wear here, as long as you wear it with conviction.

Before entering Aspen you'll pass through several communities and satellite ski resorts, starting with **Woody Creek,** a determinedly un-chic part of the valley that's most famous as the residence of Hunter S. Thompson. He isn't the only unique contribution to this area, though; if the snow's not too deep you might catch a glimpse of an Aspen landmark, the **Finger House.** Its roof sports an enormous middle finger, painted in Day-Glo colors—the owner's gesture to his wife after a particularly acrimonious divorce.

TIME OUT   A perfect example of this hip anomie is the **Woody Creek Tavern** (0002 Woody Creek Plaza, ☎ 970/923–4585), which has the temerity to sit next to a trailer park. It features pool tables, knotty-pine decor, TVs broadcasting sporting events, great burgers, nachos, and barbecue—and Hunter, who has been known to shoot target practice here every now and then. Don Henley's another habitué, though he usually keeps a low profile.

⑮ Continue southeast along Route 82, and you'll see the turnoffs (Brush Creek or Owl Creek Rds.) to **Snowmass,** one of four ski areas owned by the Aspen Skiing Company. Snowmass Village has its share of chic boutiques and eateries, but is more affordable and down-to-earth than Aspen, and predominantly caters to families. These differences apply equally to the development and to the mountain itself. Aspen Mountain is a rigorous ski experience; Snowmass is Aspen Skiing Company's family resort, with 51% of its 2,500 skiable acres designated intermediate, including the renowned classic cruiser runs off Big Burn lift, the stuff of ego massage. However, don't overlook that Snowmass is four times the size of Aspen Mountain, and has triple the black and double black diamond terrain of its famed sister, including several fearsomely precipitous gullies and Hanging Valley, accessible by a short hike. More and more skiers are discovering Snowmass's other personality, although Aspen Mountain remains the definitive test of skiing ability.

The next area, accessed by West Buttermilk Road, is **Tiehack,** unfortunately known as Aspen's "learning" mountain. It's often dissed and dismissed as a beginner's area, but the Tiehack section on the east contains several wonderfully cut advanced runs (though nothing truly expert), as well as sweeping views of Maroon Creek Valley. It also has superb powder, and deep snow sticks around longer because so few serious skiers realize what they're missing.

Aspen Highlands is the next mountain you'll reach off Maroon Creek Road, and until 1993, it was the only area not owned by the Aspen

Skiing Company. This alone made the Highlands a favorite of anti-establishment types; and though it can no longer play on its independence by billing itself as the "maverick ski area," locals ski here for other reasons as well, including the best views among the four mountains, comparatively short lift lines, and some heart-pounding runs. While not quite as hairy as Aspen Mountain, the Highlands offers thrilling descents at Steeplechase and Olympic Bowl, as well as a lovely wide-open bowl called Thunder, where intermediates play. While you're here, enjoy Aspen Highlands' anything-goes spirit, evidenced by special events such as the freestyle contests every Friday, and the now-legendary Ski Patrol Jump, over the deck—and over startled skiers—at the Cloud Nine Picnic Hut. It's held every day at noon, weather permitting.

Continue back on Route 82, and you'll finally reach **Aspen.** Originally called Ute City (after its displaced former residents), it was founded in the late 1870s during a silver rush. The most prominent early citizen was Jerome Wheeler, who in 1889, at the height of Aspen's prosperity, opened two of Aspen's enduring landmarks: the sturdily elegant redbrick **Jerome Hotel** (330 E. Main St., ☎ 970/920–1000), whose ornate lobby, bar, and restaurant today re-create fashionable turn-of-the-century living; and the elegant **Wheeler Opera House** (320 E. Hyman Ave., ☎ 970/925–2750). In 1893, however, silver crashed and Aspen's population dwindled from 15,000 to 250 people by the depression era.

In the late 1930s, the region struck gold when Swiss mountaineer and ski consultant Andre Roche determined that Aspen Mountain would make a prime ski area. By 1941 it had already landed the U.S. Nationals, but Aspen was really put on the world map by Walter Paepcke, who developed the town as a cultural mecca. In 1949, he helped found the Aspen Institute for Humanistic Studies, and organized an international celebration to mark Johann Wolfgang von Goethe's 200th birthday. This event paved the way for such renowned annual festivities as the Aspen Music Festival and the International Design Conference.

Downtown Aspen is easily explored on foot; it's best to wander without a planned itinerary, although the Aspen Historical Society puts out a walking-tour brochure. You can spend an afternoon admiring the sleek window displays and graceful Victorian mansions, many of which now house fine boutiques and restaurants.

You can obtain great insight into Victorian high life at the **Wheeler-Stallard House Museum,** which displays period memorabilia collected by the Aspen Historical Society. *620 W. Bleeker St., ☎ 970/925–3721. ☛ Adults $3.00, children 50¢. ⊙ Jan.–Apr. and mid-June–mid-Sept., Tues.–Fri. 1–4. Closed mid-June–May, mid-Sept.–Dec.*

Your next stop should be the **Aspen Art Museum,** where top local and national artists are exhibited. The complimentary wine-and-cheese-session-cum-gallery tour, held Thursdays at 5:30, is a lot of fun. *590 N. Mill St., ☎ 970/925–8050. ☛ $3 adults, $2 senior citizens and students, children under 12 free. ⊙ Tues., Wed., and Fri.–Sun. noon–6, Thurs. noon–8.*

Between galleries, museums, international conferences, and events, there's so much going on year-round that even in winter many people come to "do the scene," and don't even ski. Still, **Aspen Mountain** (also known as Ajax) is the standard by which many good skiers test themselves. Aspen is not for beginners (there are no green runs); in fact, a black diamond here might rank as a double diamond elsewhere. The narrow mountain is laid out as a series of steep unforgiving ridges with little room for error. Those wanting cruisers ski the ridge tops or valleys: Ruthie's Run, Buckhorn, and International are the classics. Bell Mountain provides some of the best bump skiing anywhere, followed by Walsh's Gulch, Hyrup's, and Kristi's. If you don't like catching air, or don't want your knees to get a workout, go elsewhere!

Aspen is equally popular in summer, with marvelous hiking and biking throughout the **White River National Forest.** One favorite jaunt is to the majestic **Maroon Bells,** twin peaks more than 14,000 feet high, so colorful, thanks to mineral streaking, you'd swear they were blanketed with primrose and Indian paintbrush. It's one of the most photographed spots in the state. Cars are only allowed partway, but Roaring Fork Transit provides shuttle buses that leave regularly in the summer from the Aspen Highlands parking lot.

What to See and Do with Children

Aspen Center for Environmental Studies (Hallam Lake Wildlife Sanctuary, 100 Puppy Smith St., Aspen, ☎ 970/925–5756) is a research center and wildlife sanctuary where children and adults alike can take refuge. The facility sponsors snowshoe walks with naturalist guides in winter, and backyard-wildlife workshops that teach children to create a minisanctuary in their own yard. In summer there are bird-watching hikes and Special Little Naturalist programs for 3–5- and 5–7-year olds, which include nature walks and arts and crafts.

Off the Beaten Path

Hut and Trail Systems
10th Mountain Hut and Trail System. During World War II a group of hardy soldiers camouflaged in white parkas practiced maneuvers in the stinging cold at Camp Hale, in the Elk Mountain Range between Aspen, Vail, and Leadville. That's where the U.S. Army 10th Mountain Division prepared for alpine fighting on hickory skis. Today, strong intermediates and experts can follow in their tracks on the 300 miles of trails crisscrossing the area. The surprisingly comfortable huts (accommodating up to 16 people in bunks; bring a sleeping bag) are solar-powered and have wood-burning stoves. Huts cost $22 per person per night, and are usually booked well in advance. For details and reservations contact the **10th Mountain Trail Association** (1280 Ute Ave., Aspen 81611, ☎ 970/925–5775).

Alfred A. Braun Hut System. This system explores the backcountry between Aspen and Crested Butte (Box 7937, Aspen 81612, ☎ 970/925–6618), and is run by the U.S. Ski Association. This is an exhilarating but grueling trek—a perfect test of skiing expertise.

Leadville
In the history of Colorado mining, perhaps no town looms larger than **Leadville**—at 10,152 feet, America's highest incorporated town. An easy detour from Copper Mountain and Vail (take U.S. 24 south from I–70, or the breathtaking Route 82 over Independence Pass from Aspen in summer), this town is a pleasant, nostalgic respite from all the prefab glitz that surrounds it. Two of the state's most fascinating figures are immortalized here: larger-than-life multimillionaire Horace Tabor and his wife Baby Doe (Elizabeth Doe McCourt), the subject of John La-Touche's Pulitzer Prize–winning opera *The Ballad of Baby Doe.*

Tabor amassed a huge fortune (by 1880s standards) of $12 million, much of which he spent building monuments throughout the state to himself and Baby. His power peaked when he purchased a U.S. Senate seat and replaced Senator Teller, who had been appointed Secretary of the Interior, well into his term. Baby Doe was his ambitious mistress and eventual second wife, after he dumped his first, the faithful but frigid Augusta. They made enemies and incurred the scorn of "high society" as only those who throw their money and weight around can. But in 1893 the repeal of the Sherman Act demonetarized silver, and, like so many other mining magnates, Tabor was ruined. He died a pauper in 1899, admonishing Baby to "hang on to the Matchless," his most famous mine, which he was convinced would once again restore her fortunes. It never did. Baby became a recluse, rarely venturing forth from her tiny unheated cabin beside the Matchless. She was discovered frozen to death in 1935.

Their legacy can be found in several attractions in town, including the **Tabor Home** (116 E. 5th St., ☎ 719/486–0551; ☛ $2; open daily 10–4), the modest dwelling where Horace lived with Augusta; the splendiferous **Tabor Opera House** (308 Harrison St., ☎ 719/486–3900; ☛ Free; open Memorial Day–Labor Day, Sun.–Fri. 9–5:30); and the **Matchless Mine** and squalid **Baby Doe's Cabin** (2 mi east of downtown on 7th St., ☎ 719/486–0371; ☛ $2; open Memorial Day–Labor Day 9–5).

Among the many other fascinating museums in Leadville are: The **Mining Hall of Fame and Museum,** which covers virtually every aspect of mining, including displays of various ores, tools, equipment, and dioramas explaining the extraction processes. *120 W. 9th St.,* ☎ *719/486–1229.* ☛ *$3 adults, $2 senior citizens, $1.50 children 6–12.* ☉ *Daily 9–5.*

Exemplifying how the upper crust such as the Tabors once lived and played are the lavishly decorated rooms of the **Healy House and Dexter Cabin.** *912 Harrison St.,* ☎ *719/486–0487.* ☛ *$2.50.* ☉ *Memorial Day–Labor Day, daily 10–4:30.*

The **Heritage Museum** also paints a vivid portrait of life in Leadville at its zenith. *120 E. 9th St.,* ☎ *719/486–1878.* ☛ *$2.50 adults, $1.50 senior citizens, $1.25 students, children under 6 free.* ☉ *Memorial Day–Labor Day, daily 9–5; Labor Day–Memorial Day, Fri. 1–5, weekends 10–5.*

Eccentricity is still a Leadville trait, as witnessed by the annual International Pack Burro Race over Mosquito Pass. The race, held the last weekend of July, ends in Fairplay, another quirky old mining town. The event is immortalized with T-shirts and bumper stickers that read, "Get Your Ass Over the Pass."

SHOPPING

Needless to say, you can find anything in these glamorous resorts except bargains. Still, window-shopping can be fun, as can a splurge every now and then.

Shopping Districts and Malls

Downtown Aspen is an eye-popping display of conspicuous consumption. Among the malls with ultra-chic stores are **Hyman Street Mall, Cooper Street Mall, Ute City Building,** and **Mill Street Plaza.**

Breckenridge also offers high-end shopping in the **Lincoln West Mall,** the **Main Street Mall,** and **Four Seasons Plaza.**

In Frisco, the **Mining Exchange Building** (313 Main St.) has several shops specializing in Americana, antiques, and collectibles.

Glenwood Springs Mall, in Glenwood, offers everything from Kmart and JCPenney to factory outlets and specialty shops.

Keystone features several top shops in the **Edgewater Mall** and **Argentine Plaza.**

Silverthorne Factory Stores Complex, in Summit County, has developed a reputation for discount shopping for Adolfo, Geoffrey Beene, Liz Claiborne, Evan Picone, Bass Shoe, Royal Doulton, Nike, and many others.

Steamboat's **Old Town Square** is a collection of upscale boutiques and retailers. On the mountain, check out **Ski Time Square, Gondola Square,** and **Torian Plaza.**

To some, Vail is one large upscale mall, but for the best of the best, head for **Gateway Plaza, Crossroads Shopping Center,** and of course, the **Beaver Creek Promenade.**

The top boutiques and galleries in Winter Park are concentrated downtown in **Cooper Creek Square** and **Crestview Place Mall.**

Specialty Stores

Antiques

Fetzer Antiques (305 S. Hunter St., ☎ 970/925–5447) carries Aspen's finest antiques, and specializes in 18th- and 19th-century English and Continental goods. **Uriah Heep's** (303 E. Hopkins Ave., Aspen, ☎ 970/925–7456) purveys an amazing assortment of antique quilts, furnishings, and clothing, as well as exotic textiles, rugs, and folk art. In Frisco, the **Junk-Tique Antique Barn** (313 Main St., ☎ 970/668–3040) is a treasure trove of odds and ends. In Georgetown, the **Georgetown Antique Emporium** (501 Rose St., ☎ 970/569–2727) specializes in oak and brass items.

Art Galleries

In the Aspen area, **Anderson Ranch Arts Center** (Snowmass Village, ☎ 970/923–3181) sells the work of resident artists. **Hill Gallery of Photography** (205 S. Mill St., Aspen, ☎ 970/925–1836) captures nature's artistry in works by leading American photographers. **Joel Soroka Gallery** (400 E. Hyman Ave., Aspen, ☎ 970/920–3152) specializes in rare photos. **Rachael Collection** (433 E. Cooper Ave., Aspen, ☎ 970/920–1313) exhibits more than 250 acclaimed American glass artists. **Stars Memorabilia** (521 E. Cooper Ave., Aspen, ☎ 970/920–2920) offers every kind of celebrity memorabilia, from Lincoln's autograph to Pete Townshend's smashed guitar.

In Breckenridge, **Skilled Hands Gallery** (110 S. Main St., ☎ 970/453–7818) is the largest art and crafts gallery in Summit County, offering everything from wood carvings to wind chimes.

Red Men Hall (U.S. 40, Empire, ☎ 970/569–3243), a few miles from Georgetown, showcases Native American art, including jewelry, paintings, and exquisite hand-painted kachina jackets.

In Steamboat, **Amer-Indian Gallery** (747 Lincoln Ave., ☎ 970/879–7116) is owned by North American Native-culture expert Mark St. Pierre (Pulitzer-nominated for his *Madonna Swan: A Lakota Woman's Story*). A wide range of Native art from Alaska to Mexico is featured. **Two Rivers Gallery** (56 9th St., ☎ 970/879–0044) sells cowboy collectibles like antler chandeliers and cow-skull lamps, as well as vintage photographs, prints, sculpture, and paintings. **White Hart Gallery** (843 Lincoln Ave., ☎ 970/879–1015) is a magnificent clutter of Western and Native American paintings and objets d'art.

In the Vail Valley, **Olla Podrida Gallery** (100 E. Meadow Dr., Vail, ☎ 970/476–6919) specializes in contemporary and antique American folk art and craft work. **Windwood Galleries** (151 Main St., Minturn, ☎ 970/827–9232) specializes in Colorado artists, as well as ceramics and artifacts. **Two Elk Gallery** (Main St., Minturn, ☎ 970/827–5307) showcases a dizzying array of items by Colorado artists, from coonskin caps to lodgepole pine furniture.

Books

Off the Beaten Path (56 7th St., Steamboat, ☎ 970/879–9127) is a throwback to the beat generation, with poetry readings, lectures, and concerts. It has an excellent selection of New Age works, in addition to the usual best-sellers and guides.

Boutiques

In Aspen, **Boogie's** (534 E. Cooper Ave., ☎ 970/925–6111) sells kitschy clothes and jewelry; you can grab a bite in their diner, too. **Chepita's** (525 E. Cooper Ave., ☎ 970/925–2871) calls itself a "toy store for adults," and the whimsy continues with kinetic clothing and wood-carved sartorially resplendent pigs, to complement the standard designer watches and jewelry. **Funky Mountain Threads** (520 E. Durant Ave., ☎ 970/925–4665) offers just that: ethnic clothes, festive hats, extravagant beadwork, and imaginative jewelry. **Gracy's** (202 E. Main St., ☎ 970/925–5131) has first-class secondhand clothing. **Scandinavian Designs** (607 E. Cooper Ave., ☎ 970/925–7299) features some of Aspen's finest hand-knit sweaters, as well as everything Scandinavian from Swedish clogs to Norwegian trolls. **Limited Additions** (205 S. Mill St., Aspen, ☎ 970/925–7112) features unique wearable art, handwoven or painted garments, and handcrafted jewelry.

In Steamboat, **Amallama** (Old Town Square, ☎ 970/879–9127) offers folk art, jewelry, and clothing from around the world, including Balinese cradle watchers, carved wooden figures believed to keep evil spirits away from sleeping children. You can make your own earrings at the bead counter. **Avalanche Ranch** (Gondola Square, ☎ 970/879–4392) sells hand-painted T-shirts, hand-knit sweaters, and unusual jewelry and ceramics. **Kirk's Kritters** (806 Lincoln Ave., in the Shirt Stop, ☎ 970/879–1288) offers a zany selection of jewelry and hand-knit sweaters. **Old Town Leather** (929 Lincoln Ave., ☎ 970/879–3558) offers every conceivable leather item, most of them handmade.

Gorsuch (263 Gore Creek Dr., Vail, ☎ 970/476–2294; 70 Promenade, Beaver Creek, ☎ 970/949–7115) is far more than a boutique or a sporting goods store; it offers everything from alpaca sweaters to buffalo coats and pottery to potpourri. **Pepi's Sports** (231 Bridge St., Vail, ☎ 970/476–5202) offers chic ski clothes and accessories, as well as evening wear from Armani to Lauren.

Ceramics

Aspen Potters (231 E. Main St., ☎ 970/925–8726) offers the latest designs from local artisans. **Geraniums 'n' Sunshine** (520 E. Durant Ave., Aspen, ☎ 970/925–6641) features Susan Eslick's colorful ceramics, as well as unique handcrafted toys and wearable art for kids. **Laughing Monkey** (223 Gore Creek Dr., Vail, ☎ 970/476–8809) has Mexican ceramics.

Crafts

Hunter Hogan Tapestries (520 W. Main St., Aspen, ☎ 970/925–8842) is named for the designer of the weavings that are sold here. Most prints have been adapted from African patterns. The aroma of hot wax percates **Handcarved Candles** (107 N. Main St., Breckenridge, ☎ 970/547–0928), where Al Kinchen fashions extraordinarily intricate tapers. **The Quiet Moose** (110 Lincoln Ave., Breckenridge, ☎ 970/453–6151) specializes in Western and rustic mountain furnishings and home accessories. **Quilts Unlimited** (Silvertree Plaza Mall, 100 Elbert La., Snowmass, ☎ 970/923–5467) sells superb handmade antique and contemporary quilts, as well as various regional handicrafts. **Art Quest** (511 Lincoln Ave., Steamboat, ☎ 970/879–1989) offers a variety of works in silver, glass, paper, ceramics, and alabaster, as well as furniture and jewelry. **Aboriginal Arts** (Crossroads Shopping Center, Vail, ☎ 970/476–7715) offers ethnic jewelry, resin-cast wood carvings, and feather masks from around the South Pacific and the Americas. **Menzel** (12 S. Frontage Rd., Vail, ☎ 970/476–6617) specializes in fanciful, intricate furniture and interiors crafted from 200-year-old pine.

Curios and Collectibles

The **Ore Rock Cart Shop** (324 S. Main St., Breckenridge, ☎ 970/453–1567) carries unique gifts made from stone, minerals, and precious metals: gold-nugget jewelry, agate bookends, crystals, even fossils and dinosaur bones. **Silver 'n Threads** (509 Rose St., Georgetown, ☎ 970/569–2965) offers a remarkable range of items, from silver ornaments, coins, and jewelry to handcrafted dolls and animals to rare tins and Navajo rock statues. The **Watersweeper and the Dwarf** (717 Grand St., Glenwood Springs, ☎ 970/945–2000) sells handicrafts and Americana fashioned from silver, gold, clay, wood, glass, stone, wool, wax, and patience.

Sporting Goods

Aspen Sports (408 E. Cooper Ave., ☎ 970/925–6331; 303 E. Durant Ave., ☎ 970/925–6332; Snowmass Mall, ☎ 970/923–6111; Snowmass Center, ☎ 970/923–3566; Silvertree Hotel, ☎ 970/923–6504) carries a full line of apparel and equipment. **Sport Stalker** (Ski Time Square, Steamboat, ☎ 970/879–2445) offers the latest fashions and gear. **Double Diamond Ski Shop** (520 Lionshead Mall, Vail, ☎ 970/476–5500) is noted not only for its wide selection of merchandise but also for its top-notch service.

Western Wear and Accessories

F. M. Light and Sons (830 Lincoln Ave., Steamboat Springs, ☎ 970/879–1822), owned by the same family for four generations, caters to the Marlboro man in us all. If you're lucky you'll find what you're looking for cheap—how about cowboy hats for $4.98? **Happy Trails** (725 Grand St., Glenwood Springs, ☎ 970/945–6076) has lots of Western-theme goods, much of it on consignment. The **Wild Wild West** (303 Main St., Frisco, ☎ 970/668–2202) has an unbridled selection of everything from bits to boots. **Into the West** (807 Lincoln Ave., Steamboat Springs, ☎ 970/879–8377) is owned by Jace Romick, a former member of the U.S. ski team and a veteran of the rodeo circuit. He crafts splendid, beautifully textured lodgepole furniture, and sells anything tasteful to do with the West: antiques (even ornate potbellied stoves), collectibles, cowhide mirrors, and new handicrafts such as Native American drum tables and fanciful candle holders made from branding irons.

SPORTS AND THE OUTDOORS

Camping

Call the U.S. Forest Service for complete information on camping in the following national forests: **Arapahoe** (☎ 970/444–6001), **Routt** (☎ 970/879–1722), and **White River** (☎ 970/945–2521).

Cycling

Blazing Pedals (Aspen, ☎ 970/925–5651, 970/923–4544 or 800/282–7238) and **Timberline Tours** (Aspen, ☎ 970/920–3217) offer downhill bicycle tours through Aspen and the surrounding countryside.

Steamboat Ski Area (☎ 970/879–6111) has expanded its trail service. **Routt National Forest** has numerous routes in its 1.5-million-acre wilderness. **White River National Forest** has the Rio Grande, Richmond Ridge, and the more strenuous Vail Pass and Independence Pass trails, among many others. **Arapahoe National Forest** offers Boreas Pass, Loveland Pass, Blue River Bikeway, and Tenmile Canyon National Recreation Trail.

Shrine Mountain Adventure (Red Cliff, ☎ 970/827–5363) offers backcountry mountain bike tours, as well as hikes, through the Vail Valley.

Winter Park is one of the leading cycling destinations in the Rockies, thanks to the 660-mile trail system created by the **Winter Park Fat Tire Society** (Box 1337, Winter Park 80482, no ☎). **Mad Adventures** (☎ 970/726–5290 or 800/451–4844) offers instruction and guided bike tours.

Fishing

Among the region's leading destinations are **Dillon Lake** and the **Blue** and **Snake rivers,** in Summit County; **Black Lakes** and the **Eagle River** in Vail Valley; the **Elk** and **Yampa rivers, Dumont Lake,** and **Steamboat Lake** near Steamboat Springs; and the **Frying Pan** and **Roaring Fork rivers** around Aspen. You'll find loads of trout, bass, walleye, pike, and others.

Aspen Outfitting Co. (☎ 970/925–3406) and **Oxbow Outfitting Company** (Aspen, ☎ 970/925–1505) run fly-fishing tours of local waterways. **Steamboat Lake Fishing Company** (Clark, ☎ 970/879–3045) arranges trips on the Elk and Yampa rivers, as well as on local lakes. **Mountain Anglers** (Breckenridge, ☎ 970/453–4665) organizes trips throughout Summit County. **Oxbow Outfitting Co.** (Aspen, ☎ 970/925–1505) runs trips for anglers. **Roaring Fork Anglers** (Glenwood Springs, ☎ 970/945–1800) leads wade and float trips throughout the area. **Summit Guides** (Dillon, ☎ 970/468–8945) offers full- and half-day trips. **Vail Fishing Guides** (☎ 970/476–3296) provides gear as well as guided tours.

The Fraser Valley was a favorite angling spot of President Eisenhower's. For information about fishing in Winter Park and the surrounding region, call the **Arapaho National Forest** (☎ 970/887–3331).

Fitness

Aspen Athletic Club (720 E. Hyman Ave., ☎ 970/925–2531) is fully equipped, and includes a steam room, tanning salon, and massage therapy. The **Aspen Club** (1450 Crystal Lake Rd., ☎ 970/925–8900) has weight-training and cardiovascular equipment, as well as indoor alpine skiing, squash, pools, basketball, and more.

Breckenridge Recreation Center (Kingdom Park, ☎ 970/453–1734) is a state-of-the-art, 62,000-square-foot facility that has a fully equipped health club, two swimming pools, and indoor tennis and racquetball courts.

Cascade Club (Cascade Village, next to Westin, Vail, ☎ 970/476–7400) and **Vail Athletic Club** (352 E. Meadow Dr., ☎ 970/476–7960) are full-service facilities, and include spas.

Copper Mountain Racquet and Athletic Club (209 Ten Mile Circle, Copper Mountain, ☎ 970/968–2882) features full-service fitness rooms, racquetball, tennis, aerobics, saunas, and tanning booths.

Hot Springs Athletic Club (401 N. River Rd., Glenwood Springs, ☎ 970/945–7428) offers Nautilus, saunas, tanning beds, and racquetball.

Golf

Beaver Creek Golf Course (100 Offerson Rd., ☎ 970/949–7123), befitting the resort's reputation, is a 6,400-yard, par-70 stunner designed by Robert Trent Jones.

Breckenridge Golf Club (200 Clubhouse Dr., ☎ 970/453–9104), the only Jack Nicklaus–designed course in America, is a 7,279-yard, par 72 beauty. Dramatically situated, it resembles a nature reserve, with woods and beaver ponds lining the fairways.

Copper Creek Golf Club (Wheeler Circle, Copper Mountain, ☎ 970/968–2339), at 9,650 feet, is America's highest course. Designed by Pete and Perry Dye, the par-70, 6,094-yard course follows the twisting, narrow, natural terrain of Copper's valley.

Eagles Nest Golf Club (305 Golden Eagle Rd., Silverthorne, ☎ 970/468–0681), renowned as the country's most mountainous course, is a par-70 with 6,698 yards, and has several daunting, challenging tee-to-green elevation shifts.

Golf Course at Cordillera (Lodge at Cordillera, Edwards, ☎ 970/926–2200), designed by Hale Irwin, is a par-72, 7,444-yard course with open meadows, ponds, and stands of pine and aspen trees; among the challenges are wandering elk and brown bears.

Keystone Ranch Course (22010 Rte. 6, Dillon, ☎ 970/468–4250) is listed as one of the top 50 resort courses in America by *Golf Digest*. The 7,090-yard, par-72 course, designed by Robert Trent Jones, winds through stunning mountain scenery.

Sheraton Steamboat Golf Club (2000 Clubhouse Dr., ☎ 970/879–1391) is a 6,906-yard, par 72, 18-hole championship course designed by Robert Trent Jones, Jr.

Singletree Golf Course (1265 Berry Creek Rd., Edwards, Vail Valley, ☎ 970/949–4240), a 7,059-yard, par-71 course, is another perennial top-50 resort course, according to *Golf Digest*.

Snowmass Lodge and Golf Club Links (239 Snowmass Village Circle, ☎ 970/923–3148) is an 18-hole, 6,900-yard championship course designed by Arnold Palmer and Ed Seay.

In Winter Park, a 7,000-yard, par-72, 18-hole **Pole Creek Golf Club** (Rte. 40 W, ☎ 970/726–8847), designed by Gary Player and Ron Kirby, is consistently ranked in the top 75 public courses by *Golf Digest*.

Hiking

Near Steamboat Springs, **Routt National Forest** offers miles of trail through aspen and conifer forests, mountain meadows, lakes, and the thunderous 283-foot cascade, Fish Creek Falls. Rabbit Ears Pass is especially beautiful, including the eroded volcanic pinnacles of Rabbit Ears Peaks. The Devil's Causeway is a vertiginous narrow isthmus along the massive ramparts of **Flat Tops Wilderness.** The **Arapahoe** (especially the Wheeler National Recreational Trail and Eagles Nest Wilderness) and **White River national forests** (including the famed Rio Grande Trail, Sunnyside Trail, Hanging Trail, and the Maroon Bells and Collegiate Peaks wilderness areas) offer a similar range of scenic trails. For further information, call the **U.S. Forest Service** (Arapahoe, ☎ 970/444–6001; Routt, ☎ 970/879–1722; White River, ☎ 970/945–2521).

Hiking opportunities in Winter Park include **Byer's Peak** and **Devil's Thumb,** but for more information contact the **Winter Park/Fraser Valley Chamber of Commerce** (☎ 970/726–4118) or **Arapahoe National Forest** (☎ 970/887–3331).

Horseback Riding

Riding trails are generally easy and wind through stunning alpine scenery. Rates begin at $12 an hour. For outfitters try: **A. J. Brink Outfitters** (Sweetwater, north of Vail off exit 133 of I–70, ☎ 970/524–9301); **All Seasons Ranch** (Steamboat, ☎ 970/879–2606); **Aspen Canyon Ranch** (Parshall, Summit County, ☎ 970/725–3518); **Beaver Stables** (Winter Park, ☎ 970/726–9247); **Breckenridge Stables** (☎ 970/453–4438); **Canyon Creek Ranch** (I–70, 7 mi west of Glenwood to exit 109, ☎ 970/984–2000); **Eagles Nest Equestrian Center** (Silverthorne, ☎ 970/468–0677); **Piney River Ranch** (Vail, ☎ 970/476–3941); **Sunset Ranch** (Steamboat, ☎ 970/879–0954); and **T Lazy Seven** (Aspen, ☎ 970/925–4614).

Rafting

Adventures Wild (Steamboat Springs, ☎ 970/879–8747) runs excursions to various rivers. Half-day to two-week trips are offered for all levels. Rates start at $30 a person. **Aspen Whitewater/Colorado Riff Raft** (☎ 970/925–1153, 970/925–5405, or 800/759–3939) offers mild to wild excursions on the Shoshone, Upper Roaring Fork, and lower Colorado. **Blazing Paddles/River Rats/Snowmass Whitewater** (☎ 970/923–4544 or 800/282–7238) runs trips to various rivers and canyons in the area and beyond. **Blue Sky Adventures** (Glenwood Springs, ☎ 970/945–6605) offers rafting on the Colorado and Roaring Fork rivers. Also, contact **Performance Tours Rafting** (Breckenridge, ☎ 970/453–0661 or 800/328–7238) and **Mad Adventures** (Winter Park, ☎ 970/726–5290 or 800/451–4844), which let you shoot the rapids of the North Platte, Colorado, and Arkansas rivers. **Rock Garden Rafting** (Glenwood Springs, ☎ 970/945–6737) runs trips down the Colorado and Roaring Fork rivers. **Whitewater Rafting** (Glenwood Springs, ☎ 970/945–8477) and **Timberline Tours** (Vail, ☎ 970/476–1414) also run trips throughout the region.

Skiing

CROSS-COUNTRY

Ashcroft Ski Touring (Aspen, ☎ 970/925–1971) features 40 kilometers (25 miles) of groomed trails in the White River National Forest. **Aspen/Snowmass Nordic Trail System** (☎ 970/923–3148) contains 65 kilometers (40 miles) of trails through the Roaring Fork Valley. **Breckenridge Nordic Ski Center** (☎ 970/453–6855) maintains 28 kilometers (17 miles) of trails in its system. **Copper Mountain/Trak Cross-Country Center** (☎ 970/968–2882) offers 25 kilometers (15.5 miles) of groomed track and skate lanes. **Devil's Thumb Ranch/Ski Idlewild** (Devil's Thumb is 10 mi north of Winter Park; Ski Idlewild in Winter Park, ☎ 970/726–8231) are full-service resorts with 53 miles of groomed trails between them. **Frisco Nordic Center** (1121 N. Summit Blvd., ☎ 970/668–0866) has 35 kilometers (22 miles) of one-way loops. **Keystone Nordic Center at Ski Tip Lodge** (☎ 970/468–4275) provides 29 kilometers (18 miles) of prepared trails and 56 kilometers (35 miles) of backcountry skiing winding through Arapahoe National Forest. **Steamboat Ski Touring Center** (☎ 970/879–8180) has 30 kilometers (19 miles) on the golf course. **Vail/Beaver Creek Cross-Country Ski Centers** (☎ 970/476–5601, ext. 4390) provide information on the many trails in the Vail Valley.

DOWNHILL

Arrowhead at Vail. West down the Vail Valley lies Arrowhead, a small mountain (1,700-foot vertical drop) with only two lifts accessing gently rolling beginner and intermediate terrain. Currently, this is an ideal place for families who just want to get away from the madding crowds for a day, although Vail Associates plans to link it with Beaver Creek by the 1996–97 season. ☎ 970/476–5601. ⊘ *Mid-Dec.– early Apr., 9–3:30.*

Aspen Highlands. Nine lifts access 597 acres of terrain with a dizzying 3,635-foot vertical drop. ☎ 970/925–1220. ⊘ *Late Nov.–early Apr., 9–4.*

Aspen Mountain. Eight lifts, including a high-speed gondola, service the 631 acres of challenging terrain, spanning a vertical of 3,267 feet. ☎ 970/925–1220. ⊘ *Late Nov.–mid-Apr., 9–3:30.*

Beaver Creek Resort. With 61 trails, 1,125 skiable acres, a 3,340-foot vertical, and 10 lifts (including 2 high-speed quads), uphill capacity is tremendous at this still-uncrowded, upscale winner. ☎ 970/476–5601. ⊘ *Late Nov.–mid-Apr., 8:30–3:30.*

Breckenridge. Sixteen lifts (including 4 speedy "SuperChair" quads) serve 1,915 skiable acres and a 3,398-foot vertical drop. It offers more than half advanced and expert terrain. ☎ 970/453–5000. ⊘ *Mid-Nov.–early May, 8:30-3:45.*

Copper Mountain Resort. Copper offers 1,360 acres of skiing on 98 trails and four back bowls, with a 2,601-foot vertical serviced by 19 lifts. The area also provides the "Extreme Experience" on 350 acres of guided adventure skiing. ☎ 970/968–2882. ⊘ *Mid-Nov.–late Apr., 8:30–4.*

Howelsen Ski Area. This tiny historic area right in Steamboat Springs is Colorado's oldest. Its three lifts, 15 trails, and 440-foot vertical aren't impressive, but it *is* the largest and most complete ski-jumping complex in America, and a major Olympic training ground. Howelsen also offers the "Champagne of Thrills" bobsled course, open daily in season 6 PM–10 PM. ☎ 970/879–8499. ⊘ *Dec.–Mar., weekdays noon–10; weekends 9 AM–10 PM.*

Keystone/Arapahoe Basin. Three mountains—Keystone (which offers an extensive night-skiing system), North Peak, and the new Outback—comprise Keystone Resort, with Arapahoe and Breckenridge available on the same lift ticket. A-Basin offers predominantly intermediate and expert terrain (90% of the 30 trails), with a 2,250-foot vertical drop serviced by five lifts. In all, there are two high-speed gondolas, three high-speed quads, 15 other chairs, and four surface lifts to connect this monstrous area, which just keeps growing. ☎ 970/468–2316. *Keystone open late Oct.–early May, daily 8:30 AM–10 PM; A-Basin open early Nov.–early June, 8:30–4.*

Loveland Ski Area. Loveland is considered small-fry, but only because of its proximity to the megaresorts of Summit County. Actually, Loveland—the nearest ski area to Denver (56 mi, just after the Eisenhower Tunnel)—offers a respectable 836 acres serviced by five lifts and spread out over two mountains: Loveland Valley for beginners, and Loveland Basin for everyone else. Basin has some excellent glade and open-bowl skiing, with a 1,680-foot vertical drop. Best of all, it opens early and usually stays open later than any other area except A-Basin. ☎ 970/569–3203. ⊘ *Mid-Oct.–May, weekdays 9–4; weekends 8:30–4.*

Ski Cooper. Seventy percent of the 385 skiable acres are rated beginner or intermediate, but the area—with a 1,200-foot vertical drop—also runs Sno-Cat tours into 1,800 acres of pristine backcountry powder. *Off Rte. 24,* ☎ 719/486–3684. ⊘ *Late-Nov.–early Apr., 9–4.*

Ski Sunlight. Yet another of Colorado's affordable gems, Ski Sunlight has 50 trails, including the super-steep glades of the East Ridge, serviced by four lifts with 2,010 vertical feet. ☎ 970/945–7491. ☉ *Late-Nov.–early Apr.*

Snowmass. This is a sprawling mountain, with five clearly defined skiing areas totalling 2,500 acres and a 4,087-foot vertical, accessed by 15 lifts. As at Breckenridge, it's a good idea to plan your route carefully, especially if you're meeting someone on the mountain. ☎ 970/925–1220. ☉ *Late-Nov.–mid-Apr., 8:30–3:30.*

Steamboat Ski Area. Twenty-one lifts, including two high-speed quads and a gondola, access 107 trails (2,500 acres), roughly half of them intermediate, with a 3,685-foot vertical drop. ☎ 970/879–6111. ☉ *Late-Nov.–mid-Apr., 9–4.*

Tiehack. This is Aspen's "learning" area, and it offers plenty of wide, gently rolling slopes for beginners and intermediates, more than 410 acres with 45 trails and a vertical of 2,030 feet. *Off Rte. 82,* ☎ 970/925–1220. ☉ *Mid-Dec.–early Apr., 9–4.*

Vail. Vail has an embarrassment of riches: 25 lifts, including a gondola and eight high-speed quads, with an uphill capacity of 41,855 per hour (and they need it—20,000 is the average skier day!); a vertical of 3,250 feet; and more than 4,000 acres of skiing on 121 runs, divided fairly evenly (32% beginner, 36% intermediate, 32% advanced/expert). ☎ 970/476–5601. ☉ *Mid-Nov.–mid-Apr., 8:30–3:30.*

Winter Park/Mary Jane. There are 1,358 skiable acres with a vertical of 3,060 feet. The resort's hub is at the base of Winter Park. Twenty chairlifts (including 4 high-speed quads) and 120 trails connect the three mountains and high alpine bowl. ☎ 970/726–5514. ☉ *Mid-Nov.–mid-Apr. 18, weekdays 9–4; weekends 8:30–4.*

SKI TOURING

Aspen Alpine Guides (☎ 970/925–6618) arranges customized multi-day tours along the 10th Mountain Hut and Trail System connecting Aspen and Vail; and the Alfred A. Braun Hut System connecting Aspen and Crested Butte (*see* Off the Beaten Track, *above*), as do **Elk Mountain Guides** (Aspen, ☎ 970/925–5601) and **Paragon Guides** (Avon, ☎ 970/949–4272). You can also contact the **10th Mountain Hut and Trail System** (☎ 970/925–5775) directly. In Steamboat, **High Country Ski Tours** (☎ 970/879–4857) leads backcountry treks.

Snowboarding

Most ski areas permit at least limited snowboarding; many offer special half pipes for performing tricks, in addition to their skiable terrain. Aspen and Keystone do not allow snowboarding.

Snowmobiling

The following companies run tours throughout the High Rockies region: **Good Times** (Breckenridge, ☎ 970/453–7604 and Frisco, ☎ 970/668–0930); **High Mountain Snowmobile Tours** (Steamboat, ☎ 970/879–9073); **Nova Guides** (Vail/Beaver Creek, ☎ 970/949–4232); **Steamboat Powder Cats** (Steamboat, ☎ 970/879–5188); **Steamboat Snowmobile Tours** (Steamboat, ☎ 970/879–6500); **Piney River Ranch** (Vail, ☎ 970/476–3941); **T Lazy Seven** (Aspen, ☎ 970/925–4614); **Tiger Run Tours** (Breckenridge, ☎ 970/453–2231); **Timberline Snowmobile** (Vail, ☎ 970/476—1414); and **2 Mile Hi Ski-Doo** (Leadville, ☎ 719/486–1183 or 800/933–1183).

Water Sports

Canoeing, kayaking, windsurfing, and sailing are done on many lakes and reservoirs, most notably Dillon (Dillon Yacht Basin, ☎ 970/468–2396; Dillon Marina, ☎ 970/468–5100; Frisco Bay Yacht Club, ☎ 970/668–3022) in Summit County.

DINING

Colorado is a melting pot of cuisines, and nowhere is that diversity and artistry better reflected than at the state's top resorts. Talented young American and European chefs are attracted to resort restaurants because of the diverse clientele and demand for variety on the menus. You can find super sushi in Aspen, terrific tahini in Vail, and blissful blinis in Steamboat Springs. All you have to do is follow your nose.

The downside, however, is that the price for this expertise can be stratospheric. As an indicator, the McDonald's in Aspen and Vail are, respectively, the third and fourth most expensive in the world (Hong Kong and Moscow beat them out). A fun, relatively new trend being offered at several resorts, such as Keystone and Copper Mountain, is a "dine around progressive dinner," which encourages guests to take in a different course at several restaurants. Most areas also have "Popcorn Wagons" that sell high-test espresso, delectable crepes, gourmet sandwiches, and snacks. For price ranges *see* the Dining chart *in* On the Road with Fodor's at the front of this guide.

Aspen/Snowmass

$$$$ **Piñons.** The food is sublime, the muted ranch decor—with a leather
★ bar, handsome Western art, and enormous brass bowls brimming with tortillas—exquisite. Unfortunately, the wait staff seems oh-so-above-it-all most of the time; maybe they think the attitude is what you're paying for. Still, the cuisine is exotic: pheasant quesadillas or lobster strudel (complemented by morels and chanterelles in phyllo) for appetizers; then segue into elk tournedos sautéed in ginger and pink peppercorn sauce or roasted Colorado striped bass in potato crust swimming on a bed of red onion sauce. ✕ *105 S. Mill St., 2nd floor, Aspen,* ☎ *970/920–2021. Reservations advised. AE, MC, V. No lunch.*

$$$$ **Renaissance.** The decor of this stunner is a coolly seductive, abstract
★ rendition of a sultan's tent. Owner-chef Charles Dale apprenticed as chef saucier to his mentor, Daniel Boulud, at New York's trendiest mineral watering hole, Le Cirque, before opening Renaissance in 1990. He dubs his cuisine "the alchemy of food," and he probably could transform leftovers into culinary gold, thanks to his magical artistry in blending tastes and textures. Opt for his *menu degustation*—six courses matched with the appropriate glass of wine. The menu changes seasonally, as well as the style of preparation for many signature dishes. Among his standouts are *ravioli à la Monegasque* (ravioli with pistachio-nut pesto), freshwater striped bass with fennel-tomato marmalade, and a roast rack of Australian lamb perfectly accompanied by asparagus, morels, and mint salsa. Upstairs, the R Bar offers a taste of the kitchen's splendors at down-to-earth prices, along with live music. ✕ *304 E. Hopkins St., Aspen,* ☎ *970/925–1402. Reservations advised. AE, D, MC, V. No lunch.*

$$$$ **Syzygy.** This posh establishment's name means the alignment of three
★ or more heavenly bodies in the solar system. It reflects personable owner Walt Harris's desire to provide a harmony of expressive cuisine, fine service, and elegant atmosphere. He succeeds, thanks to a sterling, unusually helpful waitstaff and the assured, sublimely seasoned creations of chef Alexander Kim. Kim is clearly impatient with the inevitable meat-

and-potatoes bent of the ski crowd, thus assuring that adventurous palates won't be disappointed. His food is crisply flavored and sensuously textured, floating from French to Oriental to Southwestern influences without skipping a beat. Standouts include the pheasant spring roll and lemongrass and lime-crusted prawns to start, followed by such main courses as rack of lamb with juniper glaze over polenta and sweet potato puree, or grilled John Dory with a trio of infused oils of lobster–vanilla bean, arugula, and pinot noir. The patient and knowledgeable will find a few good buys on the extensive wine list. ✗ *520 E. Hyman Ave., Aspen,* ☎ *970/925–3700. Reservations advised. AE, MC, V. No lunch.*

$$$–$$$$ **Krabloonik.** A dogsled whisks you from Snowmass Village to this cozy
★ rustic-elegant cabin (or you can ski there for lunch), where you'll dine sumptuously on some of the best game in Colorado, perhaps carpaccio of smoked moose with lingonberry vinaigrette; elk loin with marsala and sun-dried cherry glaze; pheasant breast with Gorgonzola; or wild boar medallions with morel cream sauce. The Western decor features ski memorabilia and throw rugs. ✗ *4250 Divide Rd., Snowmass,* ☎ *970/923–3953. Reservations required. AE, MC, V. No lunch in summer.*

$$$–$$$$ **Pine Creek Cookhouse.** You cross-country ski or board a horse-drawn sleigh to this homey log cabin—Krabloonik's main competition—where the emphasis is less on game and more on Continental favorites with an Oriental or Southwestern twist. ✗ *11399 Castle Creek, Aspen,* ☎ *970/925–1044. Dinner reservations required. MC, V.*

$$$ **Kenichi.** For some reason, Aspen doesn't have many good Asian restaurants, with the exception of a Thai and two Japanese spots. Kenichi was started by two "defectors" from one of the Japanese favorites. It gets the nod as much for its elegant spacious setting as for the delectable bamboo salmon and Oriental roast duck served Peking style with pancakes, cilantro, scallions, and hoisin sauce, with a side of melting asparagus tempura. ✗ *533 E. Hopkins Ave., Aspen,* ☎ *970/920–2212. Reservations advised. AE, MC, V.*

$$–$$$ **Ajax Tavern.** The brains behind Mustards Grill and Tra Vigne, two of
★ Napa Valley's finest eateries, have created this bright, pleasant restaurant with its mahogany paneling, diamond-patterned floors, leather banquettes, open kitchen, and an eager, unpretentious waitstaff. Nick Morfogen's creative, healthful dishes take advantage of the region's bountiful produce whenever possible and are reasonably priced. You might begin with house-cured Colorado lamb prosciutto with pecorino and arugula, then opt for cedar-planked rare tuna and sweet potato chips in roasted pepper vinaigrette or chicken breast slow-roasted in its own juices and served on a bed of wild mushrooms and house-smoked bacon. A typical sinful dessert might be poached pear cheesecake with pistachio phyllo crisp. The wine list, showcasing Napa's best, is almost matched by the fine selection of microbrews. ✗ *685 E. Durant Ave.,* ☎ *970/920–9333. Reservations advised. AE, D, MC.*

$$–$$$ **Farfalla.** The food is quite good and the scene spectacular at this northern
★ Italian winner. This slick, sleek L.A.-style eatery, well-lit and adorned with fine art, remained all the rage in 1995; go off-peak—at lunch when it's deserted. Specialties include tortellini with asparagus and ham in walnut pesto, and deboned quail in vegetable sauce on a bed of polenta and beans. ✗ *415 E. Main St., Snowmass,* ☎ *970/925–8222. Reservations accepted for parties of 6 or more; lines form early. AE, D, MC, V.*

$$ **Il Poggio.** This spirited trattoria suits all moods, with a light lively café and a quieter, more romantic back room. Chef Chris Blachly is a whiz at the wood-burning oven, turning out delicious grilled items such as rosemary, garlic, and cambozola pizzette; free-range chicken wrapped

in pancetta; and duck breast with polenta in honey grappa sauce. ✕ *Elbert La., Snowmass,* ☎ *970/923–4292. Reservations advised for back room. MC, V. No lunch.*

$–$$ **Little Annie's Eating House.** Everything at this charming place is ultrasimple, from the wood paneling and red-and-white checked tablecloths to the fresh fish, barbecued ribs and chicken, and Colorado lamb. Annie's is a big favorite with locals who like the relaxed atmosphere, dependable food, and reasonable prices. ✕ *517 E. Hyman Ave., Aspen,* ☎ *970/925–1098. Reservations accepted. MC, V.*

$ **Flying Dog Brew Pub and Grille.** This local hangout, with exposed brick walls and wood beams, has a pleasant ambience. The solid pub grub is a bonus, but mostly customers howl for the wonderful homebrewed beers. Try the sweet and smooth Old Yeller, the gold medal–winning Doggie-Style amber, or the malty Rin Tin Tin. ✕ *424 E. Cooper St. (downstairs), Aspen,* ☎ *970/925–7464. Reservations accepted. MC, V.*

Glenwood Springs

$–$$ **Florinda's.** The russet-and-salmon pink walls of this handsome space are graced by changing exhibits of local artists. Although most items on the menu are Neapolitan—all garlic and attitude—the chef has a deft hand with more creative fare such as veal chops delicately sautéed with shiitake mushrooms in marsala, garlic, sun-dried tomatoes, and topped with romano cheese. ✕ *721 Grand St.,* ☎ *970/945–1245. Reservations accepted. AE, MC, V. Closed Sun. No lunch.*

$ **The Bayou.** "Food so good you'll slap yo' mama," trumpets the menu
★ at this casual eatery, whose most distinctive attribute is its frog awning (two bulbous eyes beckon you in). Choose from "pre-stuff, wabbit stuff, udder stuff," such as lip-smacking gumbo that looks like mud (and is supposed to), étouffée and blackened fish, or lethal Cajun martinis and jalapeño beers. On summer weekends live music is played on the patio. ✕ *52103 Rte. 6 at Rte. 24,* ☎ *970/945–1047. Reservations accepted. AE, MC, V.*

$ **The Loft.** The decor here is soothingly Southwestern, with rough-hewn columns and lintels contrasting pleasingly with pastel linens, hanging plants, stained glass, Native American art, and elegant banquettes. The Mexican food is better and cheaper than the Southwestern specialties. Black-bean burritos are especially tasty and tangy. ✕ *720 Grand St.,* ☎ *970/945–6808. Reservations accepted. AE, MC, V.*

Idaho Springs

$ **Buffalo Bar.** No surprise as to the specialty here: steaks, burgers, fajitas, chili, Philly steak sandwiches—all made with choice buffalo. It's all part of the Western theme, with walls jam-packed with frontier artifacts and memorabilia, and the ornate bar that dates from 1886. There's often great live music that lures people from as far as Summit County. ✕ *1617 Miner St.,* ☎ *970/567–2729. No reservations. AE, MC, V.*

Steamboat Springs

$$$ **Cipriani's.** Chef Joey Bowman, a graduate of the prestigious New En-
★ gland Culinary Institute, has the ability to prepare a classic Caesar salad and then surprise with such inventive dishes as eggplant soup with *tapenade* (caper) croutons swirled with red-pepper rouille; salmon quenelles poached in white wine and served with lobster butter and pinot grigio sauce; or roast duckling with red wine, chili, coriander, garlic, and cumin. Ask to be seated in the more romantic front dining room of this cellar restaurant: Although the low ceilings and subdued lighting give it a somewhat claustrophobic feel, a more raucous atmosphere prevails in the back room, whence families are typically banished. Or go upstairs to the informal Roccioso's, little more than an upscale bar, which

shares Cipriani's kitchen and turns out affordable Italian fare. ✕ *Thunderhead Lodge, Ski Time Square,* ☎ *970/879–8824. Reservations advised. AE, MC, V.*

$$$ L'Apogee. This expert French restaurant is Steamboat's most intimate, with rose-colored walls, flickering candlelight, and hanging plants. The classic food, with subtle Southwestern and Asian influences, is lovely, especially the rock shrimp soufflé jazzed up with wasabi; roast duckling glazed with red-chili brown sugar, topped with oyster mushroom–green apple demi-glacé, and nestled in crispy rice noodles; and elk chop with kiwis and tamarinds in a roasted garlic-shallot sauce, garnished with pineapple–green peppercorn compote. Still, the menu takes a back seat to the admirable wine list. Oenophile alert: owner Jamie Jenny is a collector whose magnificent wine cellar—cited annually by the *Wine Spectator* as one of America's best—contains more than 750 labels (10,000 bottles). ✕ *911 Lincoln Ave.,* ☎ *970/879–1919. Reservations advised. AE, MC, V.*

$$–$$$ Antares. Co-owners Paul LeBrun, Ian Donovan, and Doug Enochs, who
★ cut their culinary teeth at Harwig's and L'Apogee, opened this superlative new eatery in the space formerly occupied by Gorky Park. They retained only the fieldstone walls, frosted windows, pressed tin ceilings, and stained glass, thereby calling attention to the splendid Victorian building itself. LeBrun, the chef, contributes his exciting, eclectic cuisine, which is inspired by America's rich ethnic stew. Hence, you might feast on mussels in a citrus chili chardonnay broth, pompano with a pineapple and Pommery mustard fondue, or Maine lobster over chili pepper linguine. Doug's encyclopedic knowledge of wines is reflected in the comprehensive and fairly priced list. Ian contributes his managerial acumen. Why Antares? Antares was the big red star that guided early explorers, and "we needed a star to guide us," explains Paul. "Besides, we're all Scorpios." Antares the restaurant is certainly a rising star of the first magnitude. ✕ *57½ 8th St.,* ☎ *970/879–9939. Reservations advised. AE, MC, V. No lunch.*

$$–$$$ Mattie Silk's. Named after a notorious turn-of-the-century madam, this plush split-level charmer, all velour and lace, looks like a prim wife who has loosened her corset and tarted up in an effort to win back her man. Chef Dee Conder's sauces, with fresh pungent herbs and very little butter, are assertive and zippy. Try the tender lemon-pepper veal, pounded thin, breaded, then sautéed in a fragrant lemon-cognac sauce. ✕ *Ski Time Square, Steamboat Mountain Village,* ☎ *970/879–2441. Reservations advised. AE, MC, V. No lunch.*

$$ Riggio's. This local favorite recently moved to a dramatic new space, whose industrial look (black-and-white tile, exposed pipes) is softened by tapestries, murals, and landscape photos. The menu has changed and now offers tasty pizzas (try the capra, with goat cheese, roasted peppers, garlic or clams, romano, and herbs) and lighter pastas (the sciocca, with rock shrimp, eggplant, tomatoes, and basil sautéed in olive oil, is superb). Standards like manicotti, chicken cacciatore, and saltimbocca are also well prepared. ✕ *1106 Lincoln Ave.,* ☎ *970/879–9010. Reservations advised. AE, D, DC, MC, V. No lunch.*

$$ Yama Chan's. Most people think you can't get good sushi in Colorado: Wrong. Somehow, the fish tastes fresher in the crisp mountain air at this simple, superlative Japanese restaurant. The rest of the menu is equally well-presented and prepared. ✕ *Old Town Square, 635 Lincoln Ave.,* ☎ *970/879–8862. Reservations advised. AE, MC, V. Closed Mon. No lunch weekends.*

$–$$ Harwig's Grill. This popular eatery is just next door to L'Apogee, and
★ run by the same team. You can order from the neighboring wine list, and the bar offers 40 vintages by the glass, including many lesser-known

labels. The menu here reflects owner Jamie Jenny's love of travel, with confidently prepared specialties from around the world: Colorado smoked trout to raclette, jambalaya to shu mei dim sum. The desserts are predictably sinful. ✕ *911 Lincoln Ave.,* ☎ *970/879–1980. Reservations accepted. AE, MC, V. No lunch.*

$–$$ ★ **La Montana.** This Mexican/Southwestern establishment is probably Steamboat's most popular restaurant. The kitchen is wonderfully creative, incorporating indigenous specialties into the traditional menu. Among the standouts are red chili pasta in a shrimp, garlic, and cilantro sauce; mesquite-grilled braided sausage (interwoven strands of elk, lamb, and chorizo sausage); enchiladas layered with Monterey Jack and goat cheese, roasted peppers, and onions; and elk loin crusted with pecan nuts and bourbon cream sauce. ✕ *Après Ski Way and Village Dr.,* ☎ *970/879–5800. Reservations advised. D, MC, V. No lunch.*

$ **Steamboat Smokehouse.** The loud, raucous scene, brick and wood decor, and occasional live music might fool you into thinking this joint is just a bar. Once you try the phenomenal barbecue or hickory-smoked brisket and turkey, however, you'll realize that this is a place where they really know their beans about home cooking. ✕ *912 Lincoln Ave.,* ☎ *970/879–5570. Reservations accepted. MC, V.*

Summit County

$$$$ ★ **Alpenglow Stube.** Without a doubt this is the finest on-mountain dining establishment in Colorado (just beating out Hazie's in Steamboat). The decor is warmly elegant, with exposed wood beams, a stone fireplace, antler chandeliers, and floral upholstery. At night, the gondola ride you take to get here is alone worth the cost of the meal. Dinner is a six-course extravaganza, starting with the signature pine cone paté, followed perhaps by scrumptious tuna carpaccio or smoked pheasant ragout with wild mushrooms and red pepper pasta, fresh tangy wild green salad, and such Stube specialties as smoked saddle of rabbit in tricolored peppercorn sauce or rack of boar in Poire William sauce. Lunch is equally delectable, with particularly fine pasta specials. (Removing your ski boots and putting on the plush slippers reserved for diners is a wonderful touch.) ✕ *North Peak, The Outpost, Keystone,* ☎ *970/468–4130. Reservations advised. AE, MC, V. No lunch in summer.*

$$$$ ★ **Keystone Ranch.** This glorious 1880s log cabin was once part of an actual working cattle ranch, and cowboy memorabilia are strewn throughout the restaurant, nicely blending with stylish throw rugs and Western craft work. The gorgeous and massive stone fireplace is a cozy backdrop for sipping an aperitif or after-dinner coffee. Chef Christopher Wing's rotating, seasonal six-course menu emphasizes indigenous ingredients, including farm-raised game and fresh fish. You're in luck if the menu includes rack of lamb infused with pomegranate and cardamom and encrusted with pine nuts; elk with wild mushrooms in juniper sauce and quince relish; or Gorgonzola flan. Finish your meal with an unimpeachable Grand Marnier soufflé drizzled with pistachio cream sauce. ✕ *Keystone Ranch Golf Course,* ☎ *970/468–4130. Reservations advised. AE, MC, V. No lunch in winter.*

$$$ **Jacksan's Sushi House.** The knotty-pine walls plastered with money from around the world contrast intriguingly with the black chairs and track lighting in this quaint Victorian cabin. The sushi is pricey but wonderful, as are such scrumptious offerings as tiny enoki mushrooms steamed in sake and *kani karoage* (soft-shell crab tempura in bonsai sauce). For a stratospherically priced but hedonistic meal, order the luscious lobster followed by prized Kobe beef. ✕ *318 N. Main St.,* ☎ *970/453–1880. No reservations. AE, MC, V. Closed Mon. No lunch.*

$$ Café Alpine. This bright, cheerful place offers terrific soups, salads, and sandwiches at lunch, and more substantial Continental fare with Asian flair at dinner (try the roast duck breast Santa Fe with orange mango and red pepper sauce or saffron and mushroom pheasant ravioli in roasted tomato garlic sauce). At the tapas bar (served after 4) you can sample succulent offerings from around the world, including eggplant crepes, marinated quail breast, blackened tuna sashimi, and lamb chops Szechuan. The moderately priced wine list, favoring Australian and Chilean selections, is particularly well thought out. ✕ *106 E. Adams Ave., Breckenridge,* ☎ *970/453–8218. AE, D, DC, MC, V.*

$$ Gassy Thompson's. Imagine a sports bar crossbred with a hunting lodge, and you'll get an idea of the ambience and decor of this popular mountain-base hangout. The Continental cuisine is solid if not inspired; grilled items are best, including honey-mustard chicken breast and pork medallions. ✕ *Mountain House, Keystone,* ☎ *970/468–4130. No reservations. AE, MC, V. Closed summer.*

$$ Geronimo Southwest Grill. Red tile floors and boldly colored art set the stage for robust Southwestern cuisine that draws on Mexican, Anglo-American, and Native American influences. Try the Zuni squash soup puréed with roasted pumpkin seeds, oregano, and garlic cream; beefsteak with chipotle cream sauce; or grilled turkey marinated in orange, red chili, oregano, and cumin. Or opt for solid renditions of old standbys like chili relleño. The chef uses only fresh ingredients, including many organic vegetables, which are quickly grilled for crispness and flavor. ✕ *200 W. Washington Ave., Breckenridge,* ☎ *970/453–9500. AE, D, MC, V.*

$$ Pesce Fresco. The fish is as fresh as advertised at this engaging spot, where a jazz pianist plays most nights during ski season. The decor is upscale coffee shop, but the menu is creative, with salmon dill linguine, wasabi tuna, and mixed seafood grill the winners. Breakfast is served here, as well as lunch and dinner. ✕ *Mountain Plaza Bldg., Copper Mountain,* ☎ *970/968–2882, ext. 6505. Reservations advised. AE, DC, MC, V.*

$$ Rackets. This split-level, high-tech restaurant is Copper's best, and serves predominantly Southwestern cuisine. Start with the calamari breaded with blue cornmeal; smoked duck and piñon sausage over capellini; or Southwestern ravioli (oozing Monterey Jack and green chili); then follow with tender baked cilantro lime scallops or Rocky Mountain trout in bourbon pecan sauce. Rotisserie items are also good bets. ✕ *Racquet & Athletic Club, Copper Mountain,* ☎ *970/968–2882, ext. 6386. Reservations advised. AE, MC, V. No lunch in winter.*

$ Blue Moose. Locals flock here for the hearty breakfasts, with menu highlights such as the Mexican Moose—a tortilla crammed with pork, green chili, cheese, sour cream, and scallions. Lunch and dinner are equally satisfying: Chicken vermouth and drunken chicken (marinated with tequila, lime, tomato, green chili, and jalapeño) are particularly noteworthy, as is Mother's fettuccine al pesto. ✕ *540 S. Main St., Breckenridge,* ☎ *970/453–4859. Reservations accepted. No credit cards.*

$ Frisco Bar & Grill. You'll find no frills here, just juicy burgers (nine varieties), hellacious nachos, buffalo wings, and a lively crowd in this classic pub with neon signs on the walls and sawdust on the floors. ✕ *720 Granite Boardwalk Blvd., Frisco,* ☎ *970/668–5051. No reservations. AE, MC, V.*

The Vail Valley

$$$$ Beano's Cabin. Perhaps the ultimate wilderness dining experience is traveling in a snowmobile-drawn sleigh to this tasteful, assured Beaver Creek hunting lodge. Once there, you'll choose from among seven seasonally rotating entrées and six courses. Ever since chef Chad Scothorn left to start his own restaurant (he's since moved to Utah, Beano's has seen a succession of competent chefs, but they lacked their predecessor's imagination and panache. His tradition of witty pizzas has remained a constant, however, and the convivial setting is unmatched. ✕ *Larkspur Bowl, Beaver Creek,* ☎ *970/949–9090. Reservations required. AE, MC, V.*

$$$$ **Splendido.** Even the people at Vail Associates call this ultraposh eatery
★ the height of decadence, probably because of the marble columns and statuary and custom-made Italian linens that adorn the tables. Chef David Walford, who apprenticed at Northern California's Auberge du Soleil and Masa's, is a master of the new American cuisine borrowing merrily from several different traditions. He is equally adept at turning out grouper baked with Moroccan spices, couscous, and fennel as he is preparing lobster and white bean chili with potato tortillas or elk chop in black pepper–pinot noir sauce with parsnip sweet potato pancakes and chanterelles. Pastry chef Matt Olehy excels at both standards like crème brûlée and such imaginative offerings as caramel-pumpkin *crostata* (puff pastry) with eggnog ice cream. ✕ *17 Chateau La., Beaver Creek,* ☎ *970/845–8808. Reservations advised. AE, MC, V. No lunch.*

$$$–$$$$ **L'Ostello.** The severe minimalist decor contrasts effectively with the richly textured menu at this superlative Italian eatery. The chef creates innovative variations on Italian regional favorites; specialties include blackpepper linguine with duck confit, asparagus, and wild mushrooms in a port reduction; rack of lamb with tomato herb crust, roast eggplant, and goat cheese; and fried potato gnocchi with roasted tomato Parmesan chips. The lodge offers nicely appointed, reasonably priced rooms as well. ✕ *705 W. Lionshead Cir., Vail,* ☎ *970/476–2050. Reservations advised. AE. No lunch.*

$$$–$$$$ **Sweet Basil.** Don't be fooled by the unassuming, teal-and-buff upscale
★ coffee-shop decor, enlivened by towering floral arrangements and abstract art. Chef Thomas Salamunovich, who apprenticed with such masters as Wolfgang Puck at Postrio and Alain Senderens at Lucas-Carton, has maintained the high standards of his predecessor, David Walford. His Pacific Rim–influenced Mediterranean cuisine is intensely flavored and beautifully presented. Standouts include sesame seared tuna on a bed of crisp Asian vegetables; meaty Portobello and goat cheese tart drizzled with basil-pepper and balsamic vinaigrettes; almond-crusted rack of lamb with shiitake potstickers; and honey-baked pork chop with wild rice pancakes and ruby grapefruit sauce. The menu changes seasonally, and the daily specials are invariably brilliant. At lunch, dishes are about half the price, and it's deserted on powder days. ✕ *193 E. Gore Creek Dr., Vail,* ☎ *970/476–0125. Reservations advised. AE, MC, V.*

$$$ **Alpen Rose Tea Room.** Claus Fricke's establishment started as a tearoom and bakery in 1976. He's still in the kitchen every evening, cooking feverishly until midnight; and he can still bake truly magnificent pastries. The pink, frilly decor is just as sugar-coated. This is rich, luscious, love-handle cuisine with tons of calories and drowned in butter: so good and so bad for you. The schnitzels, steak tartare, and fresh seafood specials are all home-cooking at its best. ✕ *100 E. Meadows Ave., Vail,* ☎ *970/476–3194. Reservations advised. AE, MC, V. No breakfast or lunch Tues.*

$$$ **Left Bank.** This cozy bistro, with homey touches such as family antiques and paintings, has been a Vail fixture for nearly a quarter century. Liz and Luc Meyer are the gracious hosts who consistently pamper their clientele with fresh, adroitly prepared bistro fare (the kitchen is espe-

cially good with game and lamb). How they can make the airy souf-
flés so fluffy at this altitude is nothing short of miraculous. ✕ *Sitzmark
Lodge (not affiliated), 183 Gore Creek Dr., Vail, ☎ 970/476–3696.
Reservations advised. No credit cards. Closed Wed. No lunch.*

$$$ **Michael's American Bistro.** This very sleek, stylish boîte overlooks the
atrium of the Gateway Mall, but the space is dramatic: fancifully
carved wood columns, lacquered black tables, and striking—almost
disturbing—photographs and art on the walls. The hip atmosphere is
further accentuated by the cool jazz echoing through the room and the
slinky waitstaff garbed entirely in black. They're extremely attentive
and will often let you know what the chef thinks is particularly good
that day. You could make a meal of the openers alone: grilled smoked
quail with orange chutney; gourmet spicy shrimp pizza with roasted
onion sauce; vegetable terrine with three pestos. If you can't decide,
order the tapas plate, an assortment of three appetizers that changes
daily. All courses are superbly presented, with festive colors springing
from the plate—giving equal weight to the palette and the palate. The
fine, extensive wine list (predominantly American, natch!) has several
bargains under $25. ✕ *12 S. Frontage Rd., Vail, ☎ 970/476–5353.
Reservations advised. AE, D, DC, MC, V.*

$$$ **Mirabelle.** From the crackling fireplace to the burgundy and pink
★   linens, this restaurant has achieved the ultimate in romantic, French-
country decor. Belgian Daniel Joly is the superb chef who offers as close
to classic French haute cuisine as you'll get in Colorado. His preparations are a perfect blend of colors, flavors, and textures. Try the es-
cargots baked in puff pastry with Stilton in Madeira sauce, or shrimp
and lobster mousseline accompanied by sautéed shiitakes and chives
to start; follow with shrimp nestled in spinach with tapioca caviar and
bell pepper coulis, or free-range chicken breast bursting with brie and
hazelnuts, in orange hollandaise sauce. Fairly priced wine recommendations are listed beneath each entrée. Desserts are sheer heaven, with
caramelized cinnamon pear tart kissed with passion-fruit sorbet and
vanilla ice cream the crowning achievement. ✕ *Entrance to Beaver
Creek, ☎ 970/949–7728. Reservations advised. No credit cards.
Closed Mon. No lunch.*

$$–$$$ **TraMonti.** This breezy trattoria in the Charter at Beaver Creek show-
cases the vibrant progressive cuisine of chef Cynde Arnold. She loves
experimenting with bold juxtapositions of flavors and is most successful
with her gourmet pizzas (such as shrimp, goat cheese, braised scallions,
and black olives) and pastas (penne with wild boar and veal bolog-
nese; ravioli stuffed with lobster, mascarpone, sun-dried tomatoes,
and basil in saffron cream). ✕ *The Charter at Beaver Creek, ☎
970/949–5552. Reservations advised. AE, MC, V. No lunch.*

$$ **Terra Bistro.** In the Vail Athletic Club, this sleek, airy space, with a warm
★   fireplace contrasting with black iron chairs and black-and-white pho-
tographs, is a sterling addition to the Vail dining scene. Chef Cyndi
Walt's innovative, seasonally changing menu caters to both meat-and-
potatoes diners and vegans: The pepper-crusted shell steak with wild
mushrooms, garlic-sage mashed potatoes, and Gorgonzola cabernet sauce
is delicious; the multigrain risotto with chanterelles, leeks, fontina, and
autumn squash purée would convert even the most confirmed carni-
vore. Tuna and soba rolls with a red-curry-and-lemon-chili dipping sauce,
grilled chili relleño with Moroccan spices and crisp vegetables, and
feather-light fried calamari are marvelous appetizers. Walt wants din-
ers to feel comfortable after their meals; fortunately, this doesn't mean
minute portions at stratospheric prices. Organic state produce and free-
range meat and poultry is used whenever possible. ✕ *352 E. Meadow
Dr., ☎ 970/476–0700. Reservations advised. AE, D, MC, V.*

$–$$ **Blu's.** This fun, casual, constantly hopping place is a Vail institution, with an eclectic affordable menu. The food is always fresh and zippy, from smoked duck, onion, and sage pizza to kick-ass California chicken relleño. Blu's is open for all three meals. ✕ *193 E. Gore Creek, Vail,* ☎ *970/476–3113. No reservations. D, MC, V.*

$ **The Gashouse.** This classic local hangout, in a 50-year-old log cabin with trophy-covered walls, draws up-valley crowds who swear by the steaks, delicious ribs, and sautéed rock shrimp with chili pesto pasta. Stop in for a brew and some heavenly jalapeño chips and watch how the Vail Valley kicks back. ✕ *Rte. 6, Edwards,* ☎ *970/926–2896. AE, MC, V.*

$ **Minturn Country Club.** This rustic, homey joint is a favorite hangout of racers during World Cup ski competitions, when they literally hang from the rafters. Steaks, prime rib, fish, and chicken preparations vary wildly, but you have only yourself to blame if you wanted it medium rare and it comes out well done: you cook everything yourself. ✕ *Main St., Minturn,* ☎ *970/827–4114. No reservations. MC, V. No lunch.*

Winter Park

$$–$$$ **Gasthaus Eichler.** This is Winter Park's most romantic dining spot, with
★ quaint Bavarian decor, antler chandeliers, and stained glass windows, all glowing in the candlelight as Strauss rings softly in the background. Featured are veal and grilled items, in addition to scrumptious versions of German classics such as sauerbraten. The *Rahmschnitzel*—tender veal in a delicate wild mushroom and brandy cream sauce—is extraordinary, as are the feathery light potato pancakes. The Eichler also offers 15 inexpensive, cozy, Old World rooms, with down comforters, lace curtains, armoires, cable TV, and Jacuzzis. ✕ *Winter Park Dr.,* ☎ *970/726–5133 or 800/543–3899. Reservations advised. AE, D, MC, V. No lunch.*

$$–$$$ **Peck House.** This snug, red-and-white, barnlike inn, Colorado's oldest continually operating hostelry, is actually in the quirky town of Empire, on U.S. 40 a few miles north of I–70. It began in 1860 as a boarding house built for wealthy mine investors, and the dining room is crammed with period antiques, including the original etched-glass, gaslight lamp shades from the state capitol, and evocative tinted lithographs. Game is the house specialty: expertly prepared quail and venison (try it with cabernet sauce) are among the standouts. The Peck House also offers 11 charming, inexpensively priced rooms (not all with private bath) awash in Victorian splendor. A Sunday brunch is offered. ✕ *Just off U.S. 40, Empire,* ☎ *970/569–9870. Reservations advised. AE, MC, V.*

$$ **Deno's Mountain Bistro.** In many ways, Deno's is an anomaly: It seems like a casual drinking establishment (there's a sizable selection of beers from around the world), and is by far the liveliest spot in town, yet it also has an impressive international wine list that's comprehensive and fairly priced. The wine is as much a labor of love as a folly in this unpretentious area, thanks to Deno himself, a charismatic, energetic powerhouse. The menu is as eclectic as the wine list, from spicy Szechuan beef egg roll to Cajun barbecued shrimp to veal Marsala, all well prepared and served by a friendly staff, most of whom have been working here for years. ✕ *Winter Park Dr.,* ☎ *970/726–5332. AE, D, MC, V.*

$ **Last Waltz.** This very homey place is festooned with hanging plants and graced with a crackling fireplace and tinkling piano. The huge menu jumps from bagels and lox to burritos, without missing a beat. The south-of-the-border dishes are best: zesty *calientitas* (fried jalapeños filled with cream cheese served with a devilish salsa) and black bean tostadas are especially noteworthy. Breakfast and brunch will power you for those mogul runs. ✗ *Winter Park Dr.,* ☎ *970/726–4877. No reservations. AE, DC, MC, V.*

LODGING

Choices range from rooms at humble motor inns in towns outside the main resorts to rustic luxury villas at Beaver Creek's Saddle Ridge—a series of classic Western-style lodgings complete with fireplaces, Ralph Lauren furnishings, and superb Western art and antiques. (One or two may be available to rent. At $400 per person per night, Trapper's Cabin comes replete with a private chef and activity director.) Winter is high season in Aspen, Vail, Summit County, Winter Park, and Steamboat. Prices often drop by as much as 50% in summer, despite the wealth of activities, events, and festivals. As a spa resort, Glenwood is the lone exception, with higher rates in the summer months.

Winter Park offers affordability, comfort, even luxury—but don't expect the "poshness" that the other top resorts offer. In this area, inns customarily serve both breakfast and dinner family-style, enabling guests to socialize easily. Most of the lodging is more than a mile from the mountain, but a free shuttle service runs throughout the area.

Unless otherwise noted, all accommodations include standard amenities such as phones, cable TV, and full baths in the rooms. For rates *see* the Lodgings chart *in* On the Road with Fodor's in the front of this guide.

Hotels

Aspen/Snowmass

$$$$ **Hotel Jerome.** One of the state's truly grand hotels since 1889, this is
★ a treasure trove of Victoriana and froufrou. The sumptuous public rooms alone have five kinds of wallpaper, antler sconces, and more than $60,000 worth of rose damask curtains. Each luxurious room and suite is individually decorated in soft pastel hues with period furnishings such as carved cherry armoires, with minibar and cable TV; the huge bathrooms include oversized marble baths, many with Jacuzzis and separate showers. ⌧ *330 E. Main St., Aspen 81611,* ☎ *970/920–1000 or 800/331–7213,* ℻ *970/925–2784. 44 rooms, 50 suites. 2 restaurants, bar, pool, 2 hot tubs, airport shuttle. AE, MC, V.*

$$$$ **Little Nell.** Built to be the last word in luxury, the Nell is the only truly
★ ski-in/ski-out property in Aspen, and that alone is worth something. The handsomely appointed rooms (all in mountain colors and abounding with wildlife prints) have every conceivable amenity and comfort, including fireplace, patio, marble bath, safe, cable TV, down comforters, and minibar. Equally superior is the waitstaff, who anticipate your every need. The restaurant, under new executive chef George Mahaffey, is one of the best in town. ⌧ *675 E. Durant Ave., Aspen 81611,* ☎ *970/920–4600 or 800/525–6200,* ℻ *970/920–4670. 86 rooms, 11 suites. 2 restaurants, bar, deli, pool, hot tub, health club, ski shop. AE, DC, MC, V.*

$$$$ **Ritz-Carlton.** This redbrick building seems more appropriate to Har-
★ vard than to Aspen. And although it's less formal than some Ritz-Carltons, this one is memorable, even by Aspen's exacting standards. In the august reception area, for example, are elegant burnished hickory walls, crystal chandeliers, Colorado green-granite floors, antique grandfather clocks and secretaries, and a $5 million art collection highlighted by commissioned sculptures and faux-18th-century landscapes

and portraiture. The mostly peach-color rooms are more casual than the lobby, with cherry furnishings, luxuriant marble baths, and three phones, among other amenities. The property is ski-out, though not quite ski-in. ☒ *315 E. Dean St., Aspen 81611,* ☎ *970/920–3300 or 800/241–3333,* FAX *970/920–7353. 231 rooms, 26 suites. 2 restaurants, 2 bars, pool, beauty salon, indoor and outdoor hot tubs, sauna, steam room, exercise room, meeting rooms, airport shuttle. AE, DC, MC, V.*

$$$–$$$$ **Snowmass Club.** If you like Ralph Lauren's Polo-style, you'll love this
★ elegant property with English hunting-lodge decor: guest rooms have rose-and-jade color schemes, handsome armoires and writing desks, rocking chairs, and four-poster beds. The club is equally popular with sports people: The Ed Seay–designed 18-hole championship golf course doubles as a cross-country ski center in winter, and there's a fully equipped health and racquet club on the premises. This resort is well suited for families: children stay free in their parents' rooms, and there's a fine day-care center. Sage's Bistro is the standout restaurant, featuring executive-chef Scott Phillip's sterling "Contemporary Ranchlands" cuisine. ☒ *Box G-2, Snowmass Village 81615,* ☎ *970/923–5600 or 800/525–0710,* FAX *970/923–6944. 76 rooms, 60 villas. Restaurant, bar, 2 pools, hot tub, sauna, spa, steam room, 18-hole golf course, 11 tennis courts, exercise room, racquetball, squash, cross-country skiing, ski shop, airport shuttle. AE, DC, MC, V.*

$$$ **Aspen Club Lodge.** This refined, intimate ski-in hotel has a delightfully
★ European flavor and was extensively remodeled in 1994. The rooms are tastefully outfitted in rich mountain colors and desert pastels, with polished pine woodwork and beams, French doors opening onto the patio or balcony, down comforters, and minifridges. Complimentary buffet breakfast and morning newspapers are just two of the extras. The plush Aspen Club Lodge Restaurant offers stunning views and moderately priced American fare. The management also runs several top-notch condominiums and the sunny, beautifully renovated Independence Square Hotel. Guests may use the nearby Aspen Club International, which has a weight room; pool; Jacuzzi; sauna and steam room; and tennis, squash, and racquetball courts. ☒ *709 E. Durant Ave., Aspen 81611,* ☎ *970/920–6760 or 800/882–2582,* FAX *970/920–6778. 84 rooms, 6 suites. Restaurant, bar, pool, hot tub, ski shop, airport shuttle. AE, MC, V.*

$$$ **Hotel Lenado.** This ravishing B&B is Aspen's most romantic property.
★ The smallish but quaint rooms contain either intricate carved applewood or Adirondack ironwood beds (*lenado* is Spanish for wood, and the motif appears throughout the hotel), antique armoires, even wood-burning stoves, in addition to modern amenities such as cable TV and tile bath. Gracious and graceful, the Lenado is Aspen at its considerable best. ☒ *200 S. Aspen St., Aspen 81611,* ☎ *970/925–6246 or 800/321–3457,* FAX *970/925–3840. 19 rooms. Breakfast room, lobby lounge, hot tub. AE, DC, MC, V.*

$$$ **Sardy House.** If the Lenado is full, head down the block to this equally sumptuous property under the same management. The tiny reception area opens onto an inviting parlor, with bay windows and dripping with chintz and lace. A narrow winding staircase with a magnificent oak balustrade leads to the precious rooms, decorated in aubergine, mauve, and rose, with Axeminster carpets from Belfast, cherry armoires and beds, wicker furniture, and such welcome touches as Laura Ashley bedclothes and duvets, heated towel racks, and whirlpool tubs. The new wing scrupulously duplicates the authentic Victorian feel of the original house. The restaurant serves exquisite Continental cuisine. The Sardy is straight out of a novel, the kind you read curled up by the fire on a frosty night. ☎ *128 E. Main St., Aspen 81611,* ☎ *970/920–2525 or 800/321–3457,* FAX *970/920–4478. 14 rooms, 6 suites. Restaurant, pool, hot tub, sauna. AE, DC, MC, V.*

$$–$$$ **Silvertree Hotel.** This ski-in/ski-out property is actually built into Snowmass Mountain. It's sprawling, with virtually everything you need on-site. Rooms and suites feature subdued attractive decor, with all the expected amenities of a first-class hotel. Condominium units are also available, with full use of facilities. ☎ *Box 5009, Snowmass Village 81615,* ☎ *970/923–3520 or 800/525–9402,* FAX *970/923–5192. 262 rooms, 15 suites, 200 condo units. 3 restaurants, bar, 2 pools, 2 hot tubs, spa, health club, ski shop, cabaret, meeting rooms. AE, D, DC, MC, V.*

$$ **Boomerang Lodge.** This comfortable, functional property offers a wide range of accommodations, from standard, somewhat drab hotel rooms to smartly appointed studios and deluxe rooms to three-bedroom apartments. There's even a log cabin. The nicest lodgings are the deluxe units, decorated in earth tones and with a Southwestern flair, each with a balcony, an enormous marble bath, a fireplace, and a wet bar. The staff is most hospitable. Continental breakfast is included in the rate. ☎ *500 W. Hopkins Ave., Aspen 81611,* ☎ *970/925–3416 or 800/992–8852,* FAX *970/925–3314. Breakfast room, pool, hot tub, sauna. AE, MC, V.*

$$ **Snowflake Inn.** This is another property with wildly divergent accommodations, all quite comfortable and decorated mostly in tartans or bright colors. The rustic lobby with its stone fireplace and wood beams is a convivial gathering place for the complimentary Continental breakfast and afternoon tea. ☎ *221 E. Hyman Ave., Aspen 81611,* ☎ *970/925–3221 or 800/247–2069,* FAX *970/925–8740. 38 units. Pool, hot tub, sauna. AE, MC, V.*

$ **Skier's Chalet.** This is arguably Aspen's best bargain. The location—100 feet from the ticket office and No. 1A Chairlift—can't be beat. Basic but snug rooms all have cable TV, private bath and phone, and the staff and fellow clientele are unfailingly congenial. A complimentary Continental breakfast is served every morning. ☎ *233 Gilbert St., Aspen 81611,* ☎ *970/920–2037. 20 rooms. Restaurant, pool. MC, V. Closed late-Apr.–late-Nov.*

Breckenridge

$$ **Breckenridge Hilton.** This ski-in/ski-out property, the only full-service hotel in Breckenridge, was planned as a condo development, but management ran out of financing. This pays dividends in the enormous bedrooms, which feature pleasing contemporary Southwestern decor in teal, salmon, mauve, and maroon. A half-million dollars was spent on refurbishings in 1993, with one surprising omission: air conditioning (though it's rarely necessary). Swans, on the property, is one of the town's more highly regarded restaurants. ☎ *550 Village Rd., 80424,* ☎ *970/453–4500,* FAX *970/453–0212. 208 rooms. Restaurant, bar, indoor pool, 2 indoor hot tubs, health club, ski shop, meeting rooms. AE, D, MC, V.*

$$ **Lodge at Breckenridge.** This special property has the disadvantage of being outside town, though shuttle service is provided to the town and ski area. The compensation is the breathtaking panoramas of the Ten Mile Range from nearly every angle; huge, strategically placed picture windows allow full vantage. The look is mountain chalet, with a rustic-modern decor. The well-lit, spacious rooms all have cable TV and full bath; minisuites also feature fireplace and kitchenette. The complete spa and health club facility is a bonus. ☎ *112 Overlook Dr., 80424,* ☎ *970/453–9300 or 800/736–1607,* FAX *970/453–0625. 45 units.*

Restaurant, indoor pool, 2 indoor hot tubs, 2 outdoor hot tubs, spa, health club, racquetball, pro shop. AE, D, MC, V.

$$ Village at Breckenridge. The word "village" puts it mildly, at this sprawling, self-contained resort, spread-eagled over 14 acres, and offering several varieties of accommodation from lodge-style rooms to three-bedroom condominiums. The decor runs from Southwestern color schemes to gleaming chrome-and-glass units. Studios and efficiencies have fireplaces and kitchenettes. There's even a community theater on the premises. ⚏ *Box 8329, 80424,* ☎ *970/453–2000 or 800/800–7829,* FAX *970/453–1878. 455 units. 9 restaurants, 3 bars, 2 indoor pools, 2 outdoor pools, 12 hot tubs, sauna, 2 health clubs, ski shop, meeting rooms, car rental. AE, D, MC, V.*

$ Williams House. Innkeepers Fred Kinat and Diane Jaynes spent a year ★ restoring this intimate, 1885 miner's cottage, then expanded it with utmost care. From the cozy front parlor with its mantled fireplace and floral spreads, to the exquisite dollhouselike accommodations, the Williams House is a dream bed-and-breakfast. The individually decorated rooms are as romantic as can be, with chintz or lace curtains, Laura Ashley and Ralph Lauren comforters and linens, mahogany beds, walnut wardrobes or cherry armoires, old framed magazine covers, hand-blown globe lamps, fresh flowers and sachets, and footed tubs. In 1994 they opened Willoughby Cottage next door, a perfect romantic retreat complete with scalloped lace curtains, intricately carved Victorian doors and balustrades, an elaborate mantle with hand-painted tiles, a gas-burning fireplace, hot tub, kitchenette, and rustic antique furnishings. Best of all are the affable hosts: Avid skiers ("Cold cereal on powder days," they warn), they take guests to their secret stashes, and on hikes in summer. Diane's muffins, quiches, and *huevos rancheros* (eggs with salsa) are addictive. ⚏ *303 N. Main St., 80424,* ☎ *970/453–2975. 4 rooms, 1 cottage. AE*

Georgetown

$ Hardy House B&B Inn. This 1877 Victorian has been lovingly restored by owner Sarah Schmidt, whose welcome couldn't be warmer (nor could the potbellied stove that greets you in the parlor). The cozy rooms, all with private bath, are comfortably furnished with antiques and period reproductions, as well as down comforters. ⚏ *605 Brownell St., Box 0156, 80444,* ☎ *970/569–3388. 4 rooms. MC, V.*

Glenwood Springs

$ Hotel Colorado. The exterior of this building, listed in the National Historic Register, is simply exquisite, with graceful sandstone colonnades and Italianate campaniles. The impression of luxury continues in the imposing, yet gracious, marble lobby and public rooms. Unfortunately, the sunny, individually decorated rooms and suites—most with high ceilings, fireplaces, gorgeous period wainscoting, and balconies affording superlative vistas—are a little threadbare and oddly configured. But everyone, whether notable or notorious, from Doc Holliday to Al Capone, stayed here in its halcyon days. ⚏ *526 Pine St., 81601,* ☎ *970/945–6511 or 800/544–3998,* FAX *970/045–7030. 96 rooms, 26 suites. 2 restaurants, bar, beauty salon, health club, meeting rooms. AE, DC, MC, V.*

$ Hotel Denver. Although this hotel was originally built in 1806, its ★ most striking features are the numerous art-deco touches throughout. Most rooms open onto a view of the springs or a three-story New Orleans–style atrium bedecked with colorful canopies. The accommodations are ultraneat, trim, and comfortable, and are decorated predominantly in maroon and teal. There are plenty of homey touches, such as fresh-baked cookies upon your arrival (the cordial owner also runs the best bakery in town—The Daily Bread). The Daily Bread Too is the excellent hotel restaurant. ☎ *402 7th St., 81601,* ☎ *970/945–6565,* ᴀx *970/945–2204. 60 rooms. Restaurant, bar, beauty salon, exercise room, meeting rooms. AE, D, MC, V.*

$ **Hot Springs Lodge.** This lodge is perfectly located right by the Springs, which are used to heat the property. The attractive rooms, decorated in jade, teal, buff, and rose, stress the Southwestern motif. Deluxe rooms offer a minifridge and tiny balcony, in addition to standard conveniences such as cable TV and full bath. ☎ *401 N. River Rd., 81601,* ☎ *970/945–6571. 107 rooms. Restaurant, bar, hot tub. AE, D, DC, MC, V.*

$ **Sunlight Inn.** This charming traditional ski lodge a few hundred feet from the Ski Sunlight lifts brims with European ambience, from the delightful lounge (with a marvelous carved fireplace and wrought-iron chandeliers) and fine German restaurant to the cozily rustic rooms, all with pine-board walls and rough-hewn armoires. Sunlight is a true getaway-from-it-all place, with no TVs or phones in the rooms. ☎ *10252 C.R. 117, 81601,* ☎ *970/945–5225. 24 rooms (5 share baths). Restaurant, bar, hot tub. MC, V.*

Keystone

$$–$$$ **Keystone Lodge.** The ugly cinder-block structure gives no hint of the
★ gracious living within. The lodge is a pampering place, and a member of Preferred Hotels. Rooms with king-size beds are on the small side, while rooms with two queen-size beds are enormous, with terraces. All units are beautifully appointed in rich mountain colors, with all the amenities. There are lovely thoughtful touches, like a jar of fresh-baked cookies and a teddy bear with your turndown service. ☎ *Keystone Resort, Box 38, 80435,* ☎ *970/468–4242 or 800/222–0188,* ᴀx *970/468–4343. 152 rooms. 3 restaurants, bar, indoor pool, hot tub, 2 tennis courts, exercise room, children's programs (ages 1-10), convention center. AE, DC, MC, V.*

$$ **Ski Tip Lodge.** This charming, elegant log cabin is an agreeable hostelry
★ whose rooms have quaint names such as Edna's Eyrie, and are uniquely decorated with homespun furnishings, including several four-posters, and accessories such as quilts and hand-knitted throw rugs. Breakfast and lunch are included in the room rate, and, since the kitchen vies for best in Summit County with the Alpenglow Stube and Keystone Ranch, you won't be sorry if you take advantage of the deal. You might start with pheasant, caribou, and buffalo ravioli in roasted red-pepper sauce, followed with salmon swimming in cilantro pineapple salsa or baked pheasant breast dusted with crushed pecans, hazelnuts, and sage. Be sure to adjourn to the cozy lounge for the decadent desserts and special coffees. Fortunately, nonguests can dine on a limited basis, as well. ☎ *Keystone Resort, Box 38, 80435,* ☎ *970/468–4242 or 800/222–0188,* ᴀx *970/468–4343. 24 rooms. Restaurant. AE, DC, MC, V.*

Leadville

$ **Hotel Delaware.** This beautifully restored hotel is on the National Register of Historic Places; renovations over the past three years have renewed its original 1888 Victorian condition. The lobby is graced with period antiques, brass fixtures, crystal chandeliers, and oak paneling. The comfortable rooms have lace curtains and antique heirloom quilts, in addition to modern conveniences such as private bath and cable TV. A Continental breakfast is included in the rate. ☎ *700 Harrison Ave., 80461,* ☎ *719/486–1418 or 800/748–2004,* ᴀx *719/486–2214. 36 rooms. Restaurant, bar, hot tub. AE, DC, MC, V.*

Steamboat Springs

$$$$ **Home Ranch.** You won't be roughing it at this retreat nestled among
★ towering stands of aspen outside Clark (just north of Steamboat): The
lodge is a wonderful place to relax and be pampered. The focal point
of the cozy living room is a magnificent fieldstone fireplace surrounded
by plush leather armchairs and sofas. The dining room, where Clyde
Nelson turns out gourmet Southwestern fare, is just as homey, with
saddles hanging from the rafters and a whimsical salt-and-pepper-
shaker collection displayed on the shelves. Accommodations are either
in the main lodge or in individual cabins, each with a hot tub and ter
race. Decor leans toward Native American rugs and prints, lace curtains, terra-cotta tile or hardwood floors, stenciled walls, hand-carved
beds, quilts, and such delightful touches as old steamer trunks and rocking horses. Everything from meals to the full slate of seasonal activities is included in the price; there is a seven-night minimum stay. A
member of the prestigious Relais et Châteaux group, which upholds
rigorous standards for membership, Home Ranch is the definition of
rustic chic and the ultimate in seclusion. ⊞ *Box 822, Clark 80428,* ☎
970/879–1780 or 800/223–7094. 6 rooms, 8 cabins. Dining room,
pool, hot tub, horseback riding, fishing, cross-country skiing, ski shop.
Closed late-Mar.–early June, early Oct.–late-Dec. AE, D, MC, V.

$$$$ **Vista Verde Guest Ranch.** Offering similarly deluxe digs and just as many
★ activities as Home Ranch, Vista Verde has lower rates and a more authentic Western ambience. The lodge rooms are huge and beautifully
appointed, with lace curtains, Western art, and lodgepole furniture. Cabins are more rustic, with pine paneling, old-fashioned wood-burning
stoves, horseshoe hangers, antique lanterns, and framed old news clip-
pings and photos, plus refrigerators, coffeemakers, and porches. Jacques
Wilson, a Culinary Institute of America graduate, serves up sumptuous country gourmet repasts, which include marvelous wild game, and
fresh produce from his herb and vegetable garden. Among the many
activities included in the price (along with three meals) are river rafting and mountain biking, in addition to the standard trail rides and
Nordic skiing. Optional activities (not included) are hot-air balloon-
ing and dogsledding. You can also play *City Slickers* on one of the two
genuine cattle drives held every year. ⊞ *Box 465, 80477,* ☎ *970/879–*
3858 or 800/526–7433. 3 rooms, 6 cabins. Dining room, 2 hot tubs,
sauna, exercise room, horseback riding, fishing, cross-country skiing.
Closed mid-Mar.–May and Oct.–mid-Dec. No credit cards (personal
checks accepted).

$$$ **Sheraton Steamboat Resort & Conference Center.** This bustling deluxe
hotel is Steamboat's only true ski-in/ski-out property. Rooms are Sher-
aton standard, fair-sized, with muted decor and most comforts. The
hotel also handles Sheraton Plaza (not ski-in/ski-out), economy units
with kitchens and cable TV, whose guests enjoy full hotel privileges.
⊞ *Box 774808, 80477,* ☎ *970/879–2220 or 800/848–8878,* FAX
970/879–7686. 270 rooms, 3 suites (26 units in Sheraton Plaza). 2
restaurants, 2 bars, pool, 2 hot tubs, sauna, steam room, ski shop, meet-
ing rooms. AE, D, DC, MC, V.

$$ **Ptarmigan Inn.** Convenience and comfort are the keynotes of this appealing property situated on the slopes. The modest rooms, decorated
in pleasing pastels and earth tones, have cable TV, balcony, and full
bath. If the Ptarmigan is full, consider staying at its inexpensive sister
property, The Alpiner (424 Lincoln Ave., ☎ 970/879–1430), a basic
but comfortable 32-room lodge downtown, whose guests have full use
of the Ptarmigan's facilities. ⊞ *Box 773240, 80477,* ☎ *970/879–1730*
or 800/538–7519, FAX *970/879–6044. 78 rooms. Restaurant, bar,*
pool, hot tub, sauna, ski shop. AE, MC, V.

$–$$ Sky Valley Lodge. This homey property is a few miles from downtown, amid glorious scenery that contributes to the "get-away-from-it-all" feel of the inn. Warm English country-style rooms are decorated in restful mountain colors and feature touches such as fruits and dried flowers. ⌖ *31490 E. U.S. 40, 80477,* ☎ *970/879–7749 or 800/538–7519,* FAX *970/879–7749. 24 rooms. Hot tub. AE, MC, V.*

$ Harbor Hotel and Condominiums. This charming, completely refurbished
★ 1930s hotel is smack in the middle of Steamboat's historic district. The inviting brick and wood-paneled lobby sets the tone, further emphasized by the nifty artifacts, such as the old switchboards, that dot the interior of the property. Each room is individually decorated with period furniture, combined with modern amenities for comfort. The property also runs an adjacent motel and condo complex. ⌖ *703 Lincoln Ave., 80477,* ☎ *970/879–1522 or 800/543–8888,* FAX *970/879–1737. 62 units (another 23 rooms, 24 condos in adjacent complex). 2 hot tubs, sauna, steam room. AE, D, DC, MC, V.*

$ Rabbit Ears Motel. The playful, pink-neon bunny sign outside this motel has been a local landmark since 1952, making it an unofficial gateway to Steamboat Springs. The location is ideal for those who want the springs (across the street), the ski area (the town bus stops outside), and the downtown shops, bars, and restaurants. All the rooms are kept clean and attractive and are equipped with minifridges and coffeemakers. Most have balconies with views of the Yampa River. A Continental breakfast is included in the rate. ⌖ *201 Lincoln Ave., 80477,* ☎ *970/879–1150 or 800/828–7702,* FAX *970/870–0483. 66 rooms. AE, D, DC, MC, V.*

$ Steamboat B&B. This custard and forest-green Victorian was originally a church that owner Gordon Hattersley converted into the area's nicest B&B in 1989, cleverly retaining the arched doorways and stained glass windows. The cozy, comfy rooms have floral wallpaper, lace curtains, landscape photos, potted geraniums, polished hardwood floors, and period antiques and reproductions. If you hear a polite scratching at the door, it's the house cats, Scamper and Joshua. ⌖ *442 Pine St., 80477,* ☎ *970/879–5724. 7 rooms. Hot tub. AE, D, MC, V.*

The Vail Valley

$$$$ Hyatt Regency Beaver Creek. Because this slope-side hotel has been
★ carefully crafted for guests' maximum comfort, it is considered a model accommodation. The lobby, with a magnificent antler chandelier as the centerpiece and huge oriel windows opening onto the mountain, manages to be both cozy and grand. Rooms are sizable and decorated in an appealing French provincial style, and all of them have the usual amenities and such welcome extras as coffeemakers and heated towel racks. Maintaining Beaver Creek's tradition of excellent children's programs, the Camp and Rock Hyatt day-care centers make this resort wildly popular with families. Conventioneers like the full spa and health club, ski-in/ski-out ease, and nearby golf course (with guest tee times). No wonder it's often booked months in advance. ⌖ *136 E. Thomas Pl., Avon 81620,* ☎ *970/949–1234 or 800/233–1234,* FAX *970/949–4164. 295 rooms, 3 suites, 26 condo units. 3 restaurants, 2 bars, deli, pool, 6 hot tubs, spa, 5 tennis courts, meeting rooms. AE, D, DC, MC, V.*

$$$$ Lodge at Vail. The first hotel to open in Vail remains one of the swankier addresses in town. As they say in the hotel business, it has "location, location, location," which translates to ski-in/ski-out status. The medium-size rooms are frilly and floral, a riot of pastels, with mahogany and teak furnishings and marble baths. The 40 suites are individually owned and decorated, but must meet rigorous standards set by management. The Wildflower Inn restaurant, a splendiferous space with vaulting floral arrangements and flowered banquettes, serves "postmodern Hebrew cuisine," jokes chef Jim Cohen, but it's really solidly regional American. Mickey's piano bar is still a favored après-ski spot. ☎ *174 E. Gore Creek Dr., Vail 81657,* ☎ *970/476–5011 or 800/331–5634,* FAX *970/476–7425. 60 rooms, 40 suites. 2 restaurants, bar, pool, hot tub, sauna, spa, exercise room, ski shop. AE, D, DC, MC, V.*

$$$–$$$$ **Lodge at Cordillera.** This exquisite property is purposely isolated from ★ all the activity in the valley. Surrounded by a pristine wilderness area—nearly half the property's 3,100 acres has been designated as wildlife reserve—the lodge offers privacy and spectacular sweeping vistas. The rooms are decidedly Old World, done up in mountain colors—burgundy, buff, and hunter green—with burled pine furnishings and balconies or transom windows to enjoy the views. An air of quiet luxury prevails throughout this secluded palatial retreat: prints by Picasso and Miró adorn the pine-paneled or exposed-brick walls, and ceilings are of carved recessed wood. You can luxuriate in the spa after a hard day's hiking or cross-country skiing, then sit down to a gourmet repast in the superlative Picasso restaurant. Belgian chef Fabrice Beaudoin weaves subtle magic with the healthful spa cuisine, and glorious views ensure a romantic evening out. An 18-hole Hale Irwin–designed golf course, with breathtaking valley views, opened in 1994. Nordic enthusiasts will appreciate the miles of trails in winter. The lodge operates a shuttle to the lifts. ☎ *Box 1110, Edwards 81632,* ☎ *970/926–2200 or 800/548–2721,* FAX *970/926–2486. 28 rooms. Restaurant, bar, indoor-outdoor pool, hot tub, spa, health club, cross-country skiing, meeting rooms. AE, MC, V.*

$$$ **Beaver Creek Lodge.** An atrium centerpiece highlights this all-suite property that's charmingly decorated in European style. The units graciously maintain a sky-blue-and-forest green color scheme, and all feature a kitchenette and gas-burning fireplace as well as the usual amenities. The casually elegant Black Diamond Grill offers an inventive new American menu, which includes a highly touted scallop bisque and a buffalo carpaccio garnished with rattlesnake. ☎ *26 Avondale La., Avon 81620,* ☎ *970/845–9800. 70 suites, 16 condo units. Restaurant, bar, indoor-outdoor pool and hot tub, spa, health club, ski shop, meeting rooms. AE, MC, V.*

$$$ **The Pines.** This small, ski-in/ski-out Beaver Creek winner combines posh digs with unpretentious atmosphere—and prices. The rooms are spacious, light, and airy, with blond wood furnishings, pale pink ceilings, and fabrics in dusky rose, mint, and white. Each room has a TV/VCR (tapes are free), minifridge, and coffeemaker; several rooms have balconies overlooking the ski area and mountain range. The air of quiet pampering is furthered by little extras like a ski concierge who arranges complimentary guided mountain tours and a free wax for your skis. The Grouse Mountain Grill serves up superb new American cuisine in an unparalleled setting with huge picture windows and wrought-iron chandeliers. ☎ *Box 18450, Avon 81620,* ☎ *970/845–7900 or 800/859–8242,* FAX *970/845–7809. 60 rooms, 12 condos. Restaurant, bar, pool, hot tub, spa, exercise room, laundry service. AE, D, MC, V.*

$$$ **Sonnenalp.** This property, in the midst of a pseudo-Bavarian village, ★ impresses as the real thing, and for good reason: The owning Fassler family has been in the hotel business in Germany for generations. Each of the three buildings offers a distinct look and ambience: the Swiss Chalet is quaint, with Bavarian pine armoires and secretaries and down comforters; the Austria Haus is a tad more rustic, with rough-hewn wood walls, stone floors, intricate ironwork, and Bavarian an-

tiques throughout the public rooms; and the large, sunny Bavaria Haus suites have an elegant lodge look, with stuccoed walls, wood beams, and heated marble floors. The superb restaurants include the delightful Stueberl (tiny rooms with wood paneling and sconces), the western saloon Bully Ranch (great barbecue), the enormously popular Swiss Chalet (sensational fondue), and the elegant, Continental Ludwig's. ⌧ *20 Vail Rd., Vail 81657,* ☎ *970/476–5656 or 800/654–8312,* ℻ *970/476–1639. 36 rooms (Austria Haus), 70 rooms (Swiss Chalet), 80 suites (Bavaria Haus). 4 restaurants, 3 bars, 2 indoor pools, outdoor pool, 2 indoor hot tubs, outdoor hot tub, spa, exercise room. AE, MC, V.*

$$$ **Westin Vail.** Down-to-earth yet glamorous is the best way to describe this ski-in/ski-out hotel that manages—despite its fairly large size—to maintain an intimate feel, thanks to the expert staff. Rooms in the older wing are done in mountain colors; those in the newer Terrace Wing have been beautifully redone in burgundy and mint with rich, deep plaid and floral fabrics, wicker beds, polished wood armoires, and wrought-iron lamps. Alfredo's, the hotel's restaurant, has long been one of the best Italian restaurants in the valley. Guests have access to the adjoining Cascade Athletic Club, whose facilities include indoor and outdoor tennis courts, racquetball and squash courts, and Nautilus and free-weight rooms. ⌧ *1300 Westhaven Dr., Vail 81657,* ☎ *970/476–7111,* ℻ *970/479–7025. 290 rooms, 28 suites. 2 restaurants, bar, pool, beauty salon, 2 hot tubs, meeting rooms. AE, DC, MC, V.*

$$ **Gasthof Gramshammer.** Pepi Gramshammer, a former Austrian Olympic ski racer, is one of Vail's most beloved, respected citizens, whose labor of love—Wedel Weeks—ranks among the country's best intensive ski programs. His charming rooms are done up in pastels, with original oil paintings and fluffy down comforters. Pepi's and Antlers, the property's two fine restaurants, have a European ambience, with stucco walls, wood-beamed ceilings, and waitresses in dirndls. ⌧ *231 E. Gore Creek Dr., Vail 81657,* ☎ *970/476–5626,* ℻ *970/476–8816. 28 rooms. 2 restaurants, bar, ski shop. AE, MC, V.*

$$ **Sitzmark Lodge.** This cozy lodge brims with European ambience, thanks to many repeat international guests (it's often booked months in advance). The good-size rooms look out onto either the mountain or Gore Creek. Decor is a hodgepodge, ranging from dark to blond woods and rose, teal, or floral fabrics. Each unit has a balcony, refrigerator, cable TV, hair dryer, and humidifier; some deluxe rooms have gas-burning fireplaces. The staff is ultrafriendly, encouraging guests to congregate in the sunny, split-level living room for complimentary mulled wine. A Continental breakfast is also gratis in winter. ⌧ *183 Gore Creek Dr., Vail 81611,* ☎ *970/476–5001,* ℻ *970/476–8702. 35 rooms. Restaurant, pool, indoor and outdoor hot tubs, sauna. AE, MC, V.*

$ **Eagle River Inn.** The public rooms of this delightful B&B seem straight
★   out of the pages of *Architectural Digest* or *Southwest Interiors:* painted adobe walls, traditional carved-beam ceilings, a glorious kiva, Navajo weavings, bronze coyotes, luminarias, and Zuni baskets. The guest rooms, which have unusual touches like rough-wood furnishings, ceramic lamps, and hand-painted tile baths, overflow with fresh flowers from the enchanting backyard in summer. All rooms have TVs. Scrumptious gourmet breakfasts and evening wine tastings are included in the rate. During the 19th century, the inn actually operated as a hostelry for Rio Grande railroad employees: Imagine 24 rooms with only one toilet and shower! Today, it's one of the most distinctive properties in the Vail Valley, and each room has a small private bath. The only drawback is that you'll need a car to reach the ski slopes—

Minturn lacks public transportation. ⊠ *145 N. Main St., Box 100, Minturn 81645,* ☎ *970/827–5761 or 800/344–1750,* ℻ *970/827–4020. 12 rooms. Hot tub. AE, MC, V.*

$ **Roost Lodge.** Situated on I–70 and advertising economical rates, com-
★ fortable rooms, and a heated pool, this accommodation is true to its promise—and then some, considering the price. The airy rooms are pleasing, many with four-poster beds, all with basic amenities. The staff is helpful and ingratiating, and complimentary Continental breakfast and afternoon wine and cheese are served daily in ski season. ⊠ *1783 N. Frontage Rd. W, Vail 81657,* ☎ *970/476–5451. 72 rooms, 3 suites. Pool, hot tub, sauna. AE, MC, V.*

Winter Park

$$–$$$ **Iron Horse Resort Retreat.** This ski-in/ski-out hotel/condominium complex is the deluxe address in Winter Park. All units except the lodge rooms have a full kitchen, Jacuzzi tub, and sundeck, and are furnished in an attractive, modern rustic style. ⊠ *Box 1286, 80482,* ☎ *970/726–8851 or 800/621–8190. 130 1- and 2-bedroom units. Restaurant, bar, pool, health club, ski shop. AE, D, DC, MC, V.*

$–$$ **Hidden Mountain Lodge.** The only downside of this first-rate property is its location, 20 minutes from the ski area by private shuttle (provided by the lodge). Cross-country skiing is also available in this secluded spot surrounded by the national forest. The pleasing rooms include fireplace, king-size bed, sitting room, microwave, minifridge, balcony, and plush carpeting. What really sets this property apart is the innovative kitchen. Chris Lightfoot's menu changes daily, but might highlight blackened mahimahi, yellowfin tuna in roast-pepper beurre blanc, or Texas baby-back ribs. The restaurant is open on a limited basis to nonguests with 24-hour notice. Room rates include breakfast, dinner, and lift ticket. ⊠ *Box 177, 80482,* ☎ *970/726–9266 or 800/221–9125. 18 units. Restaurant, hot tub. AE, MC, V.*

$–$$ **Timber House Ski Lodge.** This family-run property is as congenial as can be, and the staff makes you feel as though you're staying in someone's sprawling, though slightly disordered, home. The tiny rooms in the old wing have shared baths and rustic decor, with brightly colored curtains and spreads. Smallish rooms in the newer wing have private baths and huge picture windows opening onto the mountains. Dorm rooms and bunk rooms are also available. All-you-can-eat breakfast and dinner are served family-style. ⊠ *Box 32, 80482,* ☎ *970/726–8417. 35 rooms. Dining room, hot tub, sauna. AE, MC, V.*

$–$$ **Vintage Hotel.** This well-run hotel/condo complex is Winter Park's other premier resort, offering spacious, comfortable units mostly decorated in soothing earth or mountain tones. Configurations range from standard, inexpensive hotel rooms (with kitchenette and gas fireplace) and studios (with kitchen) to three-bedroom condos. ⊠ *Box 1369, 80482,* ☎ *970/726–8801 or 800/472–7017,* ℻ *970/726–9250. 118 units. Restaurant, bar, pool, hot tub, sauna. AE, D, DC, MC, V.*

$ **Sundowner Motel.** This is probably the nicest motel on the strip, and a great bargain, considering the free shuttle to the ski area. The rooms, decorated in muted earth tones, are slightly threadbare but have the standard amenities. It's right on the main drag, and convenient to restaurants and shops. ⊠ *Box 221, 80482,* ☎ *970/726–9451 or 970/726–5452. 22 rooms. Hot tub. AE, DC, MC, V.*

Condominiums

Condominiums often represent an excellent alternative to the pricier hotels, especially for families and groups. In certain resorts, like Steamboat, Copper Mountain, and Winter Park, they are often the best lodging, period. All the companies listed below represent top-notch properties, usually on or within walking distance of the slopes (or major activities in summer). Most units are individually owned and decorated, and all have full kitchen and cable TV, most with pool and/or hot tub access. **Summit County Central Reservations** (Box 446, Dillon 80435, ☎ 970/468–6222 or 800/365–6365) handles more than 2,000 units in Dillon, Frisco, Breckenridge, Copper Mountain, Keystone, and Silverthorne.

Aspen/Snowmass

Call **Aspen Central Reservations** (☎ 800/262–7736) and **Snowmass Resort Association** (☎ 800/598–2005). Among the recommended management companies are **Coates, Reid & Waldron** (720 E. Hyman Ave., Aspen 81611, ☎ 970/925–1400 or 800/222–7736, FAX 970/920–3765); **Aspen Alps Condominium Association** (700 Ute Ave., Aspen 81611, ☎ 970/925–7820 or 800/228–7820, FAX 970/925–2528); **Aspen Club Properties** (730 E. Durant Ave., Aspen 81611, ☎ 970/920–2000 or 800/633–0336, FAX 970/920–2020); **Destination Resort Management** (610 W. End St., Aspen 81611, ☎ 970/925–5000 or 800/345–1471, FAX 970/925–6891); **McCartney Properties** (421-G Aspen Airport Business Center, Aspen 81611, ☎ 970/925–8717 or 800/433–8465, FAX 970/920–4770). In Snowmass: **Snowmass Lodging Company** (Box 6077, Snowmass Village 81615, ☎ 970/923–5543 or 800/365–0410, FAX 970/923–5740) and **Village Property Management** (Box 5550, Snowmass Village 81615, ☎ 800/525–9402, FAX 970/923–5192).

Breckenridge

River Mountain Lodge (100 S. Par St., 80424, ☎ 970/453–4711 or 800/325–2342) offers fully equipped units, from studios to two-bedrooms. **Breckenridge Accommodations** (Box 1931, 80424, ☎ 970/453–9140 or 800/872–8789); **AMR Lodging** (400 N. Park Ave., No. 6A, 80424, ☎ 800/334–9162 or ☎ and fax 970/453–4432); **Breckenridge Central Lodging** (Box 709, 80424, ☎ 970/453–2160 or 800/858–5885); and **Colorado Mountain Lodging** (Drawer 1190, 80424, ☎ 970/453–4121 or 800/627–3766, FAX 970/453–0533) are a few of the reputable rental agencies. You can also call the **Breckenridge Resort Chamber Central Reservation System** (☎ 800/221–1091 or 970/453–6018).

Copper Mountain

Copper Mountain Resort (☎ 970/968–2882 or 800/458–8386) runs all 22 lodging facilities, ranging from hotel-style units to condos. All are either on the slopes or served by shuttles.

Keystone

Keystone Resort Corporation (☎ 800/222–0188) operates all the lodging facilities at the resort, which range from hotel-style accommodations at Keystone Lodge (*see* Lodging, *above*) to various condominium properties.

Steamboat

Steamboat Premier Properties (1855 Ski Time Square, Steamboat Springs 80487, ☎ 970/879–8811 or 800/228–2458, FAX 970/879–8485) lives up to its name, with the finest condominium units, from studios to three-bedroom units, in three deluxe properties: The Torian Plum, Bronze Tree, and Trappeur's Crossing. **Steamboat Resorts** (Box 2995, Steamboat Springs 80477, ☎ 800/525–5502, FAX 970/879–8060) and **Mountain Resorts** (2145 Resort Dr., No. 100, Steamboat Springs 80487, ☎ 800/525–2622, FAX 970/879–3228) also represent top properties.

fect. The tables alone reputedly cost $3,000 each. There's a wonderful selection of hot drinks, brandies, and single malts.

Garfinkel's (536 W. Lionshead Mall, ☏ 970/476–3789) is a ski-school hangout, predictably popular with the younger set—especially shredders. A young crowd can also be found scarfing down excellent and cheap pizzas until 2 AM at **Vendetta's** (291 Bridge St., ☏ 970/476–5070). The **Red Lion** (top of Bridge St., ☏ 970/476–7676), a Vail tradition, attracts a more sedate crowd, with mellow live acts and a wildly popular deck. **Sarah's** (Christiania at Vail, 356 E. Hanson Ranch Rd., ☏ 970/476–5641) showcases Helmut Fricker, a Vail institution who plays accordion while yodeling up a storm. **Mickey's** (Lodge at Vail, 174 E. Gore Creek Dr., ☏ 970/476–5011) is the place for soothing pop standards on the piano.

After attacking the moguls, the Hyatt's **Crooked Hearth Tavern** (☏ 970/949–1234, ext. 2260) in Beaver Creek is a wonderful place to wind down, usually while listening to the strains of a folk guitarist.

Cabaret

The **Crystal Palace** (300 E. Hyman Ave., ☏ 970/925–1455) is an Aspen fixture, offering two seatings nightly with fine food and a fiercely funny up-to-the-minute satirical revue. The **Tower** (Snowmass Mall, ☏ 970/923–4650) features hokey but hilarious magic and juggling acts.

Country and Western

In Aspen/Snowmass, **Cowboys** (Silvertree Hotel, ☏ 970/923–5249) usually has live country-western music and dancing nightly, as does **Shooters Saloon** (Galena and Hopkins Sts., ☏ 970/925–4567).

In Breckenridge, **Breck's** (Hilton, 550 Village Rd., ☏ 970/453–4500) offers free dance lessons each Tuesday night, and live acts Wednesday and Thursday nights.

In Steamboat, **The Saloon** (Sundance Plaza, ☏ 970/879–6303) is in no-man's-land behind a Wendy's, but it's a real cowboy joint that offers two-step lessons early in the evening. The **Loft** section of the **Ore House** restaurant (U.S. 40 and Pine Grove Rd., ☏ 970/879–1190) ropes 'em in for juicy steaks and boot-scooting.

In the Vail Valley, **Cassidy's Hole in the Wall** (82 E. Beaver Creek Blvd., Avon, ☏ 970/949–9449) is a saloon that offers live country-and-western bands nightly, to go with the authentic mouthwatering barbecue.

Discos

In Aspen, **Club Soda** (419 E. Hyman Ave., ☏ 970/925–8154) is where the beautiful people and their admirers work up a polite sweat. The **Mustang Club** (517 E. Hopkins Ave., ☏ 970/920–2111) attracts a younger—perhaps even more beautiful—crowd.

In Breckenridge, **Tiffany's** (☏ 970/453–6000, ext. 7914) has a DJ and dancing nightly. **Johsha's** (☏ 970/453–4146) offers live bands, a dance floor, pool tables, and cheap eats.

Club Med (☏ 970/968–2121) at Copper Mountain offers a $25 international dinner buffet that includes bar games, nightly entertainment (at 9 PM), and ☛ to the disco at 10:30 (☛ to the show and disco alone is $10.50).

Vail offers **Sheika's** (☏ 970/476–1515), where the young are restless on the dance floor.

Jazz Clubs

Aspen's **Ritz-Carlton Club Room** (315 Dean St., ☎ 970/920–3300) presents live jazz nightly in season. **Cottonwoods** (Snowmass Village Mall, ☎ 970/923–2748) showcases leading artists nightly in season.

Copper Mountain's **Pesce Fresco** (Mountain Plaza Bldg., ☎ 970/968–2882, ext. 6505) offers jazz piano Wednesday–Sunday nights in season.

In Vail, **Babau's Cafe** (L'Ostello Lodge, Lionshead Cir., ☎ 970/476–2050) is a piano jazz club with fine Italian specialties as a plus. **Louie's** (Wall St., ☎ 970/479–9008) is a Cajun restaurant that sizzles even more with zydeco and jazz acts.

Rock Clubs

In Breckenridge, **Alligator Lounge** (320 S. Main St., ☎ 970/453–7782) is the hot spot for acoustic, blues, Cajun, and reggae sets.

In Steamboat (on the mountain), **The Tugboat** (Ski Time Square, ☎ 970/879–7070) and **Inferno** (Gondola Square, ☎ 970/879–5111) always feature loud live acts. **Heavenly Daze** (Ski Time Square, ☎ 970/879–8080) has three levels: the ground floor is a brew pub, the second floor a restaurant, and the third floor a combination billiards parlor/rock club/disco.

In Vail, **Nick's** (bottom of Bridge St., ☎ 970/476–3433) has a frat-house feeling, especially on Mondays when shredders attend the "Board Meeting." **Garton's** (Crossroads Shopping Center, ☎ 970/476–0607) offers everything from rock to reggae, Cajun to country, and attracts a slightly older crowd (pushing 30).

The Slope (1161 Winter Park Dr., ☎ 970/726–5727) is Winter Park's most raucous venue, offering everything from rock to retro funk.

I–70 AND THE HIGH ROCKIES ESSENTIALS

Arriving and Departing by Plane

Airports and Airlines

Most of the I–70 corridor is served via Denver and its airports (*see* Arriving and Departing by Plane *in* Chapter 2, Denver). There's an extensive list of Denver-based companies that specialize in transportation to the mountain resorts (*see* Between Airports and the Resorts, *below*).

United has flights from Denver (via Aspen Aviation), as well as nonstop service to Los Angeles, Dallas, Phoenix, and Chicago in ski season. Delta flies from Salt Lake City.

Aspen/Snowmass's **Aspen Airport** (☎ 970/920–5385) is served daily by United Express (☎ 800/241–6522).

American (☎ 800/433–7300), America West (☎ 800/247–5692), Northwest (☎ 800/255–2525), and United fly nonstop from various gateways during ski season to **Steamboat Springs Airport** (☎ 970/879–1204).

The Vail Valley is served by **Eagle County Airport** (Gypsum, ☎ 970/524–9490), 35 miles west of Vail. During ski season, Delta, United, and Northwest offer nonstop flights from several gateways. American flies here year-round.

Between Airports and the Resorts
BY BUS OR VAN

To and from Aspen/Snowmass: **Roaring Fork Transit Agency** (☎ 970/925–8484) provides bus service from Aspen Airport to the Ruby Park bus station in Aspen. **Aspen Limousine and Bus Service** (☎ 970/925–9400) runs trips to Denver, Glenwood Springs, and Vail. **Colorado Mountain Express** (☎ 970/949–4227) runs trips to Vail and Aspen.

To and from Summit County (Breckenridge, Copper Mountain, Dillon, Frisco, Keystone): **Resort Express** (☎ 970/468–7600 or 800/334–7433), **Vans to Breckenridge** (☎ 970/668–5466 or 800/222–2212), and **Skier's Connection** (☎ 970/668–0200 or 800/824–1004) have regular service to and from Denver airports.

To and from Steamboat Springs: **Alpine Taxi** (☎ 970/879–8294) offers service from the airport, as well as special rates to Vail, Boulder, and Denver. **Steamboat Express** (☎ 970/879–3400) and **Panorama** (☎ 970/879–3400 or 800/545–6050) also serve DIA and the local airports.

To and from Vail/Beaver Creek: **Airport Transportation Service** (☎ 970/476–7576); **Colorado Mountain Express** (☎ 970/949–4227); and **Vans to Vail** (☎ 970/476–4467 or 800/222–2212).

To and from Winter Park: **Vanex** (☎ 970/726–4047 or 800/521–5401) offers service from Denver. **Greyhound Lines** (☎ 800/231–2222) runs from Denver to Winter Park.

Arriving and Departing by Car, Train, and Bus

By Car
If you're entering Colorado from the north or south, take I–25, which intersects with I–70 in Denver. If you're entering from the east or west, I–70 bisects the state. Idaho Springs, Summit Country, the Vail Valley, and Glenwood Springs are all on I–70. Winter Park is north of I–70, on U.S. 40, which has several hairpin turns. Leadville and Ski Cooper are south of I–70 along U.S. 24 or Route 91. Steamboat Springs is most easily reached via Route 131, north from I–70. Aspen/Snowmass can be reached via Route 82, south from I–70.

By Train
Amtrak (800/872–7245) offers service from Denver's Union Station to the Winter Park Ski Area station in nearby Fraser (where shuttles to the area are available). Glenwood Springs is on the *California Zephyr* route.

The nonstop **Denver Rio Grande Bud Light Ski Train** (☎ 303/296–4754) leaves Denver's Union Station every Sunday morning, chugging through stunning scenery and 29 tunnels before depositing passengers only 50 yards from Winter Park's lifts.

By Bus
Greyhound Lines (☎ 800/231–2222) offers regular service from Denver to several towns along I–70.

Getting Around

By Bus or Shuttle
For intercity bus service try **Greyhound Lines** (call local listings). Free shuttles serving the resorts are offered throughout the area.

Aspen/Snowmass: Within Snowmass there is free shuttle service; five colored flags denote the various routes. The **Roaring Fork Transit**

Agency (☎ 970/925–8484) provides free shuttle service within Aspen and between Aspen and Snowmass.

Steamboat: **Steamboat Springs Transit** (☎ 970/879–3717) provides transportation between the mountain and the town, and costs 50¢ per trip.

Summit County: **Summit Stage** (☎ 970/453–1339) links Breckenridge, Frisco, Copper Mountain, Dillon, Silverthorne, and Keystone for free. **Breckenridge Free Shuttle and Trolley** (no ☎) runs through town and up to the ski area, **E.A.S.E.** (☎ 970/468–2316, ext. 4200) serves the extended Keystone area, and **KAB Express** (no ☎) serves Keystone/Arapahoe Basin and Breckenridge. The **Frisco Flyer** (☎ 970/668–5276) provides service throughout Frisco.

Vail Valley: **Avon Beaver Creek Transit** (☎ 970/949–6121) runs free shuttles the length of the valley, daily, between 7 AM and 1:30 AM, every 10 minutes.

Winter Park: The **Winter Park Lift** (☎ 970/726–4163) is the area's free shuttle service.

By Car
I–70 is a fast, convenient superhighway that is remarkably well maintained. All major sights in this tour are either on I–70 or on clearly marked side routes.

By Taxi
Aspen/Snowmass: **Aspen Limousine** (☎ 970/925–2400) and **High Mountain Taxi** (☎ 970/925–8294); Glenwood Springs: **Glenwood Taxi** (☎ 970/945–2225); Steamboat Springs: **Alpine Taxi** (☎ 970/879–8294); Summit County: **Around Town Taxi** (☎ 970/453–8294) and in Dillon, **Summit Taxi Service** (☎ 970/468–8294); Vail Valley: **Vail Valley Taxi** (☎ 970/476–8294).

Guided Tours

Orientation
A romantic way to orient yourself to Aspen is by taking the **T Lazy Seven Ranch** (☎ 970/925–4614) stagecoach tour of its downtown area.

In Breckenridge, the **Breckenridge Historical Society** (☎ 970/453–9022; tours run Wed.–Sat. 11 AM) offers lively 1½-hour tours of Colorado's largest National Historic District.

Several tour companies include Idaho Springs on their itineraries, and the **Idaho Springs Visitor Information Center** (2200 Miner St., ☎ 970/567–4382) can supply information.

Special Interest
In summer, narrated bus tours from Aspen to the spectacular **Maroon Bells** are available (☎ 970/925–8484). Steamboat's **Sweet Pea Tours** (☎ 970/879–5820) and **Peak Experience** (☎ 970/879–8125) visit nearby hot springs. Vail's **Nova Guides** (☎ 970/949–4232) offers Jeep and ATV (all-terrain vehicle) tours, as well as rafting, fishing, snowmobiling, and hiking expeditions.

Important Addresses and Numbers

Hospitals
Aspen/Snowmass: **Aspen Valley Hospital** (0200 Castle Creek Rd., ☎ 970/925–1120); Glenwood Springs: **Valley View Hospital** (6535 Blake St., ☎ 970/945–8566); Summit County: **Summit Medical Center** (Rte. 9 and School Rd., Frisco, ☎ 970/668–3300); Vail Valley: **Vail Moun-**

tain Medical (181 W. Meadow Dr., Vail, ☎ 970/476–5695); **Beaver Creek Village Medical Center** (1280 Village Rd., Beaver Creek, ☎ 970/949–0800).

Visitor Information

Aspen Chamber Resort Association (328 E. Hyman Ave., ☎ 970/925–5656; and 425 Rio Grande Pl., tel. 970/925–1940); **Breckenridge Resort Chamber** (309 N. Main St., ☎ 970/453–6018); **Georgetown Visitor Center** (404 6th St., ☎ 970/569–2555); **Glenwood Springs Chamber Resort Association** (806 Cooper Ave., ☎ 970/945–6589 or 800/221–0098); **Leadville Chamber of Commerce** (809 Harrison St., ☎ 719/486–3900); **Steamboat Springs Chamber Resort Association** (1255 S. Lincoln Ave., ☎ 970/879–0880 or 800/922–2722); **Summit County Chamber of Commerce** (Main St., Frisco, ☎ 970/668–5000 or 800/530–3099); **Vail Valley Tourism and Convention Bureau** (100 E. Meadow Dr., ☎ 970/476–1000 or 800/525–3875); and a Tourist Information Center in the Vail Village and Lionshead parking structures).

4 Southwest Colorado

COLORADO" IS A SPANISH WORD meaning ruddy or colorful—adjectives that clearly describe many regions of the state, but particularly the Southwest, with the Four Corners region and the San Juans. The terrain varies widely—from yawning black canyons and desolate monochrome moonscapes to pastel deserts and mesas, shimmering sapphire lakes, and 14,000-foot mountains. It's so rugged in the Southwest that a four-wheel-drive vehicle is necessary to explore the wild and beautiful backcountry.

The region's history and people are as colorful as the landscape, from the mysterious Anasazi (meaning "ancient ones"), who constructed impressive cliff dwellings in Mesa Verde National Park to notorious outlaws such as Butch Cassidy, who embarked on his storied career by robbing the Telluride Bank in 1889. Even today, the more ornery, independent locals, disgusted with the political system, periodically talk of seceding. They're as rough as the country they inhabit.

Southwest Colorado offers such diversity that, depending on where you go, you can have radically different vacations, even during the same season. Visit the world-class resorts of Crested Butte, Purgatory, and Telluride for quality ski and golf holidays; then move on to the Old West railroad town of Durango, followed by a pilgrimage to the Anasazi ruins that dot the area. Even for Colorado, the combination of recreational, historical, and cultural opportunities is diverse.

EXPLORING

Tour 1: The San Juans, the Four Corners and the "Million Dollar Highway"

This tour spirals from the towering peaks of the San Juan range to the plunging Black Canyon of the Gunnison, taking in Colorado's most stunning alpine scenery along the way, as well as the eerie remains of old mining camps, before winding through striking desert landscapes, the superlative Anasazi ruins, and the Old West town of Durango.

Numbers in the margin correspond to points of interest on the Southwest Colorado map.

❶ Crested Butte is literally just over the mountain from Aspen, but a 15-minute scenic flight or one-hour drive in summer turns into a four-hour trek by car in winter, when Kebler Pass is closed. The town of Crested Butte was declared a National Historic District and, like Aspen, was once a quaint mining center whose exquisite, pastel, Victorian gingerbread–trimmed houses remain. Unlike Aspen, however, Crested Butte never became chic. A recent controversial ad campaign about its ski area (3 miles from town) touts it as: "Aspen like it used to be, and Vail like it never was."

That boast might make the locals seem crustier than they are; they're just proud and independent, with a puckish sense of humor. In fact, in a state that prides itself on hospitality, Crested Butte just may be the friendliest ski town of them all. Tony, the over-80 proprietor of the Sunoco station, is a font of information (some unprintable) about the place; but you won't have a difficult time finding other sources. A sense of warmth and whimsy pervades the area, most evident in the hot pink, magenta, and chartreuse facades of the buildings along Elk Avenue, the main drag. And for proof that nothing "em-bare-asses" the locals,

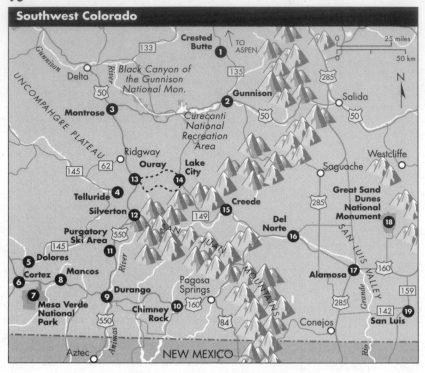

check out the diehards streaking down the mountain nude on the last day of the season, or join the mavericks (for this event fully clothed) who hike up Snodgrass (slated for development as Crested Butte West) and bomb down every full moon.

Crested Butte Mountain Resort is a trailblazer and renegade in many respects: it initiated a daring—and wildly successful—venture in which everyone skis free the first four weeks of the season, and first timers get free lessons. While many resorts are limiting their "out-of-bounds" terrain due to increasing insurance costs and lawsuits, Crested Butte is thumbing its nose at the establishment by steadily increasing its extreme skiing terrain, which now speaks for 550 ungroomed acres. The Extreme Limits and The North Face should only be attempted by experts but there are plenty of cruisable trails for recreational skiers. In the summer, mountain bikers challenge the same slopes, which are blanketed with columbine and Indian paintbrush.

Crested Butte is considered the quintessential ski bum's town: friendly, reasonably priced, cute as hell, great bars, impressive restaurants, and a gnarly mountain that remains far less crowded than its better-known neighbors.

The Route 135 scenic loop goes west from Crested Butte over Kebler Pass to **Paonia,** and south through banks of cottonwoods (which usually attract several swooping bald eagles) to **Gunnison.** At the confluence of the Gunnison River and Tomichi Creek, Gunnison has been a fishing and hunting community ever since the Utes adopted it as their summer hunting grounds. It provides economical lodging for those skiing Crested Butte and for backpackers, mountain bikers, and fishermen in summer.

The **Gunnison County Chamber of Commerce** (500 E. Tomichi Ave., ☎ 970/641–1501) issues an informative historical walking-tour brochure of downtown. Those interested in the region's history can also stop by the **Pioneer Museum,** a living history complex that includes several buildings and relics that date from the late 19th century. *U.S. 50 and S. Adams St.,* ☎ *970/641–4530.* ☛ *$3 adults, $1 children 6–12.* ⊙ *Memorial Day–Labor Day, Mon.–Sat. 9–5, Sun. 1–5.*

Aside from its easy access to Crested Butte, Gunnison is recognized for two other things. Its Western State College, the local seat of higher learning, boasts a 320-foot by 420-foot whitewashed rock shaped like a W and located on Tenderfoot Mountain, just to the north of the campus. Ostensibly, this is the largest collegiate insignia in the world. Gunnison's other claim to fame is that the town has recorded some of the coldest temperatures ever reported in the continental United States.

Nine miles west of Gunnison is the **Curecanti National Recreation Area** (☎ 970/641–2337), set amid a striking eroded volcanic landscape and stretching for more than 60 miles. The area was created in the '60s by a series of dams that resulted in three reservoirs, including **Blue Mesa**—the state's largest body of water. The reservoirs provide a wealth of aquatic recreational opportunities, as well as fine camping and hiking. At the western entrance to the recreation area, the **Cimarron Visitor Center** (☎ 970/249–4074; open daily 9–5) displays vintage locomotives, an 1882 trestle listed on the National Register of Historic Places, and a reconstruction of a railroad stockyard.

Once liberated from the restrictions of Curecanti, the Gunnison River slices through one of the West's most awe-inspiring sights, the **Black Canyon of the Gunnison National Monument,** a vivid testament to the powers of erosion. This 2,500-foot-deep gash in the earth's crust is 1,300 feet wide at its top and only 40 feet wide at the bottom. The canyon's name comes from the fact that so little sunlight penetrates its depths, the eternal shadows permitting scant plant growth on its steep walls. The Black Canyon lies 60 miles west of Gunnison, on Route 347 North, off U.S. 50. The fine **visitor center** (☎ 970/249–1915 or 970/249–7036; open Apr.–Sept., daily 9–5) includes exhibits on the region's geology, history, and flora and fauna, and schedules nature walks to the canyon's forbidding rim.

❸ Montrose, the self-described "Home of the Black Canyon," is another 7 miles west along U.S. 50. Though it sits amid glorious surroundings, it is an otherwise nondescript town with little more than a collection of truck stops, trailer parks, and strip malls. However, Montrose is perfectly placed for exploring Curecanti and the Black Canyon to the east, the San Juans to the south, the world's largest flattop mountain, Grand Mesa (*see* Exploring *in* Chapter 7, Northwest Colorado) to the north, and the fertile Uncompahgre Plateau to the west.

If you're interested in learning more about the original residents of the area, stop by the excellent **Ute Indian Museum,** a mile south of town on U.S. 550. The museum contains several dioramas and the most comprehensive collection of Ute materials and artifacts in Colorado. *17253 Chipeta Dr.,* ☎ *970/249–3098.* ☛ *$2.* ⊙ *Mid-May–Sept., Mon.–Sat. 10–5 and Sun. 1–5.*

TIME OUT Gum-cracking waitresses serve up huge portions of gravy-laden food at **Sally's Café** (715 S. Townsend Ave., ☎ 970/249–6096). The menu has it all, from Mexi-burgers, patty melts, chicken-fried steak, and grilled PB&J sandwiches to Duncan Hines cakes and dull-as-dirty-dishwater coffee. The decor, too, reflects a quirky, local flavor, with a reindeer made out of an old clock that hangs on the wall, and Sally's own diverse collection of china ("I like my dishes," says Sally with typical understatement).

Head south on U.S. 550 to Ridgway, notable mainly for its strategic location at the junction of U.S. 550 and Route 62. These two routes fan out from the town to form one of the country's most stupendously scenic drives, the **San Juan Skyway,** which weaves through a series of fourteeners (a Rockies term for peaks reaching more than 14,000 feet) and picturesque mining towns. U.S. 550 continues through historic Ouray and Silverton to Durango. Route 62 and Route 145 reach Durango via the extraordinary Anasazi cliff dwellings of Mesa Verde National Park.

Take Route 62 to its juncture with Route 145 East, to one of Colorado's hottest destinations. Tucked like a jewel in a tiny valley caught between azure sky and gunmetal mountains is **Telluride,** once so inaccessible that it was a favorite hideout for desperadoes such as Butch Cassidy, who robbed his first bank here in 1889. Some locals claim the town is named not after the mineral Tellurium, but the saying "To Hell You Ride."

The savage but beautiful terrain now attracts mountain people of a different sort—alpinists, snowboarders, freestylers, mountain bikers, and freewheeling four-wheelers—who attack any incline, up or down, and do so with abandon. As one local quips, "The Wild Bunch is alive and well."

The ski area, too, is not for the faint of heart. Telluride poses the ultimate test for skiers, with one legendary challenging run after another. In particular, the terrain accessed by Chairlift Nine, including the famed "Spiral Staircase" and "The Plunge," is for experts only (although one side of "The Plunge" is groomed for advanced skiers). Telluride has also expanded its "ultimate skiing" terrain to include more than 400 acres on Gold Hill. Forgotten in the excitement of all the challenge is that Telluride has a superb beginners' and learners' area; it's middle-of-the-road intermediates who may find themselves between a rock and a hard place.

The town's independent spirit is shaped not only by its mining legacy, but also by the social ferment of the '60s and early '70s. Before the ski area opened in 1971, Telluride had been as remote as it was back in Cassidy's day. It was even briefly included on the "Ghost Town Club of Colorado" itinerary, but that was before countercultural types moved in, seeking to lose themselves in the wilderness. By 1974 the town's orientation had changed so radically that the entire council was composed of hippies. Today there is one holdover—Councilman Rasta Stevie (he's white, but his waist-length dreadlocks might have made Bob Marley envious)—who cheerfully admits, "I came to power through the dirtbags." Regardless of future development, Stevie defends an enduring Telluride tradition called the Freebox (Pine St. and Colorado Ave.), where indigent residents can sort through and take whatever used clothing and appliances they need. (One memorable day, just after a fur shop had the temerity to open in town, surprised residents found a wide selection of minks, sables, and chinchillas at the Box. After the mysterious break-in, the furriers got the point and moved on.)

Despite such efforts at keeping such visible signs of wealth away, more and more locals are finding they can no longer afford to live here. Things were fine when the town was isolated, but thanks to the construction of the Telluride Regional Airport in the late 1980s, it's become quite accessible. Today Telluride is positioning itself as an upscale alternative to Vail and Aspen, and celebrities who need only be identified by their first names (Arnold and Oprah, for example) own homes.

Telluride is chic—and not everyone's happy about it. Many townies deplore the mushrooming Telluride Mountain Village development at the base of the ski area, and some bitterly resent The Peaks at Telluride, a glamorous resort/spa. The ambivalence felt about the influx of wealth and new buildings brings into question whether development is inevitable; whether the pristine can be preserved in this fast-paced world. For better or worse, Telluride is gorgeous. Every corner of the town yields stunning prospects of the San Juans, which loom either menacingly or protectively, depending on the lighting.

The 425-foot liquid diamond **Bridal Veil Falls,** Colorado's highest cascade, tumbles lavishly just a short hike from the end of Colorado Avenue, the main street. The town itself offers one pastel Victorian residence or frontier trading post after another, as well as the 1883 **San Miguel County Courthouse** and the 1895 **New Sheridan Hotel and Opera House.** (*Telluride Magazine* prints an excellent historic walking tour in its "Visitors' Guide" section.) Today it's hard to believe that those lovingly restored shops and restaurants once housed gaming parlors and saloons known for the quality of their "waitressing."

That party-hearty spirit lives on, evidenced by the numerous annual events held here. Highly regarded wine and wild mushroom festivals alternate with musical performances celebrating everything from bluegrass to jazz to chamber music. And the Telluride Film Festival is one of the world's leading showcases for the latest releases.

TIME OUT **The House** (131 N. Fir St., ☎ 970/728–6207) is set in a building once dubbed "The Freak House" for the colorful characters who lived here in the '70s and '80s. These days the atmosphere is more refined—likened to a European pub by owner Tom Wirth—with fine ales on tap, along with cribbage, backgammon, Trivial Pursuit, and chess.

Continue southwest along Route 145, which follows the course of the lovely Dolores River. In 1968, construction of an irrigation dam was authorized, forming the **McPhee Reservoir,** a haven for boaters and fishermen. An environmental-impact study was mandated by law, and concluded that hundreds of potentially valuable archaeological sites would be flooded. This led to massive, federally funded excavations and the creation of one of the West's model museums, The Anasazi Heritage Center, 3 miles west of Dolores.

The Anasazi, a mysterious and talented people who thrived until 1300, were probably the ancestors of present-day Pueblo tribes. They left behind a legacy of stunning ruins, both freestanding pueblos and ingenious cliff dwellings. No one knows for sure why they abandoned their homes, although most anthropologists surmise a combination of drought and overfarming sent them off in search of greener pastures.

The first white explorers to stumble upon Anasazi ruins were the Spanish friars Dominguez and Escalante, who set out in 1776 from Santa Fe to find a safe overland route to Monterey, California. The two major ruins at the **Anasazi Heritage Center** (27501 Rte. 184, ☎ 970/882–4811; ☛ Free; open daily 9–5) are named for them. The Dominguez site, right next to the parking lot, is unimpressive, although of great archaeological interest because extremely rare evidence of a "high-status burial" was found here. The Escalante site, a half-mile hike away, is a 20-room masonry pueblo standing eerie guard over McPhee Reservoir.

The state-of-the-art facility houses the finest artifacts culled from more than 1,500 excavations, as well as a theater, a library, a gift shop, and a full-scale replica of an Anasazi pit-house dwelling that illustrates how the Anasazi lived around 850. The complex is particularly notable for its Discovery Center, a series of hands-on, hologramlike interactive displays that enable visitors to weave on a Navajo loom, grind corn, even generate an Anasazi village using a computer.

⑤ Continue south along Route 145, passing through **Dolores** to its enchanting **Galloping Goose Museum** (5th St. and Rte. 145, ☎ 970/882–4018), a replica of a Victorian train station that contains an original narrow-gauge locomotive. The gentle rising hump to the southwest is **Sleeping Ute Mountain,** which resembles the reclining silhouette of a Native American replete with headdress. The site is revered by the Ute Mountain tribe as a great warrior god who, mortally wounded in a titanic battle with the evil ones, lapsed into eternal sleep, his flowing blood turning into the life-giving Dolores and Animas rivers.

⑥ At the juncture of Route 145 and U.S. 160 is **Cortez,** dominated by the northern escarpment of Mesa Verde and the volcanic blisters of the La Plata mountains to the west. The sprawling town is an unrelieved tedium of Days Inns, Dairy Queens, and Best Westerns, its architecture seemingly determined by neon-sign and aluminum-siding salesmen of the '50s. Hidden among these, however, are fine galleries and a host of pawn shops that can yield surprising finds.

There is a **Colorado Welcome Center** here (160 E. Main St., ☎ 970/565–4048), as well as the excellent **Cortez/Colorado University Center,** its exterior painted to resemble the cliff dwellings of Mesa Verde. Inside the University Center are changing exhibits on regional artists and artisans, as well as permanent displays on the Ute Mountain branch of the Ute tribe, and various periods of Anasazi culture. Summer evenings include Native American dances; sandpainting, rug weaving, and pottery-making demonstrations; and storytelling events. The related **Cultural Park** contains an authentic Navaho hogan and a Ute tepee. *25 N. Market St., ☎ 970/565–1151. ☛ Free; donations accepted. ☉ Daily 9–5.*

TIME OUT **Earth Song Haven** (34 E. Main St., ☎ 970/247–0470) is a fine bookstore, with an espresso bar and tearoom in back. Cortez seems an unlikely spot for this European touch, but the café makes wonderful coffees, sandwiches, and high-calorie desserts such as peanut-butter cream pie.

⑦ Cortez is the gateway to **Mesa Verde National Park,** an 80-square-mile area that forms one of America's most riveting attractions. In 1888, two ranchers—Richard Wetherill and Charlie Mason—set off in search of stray cattle and stumbled upon the remarkable and perfectly preserved **Cliff Palace,** apartment-style cliff dwellings built into the canyon walls. By the next day's end they had discovered two more major sites: Spruce Tree House and Square Tower House. Excitement over their find culminated in the 1906 creation of the national park by Congress, making it the first park established to preserve the works of humankind.

Mesa Verde is one of Colorado's highlights, but consider either going off-season (though many of the ruins are closed) or overnighting in the park (after the tour buses have departed) to appreciate its full effect, without the crowds. The entrance, where you can pick up information on the park's attractions and accommodations, is 10 miles east of Cortez

Valuable ski tips for a perfect season.

Fly United Airlines there and back.
There are very few runs we don't cover. We've added more flights, with more
weekend nonstops, straight to the slopes too. And on many flights you can have
all your equipment pre-delivered to and from your destination with our exclusive
Up the Hill, Down the Hill® service. No wonder we're the skier's airline.
For information, call 1-800-241-6522. Come fly our friendly skies.

 **UNITED AIRLINES**

No matter where you go, travel is easier when you know the code.[SM]

dial 1 8 0 0 CALL ATT®

Dial 1 800 CALL ATT and you'll always get through from any phone with any card* and you'll always get AT&T's best deal.** It's the one number to remember when calling away from home.

*Other long distance company calling cards excluded.
**Additional discounts available.

AT&T
Your True Choice

©1995 AT&T

on U.S. 160. From here a 15-mile drive corkscrews up the mesa, skirting canyons and plateaus, to the **Far View Visitor Center.** ☎ *970/529–4461 or 970/529–4475.* ☛ *To park: $5 per vehicle.* ☺ *Visitor center: daily 8–6.*

From the visitor center, you can head in one of two directions within the park. Your first option is to take the scenic route to **Wetherill Mesa** (open Memorial Day–Labor Day), which affords spectacular vistas of the Shiprock Formation in New Mexico and Monument Valley in Arizona and Utah. A minitram departs every half hour between 8:55 AM and 4:55 PM from the Wetherill parking lot, on a 4-mile loop to view the ruins; self-guided and ranger-led tours of Long House, the second-largest dwelling in the park, are also options. The other Far View route, **Ruins Road,** accesses the major sites on Chapin Mesa in two 6-mile loops. If you don't want to hike down into the canyons to view the ruins up close (which requires a free ticket available at the visitor center), this drive offers several strategic overlooks.

The first stop on the Ruins Road is the park's informative archaeological museum, which traces the development of Anasazi/Pueblo culture. It's a short walk from the museum to one of the most extraordinary sites, **Spruce Tree House,** the only ruin open year-round. Here you can climb down into an excavated kiva (Native American ceremonial structure, usually partly underground), symbolic of the womb of Mother Earth, for a better sense of how the Anasazis worshiped.

From the museum trailhead, one loop leads to the most famous ruin, **Cliff Palace,** the largest dwelling of its kind in the world (accessible by a moderately strenuous 15-minute hike), and to the more remote **Balcony House** (an arduous trek into the canyon below). Ranger-guided tours are available. The other loop accesses two major ruins, **Sun Temple** and **Square Tower House,** both involving a significant amount of walking and climbing.

Cortez is also convenient to two other spectacular Anasazi sites—**Lowry Pueblo** and **Hovenweep National Monument**—the latter of which straddles the Utah-Colorado border (*see* Other Points of Interest, *below*).

Driving east on U.S. 160 from Mesa Verde will take you past an endearing bit of classic American kitsch, the **Mud Creek Hogan** (U.S. 160, ☎ 970/533–7117). More than a dozen enormous arrows stuck in the ground mark the spot of this hokey trading post and museum (where you get the feeling that everything is for sale) adorned with tepees and a giant plastic horse. Beside the shop is a re-creation of a frontier town, replete with saloon, hotel, bank, jail, and livery station. Don't breathe too hard or you'll blow the town over: The "buildings" are only fronts.

❽ The highway winds through the lush Mancos Valley, passing through the small and charming town of **Mancos,** which exudes Old West ambience. There are several excellent crafts shops that offer everything from saddles to 10-gallon hats, and a cute **Cowboy Museum** (100 Bauer St., ☎ 970/533–7563) in a restored mansion that also houses a B&B and the Old Mesa Verde Inn restaurant. The **Mancos State Recreation Area** offers a wealth of activities, including **Ski Hesperus** (*see* Sports and the Outdoors, *below*), a small ski area a few miles farther east.

❾ U.S. 160 now approaches a classic Western town, **Durango,** of which Will Rogers once observed, "It's out of the way and glad of it." His crack is a bit unfair, considering that as a railroad town Durango has always been a cultural crossroads and melting pot (as well as a place to raise hell). It was founded in 1879 by General William Palmer (president of the all-powerful Denver & Rio Grande Railroad), when nearby Animas City haughtily refused to donate land for a depot; within a decade Durango had absorbed its rival completely. The booming town quickly became the region's main metropolis and a gateway to the Southwest. A walking tour of the historic downtown bears eloquent witness to Durango's prosperity in the late 19th century. The northern end of Main Avenue offers the usual assortment of cheap motels and fast-food outlets, all evidence of Durango's present status as the major hub for tourism in the area.

At 13th Avenue and Main Avenue (also known as Main Street)—the beginning of its National Historic District—the tenor changes dramatically, with old-fashioned gas lamps gracing the streets and a superlative collection of Victorians filled with chic galleries, restaurants, and brand-name outlet stores. The 1882 **Train Depot** (4th St. and Main Ave.), the 1887 **Strater Hotel** (7th St. and Main Ave.), and the three-story sandstone **Newman Building** (8th St. and Main Ave.) are among the elegant edifices restored to their original grandeur. Stop into the **Diamond Belle Saloon** (in the Strater Hotel)—awash in velour and lace, with a player piano, gilt-and-mahogany bar, and scantily clad Gay '90s waitresses—for a wonderfully authentic re-creation of an old-time honky-tonk.

The **Third Avenue National Historic District** (known simply as "The Boulevard"), two blocks east of Main Avenue, offers one of America's most outstanding displays of Victorian residences, ranging from the imposing mansions of railroad and smelting executives to more modest variations erected by well-to-do merchants. The delightful hodgepodge of styles veers from Greek Revival to Gothic Revival to Queen Anne to Spanish Colonial and Mission designs.

In Durango, the most entertaining way to relive those halcyon days is to take a ride on the **Durango & Silverton Narrow Gauge Railroad,** an eight-hour, round-trip journey along the 45-mile railway. You'll travel in comfort in restored 1882 parlor cars, and listen to the train's shrill whistle as the locomotive chugs along the fertile Animas River Valley and, at times, clings precariously to the hillside. *479 Main Ave.,* ☎ *970/247–2733.* ✒ *$42.70 adults, $21.45 children. Operates Apr.–Oct. and late Nov.–Jan. 1 daily; times vary.*

🔟 At the junction of U.S. 550 and U.S. 160 you have two options: Pick up U.S. 550 North and continue the tour, or follow U.S. 160 East for a 35-mile excursion to **Chimney Rock,** so-named for the distinctive, twin-rock spires that architecturally are more closely related to the Chaco Canyon Anasazi sites in New Mexico than to those in Mesa Verde. Anthropologists debate whether the rocks served as a trading post or as an astronomical observatory of great religious significance. Whatever the origin, many believe that the mystical ruins retain tremendous power and resonance. Access to the site is only possible with a Forest Service guide; reservations are mandatory for the free tour. For information contact the **Pagosa Springs Forest Ranger District** (☎ 970/264–2268).

If you choose to continue on the tour's direct route, take U.S. 550 North along the section of the San Juan Skyway that's otherwise known as the **Million Dollar Highway.** Depending on whom you ask, the name refers to either the million dollars worth of gold and silver mined each mile along the stretch, the low-grade ore from mining residue that was used to pave the road, the cost of the road's construction, or the million-dollar views it offers.

TIME OUT Seven miles north of Durango lies **Trimble Hot Springs** (U.S. 550, follow signs, ☎ 970/247–0111), a great place to soak your aching bones, especially if you've been doing some hiking.

Fifteen and 25 miles north (respectively) from the U.S. 160 and U.S. 550 junction are two famous recreational playgrounds: the ravishing golf course and development at **Tamarron** (*see* Lodging, *below*) and the ⑪ **Purgatory Ski Area.** Purgatory is about as down-home as it gets, with clientele that runs toward families, cowboys, and college kids on break. Purgatory's ad campaign proudly tells it like it is: "No movie stars here" and "You don't have to be a celebrity to be treated like a star."

What's unique about Purgatory is its stepped terrain: lots of humps and dips, steep pitches followed by virtual flats. This profile makes it difficult for skiers to lose control. There are some great powder days on the mountain's back side that will convince anyone that Purgatory isn't just "Pleasant Ridge," as it's derisively known in Crested Butte and Telluride. Unfortunately, the resort has had some financial problems recently, and in 1993 it narrowly avoided bankruptcy when Norwest Bank sought a more favorable repayment schedule. However, a deal was worked out that will enable the area to operate as usual at least until the 1996–97 season.

The tortuous northern route begins a dizzying series of switchbacks as it climbs over the Molas Pass, yielding splendid vistas of the Grand Turks, the Needles Range, and Crater Lake. This is prime mountain biking and four-wheeler territory. On the other side of the pass you'll ⑫ reach **Silverton,** an isolated, unspoiled old mining community ringed by glorious peaks. It reputedly got its name when a miner exclaimed, "We ain't got much gold but we got a ton of silver!" The entire town is a National Historic Landmark District. The Chamber of Commerce (414 Greene St., ☎ 970/387–5654) has issued a fact-filled walking-tour brochure that describes—among other things—the most impressive buildings lining Greene Street: **Miners' Union Hall,** the **Teller House, Town Hall, San Juan County Courthouse** (site of the county historical museum), and the **Grand Imperial Hotel.** These structures hold historical significance, but more history was probably made in the raucous red-light district along Blair Street.

Silverton has always been a rowdy town with a hardy populace, and that spirit remains. Every summer evening at 5:30, gunfights are staged at the corner of Blair and 12th streets. But the lawlessness evoked by such events is only part of the heritage that the town wishes to commemorate. If you look north toward Anvil Mountain, you'll see the community's touching tribute to miners—the **Christ of the Mines Shrine**—built in the '50s out of Carrara marble.

⑬ **Ouray,** 23 miles north, over Red Mountain Pass, is a town trapped in a narrow, steep-walled valley in the bullying shadow cast by rugged peaks of the San Juan Mountains. The ravishing setting amply explains the town's nickname, "The Switzerland of America." It was named for the great Southern Ute chief Ouray, labeled a visionary by the U.S. Army and branded a traitor by his people because he attempted to assimilate the Utes into white society. The mining town is yet another National Historic Landmark District, with a glittering array of lavish old hotels and residences. More than 25 classic edifices are included in the historic walking-tour brochure issued by the Chamber of Commerce (1222 Main St., ☎ 970/325–4746); among the points of interest are the grandiose **Wright's Opera House; the Beaumont, Western,** and **St. Elmo hotels;** and **the Elks Lodge.**

Ouray's architecture is notable, but the town's ultimate glory lies in its surroundings, and it has become an increasingly popular destination for climbers (both mountain and ice varieties), fat-tire fanatics, and hikers. One particularly gorgeous jaunt is to **Box Canyon Falls and Park,** just south of town, off U.S. 550. The turbulent waters of Clear Creek (part of the falls) thunder 285 feet down a narrow gorge. A steel suspension bridge and various well-marked trails afford breathtaking panoramic vistas.

More opportunities to immerse yourself in nature present themselves at the various hot springs in the area. It's hard to tell which is more revivifying: the 104-degree waters or the views of surrounding peaks at the **Ouray Hot Springs Pool.** *U.S. 550 at the north end of town,* ☏ *970/325–4638.* ☞ *$4 adults, $3.50 students 13–17, $2.75 children 5–12 and senior citizens.* ◷ *June–Sept., daily 10–10; Oct.–May, Mon.–Wed. noon–9.*

From Ouray, you can continue north for 13 miles on U.S. 550 on your return to Ridgway, where this tour began; or follow the four-wheel-drive **Alpine Loop Scenic Byway** (*see* Four-Wheel Driving *in* Sports and the Outdoors, *below*), which shimmies through stunning scenery on its way to Lake City, 45 miles south and east.

⑭ **Lake City** is noted for the superb hiking and fishing in Uncompahgre National Forest, especially at Lake San Cristobal. The town—with its collection of lacy gingerbread–trimmed houses and false-front Victorians—also has the largest National Historic Landmark District in Colorado. But Lake City is best known for the lurid history surrounding a notorious gentleman named Alferd Packer. Packer was a member of a party of six prospectors who camped near Lake San Cristobal during the winter of 1874. That spring, only Packer emerged from the mountains, claiming to have been deserted, and to have subsisted on roots and rabbits. Soon after, a Ute came across a grisly scene: strips of human flesh and crushed skulls. Packer protested his innocence and fled, but a manhunt ensued; Packer was finally caught nine years later, tried, and sentenced to life (he was convicted of manslaughter because of a technicality). As one wag noted at the time, "There were but six dimmocrats in Hinsdale County and he et five of 'em." To this day the event is commemorated by an Alferd Packer Barbecue, held annually in June.

Tour 2: The San Luis Valley

At 8,000 square miles, the San Luis Valley is the world's largest alpine valley, stunningly nestled between the San Juan Mountains to the west and the Sangre de Cristo range to the east. Despite its average altitude of 7,500 feet, its sheltering peaks help to create a relatively mild climate. The valley is one of Colorado's major agricultural producers, with huge annual crops of potatoes, carrots, canola, barley, and lettuce. It's so self-sufficient that local businessmen threatened to secede in the '50s to prove that the state couldn't get along without the valley and its valuable produce.

Watered by the mighty Rio Grande and its tributaries, the San Luis Valley also supports a magnificent array of wildlife, including flocks of sandhill and even whooping cranes. The range of terrain is equally impressive, from the soaring fourteener, Mt. Blanca, to the stark moonscape of the Wheeler Geologic Area to the tawny, undulating Great Sand Dunes National Monument.

The area was settled first by the Ute, then by the Spanish who left their indelible imprint in the town names and local architecture. The oldest town (San Luis), the oldest military post (Ft. Garland), and the oldest church (Our Lady of Guadalupe in Conejos) in the state are in this valley. It's no surprise that this is a highly religious, traditional area. The natural beauty is simply awe-inspiring.

⑮ Travel east on Route 149 from Lake City to **Creede,** which once earned a reputation as Colorado's rowdiest mining camp and was immortalized in an evocative poem by the local newspaper editor, Cy Warman: "It's day all day in daytime, and there is no night in Creede." Every other building was a saloon or bordello. Bob Ford, who killed Jesse James, was himself gunned down here; other notorious residents included Calamity Jane and Bat Masterson. As delightful as the town is, its location is even more glorious, with the pristine **Weminuche Wilderness** 30 miles to the south and the **Wheeler Geologic areas** 20 miles to the west, where the unusual rock formations resemble playful abstract sculptures or an M. C. Escher creation.

The **Creede Museum,** occupying the original Denver & Rio Grande Railroad Depot, paints a vivid portrait of those rough-and-tumble days. Highlights include an underground firehouse and mining museum. *6th and San Luis Sts., ☎ 719/658–2374. ☛ $3. ⊙ Memorial Day–Labor Day, daily 10–4.*

⑯ Continue along Route 149—declared the Silver Thread National Scenic Byway—on its impossibly beautiful journey east through South Fork (where Route 149 joins U.S. 160) and the **Rio Grande National Forest** to **Del Norte.** The route flirts with the Rio Grande, passes near the majestic North Clear Creek Falls, and ambles through numerous ghost towns along the way. In and around Del Norte are several historic sites, one of which is an original 1870s station on the **Barlow-Sanderson Stagecoach Line.**

The **Rio Grande County Museum and Cultural Center,** in town, celebrates the region's multicultural heritage with displays of petroglyphs, mining artifacts, early Spanish relics, and rotating shows of contemporary art. *580 Oak St., ☎ 719/657–2847. ☛ $2. ⊙ Mid-May–Labor Day, Mon.–Sat. 10–5; Labor Day–mid-May, weekdays 10–4.*

Just west of town is the gaping **Penitente Canyon,** which is usually crawling with climbers. Several miles north of town, off Route 112, near La Garita, is another marvel—the towering rock formation **La Ventana Natural Arch.**

⑰ About 20 miles farther east at the junction of U.S. 160 and U.S. 285 is **Alamosa,** the valley's major city, best known as the Olympic high-altitude training center for long-distance runners. Just outside town is the **Alamosa National Vista Wildlife Refuge;** these natural and man-made wetlands—an anomaly amid the arid surroundings—are an important sanctuary for the nearly extinct whooping crane and its cousin, the sandhill. *9383 El Rancho La., ☎ 719/589–4021. ☛ Free. ⊙ Daily 9–sunset.*

The attractive **Adams State College** complex (in town, along Main Street) contains several superlative examples of 1930s, WPA-commissioned murals in its administrative building. The admirable **Luther Bean Museum and Art Gallery,** on campus, displays European porcelain and furniture collections in a handsome, wood-paneled 19th-century drawing room, and changing exhibits of regional arts and crafts. *Richardson Hall, Main St., ☎ 719/589–7151; ☛ Free; open weekdays 1–5.*

⑱ Alamosa also serves as the gateway to the **Great Sand Dunes National Monument,** 35 miles northeast and reached via U.S. 160 and Route 150. Created by windswept grains from the Rio Grande floor, the sand dunes—which rise up to 700 feet in height—are an improbable, unforgettable sight silhouetted against the sagebrush plains and looming forested slopes of the San Juans. The dunes, as curvaceous as Rubens' nudes, stretch for 55 square miles and are painted with light and shadow that shift through the day. Their very existence seems tenuous, as if they might blow away before your eyes, yet they're solid enough to withstand the stress of hikers and skiers. The sand is as fine and feathery as you'll find anywhere; it's a place for contemplation and repose, the silence broken only by passing birds and the faint rush of water from the Medano Creek.

If you travel south from Alamosa on U.S. 285, you'll reach the little town of Romeo. From here pick up Route 142 East and travel 15 miles to **Manassa,** the birthplace of Jack Dempsey, one of the greatest heavyweight boxing champions of all time. Dempsey (also known as the Manassa Mauler) is honored in the **Jack Dempsey Museum.** *401 Main St.,* ☎ *719/843–5207.* ☛ *$2 adults, $1 children under 12.* ☉ *Memorial Day–Labor Day, Mon.–Sat. 9–5.*

⑲ Continue east along this scenic byway to the junction of Routes 142 and 159 to reach **San Luis,** founded in 1851, the oldest incorporated town in Colorado. Its Hispanic heritage is celebrated in the superb **San Luis Museum and Cultural Center,** with its extensive collection of *santos* (exquisitely decorated figures of saints used for household devotions), *retablos* (paintings on wood), and *bultos* (carved religious figures). Wonderful murals re-telling famous stories and legends of the area adorn the town's gracious tree-lined streets. A latter-day masterpiece is the *Stations of the Cross Shrine,* created by renowned local sculptor Huberto Maestas. Perched above town on a mesa called La Mesa de la Piedad y de la Misericordia (Hill of Piety and Mercy), its 15 figures dramatically depict the last hours of Christ's life. The trail culminates in a tranquil grotto dedicated to the Virgin Mary. *402 Church Pl.,* ☎ *719/672–3611.* ☛ *$3.* ☉ *Memorial Day–Labor Day, weekdays 8–4:30, weekends 10–3.*

Eighteen miles farther north, in the Sangre de Cristos (Blood of Christ, after the ruddy color of the peaks at dawn), is **Ft. Garland,** the site of Colorado's first military post, established in 1856 to protect settlers. The legendary Kit Carson commanded the outfit, and the six original adobe structures are still around, comprising the **Ft. Garland State Museum.** The venue features a re-creation of the commandant's quarters, various period military displays, and a rotating local folk-art exhibit. *Rte. 159, south of U.S. 160,* ☎ *719/379–3512.* ☛ *$3.* ☉ *Memorial Day–Labor Day, Mon.–Sat. 10–5, Sun. 1–5.*

Consider visiting a portion of the Santa Fe Trail by continuing east on U.S. 160 to the town of Walsenburg. From Walsenburg you can either go south on I–25 to the town of Trinidad; or travel north, passing through Pueblo and winding up in Colorado Springs (*see* Chapter 5, South Central Colorado).

What to See and Do with Children

The **Anasazi Heritage Center** (*see* Tour 1, *above*) features educational, hands-on displays and computer games.

The **Durango & Silverton Narrow Gauge Railroad** (*see* Tour 1, *above*)

Other Points of Interest

Four Corners Monument. A stone slab marks the only spot where four states—Colorado, Arizona, Utah, and New Mexico—meet. Of course, this is photo-op country, so smile and say "cheese"! Snacks and souvenirs are sold by Native Americans. To get here, travel south from Cortez on Route 160 for about 40 miles: You can't miss the signs. *Rte. 160 (follow signs).* ☛ *$1 per vehicle.* ☉ *Daily 7 AM–8 PM.*

Hovenweep National Monument. This site—whose literal translation from Ute means "deserted valley"—contains several major ruins, including imposing square, oval, and circular man-made towers such as Holly, Cajon, Hackberry, and Horseshoe, all of which are accessible only on foot. The most impressive ruin, called the Castle, underscores the site's uncanny resemblance to a medieval fiefdom. Hovenweep is approached via Route 160 West to County Road G (McElmo Canyon Rd.), which enters the spectacular red-walled McElmo Canyon along the way. *McElmo Canyon Rd.,* ☏ *970/749–05105 (Mesa Verde National Parks 970/529–4461).* ☛ *Free; camping entry fee $3.* ☉ *Daily sunrise–sunset.*

Lowry Pueblo. Small in comparison to Hovenweep, the Lowry site has only eight kivas and 40 rooms, and may have been a "suburb" of larger communities in the area during its occupation from about 800 to 1110. Of particular note are the Great Kiva, one of the largest such structures ever discovered, and a painted kiva, providing a fascinating insight into Anasazi decorative techniques. A brochure, which details the self-guided tour, is available at the entrance to the site. *Rte. 666, 9 mi west of Pleasant View, no* ☏. ☛ *Free.* ☉ *Daily 9–5.*

SHOPPING

Colorado's Southwest is the best place to pick up Western and Native American art and artifacts. Although there are malls and factory outlets in Durango housing the usual retailers, the following list includes only shops and boutiques with unique merchandise.

The San Luis valley offers superb examples of folk crafts, and basketry, embroidery, weaving, and beadwork adapted from Native American traditions.

Specialty Stores

Antiques
Buckskin Trading Co. (636 Main St., Ouray, ☏ 970/325–4044) sports an array of mining, railroading, Native American and cowboy collectibles.

Treasures of Time (Pacific and Davis Sts., Telluride, ☏ 970/728–3383) carries a selection of Western memorabilia, including frontier-style furnishings.

Art Galleries
Casa de Madera (680 Grand St., Del Norte, ☏ 719/657–2336) sells marvelous regional wood carvings.

Fireworks Gallery (608 Main St., Alamosa, ☏ 719/589–6064) sells fine art, collectibles, jewelry, weavings and prints.

Gallery West (718 Main St., Alamosa, ☏ 719/589–2275) carries local original paintings, photos, etchings, fiber arts, and designs in clay.

Golden West Indian Arts/Jan Cicero Gallery (101 W. Colorado Ave., Telluride, ☎ 970/728–3664) stocks a superb selection of Southwestern, Native American, and Hispanic art.

Goodman Gallery (3rd St. and Elk Ave., upstairs, Crested Butte, ☎ 970/349–5470) displays and sells Southwestern crafts from regional artisans.

Hellbent Leather and Silver (209 E. Colorado Ave., Telluride, ☎ 970/728–6246; 741 Main Ave., Durango, ☎ 970/247–9088) is a fine source for Native American arts and crafts.

North Moon (133 W. Colorado Ave., Telluride, ☎ 970/728–4145) features exquisite painted lodgepole furnishings, contemporary Native American ceramics that depart from tribal traditions, striking metallic sculptures, and petroglyph-inspired jewelry.

Something Pewter (419 Main St., Manassa, ☎ 719/843–5702) fashions what seems to be everything from bolos to belts, charms to figurines—all in pewter.

Toh-Atin Gallery (149 W. 9th St., Durango, ☎ 970/247–8277) and the related **Toh-Ahtin's Art on Main** (865 Main Ave., ☎ 970/247–4540) around the corner together comprise perhaps the best Western, Native American, and Southwestern art gallery in Colorado, offering a wide-ranging selection of paintings, pottery, prints, records, foodstuffs, clothing, and jewelry.

The Turquoise Shop (423 San Juan Ave., Alamosa, ☎ 719/589–2631) sells sterling silver and turquoise jewelry and various arts and crafts.

Books

Between the Covers Bookstore and Coffee House (224 W. Colorado Ave., Telluride, ☎ 970/728–4504) offers the perfect ambience for browsing through the latest titles while sipping a cappuccino.

Maria's Books (928 Main Ave., Durango, ☎ 970/247–1438) specializes in regional literature and nonfiction.

Boutiques

Appaloosa Trading Co. (501 Main Ave., Durango, ☎ 970/259–1994 is one of the best venues for all things leather, from purses to saddles, hats to boots, as well as jewelry, weaving, and other crafts.

Blair Street Cottage (1342 Blair St., Silverton, ☎ 970/387–5735) specializes in silk batik, with lovely scarves, ties, camisoles, and wall hangings.

Circumstance Leatherworks (306 6th Ave., Ouray, ☎ 970/325–7360) sells belts, purses, and backpacks crafted by Robert Holmes.

Shirt Off My Back (680 Main Ave., Durango, ☎ 970/247–9644) sells lovely silk-screened T-shirts (choose from more than 60 images or create your own).

Wm. Donald (220 E. Colorado Ave., Telluride, ☎ 970/728–3489) offers stylish togs, including hand-tooled leather vests, one-of-a-kind hand-spun angora/mohair jackets, limited edition sweaters with whimsical designs like chili peppers, as well as Coogis from Australia and Pendleton from Oregon.

Unicas Southwest (Ft. Smith Saloon Bldg., Ridgway, ☎ 970/626–5723; 215 E. Colorado Ave., Telluride, ☎ 970/728–4778; 703 Main Ave., Ouray, no ☎) delivers on its advertising promises of "worldly styles" and "fun, fashion, funk, and folk art."

Ceramics

Beens Pottery (145 E. 6th St., Durango, ☎ 970/247–3220) features pottery by local artist J. Milton Beens, as well as a wide selection of Western watercolors.

Creekside Pottery (126 Elk Ave., Crested Butte, ☎ 970/349–6459) show-cases local artist Mary Jursinovic's pottery and landscape lamps.

Mesa Verde Pottery (27601 Rte. 160 E, Cortez, ☎ 970/565–4492) of-fers a comprehensive sampling of ceramics from most Southwestern tribes.

The Potter's Wheel (221 E. Colorado Ave., Telluride, ☎ 970/728–4912) has a wide selection of both decorative and functional pottery crafted by local artisans.

San Juan Pottery (801 Main St., Ouray, ☎ 970/325–0319) features the work of Coloradan potters, but also carries porcelain jewelry, fig-urines, Native American baskets, gourds, and weaving.

Ute Mountain Pottery Plant (Jct. Rtes. 160 and 666, Towaoc, ☎ 970/565–8548) invites customers to watch the painstaking processes of molding, trimming, cleaning, painting, and glazing, before ad-journing to the showroom to buy pieces straight from the source.

Zappa Pottery (688 Spring Creek Blvd., Montrose, ☎ 970/249–6819) showcases the fine stoneware designs of Nick and Joan Zappa.

Crafts and Collectibles

Artesanos (115 W. 9th St., Durango, ☎ 970/259–5755) offers a mar-velous selection of eclectic furnishings from around the world (the Mex-ican crafts are remarkably fine).

The **Train Store** (501 Main Ave., Durango, ☎ 970/259–2145) sells unique train and railroad memorabilia, toys, models, books, T-shirts, and videos.

The **Candle Shop** (Blair St., Silverton, ☎ 970/387–5733) sells not only handmade candles, but also wind chimes, hurricane lamps, and local crafts.

Cortez Curiosity Shop (30 E. Main St., Cortez, ☎ 970/565–4856) sells everything from scented candles to tinctures to astrology charts to crystals.

Dietz Market (119 W. 8th St., Durango, ☎ 970/259–6030; 26345 Hwy. 160, Durango, ☎ 970/259–5811 or 800/321–6069) carries pottery, met-alwork, candles, weavings, and foodstuffs, all celebrating the region.

Images Gift Shoppe (541 Main St., Ouray, ☎ 970/325–7378) glories in tchotchkes and caters to a broad clientele, with items ranging from pottery to potpourri.

Nazca (218 N. Main St., Gunnison, ☎ 970/641–6438) has a wide se-lection of crafts, hand-carved candles, and hand-knit sweaters.

Flea Markets

Kellogg's Corner (24 Everett St., Durango, ☎ 970/247–2500) is a daily flea market.

Food

Adobe Milling Co. (Main St., Dove Creek, ☎ 970/677–2620) is in the self-styled Pinto Bean Capital of the World, and vends Anasazi beans, Dos Gringos spices, piñon nuts, and other products.

Honeyville Station (33633 U.S. 550 N, Hermosa, ☎ 800/676–7690) sells jams, jellies (try the chokecherry), condiments, and, of course, honey. You can watch how the bees make honey (in glass hives), and may be treated to a lecture by a fully garbed beekeeper.

The San Luis Valley is noted for its produce. Mycophiles should stop by the **Alamosa Mushroom Farm** (1071 South Road 5 South, ☎ 719/589–5882). **Mountain Maid Jelly** (710 2nd St., Saguache, ☎ 719/655–2824) offers a variety of unusual and delicious flavors. **Haefeli's Honey Farms** (0041 South Road 1 East, Monte Vista, ☎ 970/852–2301) sells delectable mountain-bloom honeys.

Jewelry
The **Enameling Shop** (1249 Greene St., Silverton, ☎ 970/387–5442) features original enamel works by Gary and Robert Richardson, who make buckles, earrings, and bolo ties.

Sporting Goods
Olympic Sports (150 W. Colorado Ave., Telluride, ☎ 970/728–4477) has a plethora of equipment and clothing for all seasons.

Western Wear
In Mancos, **Buck Saddlery** (106 W. Grand Ave., Mancos, ☎ 970/533–7958) is the domain of Buck, Eddie, Mark, and Sheila Proffitt, who custom build some of the sturdiest—and handsomest—saddles you'll ever find, in addition to chaps, holsters, scabbards, elk and buckskin jackets, and glamorous evening purses replete with silver, beads, and fringe. The **Bounty Hunter** (119 W. Grand Ave., Mancos, ☎ 970/533–7215; 226 W. Colorado Ave., Telluride, ☎ 970/728–0256) is the spot for leather, especially boots and vests. It also houses an astonishing selection of hats, among them Panama straw, beaver felt, Australian Outback, and just outrageous.

O'Farrell Hat Company (598 Main Ave., Durango, ☎ 970/259–2517) actually form-fits hats with a "customizer" machine; heads they've fitted include former presidents Bush and Reagan. Also in Durango, **Western Outfitters** (960 Main Ave., Durango, ☎ 970/247–0260) outfits men, women, and children from head to toe in everything from Stetson hats to Tony Lama boots.

Trail Town (U.S. 550 and Rte. 62, Ridgway, no ☎) is an entire mall devoted to the Western lifestyle, with restaurants, a dance hall, and clothing, furniture, and home accessories stores.

SPORTS AND THE OUTDOORS

Camping
The glorious wilderness area of the San Juans and Sangre de Cristos offers a diversity of camping activities. Contact the **Bureau of Land Management** (Durango, ☎ 970/247–4082), the **San Juan National Forest** (Durango, ☎ 970/247–4874), the **Curecanti National Recreation Area** (Montrose, ☎ 970/641–2337), and the **Uncompahgre and Gunnison national forests** (Delta, ☎ 970/874–7691) for more information. Campsites are also available in Mesa Verde and Hovenweep; contact the **National Park Service** at **Mesa Verde National Park** (P.O. Box 8, Mesa Verde, CO 81330, ☎ 970/529–4465).

Boating
Shorty's (Bayfield, ☎ 970/884–2768) and **Mountain Marina** (Bayfield, ☎ 970/884–9450) rent canoes on Vallecito Lake. **Beaver Creek Marina** (Cortez, ☎ 970/882–2258) rents canoes and boats on McPhee

Reservoir. **San Juan Skyway Marina** (Ouray, ☎ 970/626–5094) rents canoes and boats at the Ridgway State Recreation Area (U.S. 550, 12 mi north of town). You can also call the **Curecanti National Recreation Area** (Montrose, ☎ 970/641–2337), **Elk Creek Marina** (Montrose, ☎ 970/641–0707), and **Ridgway Reservoir** (Ridgway, ☎ 970/626–5822) for more information about boating.

Climbing

Fantasy Ridge Alpinism (Telluride, ☎ 970/728 3516) and **SouthWest Adventures** (Durango, ☎ 970/259–0370) are two climbing clubs in the region. Ouray is gaining fame in ice-climbing circles, with its abundance of frozen waterfalls. **Mountain Ouray Sports** (☎ 970/325–4284) arranges lessons and guided tours.

World-class climbing can be found outside Del Norte in the **Penitente Canyon,** as well as in the **San Juans,** and in the **Wheeler Geologic Area** outside Creede.

Cycling

Durango/Purgatory has good cycling trails, such as **Hermosa Creek** and **La Plata Canyon Road.** Top Telluride trails include **Ilium Road** and **Sawpit Road.** The entire **San Juan Skyway,** many of whose ascents are quite steep, is a favorite for cyclists.

Crested Butte Mountain offers several miles of scenic trails. **Signal Peak Loop** and **Rage in the Sage Track** outside Gunnison are also popular.

Routes around Silverton run through ghost towns and mining trails, while the Cortez area is popular for the Anasazi ruins.

Mountain Bike Specialists (340 S. Camino del Rio, Durango, ☎ 970/259–6661) arranges tours throughout the Four Corners region.

Fishing

For information on fishing in the region contact: the **Colorado Division of Wildlife** (2300 S. Townsend Ave., Montrose 81401, ☎ 970/249–3431); the **Bureau of Land Management** (701 Camino del Rio, Durango 81301, ☎ 970/247–4082); the **San Juan National Forest** (Durango, ☎ 970/247–4874); and the **Uncompahgre and Gunnison National forests** (2250 Highway 50, Delta 81416, ☎ 970/874–7691).

One of the finest sources of prime trout and bass in Colorado is the **McPhee Reservoir.** The second-largest body of water in the state, it reputedly has the best catch record in Southwest Colorado. Other well-stocked reservoirs in the area include **Jackson, Joe Moore, Taylor,** and **Groundhog.** The **Dolores, Gunnison** and **Mancos rivers,** and **Taylor** and **Bear creeks** are excellent spots as well. North of Durango are Lakes **Haviland, Lemon,** and **Vallecito.** Outside Gunnison, the **Blue Mesa Reservoir** in the Curecanti National Recreation Area (Gunnison, ☎ 970/641–2337) is another top choice, as is Lake San Cristobal.

The **Rio Grande River**—between Del Norte and South Fork—teems with rainbows and lunker browns.

The following operators run trips to various areas within the region: **Alpine Outside** (Crested Butte, ☎ 970/349–5011); **Colorado Fishing Adventures** (Pagosa Springs, ☎ 970/264–4168); **Duranglers** (Durango, ☎ 970/385–4081); **Telluride Angler** (☎ 970/728–0773); and **Telluride Outside** (☎ 970/728–3895).

Four-Wheel Driving

The inspiring **Alpine Loop Scenic Byway** joins Lake City with Ouray and Silverton. This circle is only open in summer, and is paved, except for the dirt roads over Cinnamon and Engineer passes. However, this is four-wheel heaven, dizzily spiraling from 12,800-foot passes to gaping valleys.

Golf

Alamosa Golf Course (6678 River Rd., ☎ 719/589–5330) is an 18-hole championship course.

Cattails Golf Course (State St., Alamosa, ☎ 719/589–9515), also in Alamosa, is an 18-hole course that wraps scenically around the Rio Grande.

Conquistador Golf Course (2018 N. Dolores St., Cortez, ☎ 970/565–9208) is an 18-hole public course with sweeping views of Mesa Verde and Sleeping Ute Mountain.

Dalton Ranch and Golf Club (on U.S. 5507, 7 mi north of Durango, ☎ 970/247–7921) is a Ken Dye–designed 18-hole championship course with inspiring panoramas of red-rock cliffs. The restaurant, which arranges "happy hours" with Trimble Hot Springs across the road, has become a popular hangout for both duffers and skiers, who enjoy watching the resident elk herd on its afternoon stroll.

Dos Rios Golf Club (U.S. 50, 2 mi west of Gunnison, ☎ 970/641–1482) has lovely views; water comes into play on 17 holes.

Fairfield Pagosa Resort (U.S. 160, 3 mi west of Pagosa Springs, ☎ 970/781–4141) offers both an 18-hole and a 9-hole course.

Great Sand Dunes Country Club (5303 Rte. 150, Mosca, ☎ 719/378–2357) is an 18-hole course with the billowing dunes as a backdrop.

Hillcrest Golf Course (2300 Rim Dr., ☎ 970/247–1499) is an 18-hole public course perched on a mesa.

Skyland Country Club (385 Country Club Dr., ☎ 970/349–6127) is a ravishing 18-hole course designed by Robert Trent Jones, Jr. and although it belongs to the country club, it is open to the public.

Tamarron Resort (40292 U.S. 550 N, ☎ 970/259–2000) is an 18-hole, 6,885-yard course, frequently ranked among *Golf Digest's* top 75 resort courses.

Telluride Golf Club (Telluride Mountain Village, ☎ 970/728–3856) boasts breathtaking views of Mt. Wilson and Mt. Sunshine, which dominate this 7,009-yard course.

Hiking

For general information about hiking in Southwest Colorado, contact the **Bureau of Land Management** (701 Camino del Rio, Durango 81301, ☎ 970/247–4082) or the **San Juan National Forest Ranger Districts** (100 N. 6th St., Dolores 81323, ☎ 970/882–7296; 41595 U.S. 160 E, Mancos 81328, ☎ 970/533–7716.

In the Needles Range of the San Juans, picturesque, fairly strenuous hikes include **Molas Pass** to **Crater Lake, Engineer Peak,** and the **Grand Turks.** Trails abound throughout the region, skirting waterfalls and mining ruins. The **Lizard Head Wilderness Area,** dominated by the eerie rock tooth of the same name, showcases the region's alpine scenery at its best.

The **Great Sand Dunes** are a favorite hike. The **Rio Grande National Forest** offers more than a million acres of pristine wilderness.

Horseback Riding

Fantasy Ranch (P.O. Box 236, Crested Butte 81224, ☎ 970/349–5425), **Lazy F Bar Outfitters** (P.O. Box 383, Gunnison 81230, ☎

970/349–7593), **Rimrock Outfitters** (c/o Echo Basin, 43747 County Road M, Mancos 81328, ☎ 970/533–7000), **Southfork Stables** (28481 Highway 160, Durango 81301, ☎ 970/259–4871), and **Telluride Outside** (P.O. Box 685, Telluride 81435, ☎ 970/728–3895) provide horses for riding tours, which range from one-hour walks to overnight excursions; rates begin at $20. Many outfitters also offer sleigh rides and dinners.

Rafting

River tours can last for an afternoon or for 10 days, depending on the arrangements. Rates begin at $30. **Durango Rivortrippors** (☎ 970/259–0289) runs expeditions down the Animas River. **Gunnison River Expeditions** (Montrose, ☎ 970/249–4441) specializes in Gunnison River tours. **Telluride Whitewater** (☎ 970/728–3895) explores the Gunnison, Dolores, Colorado, and Animas rivers. **Three Rivers Outfitting** (Crested Butte, ☎ 970/349–501, and Almont, ☎ 970/641–1303) runs trips down the Arkansas, Taylor, and Gunnison, and also offers kayaking lessons and raft lure fishing.

Skiing

CROSS-COUNTRY
Crested Butte Nordic Center (☎ 970/349–1707) has a 15 mile groomed track system and also offers guided tours into the backcountry.

Purgatory-Durango Cross-Country Center (☎ 970/247–9000) offers 26 miles of machine-groomed scenic trails just outside the ski area.

Telluride Nordic Center (☎ 970/728–6911) provides almost 80 miles of pristine trails. The areas around Molas Divide and Mesa Verde National Park are also popular.

DOWNHILL
Crested Butte Mountain Resort. 85 trails; 13 lifts; 1,162 acres; 2,775-foot vertical. Good beginner and extreme terrain. *Rte. 135,* ☎ *970/349–2222.* ☉ *Late-Nov.–early Apr., daily 9–4.*

Purgatory-Durango. 74 trails; 9 chairs; 729 acres; 2,029-foot vertical. A lot of intermediate runs and glade and tree skiing. *U.S. 550,* ☎ *970/247–9000 or 800/525–0892.* ☉ *Late Nov.–early Apr., daily 9–4.*

Ski Hesperus. 18 trails; 2 lifts. This small, family ski area close to Durango offers 100% night skiing. The Navahos regarded the mountain as a sacred peak, and used it as a directional landmark. *U.S. 160,* ☎ *970/259–3711.* ☉ *Dec.–early Apr., Sat.–Tues. 9–4 and Wed.–Fri, 4:30–9:30.*

Telluride. 64 trails; 9 chairs and a poma lift; 1,050 acres; 3,165-foot vertical (3,522-foot vertical if you hike to the highest ridge). *Rte. 145,* ☎ *970/728–6900 or 800/525–3455.* ☉ *Late Nov.–early Apr., daily 9–4.*

Wolf Creek. 50 trails; 5 lifts; 700 acres; 1,425-foot vertical. This is one of Colorado's best-kept secrets and a powder hound's dream: it's uncrowded with no lift lines, and gets phenomenal snow (averaging more than 450 inches a year). The 50 trails run the gamut from wide-open bowls to steep glade skiing. *U.S. 160, at the top of Wolf Creek Pass, Pagosa Springs,* ☎ *970/264–5629.* ☉ *Early Nov.–mid-Apr., daily 9–4.*

Snowboarding is also permitted at all the above ski areas.

HELI-SKIING
Telluride Helitrax (☎ 970/728–4904) offers thrilling touring through the New Eastern Powder Circuit.

SKI TOURING

San Juan Hut System (Telluride, ☎ 970/728–6935) connects Telluride with Ridgway. There are five huts equipped with beds, blankets, and stoves. Huts are about 7 miles apart.

Snowmobiling
Action Adventures (Crested Butte, ☎ 970/349–5909 or 800/383–1974); **Alpine Expeditions** (Crested Butte, ☎ 970/349–5011 or 800/833–8052); **Snowmobile Adventure Tours** (Purgatory, ☎ 970/247–9000); **Telluride Outside** (☎ 970/728–3895 or 800/831–6230).

Tennis
The following parks offer free public courts. Reservations are advised: **Crested Butte** and **Mt. Crested Butte Town parks** (no ☎s); **Durango City Park** (☎ 970/247–5622); **Ouray Hot Springs Pool** (☎ 970/325–4638); **Telluride Town Park** (☎ 970/728–3071).

DINING

Colorado's Southwest is one of those regions in the good ol' U.S. of A. that has made truck stops and their fare an indelible part of our tradition. What you'll also find here is sensational Southwestern-style cooking, especially around Durango, and superb gourmet dining in Crested Butte, about which a journalist from the *Denver Post* once opined, "There are more fine restaurants per capita in Crested Butte than anywhere else in America." Telluride isn't far behind, befitting its status as unofficial rival to Vail and Aspen. For rates *see* the Dining chart *in* On the Road with Fodor's at the front of this guide.

Even if you plan to dine in upscale establishments, Southwest Colorado makes few sartorial demands on the restaurant-goer. In general, the upscale places expect you to look neat and casual; elsewhere, jeans, shorts, or ski pants work well.

Alamosa
$$ True Grits. At this noisy steak house the cuts are predictably good, but that's not the real draw: As the name implies, the restaurant is really a shrine to John Wayne. His portraits hang everywhere: the Duke in action; the Duke in repose; the Duke lost in thought. ✗ *Jct. U.S. 160 and Rte. 17,* ☎ *719/589–9954. Reservations accepted. MC, V.*

$ Ace Inn and Old Town Bar. The decor is rough-hewn: Wood-paneled
★   walls are adorned with dried chilies and assorted kitsch such as antique pepper mills and Eiffel Tower ceramics of uncertain taste. You should definitely bring an empty stomach to this superior Mexican restaurant, for heaping portions of sopaipilla—fried stuffed with beans, rice, and beef smothered in red and green chilies burritos, and chilies relleños. Save room for the sopaipilla sundae drowned in cinnamon wine sauce. Even the margaritas are daunting: The small one is 28 ounces! ✗ *326 Main St.,* ☎ *719/589–9801. Reservations accepted. MC, V.*

Cortez
$ M&M Family Restaurant and Truck Stop. Semis and RVs jammed into the parking lot attest that M&M is the real McCoy as truck stops go. If chicken-fried steak, enchiladas, and huge breakfasts (served 24 hours a day) are your fancy, you'll be thrilled to eat here. There are posher restaurants in town, but none better—certainly not for these prices. ✗ *7006 U.S. 160 S,* ☎ *970/565–6511. No reservations. AE, MC.*

Crested Butte
$$$–$$$$ Le Bosquet. This charming Western-style Victorian bistro enjoys a sterling reputation and is wonderfully romantic. Unfortunately, it has

been woefully uneven of late: some nights brilliant, some not; some dishes extraordinary, others abysmal. For example, you might start with a French onion soup inexplicably made from beef bouillon cubes rather than from stock (and from too many at that), then feast on a sensational rack of venison with pheasant ravioli. Among the always-reliable choices are potato-and-leek pancakes with gravlax and crème fraîche, goat cheese ravioli, and such scrumptious desserts as pear tart and homemade ice cream. ✗ *2nd and Elk Aves.,* ☎ *970/349–5808. Reservations advised. AE, MC, V. No lunch weekends.*

$$$–$$$$ **Soupçon.** Soupçon ("soup's on," get it?) occupies two intimate rooms
★ in a delightful log cabin—and a cozier place doesn't exist in this town. Mac Bailey, the impish owner-chef (women fall in love nightly: "He's so cute," they gush when he trundles out from the kitchen), brings innovative variations on classic bistro cuisine and changes his menu daily. His roast duckling, usually topped with an impeccably balanced Michigan cherry sauce, may be the best in the state, and the fish dishes are sublime: Try petrale sole lightly breaded in cornmeal, glistening with black bean, ginger, and sake sauce. Desserts, however, are where Mac really shines: Order the Jack Daniel's bread pudding, the hazelnut ice-cream cake, or any souffle. ✗ *Just off 2nd St., behind the Forest Queen,* ☎ *970/349–5448. Reservations advised. AE, MC, V. Dinner only.*

$$$–$$$$ **Timberline.** This handsome, cozy split-level restaurant is set in a restored Victorian home. Among the top starters are fettuccine Alfredo with smoked trout and goat-cheese terrine. Poached salmon au jus or herb-crusted veal chops might make a perfect second course. The weekly prix-fixe menus are a good way to save money. In summer, a pleasant Sunday brunch is offered. ✗ *21 Elk Ave.,* ☎ *970/349–9831. Reservations advised. AE, MC, V. No lunch.*

$$$ **Penelope's.** The Victorian ambience at this local favorite is complemented by a pretty greenhouse. Everything on the menu is solid and dependable, from the Colorado rack of lamb to the roast apricot duck. Sunday brunch here is a Crested Butte institution. ✗ *120 Elk Ave.,* ☎ *970/349–5178. Reservations advised. AE, MC, V. No lunch.*

$$–$$$ **Powerhouse.** This is an enormous barnlike structure, with a delight-
★ ful Gay '90s bar. The cuisine is haute Mexican, with scrumptious standards such as tacos and burritos, and more exotic dishes such as soft-shell crab in cornmeal and delectable mesquite-roasted *cabrito* (kid)—a true delicacy. The margaritas are the best in town, complemented by a knockout list of more than 30 tequilas by the glass. ✗ *130 Elk Ave.,* ☎ *970/349–5494. No reservations. AE, MC, V. No lunch.*

$$ **Swiss Chalet.** The owner duplicates the true Alpine experience, right down to the *bierstube* (pub) with Paulaner on tap. The *Kalbsgeschnetzeltes* (veal loin sautéed with mushrooms and shallots in white-wine cream sauce), raclette, and fondue are luscious, as are such hard-to-find specialties as *buendnerfleisch* (savory air-dried beef soaked in wine). ✗ *621 Gothic Rd., on the mountain,* ☎ *970/349–5917. Reservations advised. AE, MC, V. No lunch in summer.*

$–$$ **The Artichoke.** From the deck of this simple, bustling establishment you can watch the skiers come down the mountain while you nibble on "high-altitude diner cuisine," with a Cajun slant. Artichokes are obviously a specialty, and are prepared in various ways. Among entrée favorites are popcorn shrimp, chicken pot pie, catfish, gumbo, and Philly cheese steak—all of which should satisfy even the heartiest appetites. ✗ *Treasury Center, on the mountain (upstairs),* ☎ *970/349–6688. Reservations accepted. AE, D, MC, V.*

$ **Donita's Cantina.** This down-home Mexican restaurant is hard to miss: It's the one in the hot-pink building. The fare isn't nearly as showy: simply good, solid standards such as fajitas and enchiladas, and a tangy salsa. It may be owing to either the bargain prices or the killer margaritas, but the crowds here are always jovial. ✗ *330 Elk Ave.,* ☎ *970/349–6674. No reservations. AE, D, MC, V. No lunch.*

$ **Slogar.** Set in a lovingly renovated Victorian tavern awash in lace and
★ stained glass, this restaurant—also run by Mac Bailey of Soupçon and Penelope's (*see above*)—is just plain cozy. Slogar's turns out some of the plumpest, juiciest fried chicken west of the Mississippi. The fixings are just as sensational: flaky biscuits, creamy mashed potatoes swimming in hearty chicken gravy, and unique sweet-and-sour coleslaw from a Pennsylvania Dutch recipe that dates back nearly two centuries. You get all that and more, including homemade ice cream, for $10.95! ✗ *2nd and Whiterock Sts.,* ☎ *970/349–5765. Reservations advised. MC, V. No lunch.*

Durango/Purgatory

$$$$ **Café Cascade.** Many locals' choice for the best restaurant on the mountain, if not in the region, this intimate split-level eatery features the Southwestern stylings of chef Tom Hamilton. Sea bass medallions with blue cornbread and red chili sauce and rabbit satay with peanut sauce are his sterling appetizers; grilled caribou with plum and sage sauce, pheasant breast stuffed with roast tomatoes and fresh oregano, and fresh grilled ahi brushed with ginger butter sauce are among the standout entrées. ✗ *50827 U.S. 550 N (1 mi north of Purgatory), Cascade Village,* ☎ *970/259–3500. Reservations advised. AE, D, DC, MC, V. No lunch.*

$$–$$$ **Ariano's.** This popular Italian place occupies a dimly lit room plastered with local art. It offers exceptional pizzas (try the pesto) and pastas, and the best fried calamari in the Four Corners. Next door, under the same ownership, is Pronto, a bright and noisy trattoria where you can get the same pastas for less money. ✗ *150 E. College Dr., Durango,* ☎ *970/247–8146. Reservations advised. AE, MC, V. No lunch.*

$$–$$$ **Ore House.** Durango is a meat-and-potatoes kind of town, and this is Durango's idea of a steak house, where the aroma of beef smacks you in the face as you walk past. This classic eatery offers enormous slabs of aged Angus—cholesterol heaven hand-cut daily. ✗ *147 E. College Dr., Durango,* ☎ *970/245–5707. Reservations advised. AE, D, DC, MC, V.*

$$–$$$ **The Red Snapper.** If you're in the mood for fresh fish, head to this congenial place, decorated with more than 200 gallons of saltwater aquariums. Try the oysters Durango, with jack cheese and salsa; salmon Joaquin with roasted garlic cumin sauce; or snapper Monterey with jack cheese and tarragon. Of course, delicious steaks and prime rib are also available. The salad bar includes more than 40 items. ✗ *144 E. 9th St., Durango,* ☎ *970/259–3417. Reservations advised. AE, MC, V. No lunch.*

$$–$$$ **Sow's Ear.** It's a toss-up between the Ore House and this Purgatory
★ watering hole for the "Best Steak House" award. The Sow's Ear gets the edge, though, for its rustic but elegant decor, with a huge fireplace, hanging plants, and—okay—statues of urinating cowboys. The mouthwatering, fresh-baked seven-grain bread and creative preparations such as blackened fillets and the daunting hodgeebaba—an 18-ounce rib eye smothered with sautéed mushrooms and onions—are a few more reasons Sow's Ear leads the pack. There's a brightly painted climbing wall at the bar for those who need to burn calories (or wait for their table). ✗ *49617 Highway 550, Purgatory,* ☎ *970/247–3527. Reservations advised. AE, D, DC, MC, V. No lunch.*

$–$$ **Lola's Place.** This delightfully whimsical space is filled with hand-
★ painted furnishings and dried flower wreaths. The mango, mint, and mauve walls are bedecked with equally colorful abstract art. The food

is just as creative. Chef David Ganley studied his trade under Wolfgang Puck at San Francisco's trendy Postrio. He turns out magnificent regional fare, using organic and indigenous ingredients wherever possible. Standouts include a free-range chicken quesadilla with zesty cilantro in an avocado salsa; vegetable tamales in mole with chipotle, dried cherries, golden raisins, and piñons; and tamales with apple cider. ✕ *725 E. 2nd Ave.,* ☎ *970/385–1920. Reservations advised. AE, MC, V. Closed Sun. No dinner Mon., no lunch Sat.*

$–$$ Carver's Bakery and Brew Pub. This microbrewery run by the "Brews Brothers," Bill and Jim Carver, offers about eight beers at any given time, including flavors such as Raspberry Wheat Ale (which brewmaster Patrick Keating nicknames "Seduction Ale"), and Colorado Train Nut Brown Ale. The front room is a well-lit coffeehouse-bakery and the back a more subdued sports bar. There's also a patio out back. From breakfast to the wee hours, the place is always hopping. Try the bratwurst, fajitas—chicken or sirloin strips pan-fried in tequila and salsa, or the homemade bread bowls filled with either soup or salad. ✕ *1022 Main Ave., Durango,* ☎ *970/259–2545. No reservations. AE, D, MC, V.*

$ Olde Tymer's Café. Locals flock to this former drugstore, which still drips with atmosphere from days gone by. The balcony, pressed-tin ceiling, and walls plastered with artifacts and locals' photos lend a '20s dance hall look to the place. You can get cheap draft beer, great burgers, and $5 blue-plate specials. ✕ *1000 Main Ave., Durango,* ☎ *970/259–2990. No reservations. AE, MC, V.*

Mancos

$$ Millwood Junction. Folks come from four states (no fooling) for the 25-item salad bar and phenomenal Friday-night seafood buffet. Steaks and seafood are featured in this upscale Red Lobster/Sizzler–style eatery. ✕ *Jct. U.S. 160 and Main St.,* ☎ *970/533–7338. No reservations. AE, DC, MC, V. No lunch.*

Montrose

$–$$ The Whole Enchilada. You'll get the whole enchilada and then some at this lively place. Portions are gargantuan, and the food goes down easily, especially the tasty chimichangas, blue-corn enchiladas, and homemade pies. The patio is a pleasant place to sit in summer. ✕ *44 S. Grand St.,* ☎ *970/249–1881. Reservations accepted. AE, MC, V.*

Pagosa Springs/Wolf Creek

$–$$ Elkhorn Café. Filling and fiery Mexican fare (try the stuffed sopaipillas), as well as robust American standards such as meat loaf and pot roast, draws people from miles around. Fill up on a breakfast burrito before attacking the Wolf Creek bowls. ✕ *438 Main St.,* ☎ *970/264–2146. Reservations accepted. AE, MC, V.*

Telluride

$$$$ La Marmotte. This romantic bistro seems transplanted from Provence,
★ with its brick walls, lace curtains, and baskets overflowing with flowers or garlic bulbs. The fish specials, such as delicate flaky salmon in saffron and mussel sauce, are particularly splendid. The only drawback here is a surprisingly skimpy wine list with criminally high prices. ✕ *150 W. San Juan Ave.,* ☎ *970/728–6232. Reservations advised. AE, MC, V. No lunch.*

$$$–$$$$ Campagna. Vincent and Joline Esposito transport diners to a Tuscan
★ farmhouse, from the decor (open kitchen, oak and terra-cotta floors, turn-of-the-century photos of the Italian countryside, and Tuscan cookbooks) to the assured, classically simple food. Everything is grilled or roasted with garlic, sage, or rosemary in olive oil, allowing the natu-

ral juices and flavors to emerge. Wild mushrooms (porcini or porto-bello) and wild boar chops are among the enticing possibilities. Finish it off with a letter-perfect tiramisù or hazelnut torte and a fiery homemade grappa. ✗ *435 W. Pacific Ave., ☎ 970/728–6190. Reservations advised. AE, MC, V. No lunch.*

$$$$ Evangeline's. This intimate boîte has only 30 seats, giving the rather formal dining room dressed in primrose and mint the air of an elegant private soiree. Chef Moore's food is haute Cajun; the nightly changing menu might include oysters Rockefeller, creamed spinach and feta ravioli in roasted red pepper sauce, or a classic shrimp Creole. There is also a $39 prix-fixe meal. ✗ *646 Mountain Village Blvd., ☎ 970/728–9717. Reservations advised. AE, MC, V. No lunch.*

$$$–$$$$ The PowderHouse. Tony Clinco (a former Golden Gloves winner who
★ found another use for his hands) bills his food as "Rocky Mountain Cuisine." In reality, this is classic Italian married to wild game. Among the winners are pheasant ravioli; smoked buffalo sausage; and the game special—stuffed quail, venison chop, and marinated elk, each in its own sauce. ✗ *226 W. Colorado Ave., ☎ 970/728–3622. Reservations advised. AE, MC, V.*

$$$ 221 South Oak Bistro. It had to happen that an ever more trendy Telluride would eventually have a "bistro." This one is very pretty, too, with high-tech Southwestern decor, spot-lit peach walls, and a blond-wood bar. Soft jazz wafts through the casually elegant space. The menu sounds exciting—for example, cured salmon and walnut ravioli—but fails to deliver on its promise. Stick to the simpler dishes such as free-range chicken with herb fettuccine and winter squash, or crispy salmon medallions with yummy roast-garlic potatoes and braised Napa cabbage. ✗ *221 S. Oak St., ☎ 970/728–9507. Reservations advised. AE, MC, V.*

$$–$$$ McCrady's. This restaurant has been a Charleston, South Carolina, institution since 1778, and the Telluride branch serves up the same enormous portions of haute Southern comfort food prepared with Southwestern flair. Enjoy a drink at the hunting lodge bar (where you'll find a good selection of reasonably priced wines by the glass), then adjourn downstairs to the handsome dining room. Popcorn shrimp with Cajun mayonnaise and crabcakes with salsa and homemade mayonnaise dipping sauces make first-rate appetizers. You can then segue into monkfish with citrus dressing, grits with shrimp and *tasso* (Cajun cured ham) sauce, or smoked pork chops with apple sage chutney. Here's a bonus: two sizes of nearly every entrée are available (5 and 7 oz. for seafood, 6 and 10 or 12 oz. for meats). ✗ *115 W. Colorado Ave., ☎ 970/728–4943. Reservations advised. AE, MC, V. No lunch.*

$–$$ Floradora. This Telluride institution is named for two turn-of-the-century ladies of the evening (although locals call it Howie's, after the owner). The rafters are draped with pennants contributed by patrons over the years. The food is nothing special, but you come here for the ambience. Southwestern and Continental specials include Southwest pizza (with three cheeses, sun-dried tomatoes, roasted red peppers, oregano, garlic, and salsa), blackened catch of the day, and tropical chicken. ✗ *103 W. Colorado Ave., ☎ 970/728–3888. Reservations accepted. AE, MC, V.*

$–$$ Roma Bar and Café. In operation since 1897, this restaurant offers tremendous value and an incomparable air of history. The 1860 Brunswick bar, with marvelous 12-foot-high mirrors, has seen everything, including cowboys riding their mounts up to the stools. Flappers even brewed rotgut whiskey in the cellar during Prohibition. The pasta specials are terrific, as are the burgers. ✗ *133 E. Colorado Ave., ☎ 970/728–3622. Reservations accepted. AE, MC, V.*

$ **Eddie's.** This ultracasual spot serves up heaping helpings of pastas, homemade soups and stews, and gourmet pizzas (choose from more than two dozen toppings). The excellent landscape photos that adorn the walls are for sale. ✕ *300 W. Colorado Ave.,* ☎ *970/728–5335. Reservations accepted. AE, MC, V. Closed Mon.*

$ **Fat Alley's BBQ.** A few family-style tables and benches, along with some old skis and ceiling fans fill this popular spot owned by Tony Clinco of the PowderHouse (*see above*). Messy, mouthwatering ribs are complemented by delectable side dishes like red beans and rice, baked sweet potatoes, snap pea and feta salad, and coleslaw. A few beers and wines are available, in addition to homemade iced tea and pink lemonade. ✕ *122 S. Oak St.,* ☎ *970/728–3985. No reservations. AE, MC, V.*

LODGING

Whatever your lodging preference, you'll be able to find a suitable property in Southwest Colorado: from motor inns in Durango to elegant Telluride bed-and-breakfasts to upscale resort developments such as Tamarron, outside Purgatory/Durango, and The Peaks at Telluride. Winter is high season in Crested Butte, Purgatory, and Telluride (with rates dropping by as much as 50% in summer despite the wealth of festivals and events). Properties in Durango, Ouray, Silverton, and the Mesa Verde area work in the opposite fashion, with many accommodations closing for all or part of the winter. Recently, properties in outlying communities such as Ridgway, Montrose, and Gunnison began offering half-price lift tickets for guests who plan to ski. Unless otherwise noted, rooms have a full bath and include cable TV and phones.

Condominiums throughout Colorado generally provide excellent value, especially for families. All the companies listed in the Lodging section represent top-notch properties, usually within walking distance of the slopes in winter (or major activities in summer). All have full kitchen and cable TV, most with Jacuzzi and/or pool access, among other amenities. For rates *see* the Lodging price chart *in* On the Road with Fodor's at the front of this guide.

Alamosa

$–$$ **Best Western Alamosa Inn.** This sprawling, well-maintained complex, scattered over several blocks, is the best hotel bet in town. Rooms are spacious and offer the standard amenities. ⌨ *1919 Main St., 81101,* ☎ *719/589–4943. 121 rooms. Restaurant, bar, indoor pool. AE, D, DC, MC, V.*

$ **Cottonwood Inn B&B.** This pretty cranberry-and-azure house was built
★ in 1908 and lovingly refurbished by an Adams State professor and his wife. Public rooms feature both original and reproduction Stickley woodwork and furnishings; regional photographs and watercolors (most of them for sale) grace the walls. In the four sunny rooms with country-French washed walls, there are hand-painted florettes, framed knits, weavings, dried flowers, lace curtains, and predominantly wicker furnishings. There are also four apartments, two with wonderful oak floors and all with claw-foot tubs. A complimentary breakfast is provided for guests. ⌨ *123 San Juan Ave., 81101,* ☎ *719/589–3882 or 800/955– 2623,* FAX *719/589–6437. 4 rooms, 2 with private bath; 4 apartments. AE, DC, MC, V.*

Antonito

$ **Conejos River Guest Ranch.** On the Conejos River, this peaceful, family-friendly retreat offers private fishing and wagon rides. The recently remodeled cabins—all fully equipped—and guest rooms are pleasantly outfitted with ranch-style decor, including lodgepole pine furnishings. A complimentary breakfast is provided. ⌧ *25390 Rte. 17, 81120,* ☎ *719/376–2464. 6 cabins, 8 rooms. Restaurant, horseback riding, fishing. No credit cards.*

Cortez

$ **Anasazi Motor Inn.** This is definitely the nicest hotel on the strip, mostly because its air-conditioned rooms are spacious and pleasantly decorated in Southwestern colors. Children under 18 stay free in their parents' room. ⌧ *666 S. Broadway, 81312,* ☎ *970/565–3773 or 800/972–6232,* ℻ *970/565–1027. 89 rooms. Restaurant, bar, pool, hot tub, meeting rooms, airport shuttle. AE, D, DC, MC, V.*

Creede

$ **Creede Hotel.** A relic of the silver days, this charming 1890s structure has been fully restored, and the rooms offer the usual Victoriana. The gracious dining room serves excellent meals, in addition to the complimentary gourmet breakfast. ⌧ *1892 Main St., 81130,* ☎ *719/658–2608. 4 rooms. Restaurant. D, MC, V. Closed winter.*

Crested Butte

$$ **Crested Butte Club.** This quaint, stylish inn is a Victorian dream: Each
★ sumptuous, individually furnished room contains a brass or mahogany bed, Axeminster carpets, and cherry-wood antiques or good-quality reproductions. All have spacious modern bathrooms and little extras such as footed copper and brass tubs or gas fireplaces. The downstairs bar is similarly delightful, but best of all is the full health club on the property, so you don't have to go far to soothe your weary muscles after a hard day's hiking or skiing. The Continental breakfast is complimentary. ⌧ *512 2nd St., 81224,* ☎ *970/349–6655,* ℻ *970/349–6654. 7 rooms. Bar, indoor lap pool, health club. AE, MC, V.*

$$–$$$ **Grande Butte Hotel.** This ski-in/ski-out property offers all the amenities and facilities of other luxury hotels at down-to-earth prices. Huge rooms are decorated in muted earth and pastel tones, and feature a wet bar, whirlpool tubs, and private balcony. The public spaces are dotted with towering plants, regional paintings and sculptures, and oversized overstuffed armchairs and sofas. Giovanni's, the gourmet restaurant, is excellent: Oddly enough, conventional fare such as saltimbocca is far surpassed by such creative, adventurous dishes as ravioli in raspberry sauce and penne with duck breast. Regrettably, while service remains as friendly as ever, the young staff can also be slow and inefficient. ⌧ *Box 5006, Mt. Crested Butte 81225,* ☎ *970/349–7561 or 800/642–4422,* ℻ *970/349–6332. 210 rooms, 53 suites. 3 restaurants, 2 bars, indoor pool, outdoor hot tub, sauna, laundry service, meeting rooms. AE, D, MC, V.*

$$ **Irwin Lodge.** The Irwin touts itself as "the best-kept secret in the Rock-
★ ies," and it's no idle boast. Talk about seclusion: In winter you must take a thrilling snowmobile ride on several switchbacks to reach this aerie, nearly 1,000 feet above (and 8 miles from) Crested Butte. The lodge sits 10,700 feet above sea level, on a remote ridge overlooking Lake Irwin and the Sangre de Cristo range. Several cozy lounge areas circle a magnificent stone fireplace at the entrance. The smallish, charmingly rustic rooms are tastefully appointed, with pine walls and mahogany furnishings. A hearty breakfast is included in the rate, and a fine Continental lunch and dinner, served family style, are available at a nominal surcharge. The repeat clientele knows that this is the premier place in America to learn powder skiing, as the surrounding area gets an average of 500 inches of fluffy white stuff a year. A Snowcat will take you up to 12,000 feet, with a 2,000-foot vertical. (Nonguests

can make arrangements on a limited basis.) Summer activities include fishing, horseback riding, and mountain biking. With no ☎ or TV, just a shortwave radio to civilization, the Irwin represents the ultimate in isolation. ⌕ *Box 457, Crested Butte 81224,* ☎ *970/349–5308. 24 rooms, 1 suite. Restaurant, bar, hiking, horseback riding, fishing, mountain bikes, snowmobiling. AE, MC, V.*

CONDOMINIUMS

Crested Butte Vacations (Box A, Mt. Crested Butte 81225, ☎ 800/544–8448, FAX 970/349–2250) can make arrangements for all condominiums on the mountain.

Durango/Purgatory

$$$–$$$$
★
Tamarron. This handsome development, nestled on 750 acres of protected land surrounded by the San Juan National Forest, harmonizes beautifully with the environment; the main lodge seems an extension of the surrounding cliffs. Units are an attractive blend of frontier architecture and Southwestern decor, and nearly all feature a fireplace, a full kitchen, and a terrace. Tamarron is famed for one of the country's most ravishing championship golf courses, and tennis and horseback riding are also available. Le Canyon, the gourmet restaurant, is a romantic spot that specializes in table-side pyrotechnics. ⌕ *Drawer 3131, Durango 81302 (approx. 10 mi north of Durango),* ☎ *970/259–2000 or 800/678–1000, FAX 970/259–0745. 411 units. 3 restaurants, 2 bars, indoor-outdoor pool, hot tub, spa, 18-hole golf course, 3 tennis courts, horseback riding, children's programs (ages 4–12). AE, D, DC, MC, V.*

$$–$$$
★
Purgatory Village Hotel. This luxurious ski-in/ski-out property offers both hotel rooms and condos, all decorated with Southwestern flair, including Native American rugs and prints. The condos include full kitchen, private balcony, washer/dryer, whirlpool bath, in-room sauna, and wood-burning fireplace. ⌕ *Box 2062, Durango 81302 (located in Purgatory),* ☎ *970/247–9000 or 800/879–7974, FAX 970/385–2116. 271 units. Restaurant, bar, pool, hot tub, sauna, steam room, exercise room. AE, D, DC, MC, V.*

$–$$
★
New Rochester Hotel/Leland House. Mother-and-son team Diane and Kirk Komick restored these two Victorian beauties that sit across the street from each other in downtown Durango, both in high Western style. The Rochester had served as a flophouse, and the Komicks rescued some of the original furniture (you can still see water and cigarette stains on the beautifully carved walnut and cherry armoires and tables), creating an atmosphere of funky chic. Steamer trunks, hand-painted settees, wagon-wheel chandeliers, and quilts contribute to the authentic feel. The halls are decorated with photos of stars and original posters of movies shot in the area, including *Butch Cassidy and the Sundance Kid* and *City Slickers;* these films provide the names for the hotel's rooms, as well. Denver and Rio Grande train windows convert the back porch into a parlor car, and gas lamps amidst towering maple trees grace the courtyard. The Leland House utilizes Southwestern pastel fabrics, weathered wood sculpture, old photos of Durango, and antique suitcases to create a similar effect. All rooms and suites here include kitchenette or full kitchen. The Leland House has a gourmet complimentary breakfast, while the Rochester's is Continental. ⌕ *New Rochester Hotel: 726 E. 2nd Ave., 81301,* ☎ *970/385–1920 or 800/664–1920, FAX 970/385–1967. 13 rooms, 2 suites (one with kitchen). Massage. MC, V.* ⌕ *Leland House: 721 E. 2nd Ave.,* ☎ *and fax same as above. 4 rooms, 6 suites. Restaurant. MC, V.*

$$
★
Strater Hotel. This Victorian beauty originally opened in 1887 and has been lovingly restored. Inside, Henry's restaurant and the Diamond Belle Saloon sport crystal chandeliers, beveled windows, original oak beams,

flocked wallpaper, and plush velour curtains. The individually decorated rooms are swooningly exquisite: After all, the hotel owns the largest collection of Victorian walnut antiques in the world and even has its own wood-carving shop on site to create exact period reproductions. All rooms feature intricate tracery and wainscoting, hand-carved armoires and beds, brass lamps, and down pillows. Your room might have entertained Butch Cassidy, Gerald Ford, Francis Ford Coppola, Louis L'Amour (he wrote *The Sacketts* here), JFK, or Marilyn Monroe (the latter two at separate times). ⌑ *699 Main Ave., Durango 81301,* ☎ *970/247–4431 or 800/247–4431,* ☒ *970/259–2208. 93 rooms. Restaurant, bar, hot tub. AE, MC, V.*

$ **Comfort Inn.** This is one of the nicer properties along Durango's strip because it's clean, comfortable, and has sizable rooms decorated in subdued teals and maroons. ⌑ *2930 N. Main St., Durango 81301,* ☎ *970/259–5373. 48 rooms. Pool, hot tub. AE, D, DC, MC, V.*

CONDOMINIUMS

In addition to **Tamarron** and **Purgatory Village Hotel** (*see above* for both), there are fine condo units at **Cascade Village** (50827 U.S. 550 N, Durango 81301, ☎ 970/259–3500 or 800/525–0896; located in Purgatory).

Gunnison

$–$$ **Mary Lawrence Inn.** This restored Victorian is an unexpected and welcome delight in Gunnison. The oversize rooms are furnished with tasteful antiques and Victorian touches such as lace curtains, hand-stencilled walls, handmade quilts, vivid local art, and potpourri. A complimentary gourmet breakfast is offered each morning, along with a smile and advice for the day's adventures from owners Pat and Jim Kennedy. ⌑ *601 N. Taylor St., 81230,* ☎ *970/641–3343. 5 rooms (4 with shared bath). MC, V.*

Lake City

$–$$ **Old Carson Inn.** This peaceful log cabin is nestled among stands of towering aspen and spruce. Don and Judy Berry offer five rooms brimming with rustic charm and nicely appointed with down comforters and private bath. The complimentary country breakfast, served family style, should get you off to a good start. ⌑ *P.O. Box 144, County Road 30, Hinsdale 81235,* ☎ *970/944–2511. 5 rooms. Hot tub. MC, V.*

Mesa Verde

$ **Far View Lodge.** The rustic rooms at this lodge include private balconies with panoramas of Arizona, Utah, and New Mexico. Soothing Southwestern pastels predominate. Another draw here is the hotel's enthusiastic arrangement of guided tours. There are also nightly talks for guests by either a local Native American or an author before a multimedia show on the Anasazi is shown. ⌑ *Box 277, Mancos 81328,* ☎ *970/529–4421. 150 rooms. Restaurant. AE, D, DC, MC, V. Closed mid-Oct.–mid-Apr.*

Montrose

$–$$ **Best Western Red Arrow Motor Inn.** This fully outfitted property is one of the nicest in the area, mainly because of the large, prettily appointed rooms adorned in greens and browns with handsome mahogany furnishings. The full baths include jetted whirlpool tubs. ⌑ *1702 E. Main St., 81401,* ☎ *970/249–9641 or 800/468–9323,* ☒ *970/249–8380. 60 rooms. Restaurant, bar, hot tub, exercise room, laundry service, meeting rooms. AE, DC, D, MC, V.*

$ **Red Barn Motel.** This friendly property offers pleasing, fair-size rooms with all the usual motel amenities, including a coffeemaker. Apart from the Red Arrow, the Red Barn boasts the most facilities in town, at a considerably lower rate than the competition. Children under 12 stay free in their parents' room. ☎ *1417 E. Main St., 81401,* ☎ *970/249–4507. 71 rooms. 2 restaurants, bar, pool, hot tub, sauna, exercise room. AE, DC, D, MC, V.*

Ouray

$$–$$$ **The Damn Yankee.** The balconies of this charming inn offer views of several soaring peaks surrounding the narrow valley in which Ouray is situated. The gracious parlor holds a baby-grand piano and a wood-burning fireplace, and informal musicales by guests are not uncommon. Rooms are a pleasing blend of english country antique and modern comfort, and all include beds draped with down comforters. The third-floor sitting room is always stocked with snacks and soft drinks. In the morning a complimentary gourmet breakfast is provided for guests. ☎ *100 6th St., 81427,* ☎ *970/325–4219 or 800/845–7512. 8 rooms. Hot tub. AE, MC, V.*

$$ **Box Canyon Lodge and Hot Springs.** The private mineral spring is the attraction here, used first by the Ute, then by the Coger Sanitarium (formerly on site). Soak away your cares in two redwood tubs full of steaming 103–107-degree water, with the stunning mountain views around you. The rooms are nondescript, but modern and comfortable, with all amenities. ☎ *45 3rd St., 81427,* ☎ *970/325–4981. 38 rooms. Hot springs. AE, DC, MC, V.*

$ **St. Elmo Hotel.** This tiny 1898 hostelry was originally a haven for "min-
★ ers down on their luck," so the story goes, thanks to its original owner Kitty Heit, who couldn't resist a sob story. Her son's ghost reputedly hovers about protectively. The rooms are awash with polished wood, stained glass, brass or mahogany beds, marble-top armoires, and other antiques. A complimentary breakfast buffet is served in a sunny parlor. The Bon Ton restaurant, Ouray's best, serves fine Continental cuisine with an Italian flair. ☎ *426 Main St., 81427,* ☎ *970/325–4951. 9 rooms. Restaurant, hot tub, sauna, recreation room. AE,D, MC, V.*

Pagosa Springs

$ **Davidson's Country Inn B&B.** This three-story log cabin is located on a 32-acre working ranch in the middle of Colorado's stunning San Juan mountains. The location is perfect, just 20 minutes from Wolf Creek Ski Area (which has no lodging of its own). Rooms are comfortable and crammed with family heirlooms and antiques. A complimentary full breakfast is served. ☎ *2763 Highway 160 East, 81147,* ☎ *970/264–5863. 8 rooms, 4 with shared bath. Recreation room. MC, V.*

Silverton

$ **Wingate Guest House.** The well-traveled Judy Graham (she hails from Wisconsin, has lived in New York, Chicago, and northern California, and has taught at two universities) is the genial hostess of this quaint inn. A prominent landscape artist as well, she adorns the walls of the inn with her own works and those of her friends, along with family photos dating from the Civil War; the entire effect is both sophisticated and homey. The breezy front porch overlooks a majestic thirteener. Large sunny rooms are filled with antiques, and sport down pillows and comforters, as well as an eclectic library culled from Judy's journeys. A complimentary breakfast is served. ☎ *1045 Snowden St.,* ☎ *and fax 970/387–5520. 5 rooms with shared bath. No credit cards.*

$ **Wyman Hotel.** This wonderful 1902 red-sandstone building has 24-inch-thick walls, cathedral ceilings, and arched windows. The attractive rooms all contain period antiques and pretty wallpapers, brass lamps, and VCR. If the Wyman is full, the owners also run the **Alma House**

(220 E. 10th St., ☎ 970/387–5336; open year-round), a charming B&B set in a restored 1902 stone house with neat, tasteful rooms and an excellent restaurant. ⊞ *1371 Greene St.,* ☎ *970/387–5372. 18 rooms. AE, MC, V. Closed mid-Oct.–early May.*

Telluride

$$$$ The Peaks at Telluride Resort and Spa. The pastel-color, prisonlike exterior and lapses in service can be excused at this ski-in/ski-out luxury resort, thanks to its invigorating, revitalizing spa facilities. The setting is glorious, dominated by fourteener Mt. Wilson (the peak on the Coors can). Rooms have balconies and are sizable, if somewhat sterile, in Norwegian wood and muted shades of green, with all amenities, including VCR, minibar, and full bath with dual marble vanities and hair dryer. The Peaks spared no expense in the pampering spa (muds and waters for hydrotherapy and facials are imported from Italy's Terme di Saturnia) and fitness center. Extras include a cardiovascular deck and climbing room. In fact, so much money was sunk into the resort, it went into receivership during its first year. The primary effect seems to be the continual turnover of staff (few of them locals) who, though eager, have difficulty answering the simplest questions about the area. ⊞ *Country Club Dr.,* ☎ *970/728–6800 or 800/223–6725,* FAX *970/728–6567. 145 rooms, 32 suites. 2 restaurants, bar, indoor-outdoor pool, beauty salon, sauna, spa, 5 tennis courts, exercise room, racquetball, squash, water slide. AE, D, DC, MC, V.*

$$$–$$$$ Pennington's Mountain Village Inn. This secluded, exclusive inn fea-
★   tures huge rooms in varying color schemes, with smashing mountain views from private decks, brass beds with cushy down comforters, handcrafted furniture, and stocked minifridges. The pampering includes concierge service, gourmet breakfast, and afternoon hors d'oeuvres. ⊞ *100 Pennington Ct., off Mountain Village Blvd.,* ☎ *970/728–5337 or 800/543–1437. 9 rooms, 3 suites. Lobby lounge, hot tub, steam room, recreation room, laundry service. AE, MC, V.*

$$$ Ice House. This property offers an appealing blend of Scandinavian and Southwestern decor: blond woods, jade carpets, fabrics in beiges, forest greens, and maroons, Native American tapestries and polished wood ceilings. The spacious rooms feature cable TV, oversized tubs, balconies, and minibars. The hotel provides a free Continental breakfast and a place to store your skis. Best of all, the Oak Street lift is just a little more than a block away. ⊞ *310 S. Fir St.,* ☎ *970/728–6300 or 800/544–3436,* FAX *970/728–6358. 42 rooms, 16 2- and 3-bedroom condominiums. Hot tub, sauna. AE, D, DC, MC, V.*

$$$ San Sophia B&B. This is a Victorian-style inn, replete with turrets and gingerbread trim, opened in 1989 by Gary and Diane Eschmann, escapees from the corporate life in Iowa City, Iowa. Pristine mountain light streams into every room, warmly accented with whitewashed oak woodwork. Rooms are on the small side, but luxurious, and offer contemporary brass beds with down comforters, tables and nightstands all handcrafted by Colorado artisans, Gary's stylish black-and-white landscape photographs, skylights in the tiled bathrooms, and stained glass windows over the oversized tubs. The color scheme differs from room to room, but favors desert pastels throughout: You might find terra-cotta with teal accents in one room, and mint or grape with blue trim in another. The amiable staff is extremely helpful. The inn is known for its fabulous gourmet breakfasts and après-ski treats. ⊞ *330 W. Pacific St.,* ☎ *970/728–3001 or 800/537–4781. 16 rooms. Hot tub. AE, MC, V.*

$–$$ New Sheridan Hotel. William Jennings Bryan delivered his rousing "Cross of Gold" speech here in 1896, garnering a presidential nomination in the process. (He was later defeated by McKinley.) Until 1994, when it was purchased by the Four Sisters Inns, the noted California chain, the New Sheridan seemed frozen in time, right down to shared baths and funky furnishings. Now it's new indeed, albeit in tasteful period style. Every room has its own bath, phone, ceiling fan, and cable TV. Decor favors exposed brick walls, old tintypes, marble-top dressing tables, faux Tiffany, crystal, or fringed lamps, and red velour love seats. A complimentary breakfast and afternoon tea complete the picture of fin de siècle gracious living. The lobby has been expanded, and the two historic dining rooms reopened. Other planned additions at press time included a meeting room, a fitness room, and ski lockers. Fortunately, the gorgeous Victorian bar, a local favorite, remains untouched. ☎ *231 W. Colorado Ave., ☎ 970/728–4351. 32 rooms. 2 restaurants, bar. AE, MC, V.*

CONDOMINIUMS

Telluride Central Reservations (☎ 800/525–3455) handles all properties at Telluride Mountain Village, and several in town. **Resort Rentals** (Box 1278, Telluride 81435, ☎ 800/LETS–SKI (800/538–7754) offers several top-notch accommodations in town.

THE ARTS AND NIGHTLIFE

The Arts

Film

The Telluride Film Festival, in September, is considered one of the world's leading showcases of foreign films.

Music

The **Montrose Pavilion** (1800 Pavilion Dr., ☎ 970/249–7015) includes a 602-seat auditorium where well-known musicians, comedians, dance companies, and regional orchestras often perform.

Telluride offers numerous festivals during the summer, including the monstrous jazz and bluegrass festivals.

Theater

In Durango, the **Diamond Circle Theater** (699 Main Ave., ☎ 970/247–4431) stages rip-roaring melodramas, and the **Durango Lively Arts Co.** (Durango Arts Ctr., 835 Main Ave., ☎ 970/259–2606) presents fine community theater productions. In Silverton, **A Theatre Group** (Miners Union Theatre, Greene St., ☎ 970/387–5337) presents a varied repertory season.

Nightlife

Bars and Lounges

In Durango, the hot spot is the **Diamond Belle Saloon** (Strater Hotel, 699 Main Ave., ☎ 970/247–4431), whose antique, gold-leafed filigree bar, honky-tonk piano player, and waitresses dressed as 1880s saloon girls pack them in.

Leimgruber's Bierstube and Restaurant (573 W. Pacific Ave., ☎ 970/728–4663) is arguably Telluride's most popular après-ski hangout, thanks to gemütlich owner Christel Leimgruber, a wonderful Bavarian ambience enhanced by barmaids in dirndls right out of "The Student Prince," and a clientele that seems on the verge of launching into "The Drinking Song." Leimgruber's offers traditional Alpine food like mixed German and wild-game sausage plates, mouth-puckering sauerbraten, and, of course, apple strudel. If you only want a brew, stop by to down a Paulaner or hoist a glass boot, which holds more than a liter of beer. The elegant turn-of-the-century bar at the **Sheridan Hotel** (231 W. Colorado Ave., ☎ 970/728–4351), the billiards parlor at **Swede-Finn Hall** (472 W. Pacific Ave., ☎ 970/728–2085), and the huge fireplaces at **Club Biota** (112 E. Colorado Ave., ☎ 970/728–6132) are the other popular après-ski nightspots.

In Crested Butte, **Kochevar's** (127 Elk Ave., ☎ 970/349–6756), a hand-hewn 1896 log cabin, is a classic pool hall–saloon. The other popular bar in town is the **Wooden Nickel** (222 Elk Ave., ☎ 970/349–6350), which has two happy hours (daily 3–6 and 10:30–midnight).

Casinos

Colorado's first tribal gaming facility, offering limited-stakes gambling—slots, poker (video and live), bingo, and 21—is the **Ute Mountain Casino** (3 Weeminuche Drive at Yellow Hat, Towaoc 81334, ☎ 970/565–8800; open daily 8 AM–4 AM). A second facility has opened at the **Sky Ute Lodge and Casino** (Ignacio, ☎ 970/563–4531), 25 miles southeast of Durango.

Country and Western

In Durango, **Sundance Saloon** (601 E. 2nd St., ☎ 970/259–2985) is a foot-stomping place to "scoot your boot." In Mancos, the **Mancos Social Club** (Main St., no ☎) can be loads of fun, but can also get wild and sometimes hairy. Ridgway's **The Big Barn** (Trail Town, U.S. 550 and Rte. 62, ☎ 970/626–3600) is just that, offering a 1,000-square-foot dance floor, free video country dance lessons, and live music.

Dinner Shows

Bar D Chuckwagon (8080 County Road 250, East Animas Valley, ☎ 970/247–5753) serves barbecued beef, beans, and biscuits, along with a heaping helping of their Bar D Wranglers singing group.

Discos

Yesterdays (Holiday Inn, 800 S. Camino del Rio, Durango, ☎ 970/247–5393) has a dance floor and live DJ nightly.

Jazz Clubs

In Durango, the **Pelican's Nest** (656 Main Ave., ☎ 970/247–4431) is a cool joint for hot jazz, with a sedate Victorian decor. The funky clientele wears anything from cowboy hats to berets. Telluride's **Café Kokopelli** (16 E. Colorado Ave., ☎ 970/728–6101) is a way-cool coffeehouse that dispenses java by day and jazz at night in an attractive space with brick and stone walls, black-and-white photos, and stained glass windows.

Rock Clubs

Farquahrt's (725 Main Ave., Durango, ☎ 970/247–5440) is decorated with antiques, but attracts a lively, youthful crowd that likes to rock and roll to the best local bands. There's also a "ski lodge" version at **Purgatory Mountain Village** (☎ 970/247–9000, ext. 3123).

In Mt. Crested Butte, **Rafters** (☎ 970/349–2298) is packed to the rafters of this big barn with cheap eats, strong drinks, and loud music (often live on weekends).

In Telluride, **One World Café** (114 E. Colorado Ave., ☎ 970/728–5530) is an eclectic club: Japanese fans and lanterns contrast intriguingly with the building's original, corrugated tin roof and stone- and brickwork. Tasty Thai is served in the front restaurant–art gallery. Exquisite stained glass doors lead to the Conga Room disco, where the DJ spins everything from Motown to salsa, and hot funk and ska bands perform regularly. The **Last Dollar Saloon** (100 E. Colorado Ave., ☏ 970/728–4800) couldn't be less chic (and couldn't care less); when it's not a pool hall–saloon, it's the best venue for local rock bands. **Excelsior Café** (200 W. Colorado Ave., ☏ 970/728–4250) is the spot to hear the best in folk rock.

Singles

Rafters in Crested Butte and **Farquahrt's** in Purgatory/Durango (*see* Rock Clubs, *above*) are the closest things to classic pick-up joints in Southwest Colorado.

SOUTHWEST COLORADO ESSENTIALS

Arriving and Departing by Plane

Airports and Airlines

Durango: The **Durango-La Plata Airport** (☏ 970/247–8143) receives daily flights from America West (☏ 800/247–5692), Mesa Airlines (☏ 800/637–2247), and United Express (☏ 800/241–6522).

Gunnison: Delta (☏ 800/221–1212), United Express, and American (☏ 800/433–7300; nonstop from Chicago, Dallas, and San Jose) fly into **Gunnison County Airport** (☏ 970/641–0526), which also serves Crested Butte.

Montrose: **Montrose Airport** (☏ 970/249–3203) is served by United and America West.

Telluride: **Telluride Regional Airport** (☏ 970/728–5313) welcomes flights from Delta, Mesa Airlines (☏ 800/MESA–AIR [800/637–2247]), and connecting flights from major airlines. At press time, there was speculation about which airlines those would be.

Between the Airport and the Resort

BY SHUTTLE

Crested Butte: **Alpine Express** (☏ 970/641–5074 or 800/822–4844); Durango: **Durango Transportation** (☏ 970/247–4161 or 800/626–2066); Montrose: **Western Express Taxi** (☏ 970/249–8880); Telluride: **Skip's Taxi** (☏ 970/728–6667) and **Telluride Transit** (☏ 970/728–6000). Shuttles average $15–$20 per person.

Arriving and Departing by Car and Bus

By Car

If you're entering Colorado from the south, U.S. 550, U.S. 160, and U.S. 666 access the Four Corners region. From the east or west, I–70 (U.S. 6) intersects U.S. 50 South in Grand Junction, to reach the San Juans and Four Corners area. From the north, I–25 intersects in Denver with I–70, for a long drive to U.S. 50. Alternatively, U.S. 40 enters northwest Colorado from Utah, connecting with Route 64 in Dinosaur, then Route 139 south in Rangely, to I–70 East to Grand Junction.

San Luis Valley can be reached via U.S. 160 from both the west (direct from Durango) and the east (via I–25), or via U.S. 285 from New Mexico.

By Bus

Greyhound Lines (☏ 800/231–2222) serves most of the major towns in the region via Salt Lake City, Denver, or Albuquerque/Santa Fe.

Getting Around

By Car

The main roads are Route 135 between Crested Butte and Gunnison; U.S. 50 linking Poncha Springs, Gunnison, Montrose, and Delta; Route 149 between Gunnison, Lake City, and Creede; U.S. 550 from Montrose to Ridgway; Route 62 and Route 145 linking Ridgway with Telluride, Dolores, and Cortez; Route 110 running from Ridgway through Ouray and Silverton to Durango; and U.S. 160, the closest thing to a major highway in the area, from Cortez to Durango via the Mesa Verde National Park north entrance.

By Bus or Shuttle

In Crested Butte, the **Crested Butte Shuttle** (no ☎) runs regularly between the town and the ski area.

In Durango, **Durango Lift** (☎ 970/259–5438) has regular bus service up and down Main Street, as well as to Purgatory Ski Area during ski season.

In Telluride, **The Tellu-Ride** (☎ 970/728–5700) offers free shuttle service between the town of Telluride and Mountain Village, as well as down-valley service to Norwood.

By Taxi

In most cases you'll need to call for a cab; taxis are plentiful and the wait is only about 15 minutes. **Crested Butte Town Taxi** (☎ 970/349–5543); **Durango Transportation** (Durango, ☎ 970/259–4818); **Montrose Taxi** (Montrose, ☎ 970/249–8880); **Skip's Taxi** (Telluride, ☎ 970/728–6667); and **Telluride Transit** (Telluride, ☎ 970/728–6000).

Guided Tours

Orientation

Adventures to the Edge (Crested Butte, ☎ 970/349–5219) creates customized treks, ski tours and alpine ascents in the Crested Butte area. **ARA Mesa Verde Company** (Mancos, ☎ 970/529–4421) runs three- and six-hour tours into Mesa Verde National Park.

Durango Transportation (☎ 970/259–4818) arranges tours of Mesa Verde, Chaco Canyon, and the San Juan Skyway.

Historic Tours of Telluride (☎ 970/728–6639) provides humorous walking tours of this historic town, enlivening them with stories of famed figures like Butch Cassidy and Jack Dempsey. **San Juan Scenic Jeep Tours** (☎ 970/325–4444 or 800/325–4385) explores the high country in open vehicles that allow unobstructed views.

Sierra Vista Tours (☎ 719/379–3277) offers tours of the area, including the Great Sand Dunes.

Special Interest

NATIVE HERITAGE PROGRAMS

Crow Canyon Archaeological Center. The center promotes greater understanding and appreciation of Anasazi culture by guiding visitors through excavations and botanical studies in the region. Also included in the week-long programs are day trips to isolated canyon sites and hands-on lessons in weaving and pottery-making with Native American artisans. Day programs are also available on a reservation-only basis to families and groups. *23390 County Road K, Cortez 81321,* ☎ *970/565–8975 or 800/422–8975.*

Ute Mountain Tribal Park. Native American guides lead grueling hikes into this dazzling primitive repository of Anasazi ruins, including the majestic Tree House cliff dwelling and enchanting Eagle's Nest petroglyphs. It's also a wonderful opportunity to learn more about the Ute tribe's culture and customs. Tours usually start at the Ute Mountain Pottery Plant, 15 miles south of Cortez, on U.S. 666. Overnight camping can also be arranged. *Towaoc 81334, ☎ 970/565–3751, ext. 282.*

Important Addresses and Numbers

Hospitals

Cortez: **Southwest Memorial Hospital** (1311 N. Mildred St., ☎ 970/565–6666); Durango: **Mercy Medical Center** (375 E. Park Ave., ☎ 970/247–4311); Gunnison: **Gunnison Valley Hospital** (214 E. Denver Ave., ☎ 970/641–1456); Montrose: **Montrose Memorial Hospital** (800 S. 3rd St., ☎ 970/249–2211); San Luis Valley: **San Luis Valley Regional Medical Center** (106 Blanca Ave., Alamosa, ☎ 719/589–2511); Telluride: **Telluride Medical Center** (500 W. Pacific Ave., ☎ 970/728–3848).

Visitor Information

Cortez Area Chamber of Commerce (925 S. Broadway 81321, ☎ 970/565–3414 or 800/346–6528); **Crested Butte–Mt. Crested Butte Chamber of Commerce** (7 Emmons Loop 81321, ☎ 970/349–6438 or 800/545–4505); **Durango Chamber Resort Association** (111 S. Camino del Rio 81302, ☎ 970/247–0312 or 800/525–8855); **Gunnison County Chamber of Commerce** (500 E. Tomichi Ave., 81230, ☎ 970/641–1501 or 800/274–7580); **Lake City Chamber of Commerce** (306 N. Silver St., 81235, ☎ 970/944–2527); **Mesa Verde National Park** (Supt. Mesa Verde Park 81330, ☎ 970/529–4465); **Mesa Verde Country** (Box HH, Cortez 81321, ☎ 800/253–1616); **Montrose Chamber of Commerce** (1519 E. Main St., 81401, ☎ 800/873–0244) and **Visitor Information Center** (2490 S. Townsend Ave., 81401, ☎ 970/249–1726); **Ouray County Chamber** (1222 Main St., 81427, ☎ 970/325–4746 or 800/228–1876); **Pagosa Springs Chamber of Commerce** (402 San Juan St., 81147, ☎ 303/264–2360 or 800/252–2204); **San Luis Valley Information Center** (Box 165, 1st St. and Jefferson Ave., Monte Vista 81144, ☎ 719/672–3355); **San Luis Visitor Center** (Box 9, San Luis 81152, ☎ 719/672–3355); **Silverton Chamber of Commerce** (414 Greene St., 81433, ☎ 970/387–5654 or 800/752–4494); **Southwest Colorado Travel Region** (call 800/933–4340 for travel planner and information); **Telluride Chamber Resort Association** (666 W. Colorado Ave., 81435, ☎ 970/728–3041).

5 South Central Colorado

THE CONTENTED RESIDENTS of Colorado's south central region believe they live in an ideal location, and it's hard to argue with them. To the west, the Rockies form a majestic backdrop; to the east, the plains stretch for miles. Taken together, the setting ensures a mild, sunny climate year-round, and makes skiing and golfing on the same day feasible with no more than a two- or three-hour drive. This easy access to diverse outdoor activities attracts tourists seeking a varied vacation: They can climb the Collegiate Peaks one day, and go white-water rafting on the Arkansas River the next.

For those who enjoy culture and history, south central Colorado has plenty to offer, its territory scouted and explored by the likes of Kit Carson and Zebulon Pike. The haunting remains of the Santa Fe Trail, which guided pioneers westward, weave through the southeastern section of the region. Towns such as Cripple Creek and Trinidad are living history. In fact, residents are so proud of their mining heritage that, despite economic hard times, they've earmarked tax revenues to preserve local landmarks. Equally alluring are cities such as Colorado Springs and Pueblo, numbered among the most contemporary in the West, with sleek shining arts and convention centers.

The region also abounds in natural and man-made wonders, such as the yawning Royal Gorge and its astounding suspension bridge; the eerie sandstone formations of the Garden of the Gods; and the space-age architecture of the U.S. Air Force Academy. However, the most indelible landmark is unquestionably Pikes Peak, from whose vantage point Katharine Lee Bates penned "America the Beautiful." The song's lyrics remain an accurate description of south central Colorado's many glories.

EXPLORING

Numbers in the margin correspond to points of interest on the Colorado Springs and South Central Colorado maps.

Tour 1: Colorado Springs/Manitou Springs and Pikes Peak

➊ **Colorado Springs,** the state's second-largest city, unfortunately made headlines in 1992 when it was identified as the headquarters for several right-wing groups behind the controversial Amendment 2, which outlawed antidiscrimination legislation that gave protection to the gay and lesbian community. With active and retired military personnel and their families comprising nearly a third of the population, it's no surprise that the Springs is staunchly conservative. Although for a brief time a state boycott was called and the Springs continues to be seen as the place where the controversy snowballed, the political situation hasn't affected tourism significantly. The Springs, after all, has a dazzling array of tourist attractions. Pikes Peak, for instance, is the state's most famous landmark, but only one of the city's many natural and man-made wonders. Other tourist draws include the Cave of the Winds, the Garden of the Gods, and historic neighborhoods such as Manitou Springs and Old Colorado City.

Colorado Springs was created by General William Palmer, president of the Denver & Rio Grande Railroad, as a utopian vision of fine living in the 1870s. The original broad, tree-lined boulevards still grace the southwest quadrant of the city. With the discovery of hot springs

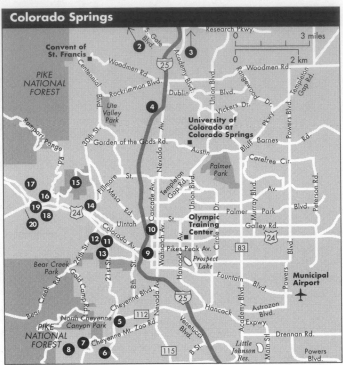

in the area, the well-to-do descended on the bustling resort town to take the waters and to enjoy the mild climate and fresh air. It soon earned the monikers "Saratoga of the West" and "Little London," the latter for the snob-appeal of its considerable resident and visiting English population. The discovery of gold at nearby Cripple Creek toward the end of the century signaled another boom for the Springs. In the early part of the 1900s, until the mines petered out just before World War I, the residents' per-capita wealth was the highest in the nation.

After World War II, the city fathers invited the military to move in, and the city's personality changed drastically. Ironically, the **U.S. Air Force Academy,** which set up camp in 1954, has become one of Colorado's largest tourist attractions. A portion of the academy is most notable for its striking futuristic design; but even more extraordinary are the 18,000 beautiful acres of land that have been dedicated as a game reserve and sprinkled with antique and historic aircraft. Most of the campus is off-limits to civilians, but there is a 13½-mile self-guided tour. At the visitors' center you'll find photo exhibits, a model of a cadet's room, a gift shop, a snack bar, and short videos on Air Force history, cadet training, athletics, and academics. Other tour attractions include a B-52 display, sports facilities, a planetarium, a parade ground (the impressive cadet review takes place daily at noon), and the chapel. The Air Force chapel is easily recognized by its unconventional design, which features 17 spires that resemble sharks' teeth or billowing sails. Catholic, Jewish, and Protestant services can be held simultaneously, without the congregations disturbing one another. *Exit 156B, off I–25 N,* ☎ *719/472–2555.* ☛ *Free.* ☉ *Daily 9–5.*

❸ Directly across I–25 from the north gate of the academy is the **Western Museum of Mining and Industry,** preserving the rich history of mining through comprehensive exhibits of equipment and techniques and hands-on demonstrations, including gold panning. This attraction is an oasis during the summer season, thanks to its stunning mountain setting. *Exit 156A off I–25 N,* ☎ *719/488–0880.* ☛ *$5 adults, $4 students and senior citizens, $2 children 5–12.* ⊙ *Mar.–Nov., Mon.–Sat. 9–4; Sun. noon–4.*

❹ Continue along I–25 South toward downtown and get off at exit 147. A bronze rodeo bull lures visitors to the **Pro Rodeo Hall of Fame and Museum of the American Cowboy.** Even a tenderfoot would get a kick out of this museum, which includes changing displays of Western art; permanent photo exhibits that capture both the excitement of bronco-bustin' and the lonely life of the cowpoke; gorgeous saddles and belt buckles; and multimedia tributes to rodeo's greatest competitors (including the unsung clowns who often save their butts!). *(Exit 147 off 1–25), 101 Pro Rodeo Dr.,* ☎ *719/528–4764.* ☛ *$5 adults, $2 children 5–12.* ⊙ *Daily 9–5.*

TIME OUT **Old Chicago** (7115 Commerce Center Dr., ☎ 719/593-7678) is one of many "concept restaurants" popular throughout Colorado. This one features a sports bar in front and a pleasant enclosed atrium and outdoor patio in back. It's a pizza, pasta, and beer (110 varieties) joint, and scores on all counts.

❺ Now take I–25 or Nevada Avenue to the southern end of the city for a glimpse of its posher neighborhoods, of which the pink-stucco, Italianate **Broadmoor,** built in 1918, stands as the most aristocratic symbol. One of the world's great luxury resorts, its 30 buildings and three championship 18-hole golf courses cover 3,500 acres of prime real estate and create a minicity unto itself. It stands as a tribute to the foresight of its original owner, the enterprising Spencer Penrose, one of Colorado Springs' wealthiest (and most conspicuously consuming) philanthropists. Having constructed the zoo, the Cheyenne Mountain Highway, and Pikes Peak Cog Railway, Penrose is credited with making the town the tourist mecca it is today.

Two superb museums are included in the Broadmoor complex: the **International Skating Hall of Fame and Museum** (20 1st St., ☎ 719/635–5200; ☛ Free; open June–Sept., Mon.–Sat. 10–4 and Oct.–May, weekdays 10–4), which documents the history of the sport and immortalizes its greatest practitioners such as Sonja Henie and the Springs' own Peggy Fleming; and the exquisite **Carriage House** (Lake Circle, no ☎; ☛ Free; open daily 9–noon and 1–5), which displays Penrose's prodigious carriage collection, from broughams (closed carriage with driver outside) to opera buses.

From the Broadmoor, make a left onto Mesa Avenue, and then turn right onto Evans. At the corner of Evans and Pine Grove, a collection of enormous abstract **aluminum sculptures** covers the lawn of Dr. Starr Gideon Kempf. The lampposts, windmills, mythical birds, and other fantastical figures are an ongoing hobby of the doctor's.

❻ Continue along Evans, and then take the Cheyenne Mountain Zoo Road to begin the ascent of Cheyenne Mountain. Aside from stunning panoramic views of the city and Pikes Peak in the distance, the road also offers two major attractions. First up is the **Cheyenne Mountain Zoo,** America's highest zoo, at 7,000 feet, with more than 800 animals amid mossy boulders and ponderosa pines. *Cheyenne Mt. Zoo Rd.,* ☎ *719/475–9555.* ☛ *$5.50 adults, $4.50 senior citizens, $3 children 3–11.* ⊙ *June–Sept., daily 9–6; Oct.–May, daily 9–5.*

❼ Continue up the spiraling road to the **Will Rogers Shrine of the Sun,** the other big attraction off the zoo road. This "singing" tower guarded by two carved Chinese dogs was dedicated in 1937 after the tragic plane crash that claimed Rogers' life. Its interior is painted with all manner of Western scenes (in which Rogers and Spencer Penrose figure prominently) and is plastered with photos and the homespun sayings of America's favorite cowboy. *Cheyenne Mt. Zoo Rd., no* ☎. ☛ *Free with zoo ticket.* ☉ *Memorial Day–Labor Day, daily 9–5:30; Labor Day–Memorial Day, daily 9–4:30.*

❽ At the base of the mountain, turn west on Cheyenne Road and follow the signs to **Seven Falls.** The road up to this transcendent series of seven cascades is touted as the "grandest mile of scenery in Colorado." Considering the state's splendors, that may be an exaggeration, but the red-rock canyon *is* stunning—though no more so than the falls themselves, plummeting into a tiny emerald pool. A set of 265 steep steps leads to the top, but there is an elevator for those who don't wish to walk. ☎ *719/632–0765.* ☛ *$4 adults, $2 children under 13.* ☉ *Daily 9–5.*

❾ Take Cheyenne Mountain Zoo Road back into town and turn north on Nevada Avenue. Colorado Springs' handsome downtown contains many historically significant buildings, including the old El Paso County Courthouse, now the admirable **Pioneers Museum.** This repository of artifacts relating to the entire Pikes Peak area is most notable for the wonderful special exhibits it mounts (or are loaned on tour from institutions such as the Smithsonian), such as a quilt competition commemorating the 100th anniversary of the song "America the Beautiful." *215 S. Tejon St.,* ☎ *719/578–6650.* ☛ *Free.* ☉ *Mon.–Sat. 10–5, Sun. 1–5.*

❿ A few blocks north is the **Colorado Springs Fine Arts Center,** an exemplary space that includes a performing-arts theater, an art school, and a room devoted to the work and life of famed Western artist Charles Russell. Also at the center are a handsome sculpture garden, a surprisingly fine permanent collection of modern art, and rotating exhibits that highlight the cultural contributions of the area's diverse ethnic groups. *30 W. Dale St.,* ☎ *719/634–5581.* ☛ *$3 adults, $1.50 senior citizens and students, $1 children 5–12.* ☉ *Tues.–Fri. 9–5, Sat. 10–5, Sun. 1–5.*

Cross under I–25 to Colorado Avenue and take it west, turning left on 21st Street, which you'll follow to the cluster of three wildly different attractions: Ghost Town, the Van Briggle Art Pottery Factory and Showroom, and the Hall of Presidents Living Wax Studio.

⓫ If you can't make it to Buckskin Joe Park and Railway (*see* What to See and Do with Children, *below*), then visit **Ghost Town,** a complete, authentic Western town with a sheriff's office, general store, saloon, and blacksmith. You can play a real player piano and nickelodeon. *400 S. 21st St.,* ☎ *719/634–0696.* ☛ *$3.95 adults, $2 children 6–16.* ☉ *May–Labor Day, Mon.–Sat. 9–6, Sun. noon–6; Sept.–Apr., Mon.–Sat. noon–5, Sun. 10–5.*

⓬ Right across the way is the famous **Van Briggle Art Pottery Factory and Showroom,** in operation since the turn of the century. Van Briggle ceramic work is admired for its graceful lines and pure, vibrant glazes. A free tour of the facility is offered, culminating—naturally—in the mind-boggling showroom. *600 S. 21st St.,* ☎ *719/633–7729.* ☛ *Free.* ☉ *Mon.–Sat. 8:30–5.*

⓭ One block south is the admittedly hokey but enjoyable **Hall of Presidents Living Wax Studio,** with more than 100 wax figures crafted at the famed Madame Tussaud's in London. The exhibits run from Washington at Trenton through Jefferson signing the "Declaration of Independence," right up to the Clintons (though there are surprising omissions, such as Herbert Hoover, for example). There's also an Enchanted Forest, alive with storybook characters from Peter Pan to Pinocchio. *1050 S. 21st St., ☎ 719/635–3553.* ☛ *$4 adults, $2 children 5–12.* ☉ *Oct.-May, daily 10–5; June–Sept., daily 9–9.*

⑭ Back on Colorado Avenue you'll find yourself in **Old Colorado City,** once a separate, rowdier town where miners caroused, today it's a National Historic Landmark District whose restored buildings house the city's choicest galleries and boutiques. Continue west along Colorado Avenue to one of the region's most riveting sights: the gnarled jutting
⑮ spires and sensuously abstract monoliths of the **Garden of the Gods.** These magnificent, eroded red-sandstone formations were sculpted more than 300 million years ago. The new (1995) visitor center has several geologic, historic, and hands-on displays.

Follow the road as it loops through the Garden of the Gods, past such oddities as the Three Graces, the Siamese Twins, and the Kissing Camels. High Point, near the south entrance, provides camera hounds with the ultimate photo-op: the jagged formations framing Pikes Peak.

As you exit the park, take U.S. 24 West; on your right are two popular tourist attractions: the Cliff Dwellings Museum and the Cave of
⑯ the Winds. The **Cliff Dwellings Museum,** an obvious tourist trap, is something of an embarrassment to locals. It's replete with Native American flute music piped through the chambers, but this minireplica of Mesa Verde is a decent (and educational) substitute if you haven't seen the real thing. *U.S. 24, ☎ 719/685–5242.* ☛ *$3 adults, $2 children 12 and under.* ☉ *June–Aug., daily 9–8; May and Sept., daily 9–6; Mar.–Apr. and Oct.–Dec., daily 9–5; Jan.–Feb., weekends 9–5.*

⑰ The **Cave of the Winds** was discovered by two boys in 1880, and has been exploited as a tourist sensation ever since. The entrance is through the requisite "trading post," but once inside the cave you'll forget the hype and commercialism. You'll pass through grand chambers with such names as the Crystal Palace, Oriental Garden, the Old Curiosity Shop, the Temple of Silence, and the Valley of Dreams. The cave contains examples of every major sort of limestone formation, from the traditional stalactites and stalagmites to delicate cave flowers, rare anthracite crystals, flowstone (rather like candle wax), and cave coral. Enthusiastic guides, most of them members of the Grotto Club (a spelunking group), also run more adventurous cave expeditions, called Wild Tours. The entrance to the cave is via **Williams Canyon,** off the highway. Summer evenings, a laser show transforms the canyon into an unsurpassed sound-and-light show of massively corny, yet undeniably effective, proportions. *U.S. 24, ☎ 719/685–5444.* ☛ *$8.* ☉ *Daily, 9–5; 45-minute tours conducted continuously.*

⑱ On the left of U.S. 24 headed west, is the lovely **Manitou Springs,** home of Manitou Springs mineral water. The **Chamber of Commerce** (354 Manitou Ave., ☎ 719/685–5089) offers free walking tours of the springs, set in this quaint National Historic Landmark District, which exudes a slightly shabby, but genteel charm. The springs are all naturally effervescent; you might stop by Soda Springs for an after-dinner spritz (it tastes and acts just like Alka-Seltzer), or Twin Springs, sweet-tasting and loaded with lithium (which, say residents, is why they're always calm and smiling). Antique trolleys ply the streets in summer. Manitou has a growing artist population; the Manitou Art Project sponsors a year-round public exhibition, and the galleries offer a delight-ful ArtWalk Thursday evenings in summer.

Among the must-see attractions in town is William Packer's grandiose estate, **Glen Eyrie.** The property is maintained by a nondenomina-tional fundamentalist sect called the Navigators, which publishes var-ious religious literary works. The original gas lamps and sandstone structures remain, many of whose rocks were hewn with the moss still clinging, to give them an aged look. Try to come here for high tea, or during the Christmas season when there's an extravagant drive-through nativity scene. *North of Garden of the Gods, 30th St., ☎ 719/598–1212. ☛ $5 over 15, $4 senior citizens; tours June–Aug., weekdays twice daily; Sept.–May, Sun.; hours vary so call ahead.*

⑲ Another Manitou Springs attraction, albeit an unusual one, is **Mira-mont Castle Museum**—a wonderfully Byzantine extravaganza com-missioned in 1895 as the private home of French priest Jean-Baptiste Francolon. The museum is a mad medley of exhibits, with 46 rooms offering a wide variety of displays, from original furnishings to antique doll and railroad collections. *9 Capitol Hill Ave., ☎ 719/685–1011. ☛ $2. ☉ June–Aug., daily 10–5; Sept.–May, daily noon–3.*

⑳ The **Pikes Peak Cog Railway,** the world's highest cog railway, departs from Manitou and follows a frolicking stream up a steep canyon, through copses of quaking aspen and towering lodgepole pines, before reaching the timberline and the 14,100-foot summit. *Ruxton Ave. (depot), ☎ 719/685–5401. Round-trip fare: $21 adults, $9.50 chil-dren 5–11. Runs May–Oct., daily 9–6.*

You can also drive the 19-mile **Pikes Peak Highway,** which rises nearly 7,000 feet in its precipitous, dizzying climb to the **Summit House,** a pit-stop café and trading post. This is the same route that leading race-car drivers follow every July in the famed "Race to the Clouds," at 100 miles an hour.

Tour 2: The Collegiate Peaks and the Arkansas River

This tour loops through stunning alpine and desert scenery, passing thrilling natural attractions such as the Florissant Fossil Beds and Royal Gorge.

㉑ Leave Manitou Springs on U.S. 24 North and West, and travel 15 miles to the town of **Florissant.** Three miles south of town (follow signs) is the little-known **Florissant Fossil Beds National Monument,** a treasure trove for would-be paleontologists, where volcanic ash has perfectly preserved the remains of a 35–40-million-year-old primeval rain for-est. The visitor center offers guided walks into the monument, or you can follow the well-marked hiking trails and lose yourself amid the Oligocene period, among 300-foot petrified redwoods. *U.S. 24, fol-low signs, ☎ 719/748–3253. ☛ $3. ☉ Daily, 10–5.*

㉒ From Florissant, a dirt road leads to **Cripple Creek,** Colorado's third legalized gambling town. Cripple Creek once had the most lucrative mines in the state—and 10,000 boozing, brawling, bawdy citizens. Today, its old mining structures and the stupendous curtain of the Collegiate Peaks are marred by slag heaps and parking lots. Although the town isn't as picturesque as Central City or Black Hawk (*see* Exploring *in* Chapter 2, Denver), the other gambling hot spots, Cripple Creek—a little rougher and dustier than the others—feels more authentic.

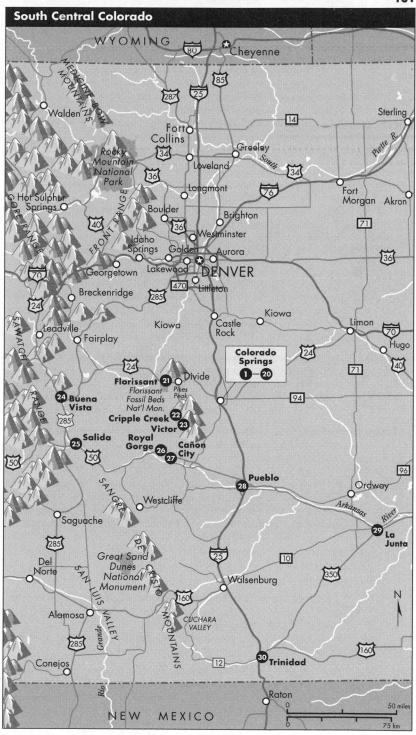

South Central Colorado

There are a few worthwhile attractions here: The **Cripple Creek District Museum** (east end of Bennett Ave., ☎ 719/689–2634; ☛ $2; open late-May–mid-Oct., daily 10–5; mid-Oct.–late-May, weekends 12–4) provides a fascinating glimpse into mining life at the turn of the century. The **Mollie Kathleen Mine Tour** (Rte. 67, north of town, ☎ 719/689–2466; ☛ $6; open May–Oct., daily 9–5) descends 1,000 feet into the bowels of the earth in a mine that operated continuously from 1892 to 1961. **Imperial Hotel and Casino** (123 N. 3rd St., ☎ 719/689–7777) offers a peek into the era's high life and a chance spin on the wheel of fortune.

A narrow-gauge railroad (depot at Cripple Creek District Museum, ☎ 719/689–2640; fare: $6; runs Memorial Day–Oct., daily 10–5, departs every 45 min) weaves past abandoned mines to Cripple Creek's former rival **Victor.** In bygone days, more than 50 ore-laden trains made this run daily. Today, however, Victor is a sad town, virtually a ghost of its former self; walking the streets—past several abandoned or partially restored buildings—is an eerie experience that does far more to evoke the mining (and post-mining) days than its tarted-up neighbor.

㉔ Back on U.S. 24 West, continue on to **Buena Vista** (or as locals pronounce it, *byoo*-na *vis*-ta), a town ringed by sky-scraping mountains, the most impressive being the **Collegiate Peaks.** The 14,000-foot giants attract alumni climbers from Yale, Princeton, Harvard, Columbia, and Oxford. A small mining town turned resort community, Buena Vista offers the usual historic buildings alternating with motels.

The most compelling reason to visit this area is for the almost unequaled variety of recreational activities. Hiking, biking, and climbing in the **Collegiate Peaks Wilderness Area** are among the favorite jaunts. Also, Buena Vista bills itself as "The White-water Rafting Capital of the World" and offers numerous excursions down the Arkansas River.

TIME OUT After a full day of activities, check out the **Mt. Princeton Hot Springs** (5 mi west of Nathrop, CR 162, ☎ 719/395–2447), for a restorative soak. The springs has three swimming pools and several private tubs.

Before leaving downtown Buena Vista, meander through the four rooms of the **Buena Vista Heritage Museum.** Each is devoted to a different aspect of regional history: One concentrates on mining equipment and minerals, another is devoted to fashions and household utensils, a third to working models of the three railroads that serviced the area in its heyday, and the last to historical photos. *E. Main St.,* ☎ *719/395–2515.* ☛ *$2 adults, $1 children under 16.* ☺ *Memorial Day–Labor Day, daily 9–5.*

㉕ If Buena Vista has any competition in the beautiful scenery and outdoors activities departments, it comes from **Salida,** approximately 25 miles south along U.S. 24 and CO 291, and situated along the Arkansas River. It, too, is dominated by imposing peaks, with fourteener **Mt. Shavano** its landmark.

㉖ Head east on U.S. 50 to reach one of the Rockies' most powerful sights. The 1,053-foot-deep **Royal Gorge,** often called "The Grand Canyon of Colorado," was carved by the Arkansas River more than 3 million years ago. It's a tribute to the powers of nature, but it's spanned by no less monumental an achievement: the world's highest suspension bridge. Near the bridge, hubristic signs trumpet, "Who says you can't improve on Nature?" Never intended for transport, it was originally constructed in 1929 as a commercial enterprise. It now attracts more than half a million visitors annually, causing a fair amount of exploitation to the area. Families love crossing the bridge, particularly on gusty afternoons when it sways, adding to the thrill. Other activities at the gorge are: riding the astonishing aerial tram (2,200 feet long and 1,178 feet above the canyon floor) and descending the **Scenic Railway** (the world's steepest-incline rail line) to stare at the bridge 1,000 feet above. There is also a theater that presents a 25-minute multimedia show, outdoor musical entertainment in summer, and the usual assortment of food concessions and gift shops. *Royal Gorge Complex,* ☎ *719/275–7507.* ☛ *$8 adults, $6 children 4–11.* ⊙ *Oct.–May, daily 9–5; June–Sept., daily 8–8.*

This site has its share of history, too: The famed Royal Gorge War between the Denver & Rio Grande and Santa Fe railroads occurred here in 1877. The battle was over the right-of-way through the canyon, which could only accommodate one rail line. Rival crews would lay tracks during the day and dynamite each other's work at night. The dispute was finally settled in court—the Denver & Rio Grande won.

㉗ Cañon City, an undeniably quirky town—and proud of it—is the gateway to the gorge. Where else would you find a shop entitled "Fluff 'em, Buff 'em, Stuff 'em"? Would you have guessed the services it provides: hairstyling, car waxing, and taxidermy? From its aggressive, even tacky, strip-mall veneer (softened, fortunately, by some lovely old buildings) you'd think Cañon City existed solely for tourism. Nothing could be further from the truth. Cañon City's livelihood stems from its lordly position as "Colorado's Prison Capital." There are 10 prisons in the vicinity, all of which the citizens lobbied to get! It might seem a perverse source of income to court, but consider that the prisons have pumped nearly $200 million into the local economy, and, as an affable former-mayor states, "You got these people walking around Denver and the Springs, here at least they're locked up."

Morbid curiosity seekers and sensationalists will revel in the **Colorado Territorial Prison Museum,** which formerly housed the Women's State Correctional Facility. Now, it exhaustively documents prison life in Colorado, through old photos and newspaper accounts, as well as confiscated inmates' weapons, contraband, and one warden's china set. The individual cell exhibits were, of course, funded by local businesses and civic organizations. There's also a video room where you can view titles such as "Prisons Ain't What They Used to Be" and "Drug Avengers." The original gas chamber sits in the courtyard. This museum is grim, grisly, gruesome, and—fascinating. *1st and Macon Sts.,* ☎ *719/269–3015.* ☛ *$3.* ⊙ *May–Oct., daily 8:30–8; Nov.–Apr., Wed.–Sun., 10–5.*

To be fair, Cañon City is also called the "Climate Capital of Colorado," for its temperate year-round conditions that attract retirees in droves. Set 12 miles north of town, amid glorious terrain, is the city-owned **Redrock Park,** a magnet for hikers and climbers thanks to its twisted sandstone formations. **Garden Park,** also city-owned, has rich deposits of dinosaur fossils.

A gravel and dirt road (open only in summer) follows the old tracks that were once used to transport ore. Running through both parks and north to Cripple Creek, the route—traversable only with a four-wheel-drive vehicle—winds through red-rock canyons and the **Rampart Range,** over a rickety (but reinforced) wooden trestle bridge. Mountains, canyons, meadows, and sky provide a background of vivid primary colors.

Tour 3: The Santa Fe Trail

This tour winds through the historic towns of Pueblo and Trinidad, in part following the route of the pioneers.

㉘ Now head east on U.S. 50 to the junction of I–25, at **Pueblo.** This is a city divided: It can't make up its mind whether to promote its historic origins or the active lifestyle it offers, with biking in the mountains and golfing in the desert. A working-class, multiethnic steel town, Pueblo lacks some of the traditional glamour of towns like Aspen, whose growth mushroomed from gold and silver. Though sizable, it remains in the shadow of Colorado Springs to the north. The resulting civic inferiority complex actually led the city council to hire an image consultant to improve its reputation at home and elsewhere.

Civic leaders, as well, have embarked on an ambitious beautification plan, encouraging citizens to volunteer their time and talents. This has especially paid dividends in the extraordinary ongoing **Pueblo Levee Project,** the largest mural in the world. The grass-roots movement began with a lone artist's whimsical "statement," and now includes all manner of witty graffiti and illustrations gracing the levee along the Arkansas River. In addition, Pueblo businesses have banded together to sponsor sculptors whose works now adorn the ramps of I–25.

This civic-mindedness extends to the historical neighborhoods of Pueblo, which have a stunning collection of Victorian homes. The **Union Avenue Historic District,** including the glorious 1889 sandstone-and-brick Union Avenue Depot, is a repository of century-old stores and warehouses, now a fashionable commercial district. Among the landmarks are Mesa Junction, which celebrates Pueblo as a crossroads, at the point where two trolleys met; and Pitkin Avenue, lined with fabulous gabled and turreted mansions attesting to the town's more prosperous times. Walking-tour brochures of each district are available at the **Chamber of Commerce** (302 N. Santa Fe Ave., ☎ 719/542–1704). Pueblo's rich history is also on display in several superlative museums.

The **El Pueblo Museum** is ostensibly a repository for the city's history, but extends its scope to chronicle life on the plains from the prehistoric era onward, as well as Pueblo's role as a cultural and geographic crossroads, beginning when it was a trading post in the 1840s. *324 W. 1st St.,* ☎ *719/583–0453.* ☛ *$2.50 adults, $2 senior citizens and children 6–16.* ☉ *Mon.–Sat. 10–4:30, Sun. noon–3.*

At the airport, the **Fred E. Weisbrod Aircraft Museum** traces the development of American military aviation, with its more than two dozen aircraft in mint condition, ranging from a Lockheed F-80 fighter plane to a McDonnell Phantom F-4. *31001 Magnuson, Pueblo Memorial Airport,* ☎ *719/948–9219.* ☛ *Free. Weekdays 10–4, Sat. 10–2, Sun. 1–4.*

Unquestionably, the glory of Pueblo is the **Rosemount Victorian Museum,** one of Colorado's finest historical institutions. This splendiferous 24,000-square-foot, 37-room mansion, showplace of the wealthy Thatcher family, features exquisite maple, oak, and mahogany woodwork throughout, with ivory glaze and gold-leaf trim; Italian marble fireplaces; Tiffany-glass fixtures; and frescoed ceilings. This museum is the height of opulence, and the rooms seem virtually intact. The top floor—originally the servants' quarters—features the odd Andrew McClelland Collection: objects of curiosity this eccentric philanthropist garnered on his worldwide travels, including an Egyptian mummy. *419*

W. 14th St., ☎ *719/545–5290.* ☛ *$3. Tours offered daily, but times vary so call ahead.*

Pueblo's equally vital concern with the present is documented in the gleaming **Sangre de Cristo Arts Center,** where several rotating exhibits in a well-thought-out space celebrate regional arts and crafts. The center also houses the superb, permanent Western Art collection donated by Francis King; a performing arts theater; and PAWS Children's Museum, which offers fun, interactive audio-visual experiences. *210 N. Santa Fe Trail,* ☎ *719/543–0130.* ☛ *Free.* ۞ *Mon.–Sat. 11–4.*

The more than 110 parks, in addition to hiking and biking trails, help to define Pueblo as a sports and recreation center. The **Greenway and Nature Center** (off 11th St., ☎ 719/545–9114), located on the Arkansas River, offers fine cycling, hiking, and canoeing. A small interpretive center describes the flora and fauna unique to the area, while a **Raptor Rehabilitation Center,** part of the nature center, cares for injured birds of prey.

TIME OUT **Café del Rio** (5200 Nature Center Blvd., ☎ 719/545–1009) boasts a sunny outdoor patio and a festive dining room. The kitchen turns out classic beans-and-burrito fare, as well as super Mexican-themed salads for lunch.

Pueblo also has an uncommonly fine **City Park** (3455 Nuckolls Ave., ☎ 719/561–9664) which has fishing lakes, playgrounds, kiddie rides, tennis courts, a swimming pool, and the excellent Pueblo Zoo—a Biopark that includes an Ecocenter with a tropical rain forest and black-footed penguins. **Lake Pueblo State Recreation Area,** off U.S. 50 West, offers more than 60 miles of shoreline and a full complement of water sports, as well as a beach. If you head east on U.S. 50, leaving the Rockies far behind, you'll be traveling toward the Eastern Plains, where rolling prairies of the northeast give way to hardier desert blooms and the land is stubbled with sage and stunted piñons. One fertile spot—50 miles along the highway—is the town of **Rocky Ford,** dubbed the "Melon Capital of the World" for the famously succulent cantaloupes grown here.

㉙ In another 15 miles, you'll reach **La Junta,** founded as a trading post in the mid-19th century. This wholesome town is notable for its tremendous **Koshare Indian Museum,** which contains extensive holdings of Native American artifacts and crafts (Navaho silver, Zuni pottery, Shoshone buckskin clothing), as well as pieces from Anglo artists such as Remington, known for their depictions of Native Americans. The Koshare Indian Dancers (actually a local Boy Scout troop) perform regularly, keeping their precious traditions alive. *115 W. 18th St.,* ☎ *719/384–4411.* ☛ *$2.* ۞ *Sept.–May, Tues.–Sun. 12:30–4:30; June–Aug., daily 10–5.*

A few miles farther east, parallel to U.S. 50 on Highway 194, is the splendid **Bent's Old Fort National Historic Site,** a perfect example of a living museum, with its painstaking re-creation of the original adobe fort, which burned down. Founded in 1833 by savvy trader William Bent, one of the region's historical giants, the fort anchored the commercially vital **Santa Fe Trail,** providing both protection and a meeting place for the military, trappers, and traders of the era. The museum's interior includes a smithy and soldiers' and trappers' barracks. The guided tours are informative and fascinating. *35110 Hwy. 194 E,* ☎ *719/384–2596.* ☛ *$2 adults.* ۞ *Memorial Day–Labor Day, daily 8–6; Labor Day–Memorial Day, daily 8–4:30.*

This area of Colorado played a major role in opening up the West, through the Mountain Branch of the Santa Fe Trail. Bent's Fort was the most important stop between the route's origin in Independence, Missouri, and its terminus in Santa Fe, New Mexico. U.S. 50 roughly follows its faded tracks from the Kansas border through the pioneer towns of Lamar and Las Animas to La Junta, where U.S. 350 picks up the scent, traveling southwest to **Trinidad.** If you detour onto the quiet county roads, you can still discern its faint outline over the gentle hump of swales and the dip of arroyos. Here, amid the magpies and prairie dogs, it takes little imagination to conjure visions of the pioneers, struggling to travel just 10 miles a day by ox cart over vast stretches of territory. We often take for granted how easily we now travel these same distances.

Initially founded as a rest-and-repair station along the Santa Fe Trail, Trinidad boomed when coal was discovered in the area, followed inevitably by the construction of the railroad. The period from 1880 to 1910 saw major building and expansion. The advent of natural gas, coupled with the Depression, ushered in a gradual decline in population, but not of spirit. Trinidad's citizens willingly contribute 1% of a 4% sales tax to the upkeep of the city's rich architectural heritage. That civic pride is clearly demonstrated in the town's four superb museums, a remarkably large number for a town its size.

Downtown, called the **Corazon de Trinidad,** is a National Historic Landmark District containing splendid Victorian mansions, churches, and the glorious, bright red domes and turrets of the **Aaron House Synagogue.** The Chamber of Commerce (309 Nevada St., ☏ 719/846–9285) publishes an excellent walking tour of the neighborhood, which even retains its original paved brick streets.

Start at the **Baca House/Bloom House/Pioneer Museum Complex.** Visited together, this facility represents the most significant aspects of Trinidad's history. Felipe Baca was a prominent Latin American trader whose 1870 residence—**Baca House**—is replete with original furnishings in the parlor, sitting room, kitchen, dining room, and bedrooms. The displays convey a mix of Anglo (clothes, furniture) and Latin American (santos, rosaries, textiles) influences.

Next door, **Bloom House** provides an effective contrast to the Baca House. Frank Bloom made his money through ranching, banking, and the railroad, and although he was no wealthier than Baca, his mansion (built in the 1880s) reveals a very different lifestyle. The railroad enabled him to fill his ornate Second Empire–style Victorian (with mansard roof and elaborate wrought ironwork) with fine furnishings and fabrics brought from New York and imported from Europe.

The adjacent **Pioneer Museum** is dedicated to the effect of the Santa Fe Trail on the community. Inside the museum are typical ranch hands' quarters, period artifacts, Kit Carson's coat, and an array of antique carriages from surreys to sulkies. *Complex: 300 E. Main St.,* ☏ *719/846–7217.* ☛ *$2.50 adults, $1.25 children and senior citizens.* ☉ *Memorial Day–mid-Sept., Mon.–Sat. 10–4, Sun. 1–4.*

The **A. R. Mitchell Memorial Museum and Gallery** celebrates the life and work of the famous Western illustrator whose distinctive oils, charcoal drawings, and watercolors graced the pages of pulp magazines and ranch romances. The museum also holds his personal collection of other masters of the genre, such as Larry Heller and Harvey Dunn, as well as a re-creation of his atelier. The community holds Mitchell in great esteem: He was responsible for saving the Baca and Bloom houses from demolition, and spearheaded numerous campaigns to restore the historic downtown. For a further glimpse into Trinidad history, be sure to see the **Aultman Collection of Photography** recently installed in the Memorial Museum Gallery. On display are photos by the Aultman family dating back to 1889; they offer a unique visual record of Trinidad. *150 E. Main St., ☎ 719/846–4224. ☞ Free. ☉ Mid-Apr.–Sept., Mon.–Sat. 10–4.*

On the other side of the Purgatoire River, the **Loudon-Henritze Archaeology Museum** takes viewers back millions of years to document the true origins of the region, including early geologic formations, plant and marine animal fossils, and prehistoric artifacts. *Trinidad State Junior College, ☎ 719/846–5508. ☞ Free. ☉ June–Sept., weekdays noon–4.*

The **Trinidad Children's Museum** is located in the delightful Old Firehouse No. 1, and displays firefighting memorabilia such as a 1936 American LaFrance fire truck (kids love clanging the loud bell) and the city's original fire alarm system. Upstairs is a fine re-creation of a Victorian schoolroom. *314 N. Commercial St., ☎ 719/846–8220. ☞ Free. ☉ Summer, weekdays 10–2.*

From Trinidad, Route 12—called the Scenic Highway of Legends—curls north through the stunning **Cuchara Valley.** As it starts its climb, you'll pass a series of company towns built to house coal miners. The first, **Cokedale,** is nestled in Reilly Canyon. The entire town is a National Historic Landmark District, and is the most significant example of a turn-of-the-century coal/coke camp in Colorado. As you drive through the area note the telltale streaks of black in the sandstone and granite bluffs fronting the Purgatoire River and its tributaries, the unsightly slag heaps, and the spooky abandoned mining camps dotting the hillsides. The impressive **Stonewall Gap,** a monumental gate of rock, roughly marks the end of the mining district.

Several switchbacks snake through rolling grasslands, and dance in and out of spruce stands whose clearings afford wonderful views of Monument Lake, as you approach **Cuchara Pass.** There is marvelous camping, hiking, and fishing throughout this tranquil part of the **San Isabel National Forest,** emblazoned with a color wheel of wildflowers in spring and summer. Four corkscrewing miles later, you'll reach a dirt road that leads to the twin sapphires of **Bear and Blue lakes,** followed quickly by a small family ski area, **Cuchara Valley,** which is closed indefinitely. Opposite the resort is **Cuchara,** a cute resort town with a rustic look that seems miles from anywhere.

You'll begin to see fantastic rock formations with equally fanciful names, such as Profile Rock, Devil's Staircase, and Giant's Spoon. With a little imagination you can devise your own legends about the names' origins. There are more than 400 of these upthrusts, which radiate like the spokes of a wheel from the valley's dominating landmark, the **Spanish Peaks.** In Spanish they are known as *Dos Hermanos,* or "Two Brothers"; in Ute, their name *Huajatolla* means "breasts of the world." The haunting formations are considered to be a unique geologic phenomenon for their sheer abundance and variety of rock types.

The Highway of Legends passes through the charming, laid-back resort town of **La Veta,** before reaching its junction with I–25 at **Walsenburg,** another city built on coal and the largest town between Pueblo and Trinidad.

What to See and Do with Children

Buckskin Joe Park and Railway. Not only is this the largest Western-style theme park in the region, but it's also actually an authentic ghost town that was literally moved here from its original site 100 miles away. Famous films such as *True Grit* and *Cat Ballou* were shot in this place that vividly evokes the Old West, especially during the re-creation gunfights and hangings that occur daily. Children love the horse-drawn trolley rides, horseback rides, and gold panning, while adults appreciate live entertainment in the Crystal Palace and Saloon. The complex includes its own scenic railway that travels to the rim of Royal Gorge, as well as a Steam Train and Antique Car Museum. *Cañon City, off U.S. 50,* ☎ *719/275–5485. Combination ticket for all attractions: $12 adults, $10 children 5–11.* ⊙ *May–Sept., daily 9–9.*

North Pole and Santa's Workshop. Energetic elves bustle about this colorful shrine to the commercialization of Christmas. Kids can feed deer, ride a Ferris wheel and carousel, try their luck in an arcade, visit Santa at the height of summer, and stuff themselves in the Candy Kitchen, Sugar Plum Terrace, or old-fashioned ice-cream parlor. *Cascade, Exit 141 off I–25, then 10 mi on U.S. 24 W,* ☎ *719/684–9432.* ☛ *$8.50 per person.* ⊙ *May, Fri.–Wed. 9:30–6; June–Aug., daily 9:30–6; Sept.–Dec. 24, Fri.–Tues. 10–5.*

Pueblo Zoo and City Park (*see* Tour 3 *in* Exploring, *above*)

Royal Gorge and Suspension Bridge (*see* Tour 2 *in* Exploring, *above*)

Off the Beaten Track

Bishop's Castle, an elaborate re-creation of a medieval castle replete with turrets, buttresses, and ornamental iron, is the prodigious (some might say monomaniacal) one-man undertaking of Jim Bishop, who began construction in 1969 and has hauled nearly 50,000 tons of rock used for the construction. Not yet complete, it soars three stories and nearly 75 feet, with plans to build a drawbridge and moat. Bishop finances this enormous endeavor through donations and a gift shop. Anyone can stop by at any time; if you're lucky he'll be there, railing against the establishment (numerous posted signs graphically express his sentiments). *To get there take I–25 south from Pueblo, turn west on Rte. 165 (exit 74) and follow the signs. CR 75,* ☎ *719/564–4366.* ☛ *Free.* ⊙ *Daily, but hours vary.*

SHOPPING

Shopping Districts and Malls

In Colorado Springs, the areas to shop are **Old Colorado City,** with numerous charming boutiques and galleries; **The Citadel** (S. Academy Blvd., at E. Platte Ave.), which counts **JCPenney** and **Dillard's** among its more than 175 stores; and the very upscale **Broadmoor One Lake Avenue Shopping Arcade.** The streets of **Manitou Springs** and **Cripple Creek** offer one souvenir shop and gallery after another.

Pueblo's **Union Avenue Historic District** and **Mesa Junction** contain several fine antiques shops and boutiques. The **Pueblo Mall** offers the usual assortment of fast-food outlets, video arcades, and franchises, including JCPenney. The **Midtown Center** mall includes chains such as Sears.

Flea Markets

There is a flea market every weekend at the **Pueblo Fairgrounds.**

ered in "green chili that won't stay with you all night, hon." The decor favors neon parrots, velvet paintings, and other tchotchkes, but nothing is as colorful as Janey herself. ✗ *807 Cyanide Ave.*, ☎ *719/275–4885. Reservations accepted. No credit cards. Closed Sun. and Mon.*

Colorado Springs

$$$ Briarhurst Manor. The symphony of cherry-wood wainscoting,
★ balustrades and furnishings, Van Briggle wood-and-ceramic fireplaces, tapestries, chinoiserie, and hand-painted glass make this one of the most exquisitely romantic restaurants in Colorado. There are several dining rooms, each with its own look and mood. Among the most charming are the former library and the garden room (a converted private chapel with granite walls). To complete the picture, classical quartets play on the patio in summer. Chef-owner Sigi Krauss is to be commended for literally rescuing this gorgeous old Victorian from the wrecker's ball, and his international clientele appreciates his diversified menu as much as they do the unparalleled ambience. Start with the house-smoked Rocky Mountain trout mousse or alligator pear (avocado stuffed with seafood, topped with both hollandaise and bordelaise sauces), then try the perfectly prepared rack of Colorado lamb or chateaubriand. ✗ *404 Manitou Ave., Manitou Springs*, ☎ *719/685–1864. Reservations advised. AE, D, DC, MC, V. Closed Sun. No lunch.*

$$$ Corbett's. Chef Corbett Reed and his father, Findlay, preside over this
★ posh eatery, the new hot spot among Springs elite. The high-tech space—halogen lamps, modern art, black tables and chairs—is matched by an equally contemporary menu (light and health-conscious). Appetizers are particularly sensational: Try house-smoked trout in tangy horseradish sauce set off by sweet pears and sassy chèvre; grilled calamari with crab stuffing and dill aioli; or seared beef roulade with antipasto platter. The wine list is extensive and reasonably priced. ✗ *817 W. Colorado Ave.*, ☎ *719/471–0004. Reservations required. AE, D, DC, MC, V. No lunch weekends. No dinner Mon.*

$$$ Craftwood Inn. This intimate, restful spot has been a restaurant for more
★ than 50 years: It once regularly hosted such luminaries as Cary Grant, Bing Crosby, and Liberace. The space has a delightful Old English feel, with wrought-iron chandeliers, stained glass partitions, heavy wood beams, and a majestic stone-and-copper fireplace. To start, try the wild mushroom and hazelnut soup, black-bean ravioli, or warm spinach salad with wild boar bacon. The mixed game bird and wild grill are particularly memorable entrées, especially when accompanied by a selection from the well-considered and fairly priced wine list. ✗ *404 El Paso Blvd., Manitou Springs*, ☎ *719/685–9000. Reservations suggested. D, MC, V. No lunch.*

$$$ La Petite Maison. This pretty Victorian abode has been divided into several romantic dining rooms. Pale pink walls, floral tracery, Parisian gallery posters, and pots overflowing with flowers create the atmosphere of a French country home. The menu offers an expert balance of old-fashioned standards and newfangled Southwestern fare. Recommended appetizers include curried shrimp crepe with banana chutney; and goat cheese-stuffed green chilies with black beans. Top-notch main courses range from pork chops with herbed demi-glacé and roasted-garlic mashed potatoes to sea scallops in a balsamic and garlic cream sauce. ✗ *1015 W. Colorado Ave.*, ☎ *719/632–4887. Reservations required. AE, D, DC, MC, V.*

$$$ Pepper Tree. From its hilltop position the Pepper Tree enjoys smashing views of the city that enhance the restaurant's aura of quiet sophistication. Interior decor features a pink-and-maroon color scheme and a mirrored wall. Table-side preparations (including the inevitable

Specialty Stores

ANTIQUES

Tivoli's Antique Gallery (325 S. Union Ave., Pueblo, ☎ 719/545–1448) sells everything from vintage clothing to furniture.

ART GALLERIES

Art of the Rockies (135 W. 3rd St., Salida, no ☎) is a co-op gallery that showcases the work of 70 regional artists. **Michael Garman Gallery** (2418 W. Colorado Ave., Colorado Springs, ☎ 719/471–1600) carries Western-style paintings and unusual figurines and dioramas. **Commonwheel Artists Co-Op** (102 Cañon Ave., Manitou Springs, ☎ 719/685–1008) celebrates the diversity of art in the region, exhibiting jewelry and fiber, clay, and glass art. **OffBroadway Art Gallery** (221 S. Union Ave., Pueblo, ☎ 719/545–8407) specializes in contemporary art by southern Colorado artists.

BOUTIQUES

Exotic Designs (112 Colorado Ave., Pueblo, ☎ 719/543–4921) sells clothing from around the world. **Heritage House Art** (320 S. Union Ave., Pueblo, ☎ 719/545–2691) has exotic wearable art. **Helstrom Studios** (330 N. Institute St., Colorado Springs, ☎ 719/473–3620) showcases beads, textiles, silks, and batiks. **The Rhinestone Parrot** (725 Manitou Ave., Manitou Springs, ☎ 719/685–5333) sells gorgeous dyed leather; brocaded and appliquéd purses, vests, and jackets; and exquisite ceramic jewelry.

CERAMICS

Pueblo Pottery (229 Midway St., Pueblo, ☎ 719/543–0720) features the lovely designs of Tom and Jean Latka. **Van Briggle Art Pottery and Showroom** (600 S. 21st St., Colorado Springs, ☎ 719/633–7729) offers free tours of its world-famous facility that end with a visit to their showroom. **Pottery by Pankratz** (366 2nd St., Monument, ☎ 719/481–3108) showcases striking raku, porcelain, and stone tableware, teapots, lamps, goblets, vases, and sinks.

CRAFTS

Simpich Character Dolls (2413 W. Colorado Ave., Colorado Springs, ☎ 719/636–3272) fashions wonderfully detailed ceramic figurines and fabric dolls, including extraordinary marionettes. Woodcarver Sophie Cowman's evocative pieces—from spoons to sculpture, made out of scrub oak, fragrant cedar, and cottonwood—are for sale at the **Wood Studio** (725 Manitou Ave., Manitou Springs, no ☎). The **Dulcimer Shop** (740 Manitou Ave., Manitou Springs, ☎ 719/685–9655) sells these instruments. **Victor Trading Co. & Manufacturing Works** (114 S. 3rd St., Victor, ☎ 719/689–2346) has everything from beeswax candles to Bull Hill baskets.

FOOD

Rocky Mountain Chocolates (2431 W. Colorado Ave., Colorado Springs, ☎ 719/635–4131) also has branches in Pueblo, Castle Rock, and Boulder. **Patsy's Candies** (1540 S. 21st St., Colorado Springs, ☎ 719/633–7215) is renowned for its saltwater taffy and chocolate. **Pikes Peak Vineyards** (3901 Janitell Rd., Colorado Springs, ☎ 719/576–0075) offers tastings of its surprisingly fine wines, including merlots and chardonnays. **Seabel's Baskets and Gifts** (105 W. C St., Pueblo, ☎ 719/543–2400) offers gourmet cookware and delicacies.

GLASSWARE

The **Mid 30s Depression Glass Shop** (225 S. Union Ave., Pueblo, ☎ 719/544–1031) has the largest selection of collectible Depression glass in Colorado.

WESTERN PARAPHERNALIA

Bandera Outfitters (2519 W. Colorado Ave., Colorado Springs, ☎ 719/635–6005) has stylish Western wear. **Back at the Ranch** (333 S. Union Ave., Pueblo, ☎ 719/544–7319) provides elegant home accessories for dudes and dudettes.

SPORTS AND THE OUTDOORS

Participant Sports

Boating

Two marinas at **Lake Pueblo State Park** (North Shore, ☎ 719/547–3880; South Shore, ☎ 719/564–1043) offer rental boats.

Camping

There are excellent camping facilities at **Pueblo Lake State Recreation Area** (☎ 719/561–9320) and **Trinidad Lake State Recreation Area** (☎ 719/846–6951). Camping is superb in the **San Isabel** and **Pike national forests.** The Forest Service (☎ 719/636–1602) or Bureau of Land Management (☎ 719/275–0631) can provide more information.

Climbing

Garden of the Gods is a popular place to test your skills, thanks to its stark spires and cliffs. Register with the visitor center at the entrance. Also, **Collegiate Peaks** around Buena Vista and Salida offer a variety of ascents from moderate to difficult. The **Royal Gorge, Redrocks Park,** and **Garden Park** outside Cañon City are alive with intrepid clamberers.

Cycling

Pueblo has an extensive **Bike Trail System,** which loops the city, following the Arkansas River part way, then goes out to the reservoir. The **Pueblo Parks and Recreation Department** (☎ 719/566–1745) can provide more information.

Cycling is popular in the **Collegiate Peaks Wilderness Area,** around Buena Vista and Salida. **American Adventure Expeditions** (228 N. F St., Buena Vista, ☎ 719/395–2409) and **Rocky Mountain Tours** (☎ 719/395–4101) provide rentals and tours.

Fishing

Pike, bass, and trout are plentiful in this region. Favorite fishing spots include **Trinidad Lake** (☎ 719/846–6951), **Lake Pueblo** (☎ 719/561–9320), **Spinney Mountain Reservoir** (between Florissant and Buena Vista), and the **Arkansas** and **South Platte rivers.** For more information, call the Colorado Division of Wildlife Southeast Region (☎ 719/473–2945).

Golf

In Colorado Springs, **The Broadmoor** (Broadmoor Complex, ☎ 719/634–7711) offers 54 splendid holes to guests and members. **Colorado Springs Country Club** (3333 Templeton Gap Rd., ☎ 719/473–1782) is another fine 18-hole course, as is the public **Pine Creek Golf Course** (9850 Divot Dr., ☎ 719/594–9999).

Pueblo City Golf Course (City Park, ☎ 719/566–1745) is a handsome, highly rated 18-hole course, and **Pueblo West Golf Course** (Pueblo West Development, 8 mi west of town on U.S. 50, ☎ 719/547–2280) is an 18-hole championship course. **Walking Stick Golf Course** (4301 Walking Stick Blvd., Pueblo, ☎ 719/584–3400) is perennially ranked in the top 50 courses by *Golf Digest.*

Hiking

Cañon City–owned **Redrocks Park,** 12 miles north of tow did hiking among the sandstone spires. You can hike tude in **San Isabel National Forest** (☎ 719/545–8737 area. There are numerous trails in the **Pikes Peak** area **Trail** up the mountain and **North Cheyenne Canyon** **the Gods,** outside Colorado Springs, is also popular. County Parks Department (☎ 719/520–6375) for furth about facilities in the Colorado Springs/Pikes Peak are

Horseback Riding

Academy Riding Stables (Colorado Springs, ☎ 719/63 trail rides through the Garden of the Gods. **Buckskin Joe** ☎ 719/275–5149) offers rides in the Cañon City area, to all day; rates begin at $20. **Cripple Creek Horse Cor** Creek, ☎ 719/689–3051) offers rides into the Rockie

In-Line Skating

Popular routes, with good paved trails, are along the **P** (*see* Cycling, *above*) and in the **Garden of the Gods.**

Skiing

DOWNHILL

Monarch. Four chairs; 54 trails; 637 acres; 1,160-foo The service, which has garnered numerous Tourism Hos ment Awards, is exceptional. Lift lines and lift ticket p nal by most comparative standards. *U.S. 50 (18 mi f 719/539–3573.* ◷ *Mid-Nov.–mid-Apr., daily 9–4.*

Rafting

Arkansas River Outfitters (Cañon City, ☎ 719/275– **Royal Gorge Rafting and Helicopter Tours** (Cañon Cit 5161), **Royal Gorge River Adventures** (Cañon City, ☎ 7 and **Sierra Outfitters** (Cañon City, ☎ 719/275–0128) the reliable outfits that line U.S. 50, between Cañor Royal Gorge.

Buena Vista and Salida are the other major rafting cent **ican Adventure Expeditions** (☎ 719/395–2409) and **R Tours** (☎ 719/395–4101), both in Buena Vista, and **Ri** 800/525–2081) and **Canyon Marine Expeditions** (☎ or 800/643–0707), in Salida, among the many recom ters.

DINING

Steak houses and Mexican cantinas are usually the m restaurants throughout South Central Colorado, th Springs and Pueblo offer a wide variety of fine eateries the Dining chart *in* On the Road with Fodor's at the fro

Cañon City

$$–$$$ **Merlino's Belvedere.** This Italian standby has ritzy co with floral banquettes, centerpieces, and a "running wa Locals swear by the top-notch steaks, seafood, and pas choice for a big evening out. ✕ *1330 Elm Ave.,* ☎ *719/2 vations advised. AE, MC, V.*

$ **Janey's Chile Wagon.** Owner Janey Workman is a forr
★ who fled the big city. *The National Enquirer* did a featur ress Builds Diner into $350,000 Restaurant!" Her food spoon, with huge portions of delicious burritos and

and delectable pepper steak) are its stock-in-trade, though the chef will go out on a limb with such daily specials as calamari stuffed with crabmeat and bacon. Still, this is one of those old-fashioned places where flambé is considered the height of both elegance and decadence. ✕ *888 W. Moreno Ave.,* ☏ *719/471–4888. Reservations required. Jacket and tie. AE, MC, V. Closed Sun. No lunch.*

$$ Margarita. Plants, adobe walls, terra-cotta tile, and mosaic tables lend an air of refinement to this fine eatery, whose constantly changing menu is an intriguing hybrid of Mexican and Continental influences. ✕ *7350 Pine Creek Rd.,* ☏ *719/598–8667. Reservations advised. AE, MC, V. Closed Mon. No dinner Sun.*

$ Adam's Mountain Café. With whirring ceiling fans, hanging plants, floral wallpaper, bucolic country garden prints, and old-fashioned hardwood tables and chairs, this cozy eatery is vaguely reminiscent of someone's great-grandmother's parlor. Come here for smashing breakfasts (wondrous muffins and organic juices); fine pastas (try the orzo Mediterranean, with sun-dried tomatoes, broccoli, onions, walnuts, and peppers sautéed in olive oil with feta, lemon, and tomato); such gourmet sandwiches as red chili–rubbed free-range chicken on grilled polenta with cilantro pesto and lime sour cream; and yummy desserts like apple crisp with dried cherries, almond pound cake, and cappuccino chocolate torte. ✕ *110 Cañon Ave., Manitou Springs,* ☏ *719/685–1430. Reservations accepted. AE, MC, V. No dinner Sun.*

$ El Tesoro. At the turn of the century, this lovely historic building served
★ as a brothel, and then for many years it was an atelier for various artists. Today, it's a restaurant that doubles as an art gallery, exhibiting especially noteworthy weavings and prints. The adobe and exposed brick walls and tile work are original; rugs, textiles, and the ubiquitous garlands of chili add still more color. The sterling northern New Mexican food is the real McQueso, a savvy, savory blend of Native American, Spanish, and Anglo-American influences. The staples of this highly evolved cuisine haven't changed in 400 years; corn, beans, squash, heavy meats like pork and goat, and, of course, chili. The *posole* (hominy with pork and red chili) is magical, the green chili heavenly, and innovative originals like mango quesadillas (a brilliant pairing of sweet and spicy elements) simply genius. ✕ *10 N. Sierra Madre St.,* ☏ *719/471–0106. Reservations advised. MC, V. Closed Sun. No lunch Sat. No dinner Mon.–Wed.*

Pueblo

$$ Irish Pub. This bustling, consistently jam-packed hot spot is a bar and
★ grill with a difference: It has a good kitchen. The owner *loves* food, and he has elevated pub grub to an art form. Even the house salad—field greens studded with pine nuts and feta—is imaginative. Among the mouthwatering appetizers is a marvelous grilled smoked-duck sausage with goat cheese, topped with a honey-mustard sauce. Sandwiches are equally creative; try the buffalo burger or beaver (yes, beaver) sandwich. The range of entrées, many of them heart-healthy, is astonishing: from a dazzling prime rib to a lip-smacking, "border grill" turkey breast lightly dusted in flour, grilled, and then poached in chicken broth and raspberry vinaigrette. ✕ *108 W. 3rd St.,* ☏ *719/542–9974. Reservations accepted. AE, D, MC, V. Closed Sun.*

$$ La Renaissance. This converted church and parsonage is the most imposing and elegant space in town, and the impeccably attired, unfailingly courteous wait staff completes the picture. The kitchen is stylish as well, offering Continental standbys such as filet mignon in mushroom sauce, superb baby-back ribs, and shrimp scampi. Desserts are sinful enough to be sacrilegious, considering the restaurant's origins.

The dinner price includes appetizer, soup, salad, and dessert. ✗ 217 E. Routt Ave., ☎ 719/543–6367. Reservations advised. AE, MC, V. Closed Sun. No lunch Sat.

$$ La Tronica's. Although it's dressed like a saloon, with mirrored beer signs and Christmas lights draping the bar, this 50-year-old restaurant is real "Mamma Mia" Italian. Waitresses, who invariably call you "sweetheart," have been here for as long as anyone can remember, and you may notice them watching approvingly as you take your first bite. Steak, scrumptious fried chicken (second-best in the Rockies, next to Slogar's in Crested Butte), and homemade pastas are the lure. ✗ 1143 E. Abriendo Ave., ☎ 719/542–1113. Reservations advised. AE, MC, V. Closed Sun. and Mon. No lunch.

$–$$ Grand Prix. A neon sign announces the location of this authentic Mexican restaurant run by the Montoya family. Red neon lights and a painted false ceiling relieve the otherwise spartan decor. The food is classic: pork and avocado, chorizo, burritos, and Mexican steak, served with heaping helpings of rice and beans, and utilizing the flavorful local Pueblo chili. ✗ 615 E. Mesa St., ☎ 719/542–9825. Reservations accepted. No credit cards. Closed Sun. and Mon. No lunch Sat.

Salida

$–$$ First Street Café. Occupying a late-19th-century building in the historic district is this café, with creative heart-healthy and vegetarian specials, in addition to the expected robust Mexican-American fare. Breakfast is served here, as well as lunch and dinner. ✗ 137 E. 1st St., ☎ 719/539–4759. Reservations accepted. AE, D, MC, V.

Trinidad

$–$$ Nana and Nano's Pasta House. This homey, classic Neapolitan eatery, with red-and-white check tablecloths, red curtains, and posters of Italy, is always saturated with the tempting aroma of garlic and tomato sauce. Pastas are uniformly excellent, with standards such as fettuccine Alfredo, gnocchi bolognese, and spaghetti al sugo among the standouts. If you don't have time for a sit-down lunch, stop in their deli next door for smashing heros and gourmet sandwiches. The Monteleones are your amiable hosts. If you want wine or beer, BYOB. ✗ 415 University St., ☎ 719/846–2696. Reservations accepted. AE, DC, MC, V. ⊘ Tues.–Fri. lunch in summer. Closed Sun.

$ La Fiesta. A few Mexican crafts, brick walls, and a fireplace in the back room (one of the nicest seating areas) lend some atmosphere to this hole-in-the-wall restaurant. The faithful clientele comes here for the subtly spicy green chili and burritos. Bring your own wine and beer. La Fiesta is open for all three meals. ✗ 134 W. Main St., ☎ 719/846–8221. Reservations accepted. No credit cards. Closed Sun.

LODGING

Colorado Springs has some of the higher-end chain properties, but, in general, the choice is usually among bed-and-breakfasts, guest houses, and motels on the strip. Unless otherwise noted, all accommodations listed below include phones, cable TV, and private baths. For rates, see the Lodging price chart in On the Road with Fodor's.

Buena Vista

$ Adobe Inn. This adobe hacienda has five charming rooms, each named for the predominant decorative motif: antique, Mexican, Native American, Mediterranean, and wicker. Some rooms have a fireplace. The airy solarium is dominated by a magnificent kiva. A complimentary gourmet breakfast is offered to guests. The owners—Marjorie, Paul, and Michael Knox—also run the charming **La Casa del Sol** Mexican restaurant down the street and can make arrangements for guests to dine there. ⚎ *303 U.S. 24 N, 81211,* ☎ *719/395–6340. 5 rooms. Hot tub. MC, V.*

Cañon City

$　**Cañon Inn.** Some of the famous people who have stayed here—John Belushi, Tom Selleck, Jane Fonda, John Wayne, Glenn Ford, and Goldie Hawn among them—now have their names emblazoned on the door of a hotel room here in their honor. Spacious and ultracomfortable accommodations are offered in two wings. All the rooms are decorated in muted pastels and earth tones. ⚎ *U.S. 50 and Dozier St., 81215,* ☎ *719/275–8676,* ℻ *719/275–8675. 104 rooms. Restaurant, bar, pool, hot tub. AE, D, DC, MC, V.*

Colorado Springs

$$$$　**The Broadmoor.** Here's one of America's truly great hotels. Completely ★　self-contained—more a village than a resort—its 30 buildings sprawl majestically across 3,500 acres. The property celebrated 75 years of deluxe service in 1993, and it maintains its exalted status through continual upgrading and refurbishment. The pink-and-ocher main building, crowned by Mediterranean-style towers, serenely commands a private lake. Rooms here are the loveliest, with period furnishings; accommodations in the other complexes, including 150 new junior suites in the Broadmoor West Tower, are more contemporary in style. The Broadmoor is renowned for its three world-class championship golf courses, former Davis Cup coach Dennis Ralston's tennis camps, and its new pampering spa. There are eight restaurants, of which the Tavern, with its original Toulouse-Lautrec posters; the elegant cranberry-and-silver Penrose Room; and the romantic primrose, mint, and buff Charles Court rank among the state's finest. ⚎ *Box 1439, 80901,* ☎ *719/634–7711 or 800/634–7711,* ℻ *719/577-5779. 483 rooms, 67 suites, 150 junior suites. 8 restaurants, 3 bars, 3 pools, beauty salon, spa, 3 18-hole golf courses, 12 tennis courts, health club, horseback riding, squash, fishing, cinema, meeting rooms, car rental. AE, D, DC, MC, V.*

$$　**Antlers Doubletree Hotel.** Two previous incarnations of this hotel once ★　competed with the Broadmoor for the rich and famous, thanks to its superb, historic location downtown. This third Antlers was completely renovated and expanded in 1991. The large airy lobby strikes an immediate note of class when you enter, and the handsome rooms sport hunting-lodge decor. ⚎ *4 S. Cascade Ave., 80904,* ☎ *719/473–5600 or 800/528–0444,* ℻ *719/389–0259. 274 rooms, 16 suites. 2 restaurants, bar, hot tub, health club, meeting rooms. AE, D, DC, MC, V.*

$$　**Embassy Suites.** This is one of the original properties in this chain, and it's among the best. The airy atrium lobby, crawling with plants, is watched over by the resident, talkative caged birds. Suites are comfortable, favoring teal and dusty rose. To complete the tropical motif, a waterfall tumbles lavishly into the indoor pool. The pool deck offers quite a view of Pikes Peak; jazz groups play here every Thursday night in season. A complimentary breakfast is offered to all guests. ⚎ *7290 Commerce Center Dr., 80919,* ☎ *719/599–9100,* ℻ *719/599–4644. 207 suites. Restaurant, bar, indoor pool, hot tub, exercise room, meeting rooms. AE, D, DC, MC, V.*

$–$$　**The Hearthstone.** Two Victorian houses joined by a carriage house comprise this famed B&B, listed on the National Register of Historic Places. The 25 no-smoking guest rooms (most with private bath) are resplendent with furnishings from the 1880s (cut glass windows, Van Briggle ceramic fireplaces, hand-carved or brass beds, glorious quilts, and rocking chairs); each is individually decorated around a theme, such as the Author's Den, complete with vintage typewriter, and the Solarium, brightened by plants and an expansive skylight. A complimentary breakfast always includes eggs, fresh fruit, and home-baked bread. ⌘ *506 N. Cascade Ave., 80903,* ☎ *719/473–4413 or 800/521–1885. 25 rooms. AE, MC, V.*

$–$$ **Holden House.** Genial innkeepers Sallie and Welling Clark realized their
★ dream when they lovingly restored this 1902 Victorian home and transformed it into a B&B. Three charming rooms in the main house and two in the adjacent carriage house are filled with family heirlooms and antiques. Fireplaces, oversize or claw-foot tubs in the private baths, and down pillows and quilts make guest rooms even more cozy. The complimentary breakfast is a gourmet's delight. ⌘ *1102 W. Pikes Peak Ave., 80904,* ☎ *719/471–3980. 5 rooms. AE, D, MC, V.*

$–$$ **Victoria's Keep.** Proud owners Marvin and Vicki Keith renovated this turreted 1891 Queen Anne in 1993 to create this unique B&B. The parlor verges on the Dickensian, with its slightly fussy, Victorian clutter. There are carved tile ceilings and intricate tracery, as well as the Keiths' impressive collections of china and Depression glass throughout the house. Each room has its own fireplace and some distinguishing feature, whether it be a Jacuzzi or a claw-foot tub, stained glass windows, or thrilling views of Miramont Castle. The decor is similarly eclectic, from ultramodern wicker furnishings to Victorian antiques. Marvin is an accomplished chef; his gourmet breakfasts might include poached eggs with brandy cream sauce or stuffed French toast. Every evening he puts out another complimentary spread, including wine, cheese, and delectable appetizers. Guests also have free use of mountain bikes. ⌘ *202 Ruxton Ave., Manitou Springs 80829,* ☎ *800/905– 5337. 5 rooms. Hot tub. AE, D, MC, V.*

Pueblo

$$ **Abriendo Inn.** This exquisite 1906 home, listed on the National Reg-
★ ister of Historic Places, overflows with character. Gracious owners Kerrelyn and Chuck Trent did most of the painting, papering, and refurbishing themselves. The house now gleams with its original, lovingly restored parquet floors, stained glass, and Minnequa oak wainscoting. The seven no-smoking rooms are richly appointed with antiques, oak armoires, quilts, crocheted bedspreads, and either brass or four-poster beds. Fresh fruit and cookies are left out for guests, and gourmet breakfast and evening cheese and crackers are included in the rate. ⌘ *300 W. Abriendo Ave., 81004,* ☎ *719/544–2703. 7 rooms. AE, MC, V.*

$$ **Inn at Pueblo West Best Western.** This handsome sprawling resort is a notch above most Best Westerns. Although it's out of the way for those who want to be close to town (about 15 minutes away by car), the golf course and activities on nearby Lake Pueblo keep guests busy. Large rooms in dark mountain colors and with terraces have an elegant woodsy feel. ⌘ *201 S. McCulloch Blvd., 81007,* ☎ *719/547– 2111 or 800/448–1972. 80 rooms. Restaurant, bar, pool, 4 tennis courts. AE, D, DC, MC, V.*

Salida

$ **The Poor Country Farm Inn.** On the Arkansas River, this cozy Victorian home has breathtaking mountain prospects. Rooms are filled with antiques and family memorabilia. A complimentary gourmet breakfast is provided to guests. *8495 CR 60, 81201,* ☎ *719/539–3818. 5 rooms, 4 with shared bath; co-ed dorm sleeps 8. MC, V.*

Trinidad

$ **Best Western Country Club Inn.** To apply the term "country club" is exaggerating this lodging's amenities. Still, rooms are clean and comfortable and are decorated in warm earth tones. ⌂ *(Exit 13A off I–25) 900 W. Adams, 81082,* ☎ *719/846–2215. 55 rooms. Restaurant, bar, hot tub, exercise room, coin laundry. AE, D, DC, MC, V.*

Victor

$–$$ **Victor Hotel.** In 1991, more than $1 million was dedicated to renovating this hotel, listed on the National Register of Historic Places. Public spaces have been restored to their Victorian splendor, adding to the list of reasons why Victor Hotel is the nicest place to stay in the Cripple Creek area. Other attributes include tastefully decorated rooms with stunning mountain views. Unfortunately, aside from the original open brickwork and a few old-fashioned tubs and radiators, the decor and furnishings are prosaically modern, and bathrooms are tiny. ⌂ *4th and Victor Sts., 80860,* ☎ *719/689–3553. 30 rooms. Restaurant. AE, D, MC, V.*

THE ARTS AND NIGHTLIFE

The Arts

Pueblo's **Sangre de Cristo Arts and Conference Center** (210 N. Santa Fe Trail, ☎ 719/542–1211) presents the **Southern Colorado Repertory Theatre, Pueblo Ballet, and Dancespectra.**

Colorado Springs' **Pikes Peak Center** (190 S. Cascade Ave., ☎ 719/520–7469) presents the **Colorado Springs Symphony,** as well as touring theater and dance companies.

Music

The **Pueblo Symphony** (503 N. Main St., Suite 414, ☎ 719/546–0333) offers cowboy to classical music throughout the year.

Salida draws some of the musicians from the Aspen Music Festival during the summer, becoming the **Aspen-Salida Music Festival,** July–August.

Theater

Air Force Academy, Arnold Hall (Colorado Springs, ☎ 719/472–4497) presents touring and local companies.

Broadway Theatre League (Memorial Hall, Pueblo, ☎ 719/545–4721) presents touring shows and specialty acts.

Powerhouse Players (200 W. Sackett St., Salida, ☎ 719/539–2455), a community theater based in Dallas, presents a variety of musical revues and straight plays throughout the summer in the town's historic steam plant.

Nightlife

Bars and Lounges

In Buena Vista, head to the **Green Parrot** (304 Main St., ☎ 719/395–8985), which has live music weekends.

In Colorado Springs, the **Golden Bee** (International Center, The Broadmoor, ☎ 719/634–7711) is an institution. The gloriously old-fashioned bar, with pressed-tin ceilings and magnificent woodwork, features a piano player leading sing-alongs. **Judge Baldwin's** (4 S. Cascade Ave., Antlers Hotel, ☎ 719/473–5600) is a lively brew pub. **Phantom Canyon Brewing Co.** (2 E. Pikes Peak Ave., ☎ 719/635–2800), in a turn-of-the-century warehouse, has colorful rotating art exhibits and great pub grub (try the sensational gourmet pizzas, barbecued shrimp braised in India Pale Ale, or the sinful black-and-tan cheesecake brownie).

In Pueblo, **Gus' Place** (Elm and Mesa Sts., ☎ 719/542–0756) is a big Yuppie hangout that once held the record for the most kegs emptied in an evening. **Peppers** (4109 Club Manor Dr., ☎ 719/542–8629) has something going on every evening, from oldies nights to stand-up comedy. The **Irish Pub** (108 W. 3rd St., ☎ 719/542–9974) is always hopping after work hours.

Casinos
Cripple Creek has several casinos that offer limited-stakes gambling (*see* Tour 2, *in* Exploring, *above*).

Comedy Clubs
Laffs Comedy Corner (1305 N. Academy Blvd., Colorado Springs, ☎ 719/591–0707) showcases live stand-up comedy; some of the performers here are nationally known.

Country and Western
Colorado Springs has several C&W spots. **Cowboys** (Rustic Hills North Shopping Ctr., ☎ 719/596–1212) is for hard-core two-steppers. **Gambler's Dance Hall and Saloon** (3958 N. Academy Blvd., ☎ 719/574–3369) attracts a younger, family-oriented clientele. **Rodeo** (3506 N. Academy Blvd., ☎ 719/597–6121) tends to have a Yuppie crowd.

Pueblo's **The Chief** (611 N. Main St., ☎ 719/546–1246) is a classic honky-tonk that has live bands most evenings.

In Trinidad, the **El Rancho Bar** (Santa Fe Ave., ☎ 719/846–9049) is a wildly popular hangout in a barn setting.

Dinner Shows
Cripple Creek's **Imperial Hotel Theater** (123 N. 3rd. St., ☎ 719/689–2922) is renowned for its Victorian melodramas. In Colorado Springs, the **Flying W Ranch** (3300 Chuckwagon Rd., ☎ 719/598–4000), open mid-May–October, ropes them in for the its sensational Western stage show and chuck-wagon dinner. The **Iron Springs Chateau** (Manitou Springs, across from Pikes Peak Cog Railway, ☎ 719/685–5104) offers stagings of comedy melodramas.

Discos
In Colorado Springs, you can dance part of the night away at **Stars** (the Broadmoor, 1 Lake Ave., ☎ 719/634–7711), a sleek, intimate boîte with a striking black granite bar, a black marble floor inlaid with gold stars, and walls covered with photos of celebrities who have stayed at the Broadmoor over the years, and **The Heat** (3506 N. Academy St., ☎ 719/591–2100), which attracts a younger, less sedate crowd.

In Pueblo, try **Images** (4001 N. Elizabeth St., ☎ 719/543–8050).

Jazz Clubs
There is usually live jazz at the **Charles Court** (the Broadmoor, Colorado Springs, ☎ 719/634–7711) several nights weekly.

Rock Clubs
In Trinidad, **The Other Place** (466 W. Main St., ☎ 719/846–9012) hires top local bands on weekends to play its intimate classy space.

Singles
In Colorado Springs, try **Old Chicago** (118 N. Tejon Ave., ☎ 719/634–8812).

SOUTH CENTRAL COLORADO ESSENTIALS

Arriving and Departing by Plane

Airports and Airlines

Colorado Springs: **Colorado Springs Municipal Airport** (☎ 719/596–0188) is served by American Airlines (☎ 800/433–4700), America West (☎ 800/247–5692), Continental (☎ 800/525–0280), Delta (☎ 800/221–1212), TWA (☎ 800/221–2000), and United (☎ 800/241–6522).

Pueblo: **Pueblo Memorial Airport** (☎ 719/948–3355) welcomes flights from United Express.

Between the Airport and the Hotels/Downtown

BY BUS OR SHUTTLE

Airport Transportation Service (☎ 719/635–3518) offers regular shuttles from the Colorado Springs airport to hotels. **Colorado Springs/Pueblo Airporter** (☎ 719/578–5232) services the stretch of I–25 between the two cities.

BY TAXI

In Colorado Springs: **Yellow Cab** (☎ 719/634–5000). In Pueblo: **City Cab** (☎ 719/543–2525).

Arriving and Departing by Car, Train, and Bus

By Car

I–25, which bisects Colorado and runs north–south from New Mexico to Wyoming, is the major artery accessing the area.

By Train

Amtrak (☎ 800/872–7245) stops in Trinidad and La Junta.

By Bus

Greyhound Lines (☎ 800/231–2222) and **TNM&O Coaches** (☎ 719/544–6295) serve most of the major towns in the region.

Getting Around

By Bus

Colorado Springs Transit (☎ 719/475–9733) serves most of the Colorado Springs metropolitan area, including Manitou Springs.

Pueblo Transit (☎ 719/542–4306) services Pueblo and outlying areas.

The **Trinidad Trolley** stops at parks and historical sites, departing from the parking lot next to City Hall (for information, call the Chamber of Commerce, ☎ 719/846–9285).

By Taxi

In Colorado Springs: **Yellow Cab** (☎ 719/634–5000); in Pueblo: **City Cab** (☎ 719/543–2525); in Trinidad: **City Cab** (☎ 719/846–2237).

By Car

Pueblo and Colorado Springs are both on I–25. Florissant and Buena Vista are reached via U.S. 24 off I–25; Cañon City and the Royal Gorge via U.S. 50. Salida can be reached via CO 291 from either U.S. 24 or U.S. 50. La Junta can be reached via U.S. 50 from Pueblo or U.S. 350 from Trinidad.

Guided Tours

Orientation

Gray Line (☎ 719/633–1181) offers tours of the Colorado Springs area, including Pikes Peak and Manitou Springs, as well as jaunts to Cripple Creek.

Important Addresses and Numbers

Hospitals

Arkansas Valley Regional Medical Center (1100 Carson Ave., La Junta, ☎ 719/384–5412); **Colorado Springs Memorial Hospital** (1400 E. Boulder Ave., Colorado Springs, ☎ 719/475–5000); **Heart of the Rockies Regional Medical Center** (448 E. 1st St., Salida, ☎ 719/539–6661); **Mt. San Rafael Hospital** (410 Benedicta St., Trinidad, ☎ 719/846–9213); **Parkview Episcopal Medical Center** (400 W. 16th St., Pueblo, ☎ 719/584–4000); **St. Thomas More Hospital** (1019 Sheridan St., Canon City, ☎ 719/275–3381).

Visitor Information

Buena Vista Chamber of Commerce (U.S. 24, Buena Vista 81211, ☎ 719/395–6612); **Cañon City Chamber of Commerce** (Bin 749, Cañon City 81215, ☎ 719/275–2331); **Colorado Springs Convention and Visitors Bureau** (104 S. Cascade Ave., Suite 104, Colorado Springs 80903, ☎ 719/635–7506 or 800/368–4748); **Cripple Creek Chamber of Commerce** (Box 650, Cripple Creek 80813, ☎ 719/689–2169 or 800/526–8777); **Florissant/Lake George Chamber of Commerce** (Box 507, Florissant 80816, ☎ 719/748–3395); **Heart of the Rockies Chamber of Commerce** (406 W. Rainbow Blvd., Salida 81201, ☎ 719/539–2068); **Huerfano County Chamber of Commerce** (Box 493, Walsenburg 81089, ☎ 719/738–1065); **La Junta Chamber of Commerce** (110 Santa Fe Ave., La Junta 81050, ☎ 719/384–7411); **La Veta/Cuchara Chamber of Commerce** (Box 32, La Veta 81055, ☎ 719/742–3676); **Lamar Chamber of Commerce** (Box 860, Lamar 81052, ☎ 719/336–4379); **Manitou Springs Chamber of Commerce** (354 Manitou Ave., Manitou Springs 80829, ☎ 719/685–5089 or 800/642–2567); **Pueblo Chamber of Commerce and Convention & Visitors Bureau** (302 N. Santa Fe Ave., Pueblo 81003, ☎ 719/542–1704 or 800/233–3446); **Trinidad/Las Animas Chamber of Commerce** (309 Nevada St., Trinidad 81082, ☎ 719/846–9285).

6 North Central Colorado

NORTH CENTRAL COLORADO is an appealing blend of Old West and New Age. More a ranching than a mining area, it's strewn with rich evocations of pioneer life, as well as turn-of-the-century resort towns such as Estes Park and Grand Lake. Yet the region is anchored by Boulder, one of the country's most progressive cities and a town virtually synonymous (some might say obsessed) with environmental concern and physical fitness. As the local joke goes, even the dogs jog.

Boulderites take full advantage of the town's glorious natural setting, nestled amid the peaks of the Front Range, indulging in everything from rock climbing to mountain biking. A short drive south brings them to the ski areas along I–70. To the west and north, the Roosevelt and Arapahoe national forests and the Great Lakes of Colorado provide a host of recreational opportunities from hiking to fishing to cross-country skiing and snowmobiling. To the northeast, Estes Park stands as the gateway to America's alpine wonderland—Rocky Mountain National Park, which spans three ecosystems that 900 species of plants, 250 species of birds, and 25 species of mammals, including elk, muletail deer, moose, bobcats, and even black bears, call home.

EXPLORING

Numbers in the margin correspond to points of interest on the North Central Colorado map.

➊ No place in Colorado better epitomizes the state's outdoor mania than **Boulder.** There are more bikes than cars in this uncommonly beautiful and beautifully uncommon city, embroidered with 25,000 acres of parks and greenbelts laced with jogging tracks and bike trails. You're also more likely to see ponytails than crew cuts: Boulder is a college town with an arty, liberal reputation. Physically fit and environmentally hip, it's a city of cyclists and recyclers who, when they're not out enjoying their natural surroundings, enjoy nothing more than sitting at a sidewalk café, watching the rest of the world jog by.

Boulder's heartbeat is the **Pearl Street Mall,** a mind-boggling, eye-catching array of chic shops and trendy restaurants where all of Boulder hangs out. As a bonus, the mall slices through Mapleton Hill, a historic district of great charm.

On the outskirts of the city there are three free attractions worth visiting. The first is the **Celestial Seasonings Plant** (4600 Sleepytime Dr., ☎ 303/581–1202; tours Mon.–Sat. 10–3), offering free tours of this well-known herbal tea company's processing and manufacturing facility. An unmistakable aroma permeates the parking lot; inside you can see the product ingredients in their raw form (the Mint Room is isolated due to its potent scent) and how they're blended. The tour ends up in the gift shop for a tea-tasting. Also aromatic are the free tours of the **Boulder Beer Company** (2880 Wilderness Pl., ☎ 303/444–8448). These run Monday–Saturday, at 2 PM, and culminate in a tasting. The last free attraction is the **Leanin' Tree Museum of Western Art** (6055 Longbow Dr., ☎ 303/530–1442; open weekdays 8–4:30)—brought to you by the folks who make wildly popular and humorous Western-themed greeting cards—whose superlative collection ranges from traditionalists in the Remington and Bierstadt manner to stylistic innovators of the Western genre. One room is devoted to the paintings of the original greeting-card genius, Lloyd Mitchell.

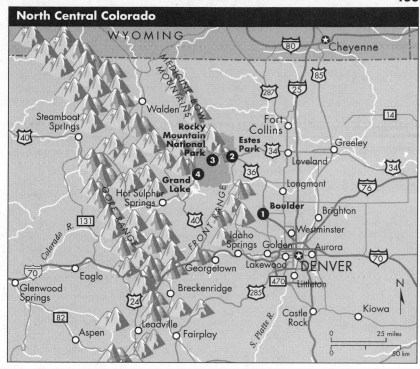

North Central Colorado

Take Broadway north to the **University of Colorado** (☎ 303/492–6301) campus, where spacious lawns separate a handsome collection of stone buildings with red tile roofs. Tours are available weekday afternoons. A favorite nearby student hangout is the bohemian neighborhood called The Hill (around 13th and College streets, west of the campus), home to lots of coffeehouses and hip boutiques, and always happening day or night.

TIME OUT **Alfalfa's** (Broadway and Arapahoe St., ☎ 303/442–0082) is a New Age organic supermarket, where one-stop shopping will net you everything from "cruelty-free" cosmetics to herbal and homeopathic remedies. The deli offers predictably healthful fare, with a crisp, fresh salad bar, homemade muffins and soups (usually something like tofu miso), and custom-blended vegetable and fruit juices.

The prettiest views of town can be had by following Baseline Drive (off Broadway) up to **Chatauqua Park,** site of the Colorado Music Festival, and a favorite oasis of locals on weekends. Continue farther up Flagstaff Mountain to Panorama Point and Boulder Mountain Park, where people jog, bike, climb, and rarely remain still. The admirable parks system also includes the trademark red sandstone **Flatirons.** These massive structures, so named for their flat rock faces, are popular among rock climbers and hikers; they can be seen from almost every vantage point in town.

The most direct route to Rocky Mountain National Park is along U.S. 36 North, via the quaint town of **Lyons.** The scenery gives little hint ❷ of the grandeur to come when you reach **Estes Park.** If ever there was a classic picture-postcard Rockies view, Estes Park has it. Even the McDonald's has glorious views and a facade that complements its surroundings, thanks to strict zoning laws that require all businesses to present a rustic exterior. The town itself is very family-oriented: Many of the small hotels lining the country roads are mom-and-pop outfits that have been passed down through several generations.

TIME OUT   At **Ed's Cantina** (362 E. Elkhorn Ave., ☎ 970/586–2919) the walls are festooned with pennants and neon signs advertising beer and ball clubs. Huge, filling breakfast burritos and tasty burgers are the more reliable choices at this popular locals' hangout.

If you would rather explore Estes' environs than the park, you have a number of options. As a resort town, Estes attracted the attention of genius entrepreneur F. O. Stanley, inventor of the Stanley Steamer automobile and several photographic processes. In 1905, having been told by his doctors he would soon die of tuberculosis, he constructed the regal **Stanley Hotel** on a promontory overlooking the town. Stanley went on to live another 30-odd years, an extension that he attributed to the fresh air. The hotel soon became one of the most glamorous resorts in the Rockies, a position it holds to this day. Incidentally, the hotel was the inspiration for Stephen King's spooky book, *The Shining,* later made into a movie by Stanley Kubrick starring Jack Nicholson.

From the Stanley, turn left to return to U.S. 36. In two blocks you'll see the **Estes Park Area Historical Museum.** The archeological evidence displayed here makes an eloquent case that Native Americans used the area as a summer resort. The museum also offers the usual assortment of pioneer artifacts and mounts interesting changing exhibits. *200 4th St.,* ☎ *970/586–6256.* ☞ *$2 adults, $1 children.* ☉ *May–Oct., Mon.–Sat. 10–5, Sun. 1–5; Mar.–Apr., Fri.–Sat. 10–5, Sun. 1–5.*

Double back on U.S. 36 where it intersects with U.S. 34; follow U.S. 34 to MacGregor Avenue and take it for a mile. The **MacGregor Ranch Museum,** in the National Register of Historic Places, offers spectacular views of the Twin Owls and Longs Peak (towering more than 14,000 feet). Although the original ranch was homesteaded in 1873, the present house was built in 1896, and provides a well-preserved record of typical ranch life, thanks to a wealth of material discovered in the attic. *MacGregor Ave.,* ☎ *970/586–3749.* ☞ *Free.* ☉ *June–Sept., Tues.–Sat. 10–5.*

❸   These sights give you a good education about the history of the area, but the real attraction in the neighborhood is **Rocky Mountain National Park** (☎ 970/586–1206; ☞ $5 weekly per vehicle), sculpted by violent volcanic uplifts and receding glaciers that savagely clawed the earth in their wake. There are three distinct ecosystems in the park, including verdant subalpine, a cathedral of towering proud ponderosa pines; alpine; and harsh, unforgiving tundra, with wind-whipped trees that grow at right angles and dollhouse-size versions of familiar plants and wildflowers. The park also teems with wildlife, from beaver to bighorn sheep, with the largest concentrations of sheep and majestic elk in Horseshoe Meadow.

The fine visitor centers at the east and west ends of the park, on, respectively, U.S. 36 and U.S. 34 (also called Trail Ridge Rd., the world's highest continuous paved highway; open only in summer), offer maps, brochures, newsletters, and comprehensive information on the park's statistics and facilities. The park is a splendid place to wander. The scenery, accessed by various trails, can be similar, but still inspiring. Trail Ridge Road accesses several lovely hikes along its meandering way, through terrain filigreed with silvery streams and turquoise lakes. The

Rocky Mountain National Park

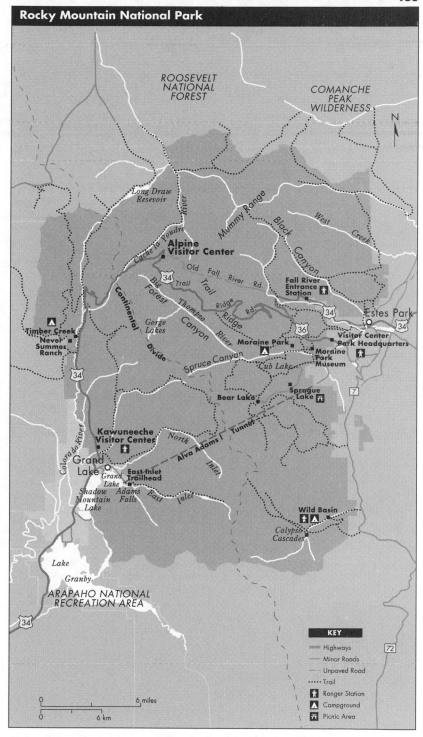

views around each bend—of moraines and glaciers, and craggy hills framing emerald meadows carpeted with columbine and Indian paintbrush—are truly awesome: nature's workshop on an epic scale.

Take U.S. 36 South for about 4 miles to Bear Lake Road and the **Moraine Park Museum** (open May–Sept., daily 10–6), which offers lectures, slide shows, and displays on the park's geology and botany. From the museum you can take the twisting, 9-mile-long Bear Lake Road as it winds past shimmering waterfalls perpetually shrouded with rainbows. The drive offers superlative views of Longs Peak (Colorado's highest) and the glaciers surrounding Bear Lake.

If you choose not to follow Bear Lake Road, head west from the museum on Trail Ridge Road. Many Peaks Curve affords breathtaking views of the crest of the Continental Divide and of the Alluvial Fan, a huge gash created in 1982 by a vicious flood after an earthen dam broke. Erosion occurred immediately, rather than over the millions of years that nature usually requires, and today it resembles a lonely lunar landscape.

❹ **Grand Lake** is the western gateway to the park, and it, too, enjoys an idyllic setting, on the shores of the state's largest natural lake, of the same name; this is the highest-altitude yacht anchorage in America. According to Ute legend, the fine mists that shroud the lake punctually at dawn are the risen spirits of women and children whose raft capsized as they were fleeing a marauding party of Cheyennes and Arapahoes. Grand Lake feeds into two much larger man-made reservoirs, **Lake Granby** and **Shadow Mountain Lake,** forming the "Great Lakes of Colorado." The entire area is a paradise for hikers and fishermen, and for snowmobilers in winter. Even the town, while it has the usual assortment of souvenir shops and motels, seems less spoiled than many other resort communities.

Off the Beaten Track

Fort Collins was originally established to protect traders from the natives, while the former negotiated the treacherous Overland Trail. Unexpectedly, however, the town grew on two industries: education (Colorado State University was founded here in 1879) and agriculture (rich crops of alfalfa and sugar beets). The Visitors and Convention Bureau has designated a historic walking tour of more than 20 buildings, including the stately sandstone **Avery House** and the original university structures. **Old Town Square** is an urban renewal project that re-creates a pioneer town, whose buildings house upscale stores and cafés set around playing fountains. The **Fort Collins Museum** (200 Matthews St., ☎ 970/221–6738; ☛ $2 adults, $1 children under 12; open Tues.–Sat. 10–5, Sun. noon–5) includes an 1860s stone cabin and an 1884 schoolhouse on the grounds.

SHOPPING

Shopping Districts and Malls

Boulder's **Pearl Street Mall** is a shopping extravaganza, with numerous upscale boutiques and galleries. **The Hill,** by the University of Colorado, is a great place for hip duds and CDs. Main Street in the tiny town of **Niwot** (northeast of Boulder on CO 119) is one long strip of antiques stores. Main Street in **Lyons** (north of Boulder on U.S. 36) also has several fine antiques shops. In Estes Park, the **Park Theatre Mall** and **Old Church Shops Mall** feature a wide variety of upscale stores that hawk primarily indigenous crafts. Fort Collins's **Old Town Square** is a pleasant collection of cafés and intriguing shops.

Specialty Stores

Art Galleries

Pearl Street Mall, in Boulder, features a number of art galleries and boutiques that carry crafts. **Art Source International** (1237 Pearl St., ☎ 303/444–4080) is Colorado's largest antique print and map dealer. **Handmade in Colorado** (1426 Pearl St., ☎ 303/938–8394) sells only the best Colorado made goods. **Boulder Arts & Crafts Cooperative** (1421 Pearl St., ☎ 303/443–3683) offers exquisite hand-painted silk scarves, handwoven garments, glass art, and pottery. **McLaren & Markowitz Gallery** (1011 Pearl St., ☎ 303/449–6807) features fine jewelry, sculpture, paintings, and pottery—primarily with a Southwestern feel. **White Horse Gallery** (1218 Pearl St., ☎ 303/443–6116) offers top-of-the-line Native American and Southwestern art and artifacts.

In Estes Park, **Michael Ricker Pewter** (U.S. 34 East, base of Lake Estes Dam, ☎ 970/586–2030) offers free tours of its casting studio and gallery, where you can see the world's largest pewter sculpture. **Glassworks** (340 Elkhorn Ave., ☎ 970/586–8619) offers glassblowing demonstrations and sells a rainbow of glass creations. **Gallery of the Winds** (222 Moraine Ave., ☎ 970/586–5514) is dedicated to promoting top regional artists in various media.

In Grand Lake, **Grand Lake Art Gallery** (1117 Grand Ave., ☎ 970/627–3104) purveys superlative weavings, pottery, stained glass, gourds, and landscapes, primarily by regional artists.

Children

The Christmas Shoppe (Park Theatre Mall, Estes Park, ☎ 970/586–2882) delights kids of all ages with every conceivable Noël-related ornament, doll, curio, and knickknack from around the world. **Jilly Beans** (1136 Spruce St., Boulder, ☎ 303/443–1757) sells enchanting handcrafted toys and furnishings. **The Printed Page** (1219 Pearl St., Boulder, ☎ 970/443–8450) presents unique and exquisite old-fashioned toys.

Clothing

In Boulder, **Alpaca Connection** (1326 Pearl St., ☎ 303/447–2047) offers Indian silks, Bolivian alpaca, and Ecuadorian merino wool garments. **Chico's** (1200 Pearl St., Boulder, ☎ 303/449–3381) traffics in funky jewelry and natural fibers and fabrics from around the globe. **Pura Vida Imports** (2012 10th St., Boulder, ☎ 303/440–5601) specializes in women's clothing and accessories with an international accent. In Estes Park, **JB Sweaters** (140 E. Elkhorn Ave., ☎ 970/586–6101) features hand-knit sweaters, shirts, and ties for men and women. In Greeley, **Ephemera Artistic Garments** (☎ 970/330–9508) sells Rachael Pitkin's wonderfully colorful and humorous hats by appointment only.

Outdoor Gear

In Boulder, visit **Hangouts** (1328 Pearl St., ☎ 303/442–2533) for their splendid handmade hammocks. **McGuckin's Hardware** (Village Shopping Ctr., ☎ 303/443–1822) is a Boulder institution that features a mind-boggling array of equipment and tools.

Western Paraphernalia

Artesanias (1420 Pearl St., Boulder, ☎ 303/442–3777) sells Zapotec rugs, Mexican santos, decorative iron, and handcrafted furniture. **Rocky Mountain Comfort** (116 E. Elkhorn Ave., Estes Park, ☎ 970/586–0512) has home accessories with the lodge look, including furniture, quilts, baskets, and throws, and even local foodstuffs. **Stage Western Family Clothing** (104 Moraine Ave., Estes Park, ☎ 970/586–3430), permeated by the pungent aroma of leather, offers imaginative cowboy hats, boots, and belts. **Aspen Kickin'** (Main St., Nederland, ☎ 303/642–7397) offers marvelous handcrafted log furniture.

SPORTS AND THE OUTDOORS

Cycling

The **Boulder Creek path** winds for 16 miles from Eben G. Fine Park, at the base of Boulder Canyon, to 55th Street, passing gardens and a fish observatory along the way. There is excellent cycling throughout the **Roosevelt National Forest** (☎ 970/498–1100).

Camping

Camping facilities abound in the 800,000 acres of **Roosevelt National Forest** (☎ 970/498–1100). There are five top-notch sites in **Rocky Mountain National Park** (☎ 970/586–1206).

Fishing

The best fishing can be found on **Grand Lake, Lake Granby,** and the **Big Thompson River** near Estes Park, and the **Horsetooth Reservoir, Red Feather Lakes,** and **Cache la Poudre River** west of Fort Collins. For more information, call the Colorado Division of Wildlife Northeast Region (☎ 970/484–2836). **Rocky Mountain Adventures** (Estes Park, ☎ 970/586–6191) offers guided fly- and float-fishing.

Golf

Collindale Golf Course (1441 E. Horsetooth St., Ft. Collins, ☎ 970/221–6651) is an 18-hole public course.

Estes Park Golf Club (1080 S. St. Vrain St., ☎ 970/586–8146) is one of the oldest and prettiest 18-hole courses in the state.

In Boulder, **Flatirons Golf Course** (5706 Arapahoe Ave., ☎ 303/442–7851) is an 18-hole public course at the foot of the eponymous mountains; and **Lake Valley Golf Club** (Neva Rd., 5 mi north of Boulder, ☎ 303/444–2144) is another 18-hole course with fine views.

Grand Lake Golf Course (CR 48, Grand Lake, ☎ 970/627–8008) is an 18-hole course 8,240 feet above sea level.

Hiking

The premier hiking, of course, is within **Rocky Mountain National Park.** The **Colorado Mountain Club** (Estes Park, ☎ 970/586–6623) sponsors day and overnight trips into the park. Other splendid hiking is within the superb **Boulder Mountain Parks** system, including Chatauqua Park and Sunshine Canyon. **Roosevelt National Forest** (☎ 970/498–1100) offers fine backcountry hiking in the Estes Park area. For information, call the **Boulder Parks and Recreation Department** (☎ 303/441–3000).

In Grand County, near Lake Granby, **Indian Peaks Wilderness Area** (☎ 970/887–3331) is another prime location.

West of Fort Collins, in truly unspoiled surroundings, the **Colorado State Forest** (☎ 970/723–8366) offers superb hiking.

Horseback Riding

National Park Village Stables (☎ 970/586–5269) and **Sombrero Stables** (☎ 970/586–4577) offer trail rides through the Estes Park region, including Rocky Mountain National Park. **Sundance Adventure Center** (Ward, ☎ 303/459–0225) offers trail rides as well as pack trips, rock-climbing trips, and mountain biking and Jeep tours in less-traveled parts of the Rockies.

Rafting

A-1 Wildwater (☎ 970/586–6548 or 800/369–4165), **Rapid Transit Rafting** (☎ 970/586–8852 or 800/367–8523), and **Whitewater Rafting** (☎ 970/586–6191 or 800/858–6808) run trips out of Estes Park up the Poudre River.

Skiing

CROSS-COUNTRY

The lower valleys of **Rocky Mountain National Park** (☎ 970/586–1206) are accessible year-round and provide miles of trails. The **Grand Lake Touring Center** (☎ 970/627–8008) offers 32 miles of trails with breathtaking vistas of the Never Summer Range and the Continental Divide. The **Never Summer Yurt System** (Box 1254, Ft. Collins 80522, ☎ 970/484–3903) is a hut-to-hut system. **Snow Mountain Ranch** (U.S. 40, 15 miles west of Winter Park, ☎ 970/887–2152) has 62 miles of groomed trails.

DOWNHILL

Eldora Mountain Resort. 43 trails; 9 lifts; 386 acres; 1,400-foot vertical. There is night skiing Wednesday–Saturday. *Rte. 119, Nederland,* ☎ *303/440–8700.* ☉ *Mid-Nov.–mid-Apr. 9–4.*

SilverCreek Ski Area. 26 trails; 3 chairs, 1 T-bar; 248 acres; 1,000-foot vertical. Here's an excellent family area with many bargains. *U.S. 40, SilverCreek,* ☎ *970/887–3384.* ☉ *Early Dec.–early Apr. 9–4.*

Snowmobiling

Grand Lake is considered by many to be Colorado's snowmobiling capital, with more than 130 miles of trails, many winding through virgin forest. Recommended outfitters, most of which can arrange guided tours, include **Catride** (☎ 970/627–8866), **Grand Lake Motor Sports** (☎ 970/627–3806), **Grand Lake Snowmobiles** (☎ 970/627–8304), **Lone Eagle Rentals** (☎ 970/627–3310), **Mustang Sports** (☎ 970/627–8177), and **Spirit Lake Rentals** (☎ 970/627–9288).

Water Sports

Grand Lake and **Lake Granby** are the premier boating centers. Call the **Spirit Lake Marina** (Grand Lake, ☎ 970/627–8158), **Trail Ridge Marina** (Shadow Mountain Lake, ☎ 970/627–3586), and **Beacon Landing** (Grand Lake, ☎ 970/627–3671) for information on renting pontoon boats and Windsurfers.

DINING

Boulder has almost as impressive a range of ethnic eateries as the much-larger Denver. Most prices are quite reasonable, thanks to a large student population that can't afford very expensive meals. There is far less diversity elsewhere in the region, although you can count on finding solid American or Continental restaurants throughout. For price ranges *see* the Dining chart *in* On the Road with Fodor's in the front of this guide.

Boulder

$$$$ **Flagstaff House.** This refined restaurant atop Flagstaff Mountain is one
★ of Colorado's finest. Sit on the enclosed patio and drink in the sublime views of Boulder to go with a selection from the remarkably comprehensive wine list. Chef Mark Monet is noted for his exquisite combinations of ingredients and fanciful, playful presentations. The

menu changes daily, but sample inspirations might include lobster ravioli and shrimp in shiitake broth; potato roll of smoked rabbit and duck with sautéed foie gras; mesquite-smoked alligator and rattlesnake; and elk dumplings with ginger and sweet onion. Those are just appetizers. Opt for the daily tasting menu. ✗ *Baseline Rd.,* ☎ *303/442–4640. Reservations required. AE, DC, MC, V.*

$$$ Red Lion Inn. Up in Boulder Canyon sits this beautiful inn, a local institution for natives and travelers alike. Ask to be seated in the original dining room with its fireplace, antlers, Austrian murals, red tablecloths, and white napery—for the feeling of being in the Alps. The stone walls and potbellied stove in the bar make it a cozy place to wait for a table. The Red Lion is revered for its excellent game: Start with rattlesnake cakes or wild game sausage, then try the elk or caribou steak. Or order a satisfying old-fashioned specialty such as steak Diane or veal Oscar. ✗ *Rte. 119,* ☎ *303/442–9368. Reservations required. AE, MC, V. No lunch.*

$$ Antica Roma. By far the most romantic restaurant in Boulder, this trattoria is a virtual stage set for *Marriage of Figaro,* replete with a spotlit balcony, tinkling fountain, exposed brick, painted beams, and ironwork lamps. Breads and appetizers such as *brescaola* (smoked meats) and *bruschetta* (thick slabs of coarse bread slathered with tomatoes, garlic, olive oil, and cheese) are sensational. Unfortunately, pastas are heavy and undistinguished, just a cut above frozen entrées; stick to such simple dishes as grilled swordfish or salmon, and drink in the wonderful ambience. ✗ *1308 Pearl St.,* ☎ *303/442–0378. Reservations advised. AE, MC, V.*

$$ Gold Hill Inn. This humble log cabin 10 miles west of Boulder hardly
★ looks like a bastion of haute cuisine, but the six-course, $19.50 prix fixe dinner is to rave about. Sample entrées may be paella or lamb venison marinated for four days in buttermilk, juniper berries, and cloves. ✗ *Sunshine Canyon, 10 mi from Boulder,* ☎ *303/443–6461. Reservations advised. No credit cards. Closed Tues. No lunch.*

$$ Imperial Mataam Fez. You eat with your hands at this lavish Moroccan restaurant that looks like it came straight from *The Arabian Nights.* The prix-fixe dinner includes five courses, with such fragrant dishes as lamb with honey and almonds and hare paprika couscous. There are branches in Denver, Colorado Springs, and Vail, but this is the original. ✗ *2226 Pearl St.,* ☎ *303/440–4167. Reservations advised. AE, MC, V. No lunch.*

$$ Mediterranean Café. After work, when all of Boulder shows up to enjoy tapas, "The Med" becomes a real scene (you may feel quite closed in, despite the restaurant's light and airy design). The decor of this yuppieteria can be described as Portofino meets Santa Fe, with abstract art, terra-cotta floors, rough-hewn painted ceilings (glittering Christmas lights twinkling against a teal "sky"), and brightly colored tile. The open kitchen turns out satisfactory food—an Italian/Spanish/Provençal hybrid—which is complemented by an extensive, well-priced wine list. Come here for a dose of local attitude or stop by just to gaze at all the pretty people. ✗ *1002 Walnut St.,* ☎ *303/444–5335. Reservations advised. AE, MC, V. No lunch weekends.*

$$ Sushi Zanmai. The restaurant section is a cool, sleek place to enjoy
★ delectable seafood and very good hibachi items, but the action's really at the zany sushi bar, where the chefs periodically burst into song: "If you knew Sushi" is a popular request. There's always karaoke here, although the official night is Saturday. ✗ *1221 Spruce St.,* ☎ *303/440–0733. Reservations advised. AE, MC, V. No lunch weekends.*

$–$$ Bangkok Cuisine. This very pretty restaurant looks more like a French bistro than a typical Thai place, with cut glass lamps, brass fixtures, and mauve tablecloths. In addition to expertly prepared staples such as satay, lemon grass soup, pad Thai (Thai noodles), and the inimitable curries, try less familiar items such as Gung Pao—juicy shrimp charbroiled with red chili paste. ✕ *2017 13th St.,* ☎ *303/440–4830. Reservations accepted. AE, D, MC, V.*

$–$$ ★ **Zolo Grill.** David Query, who was once a personal chef to Malcolm Forbes, left Q's at the Boulderado to open this superlative Southwestern restaurant. Its huge picture windows overlook one of Boulder's most active strip malls (and the Flatirons beyond); blond wood furnishings, striking abstract art, and a high-tech open kitchen complete the urbane decor. The wonderfully inventive menu offers everything from oysters with red chili to blackened shrimp cakes to barbecued red chili duck tacos. The margaritas are sassy, and there's a short but fairly priced wine list (about half the wines are available by the glass). And the way-cool T-shirts are for sale. ✕ *2525 Arapahoe Blvd.,* ☎ *303/449–0444. Reservations advised. AE, D, MC, V.*

$ **L.A. Diner.** This temple of chrome and formica calls itself the Last American Diner, and is open for all three meals. Good ol' rock and roll blasts from the speakers, waiters zip by on roller skates, and the menu runs to classic diner food, from meat loaf to malts. ✕ *1955 28th St.,* ☎ *303/447–1997. Reservations accepted. MC, V.*

Estes Park

$$ **Nicky's Cattleman Restaurant.** Elegant wood beams, oak paneling, maroon carpeting and upholstery, and a huge picture window fronting the mountain and river, make this one of the most sophisticated dining spots in town. They age and cut their own meat here, and specialties include sensational sirloin prepared Greek style with onions, peppers, and feta, and prime rib broiled in rock salt. Nicky's also offers motorlodge rooms with shag carpeting. ✕ *1350 U.S. 34,* ☎ *970/586–5376. Reservations accepted. AE, D, MC, V. No lunch.*

$–$$ **Friar's.** The name refers to the fact that the restaurant occupies a former church. The back room is woodsier and more elegant; the front room sunnier, with blackboard tables (chalk is supplied). The food ranges from dependable salads and sandwiches to fine daily fish and chicken specials. ✕ *157 W. Elkhorn Ave.,* ☎ *970/586–2806. Reservations accepted. AE, D, DC, MC, V.*

Fort Collins

$ **Rio Grande Mexican Restaurant.** One of the best Mexican restaurants in the area, the Rio Grande always satisfies with old favorites like sopaipillas, burritos, and Mexican steak, as well as more fiery Tex-Mex fare. Minimargaritas are 99¢, and strong enough to impart a pleasant buzz. ✕ *150 W. College Ave.,* ☎ *970/224–5428. Reservations accepted. D, MC, V.*

Fraser

$–$$ **Crooked Creek Saloon.** This barnlike valley hot spot is festooned with pennants and trophies, along with old roundup photos, branding irons, and Native American art. "Eat 'til it hurts, drink 'til it feels better" is the Crooked Creek motto, and you might as well succumb. Sandwiches, from blackened chicken to turkey Oscar (smoked turkey, crabmeat, broccoli, and hollandaise), are terrific, as are the burgers, pastas, salads, and Mexican specialties. There's occasional live music and nonstop conviviality from the pool-and-pinball crowd. ✕ *U.S. 40,* ☎ *970/726–9250. Reservations accepted. AE, MC, V.*

Granby

$–$$ **Longbranch Restaurant.** *The* restaurant in Granby, this stylish Western coffee shop with warming fireplace, wood paneling, and wagon-wheel chandeliers offers German, Mexican, Continental, and American fare. Not surprisingly, the quality is uneven; stick to what the German owners do best—goulash, schnitzel, and sauerbraten, with heavenly homemade spaetzle. The strudel is disappointing, but you'll probably be too full to eat dessert anyway! ✕ *185 E. Agate Ave. (U.S. 40),* ☎ *970/887–2209. Reservations advised. AE, MC, V.*

Grand Lake

$–$$ **Grand Lake Lodge.** This rustic retreat, built of lodgepole pine in 1921, calls itself "Colorado's favorite front porch," thanks to its stupendous views of Grand and Shadow Mountain lakes. The restaurant offers the same gorgeous vistas, in addition to fine mesquite-grilled fish. Cabins are comfortably but simply furnished—no TVs or phones—for those who truly want to get away from it all. ⌕ *Off U.S. 34, north of Grand Lake,* ☎ *970/627–3967. 66 cabins. Restaurant, bar, pool. AE, D, MC, V.* ☉ *June–Sept.*

$ **Bighorn Lodge.** This downtown motel has a rustic look, which helps it to blend in well with its surroundings. Mr. and Mrs. Schnittker, the owners, built the place themselves, and they set great store by the property. Their pride is reflected in the spotless rooms, all with cable TV, phones, and ceiling fans; soundproof walls; maroon carpeting; sailing prints; and pastel fabrics and wallpaper. The Schnittkers will gladly give you the lowdown on the area. ⌕ *613 Grand Ave., 80447,* ☎ *970/627–8101 or 800/621–5923. 20 rooms. Hot tub. AE, D, DC, MC, V.*

$ **Rapids Lodge.** This handsome lodgepole-pine structure is one of the
★ oldest hotels in the area. Lodge rooms—each with cable TV and ceiling fan—are frilly, with dust ruffle quilts, floral wallpaper and fabrics, and mismatched furnishings like old plush chartreuse armchairs, clawfoot tubs, and carved hardwood beds. Cabins, all with kitchenettes, are more rustic. The delightful restaurant is Grand Lake's most romantic, with stained glass, timber beams, and views of the roaring Tonahatu River; the kitchen turns out sumptuous Continental cuisine. ⌕ *Hancock Ave., 80447,* ☎ *970/627–3707. 9 rooms, 3 cabins. Restaurant, bar. AE, DC, MC, V. Closed Nov.–mid-Dec., Mon. and Tues. mid-Dec.–May.*

$ **Western Riviera.** This friendly motel books up far in advance, thanks to the low prices, affable owners, and comfortable accommodations. Even the cheapest units—while small—are pleasant, done in mauve and earth tones, with lake views and cable TV; for $13 more a night you can get a sizable, stylish room with pine furniture. Cabins, with a kitchenette (including a microwave), a bedroom, and a living room with a sleeper sofa, are a tremendous bargain for families. ⌕ *419 Garfield Ave., 80447,* ☎ *970/627–3580. 25 units. Hot tub. DC, MC, V. Closed mid-Mar.–mid-May, mid-Oct.–mid-Dec.*

Hot Sulphur Springs

$ **Riverside Hotel.** Colorado is full of fun and funky finds like this historic 1903 hotel. You enter the lobby through a jungle of plants (cultivated by owner Abe Rodriguez) and find yourself in a room dominated by a magnificent fieldstone fireplace, its mantel covered with trophies, pottery, and other tchotchkes. The lobby leads into a grand old mirrored bar and a cozy dining room with a huge potbellied stove, a piano, and landscape paintings of the kind charitably called folk art. Offering views of the Colorado River, the restaurant serves up simple but well-prepared steaks and fresh-as-can-be fish; it's worth having a meal here even if you don't stay at the hotel. Abe describes the decor of the upstairs rooms as "middle-to-late Salvation Army"; you'll find iron or oak beds, floral quilts, and heavy oak dressers or armoires. All rooms have a washbasin or a sink; corner rooms are the sunniest and most spacious. ☎ *509 Grand Ave., 80451, ☎ 970/725–3589. 21 rooms with shared bath. Restaurant, bar, fishing. No credit cards.*

Kremmling

$$$$ **Latigo Ranch.** Considerably more down-to-earth than many other Colorado guest ranches, Latigo has a caring staff that does everything it can to give you an authentic ranch experience (short of making you muck the stables). Accommodations are in comfortable but rather dowdy cabins fitted out with wood-burning stoves and full baths. While providing fewer amenities than comparable properties, the ranch offers absolutely stunning views of the Indian Peaks range, complete seclusion (10 miles—and 30 minutes on heart-stopping roads—to the nearest town), and superb cross-country trails. The owners are not your average ranchers: Jim Yost was an anthropologist, and he'll regale you with stories of Ecuadorian hill tribes; his partner, Randy George, was a chemical engineer who now engineers the "nouvelle ranch cuisine" that is served in the dining room (BYOB). Guests quickly become acquainted in the cozy dining room or the recreation center, where they play pool, watch videos, or peruse the huge library for the perfect bedtime reading. Jim and Randy also offer cattle roundups and photography workshops during the year. All activities and meals are included in the price; there's a one-week minimum stay in summer. ☎ *CR 161, Box 237, 80459, ☎ 970/724–9008 or 800/227–9655. 10 1- to 3-bedroom cabins. Dining room, pool, hot tub, horseback riding, fishing, cross-country skiing, tobogganing, coin laundry. AE, MC, V. Closed Apr.–May, mid-Oct.–mid-Dec.*

Nederland

$$ **Lodge at Nederland.** Although relatively new (1993), and ultramodern within, the lodge is made of rough-hewn timber, giving it a rustic feel. All rooms are spacious and have refrigerators, coffeemakers, hair dryers, cable TV, and balconies; rooms upstairs have marvelous cathedral ceilings; and those downstairs have gas fireplaces. The enthusiastic staff will help to arrange any outdoor activity you desire—and the possibilities are just about endless. Although there's no restaurant at the lodge, the small, arty town of Nederland—with more than its share of hippie throwbacks—has several good eateries (try Bob's Bakery for breakfast and the Pioneer Inn for dinner). An excellent choice for those who want to be centrally located, the property is within a half-hour drive of Boulder, Eldora ski area, and Central City. ☎ *55 Lakeview Dr., 80466, ☎ 303/258–9463 or 800/279–9463, FAX 303/258–0413. 23 rooms, 1 suite. Hot tub. AE, D, DC, MC, V.*

THE ARTS AND NIGHTLIFE

The Arts

Music

There are concerts throughout the summer in Boulder's peaceful **Chatauqua Community Hall** (900 Baseline Rd., 303/442–3282) including the superb **Colorado Music Festival** (303/449–1397). **The Boulder Theater** (2032 14th St., ☎ 303/444–3600) is a venue for top touring bands. **The Boulder Philharmonic** (CU Macky Auditorium and Old Main Theatre, ☎ 303/449–1343) presents its own concert season, as well as chamber music concerts, the Boulder Ballet Ensemble, and special performances by visiting divas such as Kathleen Battle.

Theater

The **Mary Rippon Theater** on the University of Colorado campus (☎ 303/442–8181) offers excellent student productions throughout the year, as well as the Colorado Shakespeare Festival each summer. **Chucho's Coffee Shop** (1336 Pearl St., no ☎) has poetry readings and an experimental theater series.

In Estes Park, concerts and top-notch semiprofessional theatrical productions are staged periodically at the **Stanley Hotel** (☎ 970/586–3371 or 800/976–1377). Concerts and performances are also staged by *Creative Ensemble Productions* (☎ 970/586–6864); call for current listings.

Nightlife

Bars and Lounges

In Boulder, the **West End Tavern** (926 Pearl St., ☎ 303/444–3535) and **Potter's** (1207 Pearl St., ☎ 303/444–3100) are popular after-work hangouts, both with fine pub grub. Potter's also offers live bands and dancing periodically. **Mediterranean Café** (*see* Dining, *above*) is Boulder's current hot spot. The microbreweries, **Boulder Brewing** (2880 Wilderness Pl., ☎ 303/444–8448), **Walnut Brewery** (1123 Walnut St., ☎ 303/447–1345), and **Oasis Brewery** (1095 Canyon St., ☎ 303/449–0363) are also popular. The **Mezzanine Lounge** (☎ 303/442–4344) in the Boulderado has Victorian-style love seats, and is a romantic place for an after-dinner drink.

In Estes Park, the watering holes of choice are the venerable **Wheel Bar** (132 E. Elkhorn Ave., ☎ 970/586–9381); the **Gaslight Pub** (246 Moraine Ave., ☎ 970/586–0994), which has occasional live music; and the locals' favorite, **J.R. Chapins Lounge** (Holiday Inn, 101 S. St. Vrain St., ☎ 970/586–2332).

In Fort Collins, the places to hang (usually with the college crowd) are **Coopersmith's Brew Pub** (Old Town Square, ☎ 970/498–0483), **Old Town Ale House** (Old Town Square, ☎ 970/493–2213), and the sports bar **Chesterfield, Bottomsley, and Potts** (1415 W. Elizabeth St., ☎ 970/221–1139), famed for its burgers and international selection of beers.

In Grand Lake, the hands-down local favorite is the **Stagecoach Inn** (Boardwalk, ☎ 970/627–8079), as much for its cheap booze and good eats as for the live entertainment on weekends.

Comedy Clubs

Comedy Works (Old Town Square, Fort Collins, ☎ 970/221–5481) is a good place to check out the local talent.

Country and Western

Boulder City Limits (47th St. and Diagonal Hwy., ☎ 303/444–6666) has dancing nightly. **Lonigans** (110 W. Elkhorn Ave., Estes Park, ☎ 970/586–4346) offers live blues and country-and-western bands several nights weekly.

Dinner Shows

Boulder Dinner Theater (5501 Arapahoe Ave., ☎ 303/449–6000) presents Broadway-style productions.

Discos

The Broker (301 Baseline Ave., Boulder, ☎ 303/449–1752) is the closest thing to a disco in these parts. In Fort Collins, try the collegiate **Fort Ram** (450 N. Linden St., ☎ 970/482–5026).

Jazz Clubs

In Boulder, the **Catacombs Blues Bar** (Hotel Boulderado, 2115 13th St., ☎ 303/443–0486) offers the best in local and national talent.

In Fort Collins, **The Page** (181 N. College Ave., ☎ 970/482–1714) offers an eclectic roundup of live rock, jazz, and blues.

Rock Clubs

In Boulder, the **Marquee Club** (1109 Walnut St., ☎ 303/447–1803) favors house music, '50s pop, and alternative bands. **Tulagi** (1129 13th St., ☎ 303/442–1369), **Club 156** (CU campus, ☎ 303/492–8888), and **The Sink** (1165 13th St., ☎ 303/444–7465) are where the college set hangs out, listening to bands like Small Dog Frenzy, Foreskin 500, the Psychedelic Zombies, and Julius Seizure. The **Fox Theater** (1135 13th St., ☎ 303/443–3399 or 303/447–0095) is an Art Deco movie palace that now hosts top touring bands as well as the wildly popular Tuesday night Disco Inferno, a sea of leisure suits—the wider the lapel the better.

In Fort Collins, **Lindens** (214 Linden St., ☎ 970/482–9291), **Sunset Night Club** (242 Linden St., ☎ 970/416–5499), and **The Mountain Tap** (167 N. College Ave., ☎ 970/484–4974) jam with the hottest rock, folk, and blues in the area. **Mishawaka Inn** (Poudre Canyon, 15 mi north of Ft. Collins, ☎ 970/482–4420) usually corrals some name bands.

Singles

Fort Ram in Fort Collins (*see above*) and **Potter's** in Boulder (*see above*) are generally the best places to meet people.

NORTH CENTRAL COLORADO ESSENTIALS

Arriving and Departing by Plane

Airports and Airlines

Boulder and Estes Park are served by **Denver International Airport** (*see* Denver Essentials *in* Chapter 2, Denver); regular shuttles are available from Denver (*see* By Bus or Shuttle, *below*). **Fort Collins-Loveland Municipal Airport** (☎ 970/221–1300) welcomes flights from **America West** and **Delta.**

Between the Airport and the Hotels/Downtown

BY BUS OR SHUTTLE

Airport Express (Fort Collins, ☎ 970/482–0505) runs shuttles from Denver and the Fort Collins airport. **Boulder Airporter** (☎ 303/321–3222) and **Boulder Ground Transportation** (☎ 303/444–4410) provide transportation from Denver. **Charles Tour & Travel Services** (☎ 970/586–5151) offers rides to Estes Park from Denver and Boulder. Costs run from $10 to $30 depending on pick-up location.

BY TAXI

Boulder Yellow Cab (☎ 303/442–2277) costs $1.50 for the first ⅙ mile and 20¢ for each subsequent mile.

Arriving and Departing by Car and Bus

By Car

The region is easily accessed via I–25, which runs north–south.

By Bus

Greyhound Lines (☎ 800/231–2222) serves most of the major towns in the region.

Getting Around

By Car

U.S. 36 North accesses Boulder and Estes Park from Denver. Fort Collins and Longmont can be reached from Denver, via I–25 North. The main thoroughfare through Rocky Mountain National Park, connecting Grand Lake with Estes Park, is U.S. 34, which is partially closed October–May. Grand Lake can also be reached by U.S. 40 into U.S. 34, from Georgetown on I–70.

By Taxi

Boulder Yellow Cab (☎ 303/442–2277) costs $1.50 for the first ⅙ mile and 20¢ for each subsequent mile; **Charles Taxi** (Estes Park, ☎ 970/586–8440) quotes individual rates; and **Shamrock Taxi** (Fort Collins, ☎ 970/224–2222) costs $2.30 for the first mile, $1.40 for each mile thereafter.

By Bus

In Fort Collins: **Transfort** (☎ 970/221–6620) runs along major thoroughfares, charging 75¢.

Guided Tours

Orientation

Doo-Dah Tours (☎ 303/449–0433) and **Explore Tours** (☎ 303/530–5116) offer tours of the Boulder area and other nearby attractions, including Rocky Mountain National Park and the Peak to Peak Highway.

Special Interest

Boulder Historical Tours (☎ 303/444–5192) sponsors tours of various Boulder neighborhoods during the summer.

Charles Tour & Travel Services (☎ 970/586–5151) runs trips to Rocky Mountain National Park.

Important Addresses and Numbers

Hospitals

Boulder Community Hospital (1100 Balsam Ave., Boulder, ☎ 303/440–2037); **Estes Park Medical Center** (555 Prospect Ave., Estes Park, ☎ 970/586–2317); **Poudre Valley Hospital** (1024 S. Lemay Ave., Fort Collins, ☎ 970/482–4111).

Visitor Information

Boulder Convention & Visitors Bureau (2440 Pearl St., Boulder 80302, ☎ 303/442–2911 or 800/444–0447); **Estes Park Area Chamber of Commerce** (Box 3050, Estes Park 80517, ☎ 970/586–4431 or 800/443–); **Fort Collins Area Convention & Visitors Bureau** (420 S. Howes, Suite 101, Fort Collins 80522, ☎ 970/482–5821 or 800/274–3678); **Grand Lake Area Chamber of Commerce** (Box 57, Grand Lake 80447, ☎ 970/627–3402).

7 Northwest Colorado

AS YOU DRIVE THROUGH NORTHWEST COLORADO, its largely barren terrain sculpted by eons of erosion, it may be difficult to imagine the region as a primeval rain forest. Yet millions of years ago much of Colorado was submerged under a roiling sea.

That period left a vivid legacy in three equally precious resources: vast oil reserves, abundant uranium deposits, and one of the world's largest collections of dinosaur remains. Throughout the area the evidence of these buried treasures is made obvious by unsightly uranium tailings and abandoned oil derricks, and the huge mounds of dirt left from unearthing valuable fossils. Some of the important paleontological finds made here have radically changed the fossil record and the way we look at our reptilian ancestors. These discoveries even fueled the imagination of *Jurassic Park* author Michael Crichton: the book's fierce and ferocious predator, velociraptor, was first uncovered here.

Dinomaniacs will have a field day in both Dinosaur National Monument in the extreme northwest corner of the state, and Grand Junction, the region's main settlement. Grand Junction also makes an excellent base for exploring the starkly beautiful rock formations of the Colorado National Monument; the important petroglyphs of Canyon Pintado; the forest and lakes of Grand Mesa, the world's largest flattop mountain; and the surprising orchards and vineyards of Palisade and Delta to the south and east.

EXPLORING

Our tour begins and ends in Steamboat Springs (*see* Exploring *in* Chapter 3, I–70 and the High Rockies), which serves as one gateway to the area's many attractions on a loop tour. If you plan to explore the area on a series of day trips, Grand Junction (*see below*) makes the ideal hub: Most of the sights covered in this section are less than a two-hour drive in various directions.

U.S. 40 winds through the lush grasslands of the Yampa Valley, the blue ribbon of the river rimmed with the color of flame-bright willows. Farther on, billowing white plumes belch from Colorado's largest coal-processing plant, the Colorado-Ute Power Station. Welcome to Craig.

Numbers in the margin correspond to points of interest on the Northwest Colorado map.

❶ **Craig** is a growing cow town, made newly prosperous by coal and oil, but it's also set in pristine wilderness, teeming with wildlife. The **Sandstone Hiking Trail** along Alta Vista Drive is a splendid vantage point for viewing the local elk and deer herds, as well as ancient Native American petroglyphs carved into the side of the cliff.

In town is the **Museum of Northwest Colorado,** with its eclectic collection of everything from arrowheads to a fire truck. The upstairs of this restored county courthouse is devoted to one man's obsession: Bill Mackin, one of the leading traders in cowboy collectibles, has spent a lifetime gathering guns, bits, saddles, bootjacks, holsters, and spurs of all descriptions. *590 Yampa Ave.,* ☎ *970/824–6360.* ☛ *Free (donations accepted).* ☉ *Jan.–Apr., weekdays 10–5; May–Dec., weekdays 10–5 and Sat. 10–4.*

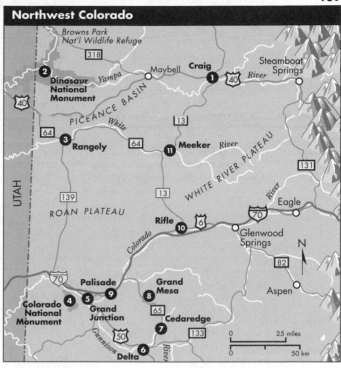

Northwest Colorado

Outside Craig, U.S. 40 gradually shifts into hillier sagebrush country. This is ideal land for raising cattle, which are about all you'll see for miles on this desolate stretch of highway. The route winds through increasingly minuscule towns every 15 miles or so, including Maybell, Elk Springs, Massadona, Blue Mountain—some not even on the map.

At Maybell, the road forks. If you follow Route 318 northwest for about 30 miles you'll reach **Browns Park Wildlife Refuge** (1318 Rte. 318, ☎ 970/365–3613; ☞ Free; open 9 AM–sunset), and pass lacy waterfalls and canyons carved by the Green River straddled by swinging bridges. The area was a notorious hideaway for the likes of Butch Cassidy and the Sundance Kid, Tom Horn, and John Bennett. This is an unspoiled, almost primitive spot, ideal for watching antelope and bighorn sheep, as well as nesting waterfowl such as mallards, redheads, and teal.

If you continue along U.S. 40, you'll note that the earth becomes increasingly creased and furrowed, divided by arroyos and broken by the mauve- and rose-streaked cliffs of **Dinosaur National Monument** (☎ 970/374–2216). The Dinosaur Quarry is actually located on the Utah side of the monument, but the Colorado section offers some of the most spectacular hiking in the West, along the **Harpers Corner/Echo Park Drive** and the ominous-sounding **Canyon of Lodore** (where rafting is available along the rapids of the Green River). The drive is only accessible in summer—even then, four-wheel drive is preferable—and some of the most breathtaking overlooks are well off the beaten track. Still, the 62-mile round-trip paved Harpers Corner Drive will take you past looming buttes and yawning sunbaked gorges etched by the Green and Yampa rivers. The dirt Echo Park Road is dotted with angular rock formations stippled with petroglyphs; the route skirts the rim of narrow 3,000-foot-deep crevasses that ripple from beige to black depending on the angle of the sun. Wherever you go, remember this austerely beautiful park is fragile: Avoid the rich black soil, which contains actual cryptoyams—one-celled creatures that are the building blocks of life in the desert; and don't touch the petroglyphs.

Dinosaur, a few miles west of the monument's visitor center, is a sad little town whose streets are named for the giant reptiles. It offers little more than pit stops and dinky motels. If you've traveled this far, though, you're almost better off camping in the park, which is first-come, first-served.

TIME OUT   **B&B Family Restaurant** (Ceratosaurus St. and U.S. 40, ☎ 970/374–2744) capitalizes on its location; a dino emblazons the side of the building. The decor is simple: one wall papered with potato sacks and another adorned with cheesy wildlife art; there are also still surprisingly beautiful remnants of an old bar with intricate carving and mirrors. However, the menu is cute and unusual. Where else can you get Brontoburgers, Stegosaurus rib-eyes, and Plateosaurus rib-eyes.

③ Drive south on Route 64 to the next sizable town, **Rangely,** which proudly touts itself as "The Oil Capital of Colorado." It's also nicknamed Strangely: As the town's primary attractions attest, a perverse sense of humor is required to live in this desolate neck of the woods. The life of oil riggers and uranium miners is a hard one, after all.

Rangely, along with Chevron Oil, cosponsors the Raven A1 Memorial Exhibit, 4 miles west on Route 64, which recounts the history of oil-field development. Back in town, the **Rangely Museum,** located in the trim 1913 green-and-white schoolhouse, offers the obligatory educational display on oil shale and a rotating display of "petroleum products that serve you every day." The museum seems to be a little desperate for related artifacts, exemplified by the exhibit of a kitchen table, with a Log Cabin syrup tin and a cherry pitter sitting upon it. Also at this venue is an explanation of the Slush Pit Country Club, a golf course created by the oil workers ("play at your own risk, not responsible for tick bites, no holds barred, a golfing nightmare, nine holes of hell"). Regrettably, their course—whose hazards included junk pits, pumps, and pipelines; and whose greens were oil and sand—no longer exists. *434 W. Main St.,* ☎ *970/675–2612.* ☛ *Free; donations requested.* ☉ *Daily 9–5, but hours vary so call ahead.*

Among Rangely's most compelling sights, however, are the superb Fremont petroglyphs—dating from between 600 and 1300—in Douglas Creek Canyon, south of town along Route 139. This stretch is known as the **Canyon Pintado Historic District,** and the examples of rock art are among the best-preserved in the West. A brochure listing the sites is available; half the fun is clambering up the rocks to find them.

Route 139 meets up with I–70 a few miles east of the Utah border. Turn east onto the highway and you'll shortly reach the western entrance of the **Colorado National Monument** (☎ 970/858–3617). The 23-mile Rim Rock Drive climbs this colorful plateau that's been nearly 1 billion years in the making, yielding sterling views of the gaping canyons and gnarled knobby monoliths below. This is dramatic, rugged country, stubbled with stunted piñon trees and junipers; populated by mule deer, gray foxes, and bobcats; and perpetually swept by ravens, swifts, and golden eagles. The starkly beautiful sandstone and shale formations include Balanced Rock, Independence Monument, and the slender, willowy sculptures of the Kissing Couple and Praying Hands.

An eccentric visionary named John Otto was instrumental in having the park declared a national monument in 1911. To get his way, the headstrong Otto frequently threatened members of Congress with everything from blackmail to beatings, acts that caused him to be institutionalized on three occasions. But as locals observed, ". . . He's the sanest man in town 'cause he's got the papers to prove it."

West of the monument, it's a treacherous 7-mile hike into **Rattlesnake Canyon;** the intrepid will be rewarded with thrilling natural arches and spires. The canyon can be accessed in summer via four-wheel drive from the upper end of Rim Rock Drive. Just opposite the western entrance to the monument is **Devil's Canyon Science and Learning Center.** This sparkling new dinosaur facility was created by the Dinamation International Society, the folks who fabricate robotic dinos. Their techno-wizardry is on vivid display in this playground for children of all ages. In addition to the amazingly lifelike robotics (including a hatching egg), there are more than 20 interactive displays. Children can stand in an earthquake simulator, dig up "fossils" in a mock quarry, or make dino prints in dirt (along with reptile and bird tracks for comparison). Kids get a special passport that's stamped as they visit each dinosaur exhibit, and they have the chance to watch local volunteers at work cleaning and preparing fossils for study.

The center does an admirable job of sustaining a sense of fun while making its exhibits relevant to a child's contemporary world. As Dr. Robert Bakker, expedition leader for the Dinamation International Society advises, "Don't think of T. rex as a 'tyrant lizard,' but as a 10,000-pound roadrunner that could eat a school bus." *Exit 19 off I–70, 550 Crossroads Ct. , Fruita,* ☎ *970/858–7282 or 800/344–3466.* ☛ *$5 adults, $3.50 children 3–12 and senior citizens.* ☉ *Memorial Day–Labor Day, daily 8:30–7; Labor Day–Memorial Day, daily 9–5.*

❺ The geographic hub for exploring this area—whose many other enticing attractions include dinosaur quarries, vineyards, and a host of recreational activities—is **Grand Junction,** caught between the gunmetal Grand Mesa to the south and the multihued Bookcliffs to the north. As the largest city between Denver and Salt Lake City, it provides a variety of services and facilities to the surrounding populace, and offers a fair amount of cosmopolitan sophistication for a comparatively small town.

TIME OUT **Mountain Roasted** (620 Main St., ☎ 970/242–5282) is the brainchild of John Price, who speculated that gourmet coffees and an arty atmosphere would go over big in Grand Junction. In addition to the rotating aromatic coffees, he sells biscotti, homemade muffins, and pastries, not to mention mugs, sweatshirts, and assorted coffee- and tea-related paraphernalia. The local art gracing the walls is also for sale, and live music is offered several evenings a week: jazz Tuesdays, acoustic guitar Wednesdays, a grab bag Fridays.

Grand Junction's cultural sophistication is readily apparent in the **Art on the Corner** exhibit, a year-round event showcasing leading regional sculptors whose latest works are installed on the Main Street Mall. Each year the community selects and purchases its favorites for permanent display. Art on the Corner is organized by the **Western Colorado Center for the Arts** (1803 N. 7th St., ☎ 970/243–7337; ☛ Free; open daily 9–5), which rotates its fine permanent collection of Native American tapestries and Western contemporary art, including the only complete series of lithographs by noted printmaker Paul Pletka. The fantastically carved doors, done by a WPA artist in the '30s, are alone worth the visit. Take time to enjoy the elegant historic homes along North 7th Street afterward.

The **Museum of Western Colorado** runs three facilities—this museum, the Cross Orchards Living History Farm, and the Dinosaur Valley Museum—as well as oversees paleontological excavations (*see* Dinosaur Valley Museum, *below*). The museum itself relates the history of the area dating from the 1880s, with an 11-decade time line, a firearms display, and two gorgeous parlor organs, among other items. *248 S. 4th St.,* ☎ *970/242–0971.* ☛ *$2 adults, $1 children 2–12.* ⊙ *Mon.–Sat. 10–4:45.*

The **Cross Orchards Living History Farm** re-creates a historic agricultural community of the early 20th century on its 24½-acre site, listed on the National Register of Historic Places. A workers' bunkhouse, blacksmith shop, country store, and an extensive collection of vintage farming and roadbuilding equipment are among the exhibits to be seen on the 1½-2 hour tours. *3073 Patterson (F) Rd.,* ☎ *970/434–9814.* ☛ *$4 adults, $3.50 senior citizens, $2.50 children 2–12.* ⊙ *Tues.–Sat. 9–5. Tours run May 1–Nov. 1. Group tours by arrangement throughout the year.*

The most fascinating facility in town is the **Dinosaur Valley Museum,** with half-size, moving, roaring replicas of the dinos found in the region. This instructive museum is designed for children and adults alike with numerous hands-on exhibits that emphasize understanding the wealth of the local fossil record. Aside from being able to handle real fossils in the open storage displays, you can also enjoy looking into a working laboratory and talking with the volunteers preparing and cataloguing the latest excavated specimens. Three working sites run by the museum are open to the public: **Riggs Hill, Dinosaur Hill,** and the **Rabbit Valley Trail Through Time.** Each is a self-guided tour that will increase your knowledge and appreciation of paleontology. You can pick up information and trail maps at Dinosaur Valley. *4th and Main Sts.,* ☎ *970/241–9210.* ☛ *$4 adults, $3.50 senior citizens, $2.50 children 2–12.* ⊙ *Memorial Day–Labor Day, daily 9–5:30; Labor Day–Memorial Day, Tues.–Sat. 10–4:30.*

❻ Head south on U.S. 50 to **Delta,** the headquarters of the **Grand Mesa, Gunnison,** and **Uncompahgre national forests.** The town is ideally located for exploring the region's natural wonders and also has an interesting attraction that has earned Delta the accolade, "The City of Murals." Seven murals, most of them lining Main Street, were painted by local artists in the late 1980s and celebrate various aspects of life in the area, from wildlife in "Delta County Ark" and ranching in "High Country Roundup," to agriculture in both "A Tribute to Agriculture" and "Labels of Delta County."

There are also museums of interest in Delta: **Ft. Uncompahgre** (Confluence Park, ☎ 970/874–8349; ☛ $3.50 adults, $2.50 children and senior citizens; open Memorial Day–Labor Day, Wed.–Sun. 10–5; Sept.–Oct. and Mar.–May, Tues.–Sat. 10–5; Nov.–Dec., Thurs.–Sat. 10–5; closed Jan.–Feb.), where docents in period attire guide visitors through this 1826 fur-trading post; and the **Delta County Historical Society** (251 Meeker St., no ☎; ☛ $1; open Tues.–Fri. 10–4, Sat. 10–1), with an eclectic display that includes local dinosaur finds, an 1886 jail, and a butterfly collection.

❼ Now loop north onto Route 65 to **Cedaredge,** where the **Grand Mesa Scenic Byway** begins. This exceptionally pretty town sits in the shadow of the Grand Mesa and is complemented by the silvery San Juans shimmering to the south. Among Cedaredge's attractions is its **Pioneer Town**

(Rte. 65, ☎ 970/856–7554; ☛ Free; open June–Sept., daily 10–4), a cluster of 23 authentic buildings that re-create turn-of-the-century life.

8 From here, Route 65 begins its ascent of **Grand Mesa,** the world's largest flattop mountain, which towers 10,000 feet above the surrounding terrain and sprawls an astounding 50 square miles. The mesa landscape is dotted with more than 200 sparkling lakes— a fisherman's paradise in summer. According to Ute legend, a great eagle carried off a Native American child, and in retaliation the father hurled its eaglets to the base of the mesa, where they were devoured by a serpent. The enraged eagle seized the serpent and tore it into hundreds of pieces, which formed deep pits upon hitting the earth. The eagle's ire caused the mesa to rattle with thunder, and torrents of rain filled the pits, creating lakes.

The stands of golden quakies (aspens) blanketing the mesa are glorious in autumn. Even on brilliantly sunny days, wispy clouds seem to catch and reflect the sun's rays, draping the summit in prismatic light. The views of the Grand Valley and the Bookcliffs (escarpments) are absolutely ravishing here, and an excellent little ski area, **Powderhorn,** takes full advantage of them. The slopes intriguingly follow the fall line of the mesa, carving out natural bowls, those on the western side being steeper than they first appear.

9 Return to I–70 (the other side of Grand Mesa), and head to **Palisade,** a hamlet nestled between the wintry Grand Mesa and the semiarid terrain. The surprisingly temperate microclimate produces delectable Elberta peaches, apples, plums, pears, and cherries, making Palisade the center of Colorado's orchard and vineyard territory. Plucky wine makers have been experimenting with several varietals since the early '80s, and the results have been encouraging. There are 14 vineyards all told in the state; the best are located right here in the Grand Valley.

You can find all the great European grapes here: Riesling, chardonnay, pinot noir, cabernet, merlot; so far, the top results have been obtained with merlot and chardonnay. Wine lovers will appreciate the heady, uncomplicated varietal bouquet and surprising depth and complexity of some of the vintages. Four vineyards are open to the public, offering regular tours and tastings (call for hours). When you tour you'll be able to meet wine makers and discuss their craft, an opportunity you generally don't have in the larger facilities in California or Oregon. The oldest, largest, and most successful commercially (to date) is **Colorado Cellars** (3553 E Rd., ☎ 970/464–7921). **Carlson Vineyards** (461 35 Rd., ☎ 970/464–5554) produces wines with fey labels— tyrannosaurus red, prairie dog—that belie their seriousness; probably the best wines to buy here are those made from other fruit (try the peach or the pearadactyl). The two most promising in quality are undoubtedly **Plum Creek Cellars** (3708 G Rd., ☎ 970/464–7586) and **Grande River Vineyards** (787 37.3 Rd., ☎ 970/464–5867), whose owner Steve Smith is experimenting with Rhone varietals (Syrah and Viognier), with tremendous returns.

TIME OUT **Slice-O-Life Bakery** (105 W. 3rd St., Palisade, ☎ 970/464–0577) is run by two of the zaniest bakers in Colorado, Mary and Tim Lincoln. All the savory, aromatic goodies are baked with whole grains and fresh local fruits. Grab a bottle of wine at one of the nearby wineries, couple it with some fresh fruit from an orchard, and you have the makings of a wonderful picnic.

10 Head east on I–70 to **Rifle.** This unassuming community (which lives up to its name with gun racks outnumbering ski racks on cars) is developing quite a reputation among mountain bikers for the series of high-quality trails along the **Roan Cliffs,** and with ice climbers for the frozen waterfalls and ice caves in the **Rifle Gap State Recreation Area.** Rifle boasts a tremendous variety of terrain that veers from semiarid to subalpine and invites both hikers, bikers, and climbers.

Take Route 325 north out of town to the **recreation area** ($3 admission), passing Rifle Gap on the way. As you gaze at the huge rock window, try to imagine a huge, orange nylon curtain billowing between the steep walls. Famed installation artist Christo did; two of his efforts were foiled due to wind, save for one amazing day when his *Valley Curtain* piece was gloriously unfolded for a brief few hours. The road wraps around a tiny reservoir before reaching the actual designated area, which officially starts with **Rifle Falls,** a triple flume cascading down moss-covered cliffs. The caves here are ideal for amateur spelunking.

Continue along Route 325, past the **Rifle Fish Hatchery** (pausing to admire the huge schools of trout being raised, including an intriguing new iridescent blue hybrid) to Little Box Canyon Road. Here is **Rifle Mountain Park,** whose sheer cliffs are stippled with holds and pocked with caves that make it a favorite among rock and ice climbers. The dirt road eventually ends up in the **White River National Forest,** a popular camping area.

⑪ Back on I–70, turn north on scenic Route 13 to **Meeker,** named for Nathan Meeker, who attempted to "civilize" the Utes with little success. When Meeker began to fear that the Utes resented his arrogant disregard for their land rights, he sent for the cavalry. The Utes became further enraged and ambushed the troops in the 1879 Meeker Massacre, which ushered in yet another period of intransigence on the part of the U.S. government. Meeker is predominantly known as an outdoorsy town, but its handsome historical buildings include the still-operating **Meeker Hotel** on Main Street and the worthy **White River Museum** (565 Park St., ☎ 970/878–9982; ☛ Free; open May–Nov., Mon.–Sat. 9–5), which features pioneer artifacts and historical photos.

East of Meeker is the **Flattops Scenic Byway,** a terrain shaped by molten lava flows and glaciers that gouged tiny jewel-like lakes in the folds of the mountains.

What to See and Do with Children

Children will adore the dino exhibits at **Dinosaur Valley** and **Devil's Canyon** (*see* Exploring, *above*).

Rim Rock Deer Park and Trading Post offers a variety of rafting and horseback-riding expeditions, as well as a petting zoo, a deer park, and a somewhat hoary wildlife museum. *Hwy. 340, Exit 19, Fruita,* ☎ *970/858–9555.* ☛ *$1.* ◷ *May–Sept., daily 8–5.*

Other Points of Interest

Tabeguache/Unaweep Scenic Byway. This 150-mile stretch of savage scenery (Rte. 141) sweeps south from Grand Junction, arcing almost to the Utah border before curling down near Naturita, where you can pick up Rte. 145 to Telluride. It slices through the Uncompahgre Plateau, an area of great geologic interest. Unaweep means "Canyon with Two Mouths," and indeed the piddling streams seem insufficient to carve these harsh gashes. Along the way you'll see an engineering marvel: The 7-mile long **Hanging Flume,** used to transport water, virtually defies gravity by clinging to the sheer cliff.

One of Colorado's oddest communities, **Nucla,** also lies along this route (3 miles north of Naturita on Rte. 97). Founded as an early experiment in communal living (though the current conservative residents could hardly be called hippies), Nucla today is famous for one thing: *The Top Dog World Prairie Dog Shootout,* held every June. Residents justify the carnage by insisting that prairie dogs are only pests and that they run roughshod over the grazing lands. The event, which is shamelessly promoted as a tourist attraction, does tend to bring out the best in Nucla humor. As one resident was quoted in the *Denver Post*. "It's a lot like sex and the Catholic Church. Everyone agrees the job has to be done; the controversy is whether we get to enjoy it."

SHOPPING

Specialty Stores

Antiques

A Haggle of Vendors Emporium (510 Main St., Grand Junction, no ☎) is just what it says; it's as if every attic you'd ever seen had emptied its contents here.

Art Galleries

Southwest Imagery (236 Main St., Grand Junction, ☎ 970/243–9906) carries Native American and Southwestern art and jewelry. **Frameworks** (309 Main St., Grand Junction, ☎ 970/243–7074) focuses on contemporary interpretations of Native American traditions and carries serigraphs, sculpture, oils, pottery, prints, and photos. **Thunderock** (128 N. 5th St., Grand Junction, ☎ 970/242–4890) offers Navajo rugs and sand paintings, Hopi jewelry, and Zuni basketry and woodcarvings. **The Apple Shed** (250 S. Grand Mesa Dr., Cedaredge, ☎ 970/856–7007) is a group of galleries that sell an impressive array of Colorado crafts.

Ceramics

Terry Shepherd (825 N. 7th St., Grand Junction, ☎ 970/243–4282) sells his own stoneware and salt-vapor designs, where the salt forms trails on the pottery.

Food

Enstrom's (200 S. 7th St., Grand Junction, ☎ 970/242–1655) makes scrumptious candy, and is world renowned for their toffee. **Harold and Nola Voorhees** (3702 G 7/10 Rd., Palisade, ☎ 970/464–7220) sell an intriguing range of dried fruits, including cherries, pears, apricots, and peaches. Also stop by the **wineries** (*see* Exploring, *above*) to sample Colorado's excellent home-grown product.

Home Furnishings

In Grand Junction, **Sunspinner** (409 Main St., ☎ 970/245–5529) specializes in stained glass; **Quilt Junction** (412 Main St., ☎ 970/245–6700) stocks a wide variety of quilts and also offers workshops; **Linen Shelf** (316 Main St., ☎ 970/242–3234) has a nice selection of bedclothes and the like. **Windfeather Designs** (1204 Bluff St., Delta, no ☎) offers Jean Madole's extraordinary weaving, a reinterpretation of designs from extinct cultures such as the Mimbre. **Mama Macumba** (Cedaredge, ☎ 970/856–7792) creates wildly imaginative furnishings in explosive colors.

Western Wear

Champion Boots and Saddlery (545 Main St., ☎ 970/242–2465), in business since 1936, is the best place in the area for the likes of Tony Lama boots or Minnetonka moccasins.

SPORTS AND THE OUTDOORS

Camping

In **Dinosaur National Monument** (☎ 970/374–3000) pristine campsites are available at **Gates of Lodore** (970/365–3693), **Deerlodge Park** (no ☎), and **Echo Park** (no ☎). Most sites are free and on a first-come, first-served basis. **Colorado National Monument** (☎ 970/858–3617) allows backcountry camping. **Grand Mesa National Forest** (☎ 970/874–7691) and the **White River National Forest** (☎ 970/625–2085), around Rifle, have several campsites available.

Climbing

Rifle Gap Falls and **Lake State Recreation Area** (☎ 970/625–1607) are magnets for rock and ice climbers, depending on the season. **Vertical Horizon Rock Guides** (Grand Junction, ☎ 970/245–8513) and **Tower Guides** (Grand Junction, ☎ 970/245–6992) both offer guided climbs and lessons in the area.

Cycling

Rim Rock Drive is the gorgeous, if strenuous 23-mile route through Colorado National Monument. **Kokopelli's Trail** links Grand Junction with the famed **Slickrock Trail** outside Moab, Utah. The 128-mile stretch winds through high desert and the Colorado River valley before climbing the La Sal Mountains. Those interested in bike tours should get in touch with **Scenic Byways** (Grand Junction, ☎ 970/242–4645) or call the **Colorado Plateau Mountain Bike Trail Association** (☎ 970/241–9561).

The biking around Rifle is gaining momentum among aficionados for the variety of trails and views around the Roan Cliffs. Call the Rifle Chamber of Commerce (☎ 970/625–2085) for details.

Fishing

The **Grand Mesa Lakes** provide some of the best angling opportunities in Colorado. For information, contact the **Grand Mesa National Forest** (☎ 970/874–7691) or the **U.S. Forest Service** (☎ 970/242–8211). The **Rifle Gap Reservoir** (☎ 970/625–1607) is plentifully stocked with rainbow trout and walleye pike. Around Craig and Meeker, the **Yampa** and **Green rivers**, **Trappers Lake**, **Lake Avery**, and **Elkhead Reservoir** are known for pike and trout; contact the Craig **Sportsman's Center** (☎ 970/824–3046) for information.

Golf

Battlement Mesa Golf Course (3930 N. Battlement Mesa Parkway, Battlement Mesa, ☎ 970/285–7274) is an 18-hole championship course with ravishing views of the Grand Valley and Grand Mesa in the distance.

Tiara Rado Golf Course (2063 S. Broadway, Grand Junction, ☎ 970/245–8085) is an 18-hole championship course set stunningly at the foot of the Colorado National Monument.

Yampa Valley Golf Course (CR 394, Craig, ☎ 970/824–3673) is an 18-hole course dotted with copses of willow and cottonwood by the Yampa River.

Hiking

The **Colorado National Monument** (☎ 970/858–3617) and adjacent **Rattlesnake Canyon** (call the Bureau of Land Management, ☎ 970/243–6561) offer superb and challenging hiking. The **Crag Crest Trail** on top of Grand Mesa (☎ 970/874–7691) affords breathtaking views of the canyons and cliffs below. **Battlement Mesa** outside Rifle, also offers rugged trails. There are numerous panoramic nature trails in **Dinosaur National Monument** (☎ 970/374−2216).

Horseback Riding

Rim Rock Deer Park (Grand Junction, ☎ 970/858−9555) offers everything from one-hour rides into Colorado National Monument to overnight pack rides.

Rafting

Adventure Bound River Expeditions (Grand Junction, ☎ 970/245−5428) runs trips on the Colorado and Green rivers (the latter through the spectacular canyons of Dinosaur National Monument).

Skiing

CROSS-COUNTRY

The acres of untracked powder amid stands of aspen and spruce on Grand Mesa are a Nordic nirvana. For information, contact the **Grand Mesa National Forest** (☎ 970/874−7691) or the **Grand Mesa Nordic Council** (☎ 970/434−9753). **Skyway Ski Touring** (Grand Mesa, ☎ 970/248−0454) offers lessons and tours.

DOWNHILL

Powderhorn. 20 trails; 4 lifts; 240 acres; 1,650-foot-vertical drop. *Rte. 65, Grand Mesa,* ☎ *970/242−5637.* ☉ *Nov.–mid-Apr., 9–4.*

DINING

The Grand Junction dining scene is fairly sophisticated, compared to other towns in the region, though it's hardly fancy or exotic. On the other hand, there's a lot of standard beef and burritos. For price ranges, *see* the Dining chart *in* On the Road with Fodor's at the front of this guide.

Craig

$–$$ Golden Cavvy. A "cavvy" is the pick of a team of horses, and this restaurant is certainly the selection in town, for the price. It's a standard coffee shop enlivened by mirrors, hanging plants, faux-antique chandeliers, and the incredible masonry of the original 1900s fireplace of the Baker Hotel (which burned down on this spot). Hearty breakfasts, homemade pies and ice cream, pork chops, and anything deep-fried (try the mesquite-fried chicken) are your best bets. ✕ *538 Yampa Ave.,* ☎ *970/824−6038. Reservations accepted. AE, DC, MC, V.*

Grand Junction

$$ G. B. Gladstone's. This local hangout sports its own style of turn-of-the-century decor: stained glass windows, faux-Victorian gas lamps, and antique skis and kayaks on the walls. It's particularly lively on Friday nights, but whatever the day, you can enjoy such savory starters as jumpin' jacks (fried jack cheese and cheddar rolls stuffed with jalapeños) and Frankie's hot steak strips, as well as the freshest fish in town (try the blackened sea bass if it's a daily special). The meat and poultry specials are good too, especially the fine prime rib; teriyaki steak; and Thai pesto linguine with broiled chicken strips, basil, garlic, and chilies. ✕ *2531 N. 12th St.,* ☎ *970/241−6000. Reservations accepted. AE, D, DC, MC, V.*

$$ River City Bar & Restaurant. Exposed brick and whitewashed walls sur-★ round you at this casual spot, where a little toy train chugs along tracks winding above the tables. The menu is eclectic and Grand Junction's most creative, with standouts such as Greek-style leg of lamb; but the pastas, salads, and appetizers (you could make a meal out of the sampler alone) are really exceptional. Try the linguine Venice Beach (with tomato, feta cheese, and basil), or pasta topped with mouthwatering shrimp jambalaya or chicken tandoori. Salads celebrate the area's produce: Palisade peach salad (field greens, walnuts, peaches, and jicama) and lime chicken salad (lime-marinated chicken strips, spinach, avocado, artichoke, olives, and homemade croutons in peanut dressing) are delicious. Marvelous appetizers include bean bites (black and pinto beans grilled in minipatties), focaccia, and artichoke hearts with sheep dip (sheep's milk, cheese, and herbs). There's an excellent selection of beers and wines (including many Colorado vineyards) by the glass, and entertainment several nights a week. ✗ *748 North Ave.,* ☎ *970/245–8040. Reservations accepted. AE, D, MC, V. No lunch Sun.*

$$ **The Winery.** This is *the* place for the big night out and special occasions. It's very pretty, awash in stained glass, wood beams, exposed brick, and hanging plants. The menu isn't terribly adventuresome, but it does turn out top-notch steak, chicken, prime rib, and shrimp in simple, flavorful sauces. ✗ *642 Main St.,* ☎ *970/242–4100. Reservations recommended. AE, D, DC, MC, V. No lunch.*

$ **Grits.** This gussied-up coffee shop (hanging plants, faux gas lamp chandeliers, leatherette banquettes, walls cleverly stenciled with petroglyphs) attempts to transform diner food into a gourmet's delight by cannily incorporating a host of international influences, from Thai to Italian. Sometimes the menu is overly ambitious, but superior choices include chunky crab cakes with red pepper mayonnaise, spaghetti with shrimp and dill cream sauce, onion rings with fiery *chipotle* (hot pepper) ketchup, and luscious baked acorn squash with multigrain stuffing. There's always Dorothy's meat loaf or mustard-fried catfish for the less adventuresome. Portions are huge and served with heaping helpings of starch and veggies (the cornbread and fried cheddar herb grits are sublime). An extensive selection of Colorado wines complements the offerings. ✗ *2704 Rte. 50,* ☎ *970/243–8871. Reservations accepted. MC, V.*

Meeker

$–$$ **Sleepy Cat Lodge and Restaurant.** The original lodge burned down in
★ 1991, but the new Sleepy Cat (owned by the same family since 1946) rose like a phoenix, and is even better than before. The huge log structure is filled with gorgeous beveled glass and the requisite trophies and bearskins mounted on the walls. Soup and salad bar accompany full and filling dinners, and you get your choice of sautéed mushrooms, corn on the cob, wild rice, fried or baked potato, and sundae or sherbet. Wonderful ribs, huge cuts of steak, teriyaki chicken, and pan-fried trout are among the top choices. There are several cozy cabins for rent as well. ✗ *CR 8, 16 mi east of Meeker,* ☎ *970/878–4413. Reservations accepted. D, MC, V. No lunch.*

Rifle

$$ **Fireside Inn.** This is a charming dining spot, with an enormous stone fireplace as its centerpiece. The owner is German, and along with Continental favorites such as veal marsala and prime rib au jus, he offers tasty Wiener schnitzel and other German favorites. The Fireside Inn serves breakfast, as well as lunch and dinner. ✗ *100 E. 4th St.,* ☎ *970/625–2233. Reservations advised. AE, D, MC, V.*

LODGING

Grand Junction offers the widest selection of accommodations; outside the town, expect motels and fairly rustic guest ranches. You'll find limited accommodations at Dinosaur National Monument; camping is probably your best bet. Unless otherwise noted, rooms include a phone, cable TV, and a private bath. For rates, *see* the Lodging price chart *in* On the Road with Fodor's at the front of this guide.

Cedaredge

$ Cedars' Edge Llamas B&B. The pretty cedar house and guest cottage offer four neatly appointed rooms. Breakfast is on a private deck or in the sunroom, which affords astonishing 100-mile views. The best part about staying at Ray and Gail Record's retreat, however, is the llama herd (yes, they accompany guests on picnics). Complimentary breakfast is provided. ▦ *2169 Rte. 65, 81413,* ☎ *970/856–6836. 4 rooms. MC, V.*

Craig

$ Holiday Inn. This property, thoroughly remodeled in 1992, is pleasant enough for a remote Holiday Inn. It boasts the usual "holidome" with pool, and rooms are a good size; they're decorated in teal and floral fabrics. ▦ *300 Rte. 13 S, 81625,* ☎ *970/824–4000,* ℻ *970/824–3950. 169 rooms. Restaurant, bar, indoor pool, hot tub, exercise room, nightclub, recreation room. AE, D, DC, MC, V.*

Grand Junction

$$ Grand Junction Hilton. By far the premier property in the area, the Hilton
★ offers quiet pampering at affordable rates, although some of the units could use refurbishing. Rooms are large and have welcome extras such as a phone *and* TV in the bathroom. The bar and nightclub are longtime local favorites. ▦ *743 Horizon Dr., 81506,* ☎ *970/241–8888,* ℻ *970/242–7266. 262 rooms, 2 suites. 2 restaurants, 2 bars, pool, hot tub, 3 tennis courts, exercise room, recreation room, travel services, airport shuttle. AE, D, DC, MC, V.*

$–$$ Ramada Inn. Management does its utmost to create a warm, inviting
★ ambience, and succeeds with plush high-back chairs in the welcoming lobby and a private library/club look in the main restaurant, Oliver's. More than $1 million was invested in refurbishment in the last five years, and it shows. Old-fashioned charm and dark mountain colors characterize the rooms. Kings and parlor quarters, with period decor, are the most appealing. ▦ *2790 Crossroads Ave., 81506,* ☎ *970/241–8411,* ℻ *970/241–1077. 157 units. Restaurant, bar, patisserie, indoor pool, hot tub, health club privileges, nightclub, meeting rooms, airport shuttle. AE, D, DC, MC, V.*

$ Budget Host. The owner continually refurbishes this property (you can occasionally catch him scrubbing the floors), whose teal-and-white exterior seems more country inn than motor lodge. Care is also lavished on the smart, fresh rooms, which sport an early-American look with Stanley cherry furniture, burgundy carpets, and floral spreads. ▦ *721 Horizon Dr., 81506,* ☎ *970/243–6050 or 800/888–5736. 54 rooms. Outdoor pool. AE, D, DC, MC, V.*

$ Junction Country Inn. Built in 1907 as the showplace mansion for a contractor, this gracious inn boasts lovely hardwood floors and wainscoting throughout. The cozy rooms all have floral wallpaper and historical prints, and three accommodations (only one has a private bath) are particularly good for families. One unit has a sunporch, one has two daybeds, another has an extra room. Complimentary breakfast is served in a sunny dining room that's dominated by a map covered with pushpins, each representing a guest's hometown. ▦ *861 Grand St., 81506,* ☎ *970/241–2817. 4 rooms. AE, MC, V.*

$ Melrose Hotel. This funky 85-year-old, brick-red-and-forest-green building functions as both a full-service hotel and a hostel. Most of the reasonably priced hotel rooms feature TV, air-conditioning, sink (some have a private shower), and the original woodwork. Most are bright and airy, with a smattering of antiques. This is a great place to connect with students from around the world. Marcus and Sabrina Bebb-Jones couldn't be more friendly and helpful, full of tips on how to save money in the area. Hostelers enjoy a pleasant common room with library, TV/VCR, and kitchen facilities. Breakfast is complimentary. ☎ *337 Colorado St., 81501, ☎ 970/242–9636. 21 hotel rooms, 10 with private bath, 5 dorms. Laundry services. MC, V.*

$ **Peachtree Inn.** This pleasant property—with pool and restaurant—offers more amenities and facilities than most "strip" motels. The appealing room decor includes grey carpeting and a mauve and light-blue color scheme. ☎ *1600 North St., 81501, ☎ 970/245–5770 or 800/525–0030. 70 rooms. Restaurant, bar, pool. AE, D, MC, V.*

Rifle

$ **Rusty Cannon Motel.** This motor lodge offers spacious accommodations, and is plain but clean and comfortable. ☎ *701 Taughenbaugh Blvd., 81650, ☎ 970/625–4004. 89 rooms. Pool, exercise room. AE, D, DC, MC, V.*

THE ARTS AND NIGHTLIFE

The Arts

Music

Grand Junction's **Country Jam** (Grand Junction Chamber of Commerce, ☎ 970/244–1480), held annually in June, attracts the biggest name acts, such as Garth Brooks and Willie Nelson. The 65-piece **Grand Junction Symphony** (☎ 970/243–6787) is highly regarded.

Nightlife

Bars and Lounges

In Grand Junction, **River City** (748 North Ave., ☎ 970/245–8040), the Hilton's **Observatory Lounge** (☎ 970/241–8888), **G. B. Gladstone's** (2531 N. 12th St., ☎ 970/241–6000), and the **Rockslide Brewery** (401 Main St., ☎ 970/245–2111), which has won awards for its ales, porters and stouts, are the preferred local hangouts.

Country and Western

Grand Junction kicks up its heels at the **Branding Iron Lounge** (2701 U.S. 50, ☎ 970/242–9897) and **The Rose** (2993 North Ave., ☎ 970/245–0606).

Discos

Bailey's (Ramada Inn, 2790 Crossroads Ave., Grand Junction, ☎ 970/241–8411) has a rather elegant ambience, much like a cozy club. **Cinnamon's** (Holiday Inn, 755 Horizon Dr., Grand Junction, ☎ 970/243–6790) is the closest thing to a disco: It has a dance floor and a DJ. For a more Western atmosphere, try **Charades** (Grand Junction Hilton, 743 Horizon Dr., Grand Junction, ☎ 970/241–8888).

Jazz Clubs

The Station (Main & 7th Sts., ☎ 970/241–4613) attracts a bohemian crowd as much for its smoking jazz and blues sets as for the righteous lattes and rotating art exhibits.

Rock Clubs

Cahoots Crossing (490 28¼ Rd., Grand Junction, ☎ 970/241–2282) features live bands several nights weekly. **Club Zephyr** (715 Horizon

Dr., ☎ 970/242–4782) attracts an even younger crowd that slams to alternative bands with names like Jesus Monkey Fish and Weird Lizard Disease.

NORTHWEST COLORADO ESSENTIALS

Arriving and Departing by Plane

Airports and Airlines

Walker Field Airport (☎ 970/244–9100) in Grand Junction is the only major airport in the region, and is served by **American, America West, Continental, Delta, TWA, United,** and **USAir.**

Arriving and Departing by Car, Train, and Bus

By Car

I–70 bisects Colorado running east–west; it's the easiest way to approach the region.

By Train

Amtrak (☎ 800/USA 7245) stops in Grand Junction.

By Bus

Greyhound Lines (☎ 800/231–2222) serves most of the major towns in the region.

Getting Around

By Taxi

In Grand Junction, call **Sunshine Taxi** (☎ 970/245–8294); **A Touch of Class** (☎ 970/245–5466) has regular service into Grand Junction and outlying communities from Walker Field.

By Car

I–70 (U.S. 6) is the major thoroughfare, accessing Grand Junction, Rifle, and Grand Mesa (via Rte. 65, which runs to Delta). Meeker is reached from Rifle via Route 13 and Rangely/Dinosaur via Route 64. U.S. 40 East from Utah is the best way to reach Dinosaur National Monument and Craig.

Guided Tours

Orientation

Coopertours (Grand Junction, ☎ 970/245–4993) specializes in tours for artists and photographers. **Eagle Tree Tours** (Grand Junction, ☎ 970/241–4792), **Western Scenic Lines** (Grand Junction, ☎ 970/242–0558), and **West of the Rockies** (Grand Junction, ☎ 970/245–4865) offer tours of Colorado National Monument and the Grand Junction area, including some with four-wheel drive, hiking, or biking.

Special Interest

Cabra d'Oro Pack Goats (1459 Grove Creek Rd., Collbran 81624, ☎ 970/487–3388) offers unique tours of Grand and Battlement mesas and the Colorado National Monument. **Dinamation International Society** (Devil's Canyon Science and Learning Center, 550 Crossroads Ct., Fruita 81521, ☎ 970/858–7282 or 800/344–3466) runs five-to six-day paleontological treks that include work in a dinosaur quarry. **Meander Tours** (Box 354, Rte. 1, Collbran 81624, ☎ 970/487–3402) offers Native American and other specially themed tours.

Important Addresses and Numbers

Hospitals

Craig Memorial Hospital (785 Russell Ave., Craig, ☎ 970/824–9411); **Grand Junction Community Hospital** (2021 N. 12th St., Grand Junction, ☎ 970/242–0920); **Pioneers Hospital** (785 Cleveland St., Meeker, ☎ 970/878–5700); **St. Mary's Hospital** (2635 N. 7th St., Grand Junction, ☎ 970/244–2273).

Visitor Information

Battlement Mesa, Inc. (Box 6000, Battlement Mesa 81636, ☎ 970/285–9700 or 800/545–6372); **Cedaredge Chamber of Commerce** (Box 278, Cedaredge 81413, ☎ 970/856–6961); **Delta Chamber of Commerce and Visitors Center** (3rd and Main Sts., Delta 81646, ☎ 970/874–8616 or 800/436–3041); **Dinosaur Chamber of Commerce** (Box 102, Dinosaur 81610, no ☎); **Greater Craig Chamber of Commerce** (360 E. Victory Way, Craig 81625, ☎ 970/824–5689); **Grand Junction Area Chamber of Commerce** (740 Horizon Dr., Grand Junction 81501, ☎ 970/244–1480 or 800/962–2547); **Meeker Chamber of Commerce** (Box 869, Meeker 81641, ☎ 970/878–5510); **Nucla/Naturita Area Chamber of Commerce** (Box 104, Nucla 81424, ☎ 970/864–7233); **Palisade Chamber of Commerce** (Box 729, Palisade 81526, ☎ 970/464–5616); **Plateau Valley Chamber of Commerce** (120 Main St., Collbran 81624, ☎ 970/487–3457); **Rangely Chamber of Commerce** (209 E. Main St., Rangely 81646, ☎ 970/675–5290); **Rifle Area Chamber of Commerce** (200 Lions Park Circle, Rifle 81650, ☎ 970/625–2085).

INDEX